MUSEUM ARCHIVES

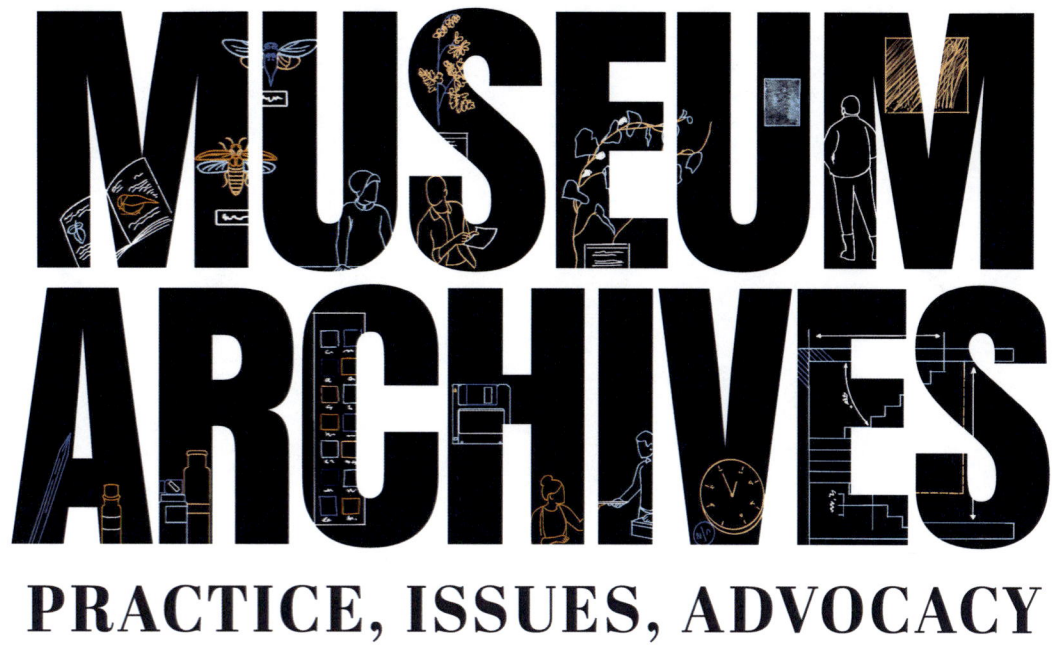

MUSEUM ARCHIVES
PRACTICE, ISSUES, ADVOCACY

Edited by Rachel Chatalbash,
Susan Hernandez, and Megan Schwenke

SOCIETY OF
American
Archivists

CHICAGO

The Society of American Archivists
www.archivists.org

© 2022 by the Society of American Archivists
All rights reserved. No part of this publication may be reproduced, stored in a retrieval system, or transmitted in any form or by any means without prior permission from the publisher.

Library of Congress Control Number: 2022940341

Printed in the United States of America.

ISBN-978-1-945246-74-6 (paperback)
ISBN-978-1-945246-76-0 (pdf)
ISBN-978-1-945246-75-3 (ePub)

Cover design by Kiki Lechuga-Dupont.
Interior design by Sweeney Design.

TABLE OF CONTENTS

PREFACE · vii

ACKNOWLEDGMENTS · ix

INTRODUCTION

1 Advocating for Museum Archives · 3
RACHEL CHATALBASH, SUSAN HERNANDEZ, MEGAN SCHWENKE, AND LYNETTE STOUDT

PART I

2 The Archival Core and Beyond · 13
MAYGENE DANIELS

3 Museum Archives: Management and Institutional Support · 17
NANCY ENNEKING AND JESSICA GAMBLING

4 Information Governance: The Importance of Being an Archivist-Records Manager · 26
SARAH R. DEMB

5 Applying Archival Fundamentals to the Museum Context · 37
SUSAN HERNANDEZ

6 Acquisition and Stewardship of Manuscript Collections · 48
BRAD BAUER AND JENNIE THOMAS

7 Providing Access and Promoting Use in Museum Archives · 59
LINDSAY TURLEY AND SAMANTHA NORLING

PART II

8 In with the Old, In with the New: Archival Processes for Audiovisual Assets and Records · 73
SETH ANDERSON AND REBECCA CHANDLER

9 Oral History: A Primer for Creation, Outreach, and Advocacy · 85
ELLEN BROOKS AND MEGAN SCHWENKE

10 Photographs: The Heart of the Museum Archives • 94
    MADELEINE THOMPSON

11 Collecting and Stewarding the Built Environment • 105
    RACHEL CHATALBASH AND SUZANNE NORUSCHAT

12 Documenting Artists in Museum Archives • 116
    RACHEL CHATALBASH AND HEATHER GENDRON

13 Negotiating Boundary Materials: Field Notes in Museums • 125
    CHRISTINA VELAZQUEZ FIDLER, REBECCA MORGAN, AND LESLEY PARILLA

PART III

14 Holistic Fundraising: A Logical Extension of Management, Outreach, and Advocacy • 141
    SUSAN ANDERSON

15 Archival Values in Museums • 152
    MELISSA GONZALES, DAWN SUEOKA, AND SUSAN HERNANDEZ

16 Provenance Research in Museum Archives: Restitution, Repatriation, and Return of Cultural Heritage • 167
    EMILY CONNELL AND MICHAEL PAHN

17 We Are What We Share, or Making the Case for Museum Archives • 180
    KATHLEEN WILLIAMS

CONTRIBUTORS • 183

INDEX • 188

PREFACE

As *Museum Archives: Practice, Issues, Advocacy* goes to print, we are at a pivotal moment in the history of museums and museum archives. The worldwide COVID-19 pandemic has forced institutions to temporarily close their gallery doors to visitors and staff alike. During this period, our museums' past and present entanglements with racism and gender biases, and legacies of colonialism and socioeconomic disparity have been laid bare. At the same time, climate change and the resulting environmental issues can no longer be ignored. Museums throughout the nation are being asked by the public and by their employees to be accountable for their actions and to make changes and reparations.

The theme of our publication—advocacy—is one we selected and considered paramount long before the present moment; however, there has perhaps never been a time during any of our careers that this topic has been more important. As some museums close and others enter periods of severe financial hardship, cultural shifts are changing the way we approach archives and institutional histories. As a result, archivists are reexamining and recontextualizing collections, and museums are engaging with diverse communities on new ground. This publication heralds the idea that museum archives, a unique type of repository, require constant and sustained advocacy to thrive and that its activities are a central component of and contributor to a museum's mission. Even in the current climate, these principles must remain steadfast for museum archives to succeed in their crucial work.

This publication originally emerged from the work that we have been leading as current and former cochairs of the Society of American Archivists Museum Archives Section's Standards and Best Practices Working Group. The majority of the book's authors have participated in the working group's activities—through volunteer membership, participation in an annual project, or presenting at the working group's annual symposium. The working group's efforts over the past decade provided the foundations for the publication's chapters, and its "Standards and Best Practices Resource Guide" is cited throughout with real-life examples contributed by museum archivists. The publication is also indebted to Deborah Wythe's *Museum Archives: An Introduction* (2004), which was the first major book on museum archives in the United States and from which ours draws its structure. While almost all of the chapters in our publication were authored prior to the events of 2020, we believe that they speak to the importance of museum archives in our time nonetheless.

The path the museum archivist travels is not always easy, and we recognize that recently it may have become even more challenging. We hope this publication helps museum archivists to better articulate their roles and the impact of their work. Our aim is to inspire museum archivists to reach higher with each new project and to continue to make significant and lasting contributions to our nation's cultural heritage, to the museum and archives professions, and to one another.

ACKNOWLEDGMENTS

This book would not have been possible without considerable support and encouragement. We would like to thank Deb Wythe for planting the seed of an idea for this book and all of the contributors to *Museum Archives: An Introduction*, second edition.

We would like to thank Chris Prom, Stacie Williams, Colleen Rademaker, Teresa Brinati, Sarah Demb, and Mary Caldera for being our sounding boards and for providing valuable feedback and guidance throughout this process. We would like to thank SAA and the entire Publications Board for supporting this project. Thank you also to our anonymous peer reviewers for helping us shape the final product.

Many archivists and colleagues provided feedback on specific chapters along the way: Kelli Bogan, Susan Anderson, Tessa Walsh, and Ines Zalduendo.

Thank you to the authors of the book for caring so deeply about the subjects of their chapters; investing their time, effort, and talents in this book; working collaboratively with us; and patiently abiding many rounds of revisions and fine-tuning.

The work of the Museum Archives Section's Standards and Best Practices Working Group in many ways laid the groundwork for this project. We would like to thank all working group members, past and present, for their work and contributions, as well as the past and present Museum Archives Section leadership for supporting these efforts.

The editors would like to thank our institutions for supporting our work on this publication, as well as our families for their encouragement throughout the project.

Rachel Chatalbash
Susan Hernandez
Megan Schwenke
Summer 2021

INTRODUCTION

1 ADVOCATING FOR MUSEUM ARCHIVES

Rachel Chatalbash, Susan Hernandez,
Megan Schwenke, and Lynette Stoudt

Museums strive to promote understanding and introspection, to advance education, and to preserve the history and heritage of our world.[1] The crucial position museums hold in society must be documented, and that documentation made available to both scholars and the public: this important work and its many facets belongs to the field of museum archives. Museum archives and the archivists who manage them have the immense responsibility of ensuring that the institutional records of museums and, in turn, the record of the cultural heritage they steward, are collected, preserved, and accessible. Museum archivists also acquire and care for manuscripts and special collections that support their museums' missions and holdings, furthering the development of significant repositories of knowledge. While museum archivists use the same methods as other archivists—they accession, arrange, describe, and preserve records in the same ways that their counterparts do at other institutions—how they situate themselves among colleagues, advocate for their role and the importance of their collections, and operate as both archivists and museum professionals set them apart.

Fundamentally, this publication articulates what museum archivists do and how they might realize their goals. It explains the set of professional skills required and the activities that all archivists might perform but views them through the lens of the museum by employing museum-specific examples. It provides practical guidance on the day-to-day management of museum archives, including creating policies, acquiring collections, and stewarding special formats, which can be of use to both novice and seasoned museum archivists. The publication goes beyond the nuts and bolts of museum archives work, however, by exploring strategies museum archivists can use to negotiate for the resources needed to successfully carry out their mandate, as advocacy for their enterprise underlies all of their work.

There is much to love about being a museum archivist. A museum archivist has an unparalleled opportunity to work with professionals from allied fields such as librarians, registrars, and curators, as well as staff at all levels of their institution, documenting both the museum's operations and the objects it stewards, simultaneously building a collection in its own right. Furthermore, a museum archivist advances the mission of the museum through research, scholarship, exhibitions, and programs. Yet, despite these contributions, the work of the museum archivist can sometimes be seen as ancillary rather than fundamental to the museum's mission-critical work. While museum archives often provide the only long-term view of an institution's most important operations and contributions, ranging from the development and stewardship of a museum's object collection to the organization and execution of its exhibitions, museum administrators and colleagues often do not consider the archives as essential to an institution's identity or future and underestimate its potential impact.

This publication argues that an essential aspect of the job of the museum archivist is to combat these perceptions to develop a functioning and fully engaged museum archives program. It addresses the vital position museum archivists should assume at their institutions, how they can and should advocate for the significance of museum archives collections—especially in the context of more highly valued object collections—and how they can position the museum archives as an indispensable hub of knowledge and activity within the museum. The ideal relationship between the museum archivist and the museum is a reciprocal one in which the archivist develops a collection as robust as the museum's object collections, which the museum, in turn, is compelled to draw from as an integral part of its exhibitions and operations. This relationship won't take shape overnight; building it is a career-long effort.

This book's chapters are full of ideas and best practices, and the museum archivist may wish to adopt many or all of them. However, practically speaking, this may not be possible, as many museum archives are staffed by a small contingent of archivists or by solo records professionals who do not have the time and resources necessary to explore all of the options outlined. Individual museum archivists will need to think strategically about the context of their particular institution and implement those initiatives that are most relevant and necessary.

To provide historical context to the current priorities and concerns of museum archives, the following sections of this introduction explain the emergence of museum archivists as a unique subset of the archival profession and highlight a selection of relevant literature before turning to an overview of this publication.

The Emergence of the Museum Archives Field

The origin of the "museum archives movement" in the United States is often traced to a 1979 meeting at the Smithsonian's Belmont Conference Center organized by archivist Arthur Breton and sponsored by the Archives of American Art and the Smithsonian Institution's Educational Outreach Program.[2] During the three-day conference, now known as the "Belmont Conference," archivists, librarians, and registrars from museums with existing archives programs came together to discuss the importance of museum archives, as well as establishing new archives, methods of storing archival records, and creating access to them for staff and scholars.[3] The Belmont Conference was a watershed moment for museum archives in the United States—not only did museum archivists and their allies assemble for the first time, but they collectively articulated their needs, strengths, and values, signaling the beginnings of a distinct museum archives profession. The National Historical Publications and Records Commission (NHPRC), which funded twenty-four museum archives seed projects between 1978 and 1988, reinforced momentum and support for museum archives programs.[4]

How did this pivotal moment in the 1970s arise? Some scholars attribute increased attention to museum archives to factors such as a revived interest in institutional history, the desire to use museum history to celebrate significant anniversaries, and the need to modernize the management of museums.[5] While these were clearly contributing factors, the professionalization of both the archives and museum professions during the second half of the twentieth century should also be considered.

Although museums had been acquiring archival collections and creating institutional records for many years, standards-based archives management and preservation were not prevalent until the middle of the twentieth century.[6] Furthermore, not until the 1970s did guidance on archival education begin to emerge from the Society of American Archivists and broad-based educational resources, such as the Archival Fundamentals Series, were published.[7] The promotion of the profession's first widely accepted standards and educational programs, as well as its emerging professional identity, encouraged the growth of many kinds of institutional archives programs as well. Just as museum archives were being established and developed, so too were university archives programs and the archives of other types of institutions, ranging from nonprofits to corporations.[8] Additionally, the establishment of regional professional organizations, such as the Midwest Archives Conference (1972) and the New England Archivists (1973), as well as more locally regionalized groups such as the NYC-based Archivists Round Table of Metropolitan New York (1979), can be traced to this time. Thus, the emergence of museum archives in the United States should be viewed within the larger context of a burgeoning archives profession, replete with different types of institutional repositories, and not in isolation.

The museum field also underwent changes in the 1960s and 1970s that led to increased specialization among museum professionals. Museum studies scholar Stephen Weil has demonstrated that during this period, museums shifted their focus from solely collection-based work carried out primarily by curators to the services they could provide to their communities, which required the introduction of other distinct professionals and professional departments into the museum's organizational structure.[9] Simultaneously, the role of the curator became characterized as more intellectual, authorial, and discursive, further divorced from the responsibilities of other museum functions ranging from education to marketing to graphic design.[10] These changes to institutional infrastructure and operations, as well as the transformation of curatorial roles, may also have provided room for professional archivists within the museum structure and contributed to the rise of the museum archivist as a discrete professional entity within the museum environment.

The rise of the museum archives profession can also be tracked through the development of its role in the Society of American Archivists. Since 1981, museum archivists have strived to establish a distinct and formal identity for themselves in the broader landscape of the national archival professional organization and continue to do so today; see "Key Moments in the Development of the Society of American Archivists Museum Archives Section" on page 6 for a detailed history.

As the museum archives field matured, its evolution can be further tracked by way of related literature.[11] Much of the scholarship on museum archives has been dedicated to their establishment and value. After the professional principles and guidelines set forth by the Belmont Conference in 1979, SAA's first edition of *Museum Archives: An Introduction* by William Deiss was published in 1984 as a "manual" written "to encourage museums to preserve their historically valuable records and to offer guidelines for the establishment of museum archives."[12] Similarly, the NHPRC's Laurie Baty authored a technical paper demonstrating the importance of funding the development of museum archives programs in 1988.[13] In championing the value of museum archives, others have primarily advanced two discrete arguments for why their archives are important to museums. First, that archives can serve as a repository of research materials related to the museum's collections that are of interest to scholars and researchers.[14] Second, the museum's institutional records are useful to museum operations and museum staff.[15]

Another strand of museum archives literature examines museum archivists' relationships with museum colleagues, such as curators, registrars, and conservators, and also with other professional standards.[16] In it, the role of the museum archivist is defined relative to other positions at the institution, highlighting areas of overlap and collaboration while also identifying key differences.[17] That examination has since broadened beyond the museum itself to include cross-sector professional convergences and opportunities among libraries, archives, and museums: in 2015, a panel comprised of eight professionals from libraries, archives, and museums, and moderated by museum archivists David Farneth and Lorraine Stuart, investigated the challenges of metadata integration across galleries, libraries, archives, and museums; proceedings were published under the title, "How Can We Achieve GLAM?"[18] Continuing this trend, in 2018, the UK journal *Archives and Records* published a special issue on archives in museums, edited by archivist Charlotte Berry, that considered cross-professional approaches to professionalization, documentation, collection management, and exhibitions through five articles authored mainly by archivists.[19]

Still, treatment of museum archives in museum literature is scant in comparison to the voluminous number of publications focused on museum work. When addressed, the presentation of the topic is often cursory, casting the museum archives' position as ancillary to other foregrounded museum and museum library functions.[20] Some notable exceptions, ranging in approach from the theoretical to the instructive, do exist, however. For example, Smithsonian curator Lois Marie Fink's "Museum Archives as Resources for Scholarly Research and Institutional Identity" discusses how museum archives must be considered within the context of museum theory and operations because they provide essential research resources in various subject areas while also aiding in the study of the museum field and its practices through stewardship of institutional records.[21] Other examples include "how-to guides" meant for a museum audience, such as "Successfully Managing Archives in Museums" produced by the UK Association of Independent Museums in 2015.[22] While this literature is important in bringing attention to the role of museum archives within the broader museum environment, its depth and breadth are not sufficient for already operational museum archives staffed by professional museum archivists who require a more critical and significant body of literature with which they can engage and on which to base their practice.

KEY MOMENTS IN THE DEVELOPMENT OF THE SOCIETY OF AMERICAN ARCHIVISTS MUSEUM ARCHIVES SECTION

YEAR	EVENT
1981	Society of American Archivists (SAA) approves the formation of a Museum Archives Task Force, chaired by museum archivists Alain Bain and Carole Schwartz, to gather information on archival programs, connect with allied groups, and establish a set of guidelines for the creation and maintenance of museum archives.
1983	The task force sends out a questionnaire to more than 500 institutions accredited by the American Association of Museums (AAM) about access to museum archives resources.[23] Out of the 54% of recipients who respond, 88% want more information about museum archives. The task force starts to develop materials and distributes them in 1984.
1984	SAA publishes William Deiss's *Museum Archives: An Introduction*. It is the first book to cover techniques and strategies specific to museum archives and is oriented toward those establishing museum archives programs.
1985	AAM adds questions about museum archives to the self-study portion of the accreditation process.
1986	SAA Council ends the task force's term in June 1986. At the August Annual Meeting, 28 SAA members attend the first meeting of the SAA Museum Archives Roundtable, established as a forum devoted to the work of museum archives. In December, the first issue of the Roundtable newsletter, *The Museum Archivist*, is distributed.
1990	SAA Council approves the Museum Archives Roundtable's request to transition from a roundtable to a section, which awards museum archivists greater status within SAA. The section has its first meeting on September 9, 1990, and establishes bylaws in 1991.

YEAR	EVENT
1997	The section establishes a working group to investigate issues of appraisal in museum archives. Subsequent working groups meet annually on different topics of interest until 2006.
1998	The section approves the revision of the museum archives guidelines created at the Belmont Conference (1979), which SAA never formally approved. A committee is formed to oversee the process, and a proposed new version is published in the September 1998 issue of *The Museum Archivist*.
2003	The section finishes its revised set of guidelines, and SAA Council endorses them; these guidelines are still in use at the time of this writing.[24]
2004	SAA publishes *Museum Archives: An Introduction* (2nd ed.), edited by Deborah Wythe. It greatly expands on the previous edition, covering many aspects of establishing and administering a museum archives program.
2010	The Museum Archives Section's Standards and Best Practices Working Group is formally established. The group, which embarks on a new focused project each year, is devoted to exploring, discussing, and documenting examples of museum archives' shared practices. It also maintains an online resource guide for museum archivists consisting of sample documentation contributed by museum archivists.

Museum archivists have only begun to author significant literature that truly articulates their vital role within their institutions.[25] The second edition of *Museum Archives: An Introduction* (2004), edited by Deborah Wythe, and Charlotte Brunskill and Sarah Demb's *Records Management for Museums and Galleries* (2012) are currently the only books in print dedicated entirely to museum archives and/or records management.[26] The former provides an overview of establishing and managing a museum archives program, while the latter focuses exclusively on records management, which is relevant to most museum archives but does not represent the full extent of their activities. Furthermore, in 2012, two essays by museum archivists—David Farneth and James Moske—were published online as part of the proceedings of the Art Museum Libraries Symposium held at the Peabody Essex Museum that same year. Later in 2019, Samantha Norling's chapter on management and leadership in a museum archives appeared.[27] These essays begin to grapple with many of the concepts addressed by this publication, including advocacy, leadership, and the active role museum archives must play within their institutions.

Museum Archives: Practice, Issues, Advocacy Overview

The editors hope that *Museum Archives: Practice, Issues, Advocacy* will be useful to archivists at all types and sizes of museums.[28] In particular, it may interest archivists tasked with managing archival materials created by their parent institution, working within what is often referred to as an "institutional" museum archives. The book summarizes relevant archival literature as well as fundamental theory and practice to provide context for discussions of issues specific to museums and to connect the topic of museum archives to the broader professional discourse, from which museum archives and archivists are almost always absent. Each chapter concludes with a list of suggested additional resources.

This publication argues that museum archives should be staffed by professional archivists. In practice, however, this is not always possible, and, in many cases, museum professionals who are not trained as archivists run or oversee museum archives programs. Part I of this book, which outlines archival theory, functions, and processes and applies them to the museum context, will be especially useful to these professionals. It also provides a refresher for professionally trained archivists and is intended to assist them with articulating archival methodology to museum colleagues who may not be familiar with archives or archivists. Part I also provides an overview of the policies and relationships that a museum archivist must maintain to run an effective program; argues that museum archives are not possible without a records management program; describes broad archival topics like appraisal, access, and preservation; discusses acquisition and management of materials obtained from outside the museum; and addresses the use of museum archives by external and internal constituents.

Part II turns to the concerns of the following types of records often encountered in museum archives: audiovisual records, oral histories, photographs, architectural records, artists' records, and field notes. These chapters focus on how museum archivists can properly steward these records in their care while actively collaborating with records creators and other museum departments.

Part III consists of several issue-based chapters covering fundraising, ethics and values, provenance research, and the museum archives' role in repatriation, restitution, and the return of cultural objects. The book's conclusion summarizes the ways in which museum archivists can advocate for their repositories and collections by employing "aggressive sharing."

Conclusion

The distinctive role of museum archives is one that must be actively promoted with museum administrators and colleagues, the public, and fellow archivists working in alternate settings. A museum archives program only succeeds when its value is recognized and its operations are supported. As museums endeavor to engage new audiences and examine their world in innovative ways, the charge of the museum archives is to document not only where the museum has been, but to imagine and help others imagine where it will go. The potential for a museum archives to effectively support and lead within its parent institution is limitless.

NOTES

1 Many types of organizations fall into the category of "museum," including art museums, halls of fame, military museums, zoos and aquariums, arboretums, and historical societies among others. Museums may be nonprofit or privately funded or may be attached to an academic institution or a government agency. This organizational diversity extends to the collections museums maintain, which illustrate topics such as art, science, culture, and history.

2 For a detailed recounting of the event, see Ann Marie Przybyla, "The Museum Archives Movement," in *Museum Archives: An Introduction*, ed. Deborah Wythe (Chicago: Society of American Archivists, 2004), 4–5.

3 It was collectively acknowledged that widespread establishment of museum archives was necessary; according to the conference report: "While the significance of museum records is widely acknowledged, they have been and still are sadly neglected. The number of museums with even minimally adequate archival programs is small indeed." "Conference on Museum Archives," *Archives of American Art Journal* 19, no. 4 (1979): 25, http://www.jstor.org/stable/1557319, captured at https://perma.cc/53FL-TAM9. Recognizing this disparity, the conference culminated in the creation of "Draft Guidelines for Museum Archives." These guidelines were oriented toward museum administrators and were distributed to museums across the country to create awareness and advocate for the establishment of museum archives. "Conference on Museum Archives," 25. These guidelines were revised and formally approved by SAA Council in 2003. For current guidelines, see "Museum Archives Guidelines," Society of American Archivists, http://www2.archivists.org/groups/museum-archives-section/museum-archives-guidelines, captured at https://perma.cc/2SES-NALP.

4 Laurie A. Baty, *Federal Funding for Museum Archives Development Programs: A Report to the Commission* (Washington, DC: National Archives and Records Administration, 1988).

5 Michael Steven Shapiro and Louis Ward Kemp, *The Museum: A Reference Guide* (New York: Greenwood, 1990): 367–68; and Maygene Daniels, "Developing New Museum Archives," *Curator: The Museum Journal* 31, no. 2 (1988): 99–105.

6 For an overview of the development of standards in archival practices in the United States, albeit within a science context, see R. Joseph Anderson, "The Organization and Description of Science Archives in America," *Isis* 104, no. 3 (2013): 561–72, https://doi.org/10.1086/673275.

7 The series was first published in 1976–1977. For a summary of the development of archival education and subsequent professionalization in the United States, see Robert Martin, "The Development of Professional Education for Librarians and Archivists in the United States: A Comparative Essay," *American Archivist* 57, no. 3 (1994): 544–58, https://doi.org/10.17723/aarc.57.3.116720kn81j25108; and Mott Linn, "Not Waiting for Godot: The History of the Academy of Certified Archivists and the Professionalization of the Archival Field," *American Archivist* 78, no. 1 (2015): 96–132, https://doi.org/10.17723/0360-9081.78.1.96. See Roy Schaeffer, "From Craft to Profession: The Evolution of Archival Education and Theory in North America," *Archivaria* 1, no. 37 (1994): 21–34; for a discussion of training based on experience in the United States, see page 28.

8 For a discussion of the growth of institutional archives by type, see Richard Cox, *Managing Institutional Archives: Foundational Principles and Practices* (Westport, CT: Greenwood Press, 1992): 12–18. According to Cox, between the mid-1960s and early 1980s, the number of institutional archives programs at colleges and universities grew from over 500 to nearly 1,000. Since the 1970s, the number of corporate archives increased as well due to factors including the United States' bicentennial, attention to corporate anniversaries, and advocacy efforts by archivists.

9 For a discussion of this shift from a collection focus to an education focus, see Stephen E. Weil, "From Being about Something to Being for Somebody: The Ongoing Transformation of the American Museum," *Daedalus* 128, no. 3 (1999): 229–58, http://www.jstor.org/stable/20027573, captured at https://perma.cc/BNX2-YD7C.

10 Speaking of art exhibitions and the role of the art museum curator, scholars Paul O'Neill and Mick Wilson note, "having moved, since the late 1960s, from an activity primarily involved with organizing exhibitions of discrete artworks to a practice with considerably extended remit, contemporary curating may be distinguished from its precedents by an emphasis upon the framing and mediation of art and the circulation of ideas around art, rather than on its production and display. Paul O'Neill and Mick Wilson, *Curating and the Educational Turn* (London: Open Editions, 2010): 18–19.

11 The remainder of this section charts key ideas in museum archives scholarship but does not serve as a comprehensive review of all related literature.

12 William Deiss, *Museum Archives: An Introduction* (Chicago: Society of American Archivists, 1984), 7.

13 Laurie Baty, *Federal Funding for Museum Archives Development Programs* (Washington, DC: National Historical Publications and Records Commission, 1988). In the report, Baty identifies a need for museum archives funding. Baty concludes the report by suggesting that NHPRC continue to support museum archives by encouraging national or regional workshops in museum archives, supporting national or regional work on documentation strategies and standards for museum archives, educating museum administration about the importance of archives, and engaging with archivists to determine what role they see the NHPRC taking in advancing museum archives. In Baty, *Federal Funding for Museum Archives Development Programs*, 7–9.

14 The earliest articles about museum archives, specifically about the archives of the Hagley Museum for the DuPont Company and the National Portrait Gallery, describe items in archives that could displayed in museums or used by researchers. See Walter J. Heacock, "Business Archives and Museum Development," *American Archivist* 29, no. 1 (1966): 40–43, https://doi.org/10.17723/aarc.29.1.f2ll2x12xx51n678; and Lyndon Ormond-Parker, "Access to Museum Archives: Whose Information Is It Anyway?," *Museum National* 7, no. 1 (1998): 9.

15 See Claudia Hommel, "A Model Museum Archives," *Museum News* (November/December 1979): 66. See also Kristine Haglund, "Documenting Our Past," *Highlights* 2, no. 4 (1980): 4, in which Haglund says that the "primary purpose of any archives is to improve administrative efficiency. See also Carole Schwartz, ed., "Keeping Our House in Order: The Importance of Museum Records," *Museum News* (April 1983): 42.

16 For example, see John A. Fleckner, "Archives and Museums," *Midwestern Archivist* 15, no. 2 (1990); and Shelley McKellar, "The Role of the Museum Archivist in the Information Age," *Archivaria* 35 (September 1992): 347–52. See also Melanie Tran, "Institutional Knowledge Sharing of Museum Records" (master's thesis, University of California, Los Angeles, 2012), which discusses the benefits of sharing resources and knowledge between archivists and registrars.

17 More recent scholarship on the general relationship among archives, museums, and libraries, while copious, has mostly neglected the role of museum archives and the museum archivist. The following article is an exception to that: Mike

Jones, "Artefacts and Archives: Considering Cross-Collection Knowledge Networks in Museums," *MWA2015: Museums and the Web Asia 2015*, August 15, 2015, http://mwa2015.museumsandtheweb.com/paper/artefacts-and-archives-considering-cross-collection-knowledge-networks-in-museums/, captured at https://perma.cc/CWB5-A489.

18. David Farneth et al., "How Can We Achieve GLAM? Understanding and Overcoming the Challenges to Integrating Metadata Across Museums, Archives, and Libraries," CIDOC, New Delhi, India, September 8, 2016, http://network.icom.museum/fileadmin/user_upload/minisites/cidoc/AGM_2015/CIDOC_GLAM_Panel_Report_6__4_.pdf, captured at https://perma.cc/H529-45AU. Farneth published a follow-up paper on the same topic: "How Can We Achieve GLAM? Understanding and Overcoming the Challenges to Integrating Metadata across Museums, Archives, and Libraries: Part 2," *Cataloging & Classification Quarterly* 54 (2016): 5–6, 292–304, https://doi.org/10.1080/01639374.2016.1192078.

19. *Archives and Records* 39, no. 1 (2018).

20. For example, Michael Shapiro and Louis Kemp, eds., *The Museum: A Reference Guide* (New York: Greenwood Press, 1990), 367–76, which provides theoretical grounding and a historical overview for museum professionals on many types of museum work, relegates museum archives to an appendix, which, despite a short introduction to the subject, mostly offers information about specific museum archival repositories. Timothy Ambrose and Crispin Paine, *Museum Basics* (New York: Routledge, 2012), 208–10, similarly includes museum archives but gives them a very basic treatment, focusing primarily on a list of the types of institutional records that a museum archives might keep. Publications on the museum library field, if they address museum archives, typically limit the topic to one chapter or section among many others devoted to library subjects. For example, Joan M. Benedetti, ed., *Art Museum Libraries and Librarianship* (Lanham, MD: Scarecrow Press, 2007), does just that.

21. Lois Marie Fink, "Museum Archives as Resources for Scholarly Research and Institutional Identity," in *New Museum Theory and Practice: An Introduction*, ed. Janet Marstine (Malden, MA: Blackwell, 2010), 292–307.

22. Emma Chaplin and Janice Tullock, *Successfully Managing Archives in Museums* (Ludlow, Shropshire: UK Association of Independent Museums, 2015). This publication is very much in the vein of those distributed by the SAA Museum Archives Task Force beginning in 1984—instructional materials about museum archives created for museums rather than archives audiences.

23. The American Alliance of Museums was formerly called the American Association of Museums. The name change took place in 2012.

24. The Museum Archives Section's Standards and Best Practices Working Group initiated a project in 2019 to update the Museum Archives Guidelines.

25. Despite the increase in scholarship on both museums and archives since the 1990s, the majority of writing on museum archives continues to appear mainly in professional trade newsletters such as SAA Museum Archives Section's *Museum Archivist*. A full run of these newsletters is available on the Society of American Archivists website, "Museum Archives Section," Society of American Archivists, http://www2.archivists.org/groups/museum-archives-section#.VyYhIj_OSqA, captured at https://perma.cc/72HN-NBMW.

26. Deborah Wythe, ed., *Museum Archives: An Introduction* (Chicago: Society of American Archivists, 2004); and Charlotte Brunskill and Sarah R. Demb, *Records Management for Museums and Galleries: An Introduction* (Oxford: Chandos, 2012). While Brunskill and Demb's book is primarily written for a British audience, much of its content also applies to a US audience.

27. Judy Dyki and Sidney E. Berger, eds., *Proceedings of the Art Museum Libraries Symposium*, The Phillips Library, Peabody Essex Museum, Salem, MA, September 20–21, 2012, https://web.archive.org/web/20140209114946/http://pem.org/aux/pdf/library/AMLS2012.pdf. Also see Samantha Norling, "Management and Leadership in a Non-Profit Archives: A Lone Arranger, New Professional Perspective," in *Leading and Managing Archives and Manuscript Programs*, Archival Fundamentals Series III, vol. 1, ed. Peter Gottlieb and David W. Carmichael (Chicago: Society of American Archivists, 2019).

28. It does not explicitly address the unique context of some special types of museums such as historical societies or historic houses, although much of the book will be useful to archivists working in these types of museums. Historical societies, in particular, have an extant body of literature from which readers can draw. This omission does mean, however, that this publication does not address topics such as community archives and archival contexts such as state and local agencies.

PART I

2 THE ARCHIVAL CORE AND BEYOND

Maygene Daniels

Museum archivists balance multiple responsibilities to the archives and to their parent institutions. They must be consummate professionals with a deep understanding of archival work, powerful advocates for the archives program in a competitive bureaucracy, and effective collaborators, teachers, and interpreters. To meet these multiple demands, their knowledge must encompass the archival core and go far beyond.

Guidelines for graduate education established by the Society of American Archivists (SAA) define the body of thought unique to the profession that every archivist needs to master.[1] This corpus includes appraisal and acquisition, arrangement and description, reference service and access, and preservation, as well as other subjects. Similarly, the Academy of Certified Archivists (ACA) Role Delineation Statement outlines seven domains of archival activity that closely track the SAA guidelines.[2] The ACA amplifies these domains with statements of associated knowledge and lists of archival tasks. Together, these documents comprehensively define the core elements of archival work. Broad competence in this body of knowledge is essential for museum archivists, who are likely to be responsible for every area of archival endeavor.

To perform their basic functions, archivists also must engage with departments throughout the museum. A strong mission statement that defines archival authority is a necessary place to begin, but directives relating to records and archives are notoriously difficult to enforce. To gain allies and to perform core functions, archivists need to understand the programs, sensitivities, and perspectives of other museum departments. Persuasion built on sympathetic knowledge of the missions of other departments is the museum archivist's most effective tool.

Registrars, for example, are natural archival colleagues. They are meticulous keepers of records concerning the receipt and location of museum objects, and they fully comprehend the critical value of museum information. Registrars also readily understand the historical value of documents and information and create important records that, when noncurrent, should become an archival responsibility. Nonetheless, the primary focus of registrars is current management of individual museum objects, in contrast to archivists' concern for context and the past. Data systems designed for registrars seek to provide quick access to current data, often with sophisticated search and physical description components, but without the hierarchical and relational features needed for archives. As a result, recordkeeping systems designed for registrars rarely work well for archives, despite shared interests.

Lawyers' and counsels' offices are also important users, advisers, and allies for museum archives. Lawyers are taught to recognize the significance of evidence in recorded documents to protect the rights and interests of their clients, and they intuitively understand the value of the written record and its importance in risk management. Lawyers also provide important support to archives as they confront thorny rights and access issues. To work with these colleagues effectively, museum archivists must be alert to institutional legal issues and conversant with legal requirements for deeds of gift, copyright, and fair use. With this preparation, archivists can turn to counsel for advice, and lawyers in turn will be effective and influential advocates for the archives program.

Yet, work with counsel can also bring particular challenges, as the legal point of view is markedly different from that of archivists. Lawyers are responsible for protecting the interests of the museum and are more inclined to restrict records than to make them available to users. They are notoriously risk averse. By recognizing this professional bias and working in advance toward written institutional policies, archivists can meet lawyers on their own terms. Knowledge of archival standards and the practices of other museums also can lend credibility to their arguments.

The work of archivists also can be enhanced through the knowledge of other professional colleagues in the museum. Conservators, for example, are trained in collection care and have deep knowledge of issues affecting the physical condition and preservation of paper, film, and other archival materials. They are experts in analyzing storage conditions, as well as important sources of information and partners in advocating for environmental improvements throughout the museum, in monitoring fire suppression and other safety systems that impact archives, and in developing exhibition standards for archival materials, among other museum collections.

Despite these shared interests, conservators also have their own particular point of view that archivists should recognize. Conservators typically restore individual, high-value items and may not understand the trade-offs needed to protect large volumes of documents. Thus, while working with conservators to restore or repair archival treasures, archivists also must be prepared to defend the need to focus resources broadly to preserve all materials in the archives so that costly restoration treatments will not be required.

Museum archivists also must be deeply engaged with the departments that create photographs, video and audio recordings, and other media, now essentially all in digital form. While always important, in the digital age, these archival materials are in increasingly high demand as museum websites depend on media, and exhibitions make dramatic use of oversized historical images and multimedia displays. Archivists also must continually work to manage and preserve increasing volumes of media materials in ever-evolving forms.

To hold their own in this environment, archivists must be conversant with digital media technologies and passionate advocates for comprehensive metadata. This includes technical data such as digital media formats, pixel dimensions, color space, or recording speed, as well as descriptive metadata including subject, place, date, and creator. Archivists also must be attuned to varied needs of media users.

Photographers and audio engineers are specialists in producing media, but they may not be conversant with preservation formats, bibliographic metadata, and strategies for long-term digital preservation. Collaboration between archivists and these media producers is needed to ensure that digital assets are appropriately created, safely stored, and ultimately transferred to the archives for long-term preservation.

Management is considered an element of core archival knowledge, and, at root, the archival enterprise is practical and administrative. Excellent skills are needed to manage arrangement, description, preservation, and reformatting projects. Like other museum professionals, archivists also must work with personnel offices, contracting officers, budget managers, and other administrators. A sound grasp of numbers and an ability to prepare succinct and pithy documents that translate archival jargon into management terms are important to success in the inevitable competition for staff and budget. Although bureaucratic hurdles may be challenging, they compel archivists to learn how to interpret the value of archives to new, and not necessarily sympathetic, audiences.

Records and information management is also part of the core archival curriculum, and traditionally, archivists have recognized the significance of institutional recordkeeping systems to ensure full and complete historical documentation. In the digital era, knowledge of records management has become increasingly critical as museums implement digital document management systems, which will have a huge impact on the future historical record.

Yet, development of office document management systems is often viewed as an IT responsibility, and decisions are technology-driven, despite the critical importance of these systems to archives. To participate meaningfully in discussions, archivists must remain up to date on digital developments and constantly alert to new laws, standards, and requirements for digital records retention, email preservation, and technologies for organizing and storing digital files. Inevitably, this involves time and effort but should result in productive collaboration as both departments face new technical frontiers.

Museum archivists also must have practical knowledge of digital systems for their own day-to-day archival functions of arrangement, description, preservation and reference service. For example, archivists should have solid knowledge of methods to manipulate large data sets. They should be able to apply checksums to validate file accuracy during import or export. To serve researchers, they need to manipulate media files.

Archivists also need structural knowledge of databases and other information systems to manage the museum's archival data. The relational, hierarchical structures of finding aids based on record groups, series, and folders fit naturally with relational database structures, making them intuitive to archivists and readily adapted for legacy archival information. This offers fruitful opportunities for collaboration with specialized data managers and is particularly significant as museum-wide collections management systems and digital preservation are explored and implemented.

Shared and linked data systems are important developments that offer previously unknown opportunities for archivists to collaborate with colleagues within the museum and to reach new audiences. With appropriate software and cross-disciplinary access points, historical photographs can be seen with images of related museum objects. Oral histories can be listened to with recent lectures or podcasts on related subjects. Information about historical materials can be revealed at the same time as users explore library holdings.

This promise of new possibilities to link and access information across disciplines has led to a new emphasis on breaking barriers between professions. The Coalition to Advance Learning in Archives, Libraries, and Museums, for example, was founded to advocate for education that deliberately crosses professional boundaries.[3] With firsthand knowledge of archives and museums and familiarity with library practice, museum archivists are in a favored position to develop partnerships across the museum and information disciplines. This is useful and productive, yet, at the same time, archivists should be aware that the blurring of professional boundaries can also conflate and confuse the work of archives with that of libraries. Both professions serve users and have similar needs for research rooms, storage, and controlled preservation environments. Furthermore, collaboration with libraries is necessary and important, and shared efforts in such areas as digitization and outreach can be efficient and practical.

Yet beneath the surface, archives are fundamentally different from libraries, and archivists must be ambassadors and educators to explain why this is so. Most museum staff have worked in libraries and are comfortable with their systems and organization, yet relatively few have worked with archival finding aids or understand the basic requirements of archives management. This places an additional responsibility on archivists to explain and interpret archival practice and tools for users.

In the digital world, the ability to communicate the essential nature of archives in contrast to libraries is especially important. Library information systems are designed for the particular requirements of books, for which subject access is critical but context less so. In contrast, archival information must be understood in its hierarchical, organizational context. Historically, when library systems are applied to archives, the result is awkward and unsatisfactory, a wasteful and frustrating outcome. To avoid this, museum archivists must profoundly understand the different needs of archives and libraries and must be able to explain these requirements to others.

Just as archives and libraries have closely related functions, the relationship between archives and curatorial offices is natural and supportive. Many curators are archives users and understand the importance of preserving historical materials and transferring them to the archives. They are partners in pursuing the museum's public mission. Even when understanding is not easy or mutual, archivists have professional knowledge that can help curatorial offices and lead to increased support and collaboration, especially in digital document management, imaging, records access and organization, and preservation.

Perhaps above all, museum archivists must have a sympathetic understanding of their institution's field of collecting to contribute fully to the museum enterprise. Knowledge of the terminology, scope, current trends, and history of the museum's academic area, whether art, history, natural science, anthropology, or any other field, is essential to ensure that the archives fully preserves the museum's significant records. Wise digitization decisions within the archives also depend on the archivist's intimate understanding of the museum's mission and the meaning of its records in the broader intellectual context of curatorial responsibilities.

Archives administration has its own principles and unique body of knowledge and practice, which must be the fundamental core skill set for every museum archivist. Yet, archivists also must go beyond this foundation to know and understand the varied professions and scholarly interests of the museum's staff. The special rewards of being a museum archivist such as writing, lecturing, and creating exhibitions depend on deep engagement with the museum's mission. Museum archivists also must master developments in digital technologies and should be skilled in meeting user needs. They must be adept at navigating the museum's competitive bureaucratic structure. This unique combination of skills and knowledge is not easy to achieve, but the challenge brings with it great rewards.

NOTES

1   "Guidelines for a Graduate Program in Archival Studies (2016)," Society of American Archivists, last modified December 7, 2017, https://www2.archivists.org/prof-education/graduate/gpas, captured at https://perma.cc/T5ZW-S6SK.

2   "Role Delineation Statement," Academy of Certified Archivists, last modified 2014, https://www.certifiedarchivists.org/get-certified/role-delineation-statement, captured at https://perma.cc/8AFC-BMWV.

3   About Learning, www.coalitiontoadvancelearning.org, captured at https://perma.cc/4ZCG-XEKH.

3 MUSEUM ARCHIVES: MANAGEMENT AND INSTITUTIONAL SUPPORT

Nancy Enneking and Jessica Gambling

For a museum archives to function most effectively, its parent institution must provide resources, infrastructure, and organizational support, and the museum archivist must clearly communicate the mission and vision of the museum archives and how the program complements the organization as a whole. The first part of this chapter will address the institutional support and resources essential to a successful museum archives program, including placing it strategically within its organizational structure and providing it with appropriate professional staffing, the authority to establish and advance archival policy and programmatic decisions, and broad support for its physical and technical infrastructure. The second part will concentrate on the leadership the archivist must bring to the museum, by creating and communicating such policies, planning for the future of the archives, and establishing and meeting goals.

Institutional Support

Financial and programmatic institutional support for the museum archives and its staff are essential to the success of the program. This support should encompass a variety of executive and administrative functions and requirements, from staffing and endorsement of the archives mandate across the museum, to financial resources and infrastructure needs. First and foremost, support must begin with the employment of a professional museum archivist, with the skills and education recommended in chapter 2, "The Archival Core and Beyond," to manage the archives. If the role of archivist is assigned to a nonarchivist museum employee, the institution should provide administrative and financial support to allow the individual to grow into the position, enabling them to seek the advice of experts in the field and take advantage of the wide variety of professional archival in-person and online training and continuing education opportunities.[1] Involvement in the wider professional archives community, through regional and national professional societies such as the Society of American Archivists (SAA), and knowledge-sharing with their community of peers at other museums are crucial to the success of the museum archivist at every stage of their professional career. It is in the museum's best interest to have its archivist maintain currency in standards, practices, and legal and ethical archival issues, ensuring the best possible decisions are made for the museum's archives program and, by extension, the museum as a whole. Remaining well acquainted with and in a position to clearly communicate best practices to nonexperts is especially important when the museum archivist is the only archivist within the institution and possibly the first archivist many staff have ever met.[2]

Administrative Placement

While the placement of the museum archives and archivist within the organization can vary, reporting through an executive level is ideal. A successful museum archives requires the creation and implementation of institution-wide policy, thus optimally the museum archives is an independent department, headed by a museum archivist with the rank and authority to interact with other senior managers. Placement within another department such as the museum's registrar's office, based on perceived functional alignment, may position the archivist and archival functions too deep within the organizational hierarchy, hindering the establishment of the authority and visibility of the archives. In some institutions where the ideal situation is not immediately feasible, it may be appropriate to consider where other departmental missions and resources align well with the archives. For example, if the museum has a library with professional staff and appropriate systems, facilities, and processes, placing the archives in organizational proximity may be beneficial. Wherever the archives is placed within the institution, the museum archivist should advocate for a reporting line that will result in active sponsorship of archives initiatives via introductions to higher-level staff, assistance with policy promulgation and enforcement, and strong advocacy for physical, financial, and human resources.

Mandate

The museum archives must be granted a mandate to govern all museum records of permanent historical value in all formats. It should specify whether or not the archives is charged with acquiring special collections in addition to institutional records and whether or not the archives is responsible for the museum's records management program.[3] The mandate should acknowledge the fact that some records permanently and legitimately reside within departments, such as object files in the registrar's office, in which case the archives should be prepared to provide guidance for the long-term care of those materials or collaborate with other museum staff on their management, rather than directly oversee them.

Financial Resources

The museum archives should have an independent budget with specific line items overseen by the archivist, with full expenditure authority up to the limit allocated to other museum department heads. If a budget must be shared, it is the responsibility of all parties to engage in close communication and collaboration to ensure that, say, commingled reformatting and conservation funds are allocated in fair and agreed-upon amounts. Wherever possible, the archives should work with the museum's grant administrators to develop opportunities specifically for the archives to be included as a participant in broader grant initiatives. The archives and its staff positions should also be seen as a potential endowment naming opportunity for the institution.[4]

The museum archives should be afforded full opportunity to participate in any paid museum internship and work-study programs. This places the archives in a position of equity with other museum departments in terms of both obtaining additional human resources as well as a similar opportunity to promote the work and importance of its program to others who might eventually wish to join the museum field.

Archival Infrastructure in the Museum Setting

Archives Systems

To manage the archives collection inventory, the museum archivist should leverage any existing library OPAC, collection management system, and/or digital asset management system already used at the museum. A digital asset management system designed to support the entire museum is likely to receive more support and resources than one intended solely for the museum archives. Collection management systems commonly used by museums are very good at managing discrete objects and activities such as loaning and exhibiting materials, and the museum archives should use them for these purposes, as needed, taking advantage of existing workflows and processes. With access to these systems, a museum archives may have the opportunity to manage significant archival materials in the same manner as museum collection objects and to more easily facilitate loans to other institutions and organize exhibitions around its collections. Systems intended to manage discrete objects are not, however, well suited to some of the most fundamental tasks performed by the museum archives, and it is vitally important for the archivist to know the limits of these systems and advocate strongly for collection management tools that have well-developed archives-specific functionality. Archival management systems should focus on the ability to efficiently track accessioned records, effectively describe hierarchical and collection-based relationships common in group-level archival description, document the extent and volume of collections, and manage locations of materials and available space.

The systems should facilitate the sharing of archival data, as appropriate, on the museum's intranet, websites, and media platforms and with state or national consortial archival databases. Ideally, the archival systems will also assist in generating trusted collection metrics to aid in setting goals and planning for the future.

Digital Preservation

As stated by digital studies scholar Matthew Kirschenbaum, "our born-digital archives of today will be the cultural heritage of tomorrow."[5] Digital preservation is a universal need and a profound challenge. When a museum commits to the creation and maintenance of a museum archives, that commitment must extend to the stewardship of records in all formats.[6] If the museum archives has not already established methods of capturing and storing born-digital and digitized content, however imperfectly, it must do so.[7] Museums may have structured data in stand-alone databases and enterprise systems, and unstructured information on a variety of storage media such as servers, internal and external hard drives, flash drives, floppy discs, and cloud servers. The institution may also have digital or time-based media collections with their own unique and challenging preservation needs.

The museum archives should communicate the data storage, technology, and policy needs required for digital preservation to the museum's technology staff and explain how they differ from routine backup and recovery procedures.[8] If digital preservation systems or infrastructure have been adopted for technology-based artworks or objects within the museum collection, it must be made clear that born-digital records require the same level of support if they are to survive in perpetuity.

Managing digital content requires a level of infrastructure and labor far in excess of that required for paper records; passive neglect and chance will not protect born-digital records from accidental alteration, ensure that external media such as CDs and floppy discs can be accessed, or guarantee that a jpeg stored on the museum's network will not become corrupted. A robust combination of technology, expertise, and policy is called for, and collaboration across departments is essential to make this work possible.

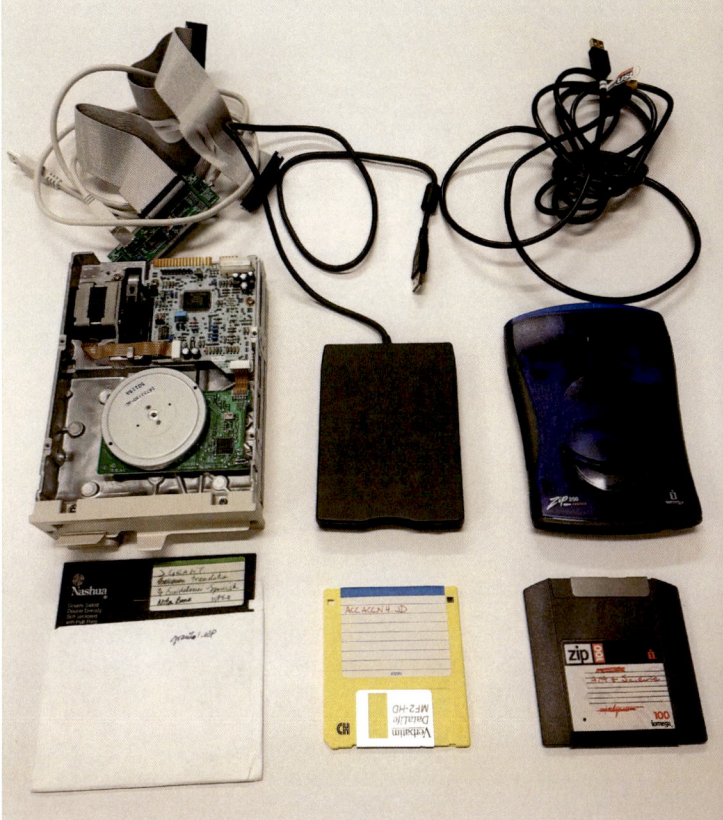

FIGURE 3.1. Examples of external media housing administrative correspondence and financial records.
© J. Paul Getty Trust. Getty Research Institute, Los Angeles.

Facilities and Equipment

Museum administration should afford the archives program the opportunity to take advantage of the skills, systems, and facilities already present within the institution. Collections management staff, along with climate-controlled storage facilities already in place at a museum, may support or even absorb the work of paging and storing archival materials. In many cases, though, archives-specific facilities will be required, as the museum may be uncomfortable sharing object storage areas with archival holdings, and object storage and retrieval procedures may be unnecessarily cumbersome for the frequent and broad access desirable for archival collections. The museum administration may not be familiar with the standards and specifications for safe and appropriate handling of archival materials so, when advocating for physical resources, the museum archivist should reference professional guidelines, such as those adopted by SAA, to demonstrate that the request is backed by professional consensus.[9]

The need for storage of both unprocessed records and processed collections is significant. No other physical space need for the museum archives will

FIGURE 3.2. A multipurpose workspace, with a worktable used for staff meetings, processing, and reference. The space includes a staff workstation, a digital capture station, and (out of view) a scanner and workstation for interns and volunteers. © J. Paul Getty Trust. Getty Research Institute, Los Angeles.

be greater, and it is the most common reason for building or remodeling an archival facility.[10] The museum archivist should begin advocating for additional space about two to five years in advance, depending on the institutional planning cycle, and be sure to make distinctions between immediate needs and long-term projections, providing specifics as they pertain to technological infrastructure, storage furniture, and climate control. This is particularly important in regard to physical space planning because the capital investment process is expensive and time consuming, and the museum will not want to repeat the process regularly.

Planning and equipping storage spaces will have a significant impact on the museum archives' ability to manage its holdings. An inverse relationship can exist between the efficiency of storage methods and their ease of accessibility, so these considerations should be weighed carefully. Spaces and the management of space in a museum archives should be kept as flexible, configurable, multipurpose, and efficient as possible. While not ideal, it is common for work,

FIGURE 3.3. Example of a workspace in an off-site warehouse, with laptop docking stations and tables on wheels, allowing for flexibility in configuration. © J. Paul Getty Trust. Getty Research Institute, Los Angeles.

user access, and even storage areas to do double or triple duty.

Sufficient space for processing and staging paper records, computer workstations, and equipment and supplies needed to engage in regular work will be required. If the space is also used as a reading room, ensure it has clear sight lines, extra chairs, a secure space earmarked for user belongings, electrical outlets in proximity, and necessary equipment such as a lightbox and a nonnetworked computer for users to access digital content. All museum archives work, access, and storage areas should meet basic health and safety requirements.

The solution to some space issues may be storing materials in an off-site facility or with a storage vendor. If the storage area is in an institutionally owned building, make sure museum archives staff have access and develop retrieval and storage procedures. To assist with circulation, other staff may need to access archival storage areas and be trained accordingly. If using an external vendor, the museum's procurement department and/or general counsel should review the contract to make sure all expectations in regard to climate, insurance, security, frequency of retrieval services, facilities, and service costs are clear and specified. Identifying and designing such a facility can be an advocacy opportunity for the museum archivist to promote appropriate security, shelving, physical access points and logistics, and even floor loads.

Accountability and Evaluation

The expectations of the museum archives and museum administration are mutual, and the administration has the right to expect leadership, management, and measurable accomplishments from its archival program, even when a solo records professional oversees that program. The museum archives was created to accomplish goals and solve problems perceived by museum executive leadership and administration. The museum archivist's task is to understand those drivers, address them, and take the opportunity to demonstrate the additional value the archives can bring to the table. As David Carmicheal frankly states,

> Though it may seem counterintuitive that a repository's vision needs to be communicated to higher administrators, these people must share the vision of the archives if they are to support the repository adequately. In fact, the strength of their support is likely to depend on the extent to which they see their own needs and desires reflected in the archives leadership's vision. For that reason, the best question to ask before communicating with people in such roles might be, "What's in it for them?" Archival leaders who can answer that question are likely to communicate effectively.[11]

Archival Policy in the Museum Context

While the collections and work of the museum archives are unique within the museum context, archives-specific policies should complement existing museum policies, standards, and practices in regard to collection development, access and use, and other overlapping activities. Upper management should periodically review and approve museum archives policies, enabling iterative conversations about the content and scope of the policies, providing an important opportunity to achieve buy-in, and demonstrating to museum staff that the authority of museum administration fully supports and backs the archives.

Because the museum has both legal and ethical requirements to keep some information permanently, policies help ensure that these requirements are met and that all museum information is cared for and handled properly while directly reflecting and serving the museum archives' mission. Reviewing policy regularly will ensure that procedures are not too specific, restrictive, or labor intensive for nonarchives staff to fit into their workflows and that archives' policy does not conflict with other administrative policies.

Collaborating in ways that allow other departments to support museum archives policies and procedures is good practice. For example, the museum archivist might ask human resources to include records policies in the employee handbook, fold the museum archives into new employee orientations or tours, and require that departing employees meet with museum archives staff as part of the separation process. It is also good practice for the museum archivist to work with museum IT so that policies regarding the use of network servers, systems, and email align with good records management practice.

Museum archivists should be confident and firm when creating policies. Suggestions and concerns from throughout the organization should be taken seriously and incorporated whenever feasible, but museum archives staff are responsible for using their knowledge and experience to drive policy creation in the area of information management. In a museum environment, other staff may believe they understand the boundaries of a museum archivist's position because its responsibilities and day-to-day tasks seem very similar to theirs; thus, to create and enforce policy that will work explicitly for archival collections, the museum archivist must understand and explain where archival and museum practices diverge.

Compliance

Keep in mind that while museum staff have recordkeeping responsibilities, they were hired to be experts in their own fields and have their own mission-critical work. Full and unfaltering staff adherence to archival policy is difficult to achieve and must be encouraged by collegially supporting staff with training, guidance, and clear documentation. Staff may only infrequently engage in records- and archives-related activities, such as depositing materials or taking part in a file purge, and require retraining each time. They may rely on museum archives staff to remind them how to apply records retention schedules and when to act on disposition. The museum archivist should have multiple lines of approach prepared, tailoring the message to the particular concerns of an individual staff member or department, whether these are information needs, a dearth of filing space, or an unorganized shared drive. Achieving success with these initial challenges can drive a willingness among staff to follow policies going forward and help achieve compliance.

Mission Statement

Creating policy for a museum archives begins with drafting its mission; all aspects of the archives' program should flow from and directly relate back to its mission. When creating a mission statement, the museum archivist should emphasize what aspects of the museum's mission can be supported, complemented, or expanded on by the activities of its archives. Thus, the final version should describe the purpose of the archives and reinforce the ways in which it serves the overall mission of the museum, making it an integral part of the museum's activities and identity. In keeping with the goal of both the museum and archival fields to promote broad diversity in collecting, staffing, and breadth of programming, the statement should reflect the museum archives' commitment to inclusion.

Core Policies

For the museum archives to have an acquisitions and collection development policy governed by concepts of records management, collection scope, and appraisal is critically important.[12] The policy should state whether or not the museum archives is able to purchase collections, accept outside gifts, and deaccession holdings. A well-written policy document enables the archivist to make a consistent case for accepting materials of value to the archives' collection as well as reject materials that are out of scope, such as unremarkable items belonging to the parents of the museum's founder.

The museum should have a records management policy, and the archives is well placed to oversee and administer the related program. A records management policy codifies ownership of museum records, states staff recordkeeping responsibilities, determines records retention periods based on legal and operational needs, encourages destruction of records in a consistent and sustainable manner, and places the museum in a strong position in the event of a legal discovery request. In archivist Richard J. Cox's opinion, "... an institutional archives program must be closely linked with a records management operation in order to ensure that all records that have archival value are identified, preserved, and made available for use."[13] Holding records management training sessions, assisting departments with interpreting the policy, and maintaining records retention schedules also give the archives an opportunity to build relationships with other departments.

Access, use, and exhibition and loan policies govern use and reuse of materials.[14] This documentation enables the museum archivist to address the challenge of promoting and providing the widest possible equitable access to archival records, the first core value of archivists, in the museum environment where access to information is generally more mediated.[15] Access and use will largely be determined by a complex equation of organizational status (public, private, nonprofit, subject to open records statutes);

the internal institutional sensitivities concerning collection acquisition, management, security, and current operations; the risk tolerance of the organization; the processing status of materials; and whether the researcher is a member of the staff or public. As more records are opened and low risk to the museum's reputation or security in comparison to the benefit to scholarship and the museum's mission overall can be demonstrated, a case for wider access can be made.

Strategic Planning and Goals

The museum archivist should establish institutionally appropriate goals and objectives for each major segment or activity of the museum archives program. The goals should be used to advocate for additional resources, but results should only be promised when they can be achieved under existing circumstances. The strategic goals and objectives of the museum should be referenced when drafting archives-specific goals; this will familiarize the archivist with the institution's administration and political landscape, which is helpful when determining the best line of approach when advocating for new or additional resources to, for example, create a digital exhibition on the museum's founder. Goals may be separated into those achievable in the next one to five years with existing resources and aspirational goals achievable with, for example, more staff, specific equipment or software, and/or the opportunity to further develop professional skills. Conservators and preparators, exhibition coordination staff, curators, specialized IT staff, education staff, and robust marketing and communications teams are commonplace at museums and accessible to the museum archives in ways hard to replicate in a business or even university environment; when planning and setting goals, the museum archivist should utilize these connections and explore opportunities for collaboration and resource sharing. As an innate part of all goal setting, the museum archives should strive to develop a reputation for service-oriented responsiveness, accuracy, robust communications, and the ability to complete tasks on deadline and in budget.

Disaster Planning

Records in the archives may be crucial to both planning for and recovering from a disaster. Building plans may be used to assess facilities for damage or to plan emergency egress, while ownership records of assets and collections will be needed to begin insurance claims. The museum archives should be integrated into the museum's overall disaster and business continuity plans and designated as an irreplaceable asset similar to museum collections. In the course of this planning, the museum archivist should consider multiple salvage and preservation strategies, from digitizing vital records to developing a salvage priority list.[16]

Communicating Results

Generating reports and maintaining statistics in a way that speaks to the overall mission of the museum can aid in communicating the forward progress and successful completion of both tangible and aspirational goals. As noted by Peter Gottlieb, archival "leadership pays attention to measurement and evaluation for the simple reason that it has the responsibility to monitor the progress of strategic work. The authorities to whom leaders and managers report expect them to show the results a strategy is producing."[17] The more targeted, focused, and thoughtful this communication is, the more likely it will result in additional support and, possibly, resources.

Desirable measurements will vary from museum to museum, but they might include use statistics and the ability to demonstrate an increase over time through reading room visits by staff and the public or citations in exhibitions, publications, and internal reports. Additional metrics might include the number of visitors to an exhibition on the history of the museum, the number of collections made available to the staff/public, frequency of assistance with institutional provenance research, collection growth in strategic areas, or even a reduction in the off-site records storage budget as older records are evaluated and dispositioned. The museum archivist should be sure not to limit the communication of results to a direct reporting line. Sharing the activities and abilities of the archives at general staff meetings will also help raise awareness and encourage support.

Conclusion

Every museum archivist should expect to provide vision and leadership for their archives program, in addition to managing the detailed ongoing practical work. It can seem as though one is always trying to draw attention to the repository's functions, negotiate relationships, communicate value, and position the museum archives to fully participate in the museum environment. This work is highly iterative and not always smooth, requiring ongoing attention, patience, and dedication, with the recognition that appreciation for the archives may come slowly, following a successful exhibition, assistance with an internal provenance research project, or a timely fact check for a major news story or press release. As Gottlieb concisely notes,

> There is as much art as engineering in how archival leadership pursues strategy, and there is no master blueprint that works for all archives. Persistence and learning from missteps are more important than any other keys to progress.[18]

Further Reading

Behrnd-Klodt, Menzi L. *Navigating Legal Issues in Archives*. Chicago: Society of American Archivists, 2008.

Corrado, Edward M., and Heather Lea Moulaison. *Digital Preservation for Libraries, Archives, and Museums*. Lanham, MD: Rowman & Littlefield, 2014.

Cox, Richard J. *Managing Institutional Archives: Foundational Principles and Practices*. Westport, CT: Greenwood Press, 1992.

Gottlieb, Peter, and David W. Carmicheal, eds. *Leading and Managing Archives and Manuscripts Programs*. Archival Fundamentals Series III, vol. 1. Chicago: Society of American Archivists, 2019.

Kurtz, Michael J. *Managing Archival & Manuscript Repositories*. Archival Fundamentals Series II. Chicago: Society of American Archivists, 2004.

Wilsted, Thomas P. *Planning New and Remodeled Archival Facilities*. Chicago: Society of American Archivists, 2007.

NOTES

1 Society of American Archivists Museum Archives Section, "Museum Archives Guidelines," Section 4, https://www2.archivists.org/groups/museum-archives-section/museum-archives-guidelines, captured at https://perma.cc/E97R-8HEA.

2 Samantha Norling, "Management and Leadership in a Nonprofit Archives: A Lone Arranger, New Professional Perspectives," in *Leading and Managing Archives and Manuscripts Programs*, Archival Fundamentals Series III, vol. 1, ed. Peter Gottlieb and David W. Carmicheal (Chicago: Society of American Archivists, 2019), 147–48.

3 Later chapters of this publication discuss in detail the museum archives' possible role in acquiring and managing the papers of external parties, such as artists, galleries, and former staff. According to the "Museum Archives Guidelines" endorsed by the Society of American Archivists in 2003: "The archives should have a mission statement, approved by the director of the museum or the institution and ratified by appropriate governing bodies of the museum or its parent institution, which defines the authority of the archivist within the museum and the parameters of the archival program. The statement should explicitly recognize the archivist's role in the museum and/or parent institution's records management program. All general policy statements concerning the archives should be in writing and approved by the appropriate authority." Society of American Archivists Museum Archives Section, "Museum Archives Guidelines," approved August 2003, https://www2.archivists.org/groups/museum-archives-section/museum-archives-guidelines, captured at https://perma.cc/E97R-8HEA.

4 For more discussion on fundraising for museum archives, please see chapter 14 of this publication.

5 Matthew Kirschenbaum, abstract for "Born-Digital Humanities: Toward a Research Agenda" (paper presented at the UCLA Information Science Colloquium Series, April 21, 2011).

6 Jeremy Leighton John, "Adapting Existing Technologies for Digitally Archiving Personal Lives: Digital Forensics, Ancestral Computing, and Evolutionary Perspectives and Tools" (paper presented at iPRES 2008: The Fifth International Conference on Preservation of Digital Objects, London, UK, September 29–30, 2008), http://www.bl.uk/ipres2008/presentations_day1/09_John.pdf, captured at https://perma.cc/U968-JYWU. Though focused on personal archives, the author's considerations and suggestions apply equally well to institutional settings and the acquisition of digital art. See also Edward M. Corrado and Heather Lea Moulaison, *Digital Preservation for Libraries, Archives, and Museums* (Lanham, MD: Rowman & Littlefield, 2014), 182.

7 Archivist Elizabeth Dow points out that all future archivists will be, at least in part, digital archivists. See Elizabeth H. Dow, *Electronic Records in the Manuscript Repository* (Lanham, MD: Scarecrow Press, Inc., 2009). See also Richard Pearce-Moses and Susan E. Davis, *New Skills for a Digital Era* (proceedings from colloquium sponsored by National Archives and Records Administration, Society of American Archivists, and Arizona State Library, Archives and Public Records, Washington, DC, May 31–June 2, 2006, http://files.archivists.org/pubs/proceedings/NewSkillsForADigitalEra.pdf, captured at https://perma.cc/Q8HK-49T6.

8 Corrado and Moulaison, *Digital Preservation*, 3–4.

9 Michele F. Pacifico and Thomas P. Wilsted, *Archival and Special Collections Facilities: Guidelines for Archivists, Librarians, Architects, and Engineers* (Chicago: Society of American Archivists, 2009).

10 Thomas P. Wilsted, *Planning New and Remodeled Archival Facilities* (Chicago: Society of American Archivists, 2007), 116.

11. Peter Gottlieb and David W. Carmicheal, eds., *Leading and Managing Archives and Manuscripts Programs*. Archival Fundamentals Series III, vol. 1 (Chicago: Society of American Archivists, 2019), 16.

12. Examples of collection development policies as well as other useful documentation pertaining to the appraisal and acquisition of records can be found on the Society of American Archivists Museum Archives Section Standards and Best Practices webpage at https://www2.archivists.org/groups/museum-archives-section/2-appraisal-and-acquisitionaccession, captured at https://perma.cc/WEL4-K78G. For records management policy guidance, see chapter 4; for acquisitions and collection development considerations, see chapter 6; and for guidance on access and use of museum records, see chapters 7 and 15.

13. Richard J. Cox, *Managing Institutional Archives: Foundational Principles and Practices* (Westport, CT: Greenwood Press, 1992), 80.

14. Access and Use policies, procedures and documentation can be found on the Standards and Best Practices webpage at https://www2.archivists.org/groups/museum-archives-section/6-reference-and-accessuse-services, captured at https://perma.cc/WM6G-8CVU.

15. Society of American Archivists, *Core Values of Archivists*, approved by SAA Council in May 2011, https://www2.archivists.org/statements/saa-core-values-statement-and-code-of-ethics#core_values. Captured at https://perma.cc/F9BB-2SZN.

16. Northeast Document Conservation Center, "Preparing for Disaster" part of "Session 8: Emergency Preparedness," in *Preservation 101: Preservation Basics for Paper and Media Collections* (2015), https://www.nedcc.org/preservation101/session-8/8preparing-for-disaster, captured at https://perma.cc/48MQ-SAT8. The Northeast Document Conservation Center (NEDCC) offers a helpful overview of disaster preparedness for libraries and archives as a part of its Preservation 101 curriculum, available for free on the NEDCC website, https://www.nedcc.org/preservation101/session-8, captured at https://perma.cc/QN2P-878P.

17. Gottlieb and Carmicheal, *Leading and Managing Archives and Manuscripts Programs*, 33.

18. Gottlieb and Carmicheal, *Leading and Managing Archives and Manuscripts Programs*, 38.

4 INFORMATION GOVERNANCE: THE IMPORTANCE OF BEING AN ARCHIVIST-RECORDS MANAGER

Sarah R. Demb

The development of records management in museums generally follows on from the growth of museum archives.[1] It has been divorced from the uptake of records management in other sectors, usually highly regulated industries that include banking and finance, insurance, and pharmaceutical research. Those for-profit sectors have traditionally benefited from consistent records-keeping methodologies and the recognition of records and proprietary information as critical to the bottom line, which in turn helped to develop many of the electronic records and document management systems now available as turn-key applications from a variety of national and international vendors.

Traditionally, records-keeping in museums has focused on object collections.[2] But this aspect of records-keeping, while often central to museums' missions, was not generally broadened to the rest of museum functions or business activities until recently.

As described in the introduction, the Museum Archives Section of the Society of American Archivists grew out of the Museum Archives Roundtable, established in 1985 by vote of the members in response to the growing need to address the issues within a formal cohort.[3] That group, alongside the SAA Records Management Section, has grown exponentially over the past thirty-five years, and best practices and ideas are shared across emails lists, meetings, and SAA educational sessions. Similarly, even in the United Kingdom, where the predominance of public institutions meant that records management was often galvanized by regulatory requirements such as the Freedom of Information Act (2000) and the Data Protection Act (1998) that support access to information and individual privacy rights, museum records management was not systematically addressed until 2007.[4] One project aimed to increase capacity for records management via training, consultancies, and guidance, to give museum staff, especially in those institutions too small to hire records professionals, the tools and skills needed to improve their practices. Picking up where a Standing Conference on Archives and Museums publication had left off in 2003, the project provided a template for other regions to follow and ensured that all its publications were freely available online to museum records professionals all over the globe. These resources are still available, although the project funding, along with the agency, were devolved in 2012–2013.[5] Even as of 2018, many museums had very new records management programs, and many of those are carried out by personnel originally hired as archivists. An informal snapshot poll of a self-selected subset of the Society of American Archivists' Museum Archives Section members carried out in July 2018 indicated that records management as a formal program was still relatively new, where it existed at all, and that records management schedules were not always in place.[6] It is still an emerging but essential practice in museums.

This chapter of the book seeks to consolidate the lessons archivists and records managers have learned from each other over the last thirty years and to place records management within the context of best practice within museums. All museums manage their records. Whether those records are managed effectively, however, depends on the comprehensive implementation of the systematic approach known as records management.

The usual business case for records management is that it strengthens museum archives by enabling the transfer of records from museum departments into the archives on a regular and consistent basis. This is very true but is only one element of the relationship between the functions of records management and museum archives. This chapter will explain why museum archives cannot really exist without records management and how records management is directly related to a museum's information security and risk management activities, as well as museum-specific workflows and business systems.[7]

This book exists because archives are a core function of the museum, which itself is an information (or information-based) business, one that exists to collect, generate, interpret, and disseminate information about its collections, its social and historical contexts, and wider trends in society.[8] Museums cannot operate without the many types of information they collect, generate, use, share, and preserve. Museums do more than just collect and codify information; through educational, curatorial, and conservation activities, they synthesize it into knowledge promulgated through exhibitions, events, and publications. Information is the "value added." For example, object collections management relies on complex informational holdings concerning provenance, exhibition/loan histories, and internal use/preservation audit trails. Much of this information is held in collections management database systems. It is cumulative and iterative, and often related to or extracted from paper-based materials. Databases allow all of this information to be held in one easily accessible place and, to this extent, museums are starting to digitize their paper records so that the electronic documents can be attached to the object record.

However, neither digitizing every item nor linking every record to additional born-digital information is always feasible or necessary. And using a business system such as a proprietary collections management database as a long-term preservation tool for electronic records is almost impossible. That is where archives come in. As demonstrated in other chapters in this book, archival repositories delicately balance practical necessity (space savings) and informed decisions about when offices no longer need records of permanent value on a regular basis. Records management allows for the implementation of decisions about how and when defined types of information move through their life cycle (or the records continuum) to ultimately either be disposed of or designated as having archival value.[9] Records management is the systematic process of implementing policy via tools and guidance to enable an organization to locate and retrieve the right information in the right format by the right person at the right time at the lowest possible cost with the least amount of effort.[10] Effort is still required, but records management endeavors to reduce it as much as possible![11]

Without records management practices, museums, like most other organizations, often end up with archives that have large gaps in documenting business activities over time, duplicate records, and/or records that are difficult to understand in context or to easily access. This is one reason that museum archives are often relegated to inferior spaces, seen as a low priority and inadequately resourced, or suffer from benign neglect (including being seen as a dumping ground for anything other departments no longer want to keep). However, many areas exist where museum archivists can contribute to the larger institution, and records management is a vehicle to build the relationships necessary to make archives an institutional priority. These areas include:

- understanding workflows and business systems, and therefore the records they create, across the museum through governance structures and a consultative model;
- developing a records management policy[12] and records schedules as an element of the museum's information governance program (in turn related to the museum's risk management) to underscore the importance of records-keeping as a core museum function; and
- implementing strategic approaches to support integration of records management into those workflows and business systems.

This means that solo records professionals in a museum environment are usually *de facto* records managers. They can't afford to ignore records management, and, in fact, must not ignore it, because records management work will support the archives and secure its role as a core function of the museum.

The "extra" effort directly contributes to archival work and often provides a business case for additional resources. In the end, records management is not only an archival collections development tool, but a key aspect of the museum's larger information governance structure and activities. Information governance and governance structures are outlined in the following sections.

Understanding Workflows and Business Systems in the Context of Governance Structures

To help colleagues understand the archives and to make informed decisions about which of their records have archival value, records professionals should fully understand the many workflows and business systems across the entire spectrum of its activities, in every department, from the top of the museum's governance structure through every operational function. The ways to do this are multifaceted and reach beyond the traditional analysis of the documentation—such as annual and financial reports, board/advisory committee reports, departmental reports, museum publications, and all-staff memos—used to understand museum functions.

HOW REPORTS CAN HELP YOU

Don't just collect the annual, board, or advisory committee reports; analyze them in terms of where records management could be applied. What systems created the information in the report? Where are the intermediary reports or statistics held before they are edited for publication? Who is responsible for those systems? How can the museum archives support their work?

These documents are important and advance an understanding of how the museum functions, but to truly grasp how workflows are carried out and how colleagues see the information they create, use, and document, the records professional needs to know about, develop, and/or be a part of governance structures such as board and/or museum advisory committees and core funding structures. What is the best way to achieve these goals? The pop-out example "How Reports Can Help You," and the bullet points and figure that follow show the relationship between workflow systems and governance structures, and illustrate why understanding each of them is key to collecting pertinent records (knowing who creates them and why, and in which systems they are held).

- *Board and/or museum advisory committees:* Depending on the size of the organization, board and museum committees may be more or less opaque; they may be listed in and contribute to annual reports, or they may be more ad hoc structures that aren't discussed outside the board/advisory committee or senior management meetings. Even knowing they exist—and understanding what they are responsible for—will provide valuable information about how the museum operates and what the board or advisory committee sees as museum-wide priorities. They also facilitate or enhance access to the information the committees may rely on. If the museum archivist reports to a senior manager or is a senior manager, then a ready-made conduit exists for finding out how committees are structured. This doesn't necessarily mean asking for confidential or privileged information; the intention is merely to find out what the committees are responsible for and which job roles sit on them.
- *Core funding structures:* Again, depending on the complexity of the organization and whether it is public or private, core funding can seem mysterious. However, knowing where the funds come from and how the requirements for receiving and using them work is invaluable to understanding why the museum functions in the ways that it does. This, in turn, can inform the way an approach embeds records management into the museum; for example, the annual financial report is key to analysis, in conjunction with information on any financial-related committees discussed.

The questions in the core funding pop-out can be transposed to other business systems and inform the survey and interview processes necessary for understanding how the museum operates. No better

EXAMPLE: CORE FUNDING STRUCTURES INFORMATION WORKFLOW FOR REPORTING

In the diagram here, how does records management interact with or impact each of the informational elements required for reporting? The end information "product" is a summary of very granular figures held in different business systems. Understanding the different workflows employed to extract these elements into a summary description results in knowing which systems are used to hold each informational element, so as to determine:

- How long the raw data, each information element, and the summary data should be kept (the records retention period) and by which department (the office of record); whether the raw data, information element, or reported summary will eventually come to the archives (a combination or all of these?); and if information is duplicated across any of the systems.
- If records are going to be exported from a business system such as a finance system, a ticketing system, an attendance tracking system, or a collections management system, how does that occur? Will the information be deleted from the system once the appropriate records are transferred to the archives? Do system constraints dictate how the records are exported and in what form(at) they will come to the archives? Even if the system's export functionalities are complex or limited, knowing how they work is an important part of determining where the workflow ideally needs to change going forward.
- To what extent expertise in archival preservation can inform the museum's choice of business systems and the way information is extracted/exported from the systems, and how the reporting workflow is carried out and validated.

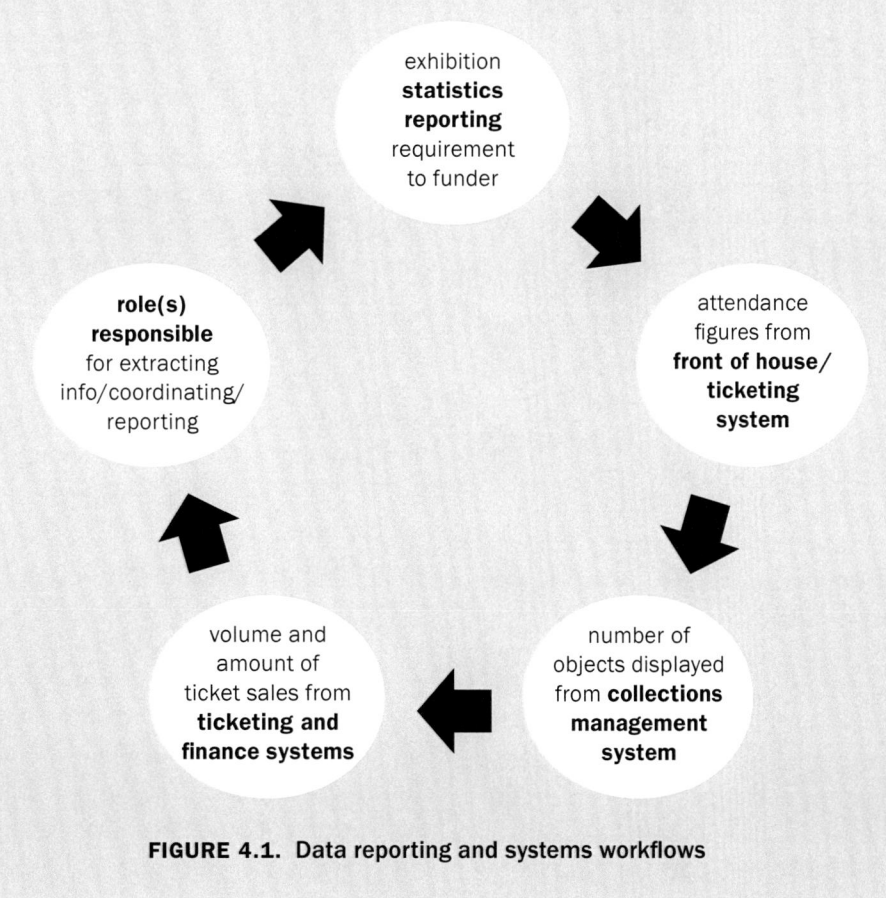

FIGURE 4.1. Data reporting and systems workflows

way exists for getting buy-in for records management from colleagues than by asking them about their work and showing that it is appreciated and that records management is invested in the information they create and use. Everyone learns from this outcome, so it is a win-win environment. This is the consultative model, as further described in this chapter.

Understanding Governance Structures

One understandable tendency is to leave out governance structures and to focus on individuals when conducting records surveys or interviews. Senior management is busy, and the governance processes that enable executive oversight and steer the direction of the museum can be seen as private or privileged. Organizing a decade's worth of board or committee reports is a very different—but related—task from understanding exactly how they were produced and/or how they will be created going into the future.

Choose one or two board/advisory committees and ask to sit in on a meeting to better understand both the way decisions are made and documented and also the larger context that impacts those decisions. This has the dual purpose of increasing the visibility of the museum archivist and the work of the archives and allowing the archivist to acquire necessary information. Typical governance committees include audit and risk, finance, fundraising or development, and special projects. Some museums have board/advisory–level collections acquisitions or exhibition committees; at others, these committees are internal working groups comprised of staff members.

Understanding governance will help leverage existing internal communications to publicize the records management program, including an initial records survey and staff interview initiatives. Knowledge of the existing state of records-keeping and what activities would be most beneficial to it will require not just an initial survey and interviewees, but a regular program to keep this understanding current.[13] Whether a records position or function is new to the museum, or whether it is being added to an existing job or to the roster of existing museum functions, communication is key. Internal working groups (usually comprised of cross-departmental teams) typically relate to collections management/

KEY CONTACTS

Your key contacts are often colleagues who will benefit most immediately from records management—IT staff and managers of the business systems across the museum:
- finance systems
- human resource systems
- collections management systems
- exhibition ticketing, admissions, and venue-hire systems
- building and facilities management and environmental monitoring systems

Even small museums will have at least one of these systems. It may be a single database that holds and exports critical information. It may be a complex relational database that interacts with others. Museum archivists do not need to be database administrators—but they do need to know what systems are in use, who manages them, and how the information they hold is used. Key contacts who benefit from records management practices will become the archivist's records management advocates.

acquisition, exhibitions, information security, buildings and facilities, and development/events/education programming. These groups are the operational counterparts to the governance structures; they are made up of staff that put the strategic plans approved by the board or advisory committees into action.

Solo records professionals at small museums have an instant "in" to many of the functions described here. On the surface, the role of museum archivist may not seem to touch on those functions, but there is a smaller governance table to sit at and more immediate opportunities to ask questions and implement records management "quick-wins" to help support the museum's goals (addressed in the next section of this chapter).

Working to discover how functions are carried out is not a linear process. Museum archivists can pursue this knowledge at a board or advisory committee meeting, find out what areas have internal working groups, promote records surveys and interviews, and investigate key contacts to support records management simultaneously.

Information Governance and Risk Management

Museum governance is ultimately a mechanism to reduce or mitigate risk to the organization. As an information-based business, the museum therefore incurs informational risks. Just like all other parts of governance, information governance is a strategic approach to the way that museum information is created, used, shared, and managed over time, taking into account the larger informational context of the museum as a whole.[14] This means that the governance structures that oversee museum policy development should recognize information and records, and thus records management, as a core function of the museum. Information governance provides a way to integrate records management with the strategic goals of the museum. Through information governance, records management is shown to support the strategic goals of the museum and is therefore a key part of all museum activities. Remember that information and records already figure in almost every part of the museum's operation. The *management* of the records and information is the "ask"—this work needs to be recognized as a core museum function, included in policies, and subsequently embedded into workflows.

Ideally, information governance is a top-down program that allows for implementation of records management within a larger information policy context. Yet, more often than not, museum archivists must advocate for information governance from the bottom up. It can be done! Transposing the strategic planning mindset that already should exist for other areas at the museum to information governance will enable integration of records and archives management with many business functions so that colleagues see it as a natural outcome of what they do. Consider the records and information aspects of every policy that is developed and disseminated across the organization. Are the relevant records and information included in the policies? Do the policies lack a reference to existing records and archives policies? (Information security policies are a classic example of the latter as, when drafted by IT professionals, they tend to state, "Personal data [collected for museum business purposes] should be destroyed when no longer needed," without referencing records management policies that contain exceptions that will end up in the archives.) Keeping personal data on ticket buyers (such as credit card numbers) for longer than two years is illegal[15] and increases risk of litigation, while keeping personal data related to object donors is often key to proving transfer of title and object provenance, should a lawsuit occur. Policies must reflect this type of information complexity by referencing specific guidance in the form of retention schedules, especially if they include blanket statements. Pointing out relevant gaps in policy language enables non-records colleagues to see the bigger information governance picture and to make it more robust by filling the gaps with this support.

Not taking a strategic approach to information increases visible information risk to the museum. These risks are both tangible and intangible:

- Uninformed decisions about information services divert from goals and consume vital resources (funds, staff time, technology).
- Resources are diverted to a "technology-led" approach to information solutions (rather than knowing what the museum's information goals are and then choosing the most appropriate technology).
- Opportunistic projects are mooted just to take advantage of funding opportunities rather than being intentionally designed to further museum requirements.
- IT infrastructure does not accurately reflect the museum's requirements.
- Information access is uncoordinated and inconsistent across the museum.
- Museum staff are unaware of or not trained to deal with legal[16] and ethical issues relating to information creation, use, and management.[17]

These risks won't come as a surprise—they will be recognizable in the records surveys and interviews conducted as part of a records and archives program. Therefore, articulating what information governance enables the museum staff to do becomes possible. Staff can:

- avoid duplication of information over multiple places, whether virtual or physical space;
- decrease time spent searching for information;
- prioritize information assets;
- implement strategic objectives and prioritize workflows;

- know who is responsible for creating different information assets;
- understand why the long-term viability and preservation of certain information and records need to be ensured; and
- understand what information and records can and should be shared, and what needs a higher level of security or confidentiality. This can lead to a more efficient and effective relationship with the museum's IT staff.[18]

Policy that guides information governance for museum staff may also be instructed by an information map, which enables records management to be implemented through a related records management policy and a records (retention) schedule.[19] Active use of these tools should result in decreased risk to the museum and increased visibility and reputation of the museum archives. When the museum archivist takes on tasks that inform archival work but that may not have previously fit into any one area, such as mapping out how records are duplicated across functional areas in the course of routine work (for instance, multiple instances of object photographs used to document accession, inform exhibition planning, and publicize collections), their value as an information professional will be especially apparent to more colleagues.

RISK REGISTERS

A helpful tool to track risk is called a *risk register*. Registers are often used at a granular level for specific projects, but they are easy to create on a departmental or even museum-wide level. Information risk registers use the same "likelihood x impact" formula as any other risk register to help mitigate and monitor risks once the records management program identifies them by in tandem with consultations across the museum.[20]

Strategic Approaches and the "Policy Umbrella"

Marty and Jones's work mentions the relationship of the information policy to other policies such as those covering IT, intellectual property rights, and collections management.[21] This is the "policy umbrella" model, in which under the umbrella-like cover of the information policy, all related work is governed in collaboration across the many museum functions that implement it. Figure 4.2 illustrates how records management (and therefore archives) sit within the information governance structure as manifested by agreed policies. Under the example policies, sample procedures and tools used to implement them are shown.

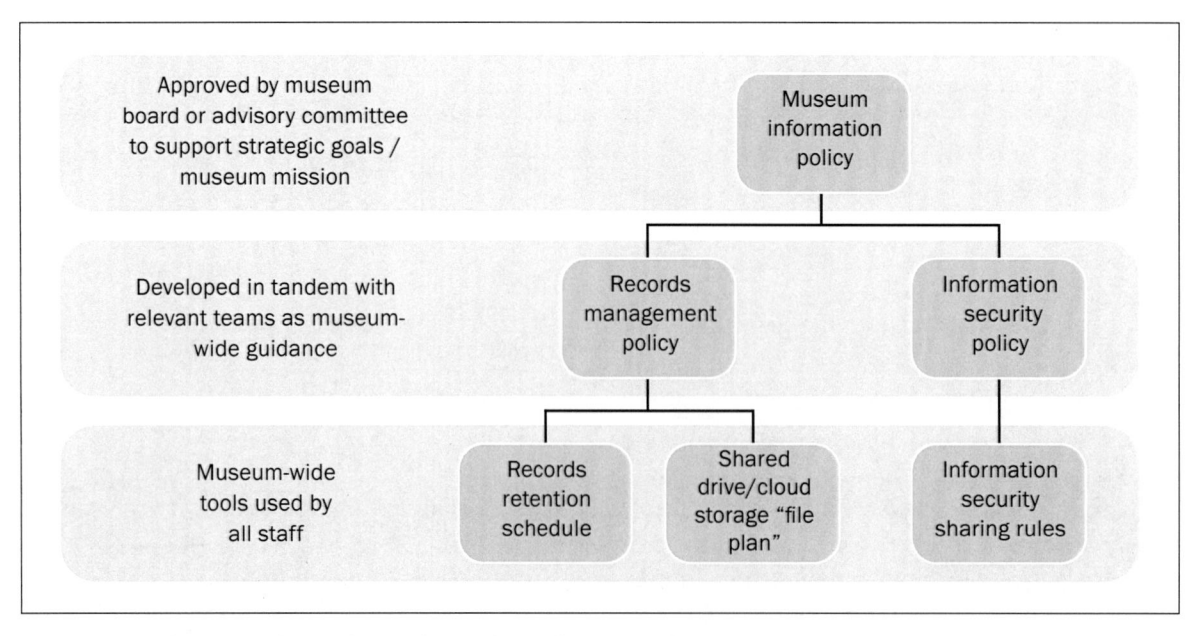

FIGURE 4.2. Sample information and records "policy umbrella"

This strategic approach prevents information and records risks from being siloed or sidelined. Instead, progress toward the integration of records management into workflows and business systems via the policy model means that problems can be prevented by collaborative work with all the relevant stakeholders: colleagues who use the business systems creating and holding information, as well as the person responsible for ensuring that the records in which the information is preserved are central to museum programs. This allows several types of issues to be addressed:

- Unnecessary duplication of information held in digital asset management systems (DAMS), increasingly used to manage picture or photo libraries and exponential copies of images on the museum's shared drive or cloud storage. The policy and subsequent procedures will allow everyone to agree which system is the "system of record"; which system holds the working papers/data/images while an exhibition, conservation project, or other workflow is in process; and who is responsible for ensuring that long-term preservation of the correct digital asset occurs via records transfer to the archives.
- The museum archivist ending up with non-permanent records in large digital archival collections. A thorough records schedule defines which records must be weeded before ingest into any digital preservation system (whether it is a read-only shared drive or a more sophisticated system).[22]
- When it is good value to digitize records—the tendency to digitize is fierce! Having all the information readily at hand is an attractive proposition; strong information and records policies, and the research on workflows that inform them, will help determine the extent to which colleagues really need the materials under consideration to be digitized. Is it possible to make the records available from the archives on an as-needed basis and save money and time? Or are the records vital enough on an ongoing basis that digitization is worth both the initial investment and migration/storage costs over time?[23]

Linking the museum's strategic goals to information risk management via the information policy is the bedrock upon which the museum archives' programs will flourish. An information policy derives from the museum's mission statement, goals, and priorities, and defines:

- the objectives of information use;
- the technologies used for managing information;
- the persons responsible for managing information; and
- the criteria used for monitoring implementation of the policy.[24]

This type of policy will benefit from comment by nonrecords colleagues, after which it can be brought to the most appropriate governance structure for approval. This action on its own may result in or encourage a new governance area for information in the museum. In the United Kingdom, the impetus for information governance over the past fifteen years has been linked to strong data protection and freedom of information legislation, which impacted both the public and private sectors. In the United States, similar legislation and initiatives surrounding repatriation of Native American grave goods and cultural patrimony and restitution for Nazi-looted art have played similar roles since the late 1990s.[25] However, the case for information governance, and good practice in records and archives management, does not need to rest on such specific areas (although they are powerful arguments). The reality is that good information governance supports all the museum's strategic goals, and poor information governance can increase financial, legal, and reputational risks to the organization.

Once records management is linked to the strategic goals of the museum, it shows how records management is integrated into the many granular (but museum-wide) workflows, and the activities that support the development of museum archives will become more routine. These activities might include:

- ensuring that new employees understand how information systems work, how they should store the information they create, and what information security measures may apply to their work;
- ensuring that the records of departing employees are shared appropriately,

transferred to the archives, and/or destroyed as scheduled in a timely manner;
- organizing records on shared network drives according to an agreed plan that reflects the way colleagues use the information;
- decreasing duplication between paper and digital records and instances of multiple digital records "just in case";
- including museum information management requirements (such as data export) in user requirements and third-party contracts for shared services (such as membership database management, email and website hosting, or even HR systems);
- distinguishing between materials in the picture or photo library for licensing and marketing purposes, the photograph archives, and the active (or semi-active) records kept by museum photographers;
- establishing a workflow for exhibitions projects that allows curators to reuse their research notes for future work, while at the same time providing a comprehensive and definitive record of the exhibition available for reuse as part of the archives; and
- linking related records and archives to the appropriate object record in the collections management database.

These are just a few examples of the way increased awareness of information opportunities and risk benefit the museum and ultimately the museum archives. This awareness is one of the main goals of establishing or managing a records and archives program within the context of information governance. In turn, this means that colleagues are more likely to understand and use records management tools such as a records retention schedule.

Being an archivist-records manager brings more than one advantage: the museum archivist is informed about and can effectively plan for the records that are accessioned into the archives; is strategically positioned to provide guidance to colleagues on a wide range of information and records decisions; and can bring museum archives to join core institutional functions in a highly visible and effective way that benefits all staff while enhancing the organization's reputation and reducing financial and informational risk. The result is that the museum archives benefits from comprehensive and regular transfers of material, instead of being a well-meant afterthought repository of last resort.

Further Reading

American Association of Museums. *Proceedings of the American Association of Museums.* Pittsburgh, 1907, 77–82.

Brunskill, Charlotte, and Sarah R. Demb. *Records Management for Museums and Galleries: An Introduction.* Oxford: Chandos Publishing, 2012.

Franks, Patricia C. *Records and Information Management.* Chicago: Neal-Schuman, 2013.

Lomas, E. "Information Governance: Information Security and Access within a UK Context." *Records Management Journal* 20, no. 2, 2010, 182–98. https://discovery.ucl.ac.uk/id/eprint/1543932/1/Lomas_information_governance_information-security.pdf, captured at https://perma.cc/A5B7-VQH2.

Marty, Paul F., and Katherine Burton Jones. *Museum Informatics: People, Information and Technology in Museums.* New York: Routledge, 2008.

Renaissance London Information and Records Management Project Toolkits and Fact Sheets:
- Demb, Sarah, and Samira Teuteberg. *Museum Records Management Toolkit*, 2010. http://www.museuminfo-records.org.uk/toolkits/RecordsManagement.pdf, captured at https://perma.cc/3UPK-8JM3.
- Fact Sheet: Records Management in Museums—What Is It? Why Should Museum Managers Care? http://www.museuminfo-records.org.uk/factsheets/managers.pdf, captured at https://perma.cc/P3DY-9YD8.
- Fact Sheet: Records Management in Museums—What Is It? Why Should Museum Staff Care? http://www.museuminfo-records.org.uk/factsheets/staff.pdf, captured at https://perma.cc/2P6K-93HU.

- Fact Sheet: Records Management in Museums—Managing Your Email. http://www.museuminfo-records.org.uk/factsheets/email.pdf, captured at https://perma.cc/GSW3-DR89.
- Fact Sheet: Records Management in Museums—Version Control. http://www.museuminfo-records.org.uk/factsheets/versioncontrol.pdf, captured at https://perma.cc/M3C4-ZELL.
- Fact Sheet: Records Management in Museums—Naming Your Files and Folders. http://www.museuminfo-records.org.uk/factsheets/naming.pdf, captured at https://perma.cc/MVF6-AHQF.
- Fact Sheet, 2010: Museum Information Management: Adapting to Change—Quick Guide 4: Assessing [information management] Risk. http://www.museuminfo-records.org.uk/downloads/4AssessingRisk.pdf, captured at https://perma.cc/9THJ-BVRB.
- Grant, Alice, and Claire Sussums. *Museum Information Policy Toolkit*. London: Renaissance London/MLA, 2010. http://www.museuminfo-records.org.uk/toolkits/InformationPolicy.pdf, captured at https://perma.cc/BK66-EKPT.

Robek, Mary F., Gerald F. Brown, and David O. Stephens, *Information and Records Management: Document-Based Information Systems*. New York/Glencoe: McGraw-Hill, 1995, 20–21.

NOTES

1 Records management in its formal sense as the practice of work described in this chapter began within a governmental context within the National Archives and Records Administration (NARA) in the 1930s. (Patricia C. Franks, *Records and Information Management*, 2nd ed. [Chicago: Neal-Schuman, 2018], 5). The function was a division of NARA by 1949, and a national system for inactive records was in place by 1952 (Mary F. Robek, Gerald F. Brown, and David O. Stephens, *Information and Records Management: Document-Based Information Systems* [New York, Glencoe: McGraw-Hill, 1995], 20–21). However, even a significant and regulated government museum such as the Smithsonian Institution (established in 1846) only hired its first archivist in the 1890s; records management came much later. The American Association of Museums (AAM, now American Alliance of Museums) held what was probably its first session on museum records in 1907 (American Association of Museums. *Proceedings of the American Association of Museums*, Pittsburgh, 1907, 77–82). Museum archives were not generally formalized or separately resourced from libraries until the late 1970s, when the Belmont Conference included twenty-two archivists from eighteen repositories (Deborah Wythe, ed., *Museum Archives: An Introduction* [Chicago: Society of American Archivists, 2004], 4–5). Even in the United Kingdom, where public museums vastly outnumber their private counterparts, a similar meeting (the Standing Conference on Archives in Museums, or SCAM) was not held until 1989 (Charlotte Brunskill and Sarah R. Demb, *Records Management for Museums and Galleries: An Introduction* [Oxford: Chandos, 2012], 7).

2 This focus was to provide evidence of transfer of title and best preservation practices combined with the need to understand their holdings as they have grown, often exponentially, over the last 150 years. The emergence of the registrar role is a testament to the meticulous recordkeeping of curators as both continue to work closely to document and preserve object histories over time. Collections managers, registrars, curators, and archivists rely on each other for the herculean efforts demanded by the Native American Graves Protection and Repatriation Act (NAGPRA) of 1990, which continues to impact the work of anthropology, natural history, art, and local history museums.

3 Society of American Archivists, *Museum Archivist: Newsletter of the Museum Archives Roundtable* 1, no. 1 (1986), http://files.archivists.org/groups/museum/newsletter/pastissues/pdfs/198612_vol01n1.pdf, captured at https://perma.cc/EPD9-YDPF.

4 The Museum Library and Archives Council (MLA; later rebranded as Renaissance London) funded a records management project for the London Museums Hub, a consortium of regranting agencies made up of four larger museums that coordinated collaborative projects among the 240+ smaller museums within the greater London area.

5 Renaissance London, http://www.museuminfo-records.org.uk, captured at https://perma.cc/95ZD-YXWR.

6 Personal communication, Doodle Poll.

7 The basic principles and tools of records management for museums and related issues common to museums are described in the 2012 companion volume (see footnote 10) of sorts to the 2004 version of this book. Additional resources are available online as listed at the end of this chapter.

8 Brunskill and Demb, *Records Management for Museums and Galleries*, 35.

9 Brunskill and Demb, *Records Management for Museums and Galleries*, 44.

10 Wythe, *Museum Archives*, 112.

11 The records "life cycle" is based on the idea that records become less immediately useful over time and that different people in the organization are responsible for managing the record as its usefulness changes; the records "continuum" approach assumes that records may be kept and used for multiple purposes simultaneously and that therefore multiple people must collaborate to manage the records over the medium and perhaps long term (Wythe, *Museum Archives*, 112). These concepts are based on those described in Hilary Jenkinson, *A Manual of Archive Administration* (London: Percy Lund, Humphries and Co., 1922, 1937); Theodore R. Schellenberg, *Modern Archives: Principles and Techniques* (Chicago: University of Chicago Press, 1956, 1996); and Frank Upward, "Structuring the Records Continuum—Part 1: Post-custodial Principles and Properties," *Archives and Manuscripts* 24, no. 2 (1996): 268–85.

12 See https://www2.archivists.org/groups/museum-archives-section/3-records-management for policy and schedule examples.

13 In the digital decade-plus since 2004, archivists with records management responsibilities no longer have the luxury of

"recognizing [their] limitations" (Wythe, *Museum Archives*, 112). That is, by all means, know your limitations—and then get out there and overcome or surpass them! I have been a sole records professional in all three of my museum archives jobs—you can do it—and benefit from it—the "it" being records management. In many ways, electronic records demand that we all—including every staff person in the museum—be records managers. Embrace it! A good records management program educates your colleagues to do what you cannot.

14 "... information governance solutions and thinking, which balance risks, present many of the practical answers for the development of records and information management systems within the context of current and future challenges." See Elizabeth Lomas, "Information Governance: Information Security and Access within a UK Context" (article as submitted to *Records Management Journal*, 2010), 3, https://discovery.ucl.ac.uk/id/eprint/1543932/1/Lomas_information_governance_information-security.pdf.

15 Fair and Accurate Credit Transactions Act of 2003 (FACTA) § 628; 15 U.S.C. § 1681w; 16 C.F.R. § 682; 12 C.F.R. § 205.13, https://www.congress.gov/108/plaws/publ159/PLAW-108publ159.pdf.

16 An additional argument for consistent and comprehensive policy is that, in any organization, records destruction of eligible, relevant (as defined by legal counsel) records should always stop (be put "on hold") when a lawsuit is underway and should not resume until legal counsel has advised it is safe to do so.

17 Alice Grant and Claire Sussums, *Museum Information Policy Toolkit* (London: Renaissance London/MLA, 2010), 9, http://www.museuminfo-records.org.uk/toolkits/InformationPolicy.pdf, captured at https://perma.cc/BK66-EKPT.

18 Grant and Sussums, *Museum Information Policy Toolkit*.

19 An *information map* can be a simple spreadsheet listing who is responsible for which information asset, or a more complex visualization of the relationship between assets and responsible staff at various points of the appropriate workflows. No matter what form it is in, the map must be made available to all staff—on a shared drive, intranet, or similar platform, whichever is most easily accessible in the museum. Traditionally, museum librarians often ended up *being* the information map. This was a fine idea, until they left the museum, or exponential growth occurred, and suddenly one person's undocumented knowledge was incomplete or no longer held within the organization. If the map is mandated within *information governance*, then this knowledge becomes *information*—and more accessible to everyone who needs to access it.

20 A sample information risk register can be found in Brunskill and Demb, *Records Management for Museums and Galleries*, 51.

21 Paul F. Marty and Katherine Burton Jones, *Museum Informatics: People, Information and Technology in Museums* (New York: Routledge, 2008), 105.

22 Here, the archivist may decide that a "big bucket" approach to the records schedule may not work for certain types of records created in specific workflows or business systems. For example, one retention period for all HR or financial records may be workable for those functions (*caveat emptor!*); but when it comes to multiple iterations of exhibition plans or draft exhibition panel text and images, a more granular approach may be necessary to avoid keeping duplicates or nonfinal versions in the archives. The traditional approach to records schedules has often been departmental, when in fact, the same types of records with the same functions are kept across departments. In this case, a "big bucket" approach to, for example, invoices, will usually work; when it comes to retention, where the invoice is held may not matter. The idea is to simplify the records schedule to encourage its use. See Brunskill and Demb, *Records Management for Museums and Galleries*, for more detailed guidance on records schedules.

23 The COVID-19 pandemic brought these questions into sharp relief as many museums prioritized rapid digitization projects to enable their staff to work from home. The sector may experience hard lessons learned from forthcoming quality evaluations of quick-turnaround digitization projects carried out on museum records and archives.

24 A sample information policy can be found at http://www.museuminfo-records.org.uk/toolkits/InformationPolicy.pdf, captured at https://perma.cc/BK66-EKPT; Marty and Jones, *Museum Informatics*, 103.

25 Compliance with the EU General Data Protection Regulation (GDPR) 2016, which came into effect on May 25, 2018, and protects the personal data of EEA residents *no matter where it is held*, may also help drive more strategic information governance in the United States going forward, as many American museums offer services to EEA residents that require collection of personal data—such as the email or street addresses necessary to fulfill research requests. For more information on GDPR compliance in UK museums (the United States is still coming to grips with compliance), see Helen Shone Development Partners, *Success Guide: Successfully Managing Privacy and Data Regulations in Small Museums* (Shropshire, UK: Association of Independent Museums, 2017), http://www.aim-museums.co.uk/wp-content/uploads/2017/10/2-Successfully-managing-privacy-and-data-regulations-in-small-museums.pdf, captured at https://perma.cc/V2XT-R298.

5 APPLYING ARCHIVAL FUNDAMENTALS TO THE MUSEUM CONTEXT

Susan Hernandez

This book strongly contends that museum archives should be administered and staffed by professional archivists. In practice, however, this is not always possible, and, especially in small museums, it is not uncommon for archives to be administered by nonarchivists. Even when an archivist runs the museum archives, that archivist will likely report to a nonarchivist like a librarian, registrar, curator, or museum administrator. Working with museum colleagues who are unfamiliar with archives makes it necessary for museum archivists to be able to clearly articulate what an archives is and what it does and why to properly advocate for the support the archives program needs from its parent institution. This chapter is written with this audience—those nonarchivists in charge of museum archives and the archivists who need to explain archives to nonarchivists—in mind. The chapter will also be useful to museum archivists looking for a refresher on fundamental archival topics or preparing explanations of the archival enterprise for museum colleagues. It will discuss fundamental topics like selection and appraisal, description, and preservation in the museum setting and will explain basic archival concepts with brief summaries and more detailed footnotes. The chapter will also explore the idea of convergence of libraries, archives, and museums and discuss its implications for description in the digital age.

Selection and Appraisal

Archival selection and appraisal are not concepts with which most nonarchivists are familiar, and museum archivists need to be prepared to explain their rationale to colleagues.[1] Beyond the basic argument that space is not infinite and should be used strategically, museum colleagues will be familiar with the notion that best practices should be used to guide professional conduct. A curator wouldn't keep just anything offered to them, instead they would carefully vet, research, and understand objects before acquiring them as is consistent with established curatorial practice. Similarly, museum archivists do not just keep everything—if they did, they would not be following established archival practice. This section considers several models for appraisal and applies them to the museum archives context. Not all theories will apply to each museum archives. Instead, museum archivists should choose an appropriate combination of approaches for their institutions.

The goal of selection and appraisal in museum archives is to support the mission of the museum by retaining records that are essential to operations, decision-making, and research. Museum archives may collect internally, externally, or both depending on the mission of both the museum and the archives. Internal collecting refers to the retention of institutional records, or those records created by the parent institution. These records preserve institutional identity and memory, support decision-making, and are essential to internal and external researchers. Museum archives may also, or exclusively, collect materials originating from outside the museum. These external collections are often referred to as manuscript or special collections. They support the research mission of the museum and may augment the understanding of the museum's object collection. For example, a museum archives may collect the personal papers of museum staff and affiliated individuals such as board members; records of notable scientists, historians, artists, or politicians; or records of organizations and individuals from a specific geographic region.

The following sections will summarize several models commonly used in archival selection and appraisal. Before beginning, note that appraisal decisions in institutional museum archives are often codified by the museum's records management policy and records schedules. For institutions with a records management program in place, records schedules will outline appraisal decisions long before records are transferred to the archives.

Life-Cycle Model

The life-cycle model assumes records go through stages of active use, inactive storage, and finally disposition or acceptance into the archives. In this model, archivists select records once their primary purpose has ended, an approach that is appropriate for many situations in museums. For example, when a staff member separates from the museum, archivists are often called in to go through the employee's cabinets and network drives to select appropriate records for retention. Similarly, files for projects like

TYPES OF INSTITUTIONAL RECORDS TYPICALLY FOUND IN MUSEUM ARCHIVES

Although museums are organized differently and the list below is hardly exhaustive, the following types of records are characteristic of museums and can often be found across collections.[2] The museum archives' collection development policy and records management policy will determine whether or not records are kept permanently.

MUSEUM FUNCTION	WHAT TYPES OF RECORDS MIGHT DOCUMENT THE ACTIVITY?	MUSEUM FUNCTION	WHAT TYPES OF RECORDS MIGHT DOCUMENT THE ACTIVITY?
Governance	Board of trustees minutes and accompanying reports; correspondence from the director's office and other executive offices	Research	Correspondence; publications; surveys; scientific studies; presentations; lectures
Acquiring objects	Correspondence between museum staff and dealers or donors; deeds of gift or sale; payment vouchers; receipts; shipping orders; press releases	Programs and projects	Program development materials such as meeting minutes; program evaluation materials; lesson plans; correspondence; recordings of lectures, symposia, and performances; printed programs
Caring for objects	Conservation reports; environmental and security reports for gallery and storage spaces	Development and outreach	Grant applications and administrative materials; special event records; donor files; membership records; press releases; advertisements; social media posts
Disposition of objects	Correspondence and other records documenting the case for repatriation, return, or deaccessioning of objects	Maintenance and construction of the museum building	Architectural drawings; correspondence; change orders; specifications
Exhibitions	Planning materials; meeting minutes; checklists; loan materials; installation photographs; appraisals; marketing materials		

exhibitions are often appraised after their conclusion. Manuscript collections may also be acquired by archives at the end of their life cycles, perhaps after the death of the creator.

Records Continuum and Postcustodial Approaches

The records continuum approach grew out of the realities of an increasingly digital workplace. It de-emphasizes the time-bound stages of the life-cycle model and urges archivists to be involved earlier, perhaps selecting records for retention at the point of creation. Postcustodial thinking often aligns with this records continuum approach; it contends that records are continuously active, shifts the role of archivist from caretaker to manager, and challenges archivists to be involved in tasks like system selection and implementation.[3] This model may be especially appropriate for museum archivists because some critical museum records, such as object files, are seen as permanently active and are thus rarely transferred to museum archives. However, as object documentation becomes increasingly born digital, museums must confront the question of how to manage hybrid object files. Some may advocate for the print and file approach, and this could be appropriate for some situations. However, some born-digital formats, such as complex spreadsheets or three-dimensional photography, do not lend themselves to analog conversion, and the sheer bulk of digital documentation may make it infeasible to print everything. As museums grapple with the problem of preserving born-digital object documentation, archivists, who are concerned with the preservation of these vital museum records, can be valuable partners. Archivists will ask questions that other museum professionals may not, such as: What file formats would be acceptable to include in a digital object file? What metadata is necessary to ensure that digital documentation is authentic and reliable? What preservation steps should be taken to ensure the integrity of digital files? The fact that archivists do not traditionally manage object files need not deter or disqualify them from being involved in their preservation.

Other born-digital documentation such as financial, human resources, donor, and library records may also remain active in systems and be transferred from system to system in perpetuity. Institutional museum archivists will want to be familiar with the systems used in their museums and the types of records they contain. It may be possible, and even preferable, to designate records for retention or destruction at the point of creation. Participating in system selection and design can facilitate the inclusion of records management and digital preservation into core museum systems.

Functional Analysis and Macro-Appraisal

Because functional analysis comes out of an institutional context, it may be particularly well suited to the appraisal of institutional museum records.[4] Linking appraisal decisions to functions instead of to individuals or departments can help museum archivists stay ahead of sometimes quickly changing organizational charts. Even though department names and reporting structures may change at a brisk pace, the major functions of a museum can stay relatively stable.

Citing storage space shortages and a rapidly shifting organizational structure, the Smithsonian Institution set out to apply functional analysis as an appraisal criterion in the late 1990s. The resulting report defines four main institutional functions: assuring institutional continuity, acquiring and maintaining national collections, conducting and supporting original research, and diffusing knowledge. Subfunctions are also defined, for example, exhibitions are a subfunction of diffusing knowledge, and types of records associated with each function as well as offices expected to produce them are outlined.[5]

Functional analysis and macro-appraisal can be particularly appropriate for complex digital collections such as email. Some archives have taken a "capstone" approach to email appraisal in which the email account is appraised in its entirety based on the job function of its creator. For example, accounts such as the museum's director and department heads would be kept permanently because they document decision-making functions, while routine accounts like administrative staff document less significant functions and therefore would not be retained.[6]

Documentation Strategy

Instead of beginning appraisal work by asking what documentation exists through a records survey, documentation strategy asks archivists to focus on what documentation should exist.[7] Museum archivists can keep documentation strategy in mind as they proactively seek out records from important events like museum anniversaries or work to document interinstitutional projects such as exhibitions organized by multiple museums. Museum archivists looking for ways to expand inclusive collecting could also look to documentation strategy, which rejects the idea that archivists should be impartial and asks them to proactively develop strategies to better document society, especially focusing on subjects, issues, or geographic areas. Adopting documentation strategy could lead museum archivists to broaden collection criteria to include activities that may historically have been less completely documented, such as educational programming for underserved populations, records of museum departments not normally solicited, or external collections documenting underrepresented constituencies.

Minnesota Method

Externally collecting museum archivists, especially those faced with a broad collecting scope, who find themselves contending with an overwhelming number of potential acquisitions or donations could benefit from consulting the Minnesota Method.[8] Perhaps the museum archives is tasked with collecting the personal papers of museum staff, such as curators, and must decide which collections should be accepted, and further, which collections should be actively solicited. The museum archivist could use the Minnesota Method to develop a framework by which the relative merits of different collections of personal papers could be judged taking into account factors like which curatorial areas are already well documented, how influential the staff person in question was to their discipline as measured by the number of their scholarly publications and noteworthy exhibitions, how significant the staff person was to the museum's history, how useful the collection of papers would be to the archives' user base, and so on. Archivists working in historical societies or other museums focused on a specific time period or geographic region could similarly use this method to create a collecting rationale based on factors like the strengths and weaknesses of collections currently in the archives, an analysis of the relative importance of different topics, and consultation with users of the collections.[9]

Receiving Acquisitions

In an institutional archives, acquisitions are received from fellow museum staff members. These internal transfers present an opportunity to build relationships and promote understanding of the archives' role within the institution. Procedures will vary based on institutional context, but generally, the transfer process includes some method for museum staff to convey to the museum archivist the information needed to create an accession record.[10] Depending on the organizational culture of the institution, this information sharing can be facilitated by a form, an email, or, practically speaking, can be initiated by the archivist in "crisis" situations like an unexpected departure of a staff member. Whatever the method, general information about the records such as transfer date, department of origin, records creator, contact person (the person transferring the records), description of the records, and extent of the records (for example, number of boxes or digital extent) should be recorded. To avoid confusion between museum object collections and museum archives collections, museum archivists should adopt a method of assigning unique identifiers that prevents duplication with museum object accession numbers. This will ensure that museum and archives collections can be easily differentiated even if they are described in the same system or are stored in the same area. Born-digital records may be transferred by a records creator or IT staff member, or they may be collected directly by the archivist from a website, network drive, or museum system. If the museum archives obtains custody of born-digital records, steps should be taken to ensure the records maintain their integrity and authenticity during transfer.[11]

External collections may be donated or purchased and will require different policies and procedures from institutional records because they originate outside the museum. For more information on external collecting, see chapter 6.

Arrangement and Description

The concept of archival arrangement and description might seem strange to museum colleagues who are used to describing objects at the item level. Usually in museums, a one-to-one correlation exists between an object and its descriptive record, so care will need to be taken when explaining aggregate description to museum colleagues. The following sections will consider arrangement and description in a museum archives context through a discussion of extensible processing and baseline description; convergence among museums, archives, and libraries; and an exploration of the descriptive relationship between museum archives and museum object collections.

Accessioning, Extensible Processing, and Baseline Description

Most museum archivists collect institutional records, many of which are sensitive or confidential and must remain restricted to the public for many years, or even forever. When records are assigned long restriction periods, the goal of arranging and describing them is not to make them publicly accessible. However, just because records are not publicly available does not mean they are not used. Internal staff regularly use materials that are restricted from public use, and museum archives staff routinely use unrestricted information included in restricted collections to answer a wide variety of reference requests from external researchers as well as museum staff. Instead of visiting the archives and performing in-depth research using finding aids and processed collections as other researchers tend to do, museum staff often ask the archivist specific, fact-based questions. Perhaps they are looking for a certain document such as an invoice or contract, or they need to know the date an event occurred. In these cases, the archivist is the direct user of institutional records, and, to supply a speedy response to requests by museum staff, the museum archivist must be able to quickly locate information in institutional accessions. Because of this need to provide immediate access to all accessioned materials, museum archivists can benefit from a familiarity with the concepts of baseline description and minimal processing. Advocates of a minimal processing approach (also known as "more product, less process" or MPLP) believe that facilitating discovery of collections and access to them is the most important function of an archives and argue for making collections accessible as quickly as possible. They contend that traditional analog processing tactics, such as removing paper clips and refoldering materials, are not practical given the scope of modern collections, slow down processing, create unwieldy backlogs, and prevent archivists from making the best use of available resources.[12] Some archivists have eliminated traditional processing for most collections from workflows altogether and instead carry out all arrangement and description during accessioning.[13]

Employing minimal processing and baseline description is often referred to as creating an extensible processing program. Archivist Daniel A. Santamaria writes that an extensible processing program "ensures that baseline descriptions of all collections material held by an archives or library are available as quickly as possible, with more detailed descriptive work conducted later based on user demand and assessment of the research value and state of collections."[14] Museum archivist Deborah Wythe encourages museum archivists to create a consistent descriptive program to establish "an adequate level of access for *all* records under your care" and from there move "on to enhanced access to top priority materials." Furthermore, she writes that such a descriptive program "will also help you avoid the pitfall of using scarce resources to create highly detailed access to certain collections and little or none to others."[15]

Museum archivists may therefore decide to perform arrangement and description to a level deemed appropriate during accessioning. Furthermore, immediate description is especially important when the museum archivist is also the records manager and must keep track of records marked for destruction. As Wythe notes, "Both the beauty and the challenge of archival description lie in its flexibility. No one method will be appropriate to every collection or item in the archives."[16] Museum archivists should adapt procedures to their particular environments by leveraging their knowledge of their users, institutional priorities, and available resources to decide which collections would benefit from added description and more granular arrangement.

Convergence and Discovery

Arguing that museums, archives, and libraries would all benefit from sharing resources and information, some advocate for greater integration between professions.[17] This call for integration, particularly in the areas of professional training and online discovery, is often referred to as "convergence," and the libraries, archives, and museums toward whom the message is geared are often referred to as LAMs (libraries, archives, and museums).

The digital era has allowed archives, museums, and other collecting institutions like libraries to present their collections online, and convergence advocates believe that integrated discovery of these online resources will allow users to uncover previously hidden relationships between materials. However, challenges in implementation arise in large part because of different descriptive practices.[18] Whereas archives are described in the aggregate using contextual information and standards such as Describing Archives: A Content Standard (DACS) and Encoded Archival Description (EAD), museum objects have traditionally been described individually using cataloging methods designed to allow the museum to maintain physical and administrative control rather than to create and share contextual information.[19] Furthermore, museums each have their own specialties, which can result in various methods of description, and are generally focused on interpretation and exhibition rather than on providing users direct access to materials.[20]

However, the progressively educational focus of museums has contributed to a growing interest in making information about museum collections widely available. Many experts note that museums in the United States have gradually undergone a paradigm shift, changing from inward-looking institutions primarily concerned with acquiring, studying, and preserving objects to outward-looking institutions focused on providing educational opportunities and other services to the public.[21] As museum professional Stephen Weil put it, museums have shifted "from being about something to being *for* somebody."[22] Increasingly, museums are expected to demonstrate their worth to their communities, and one way to do that is by sharing their intellectual resources for the public good.[23]

User expectations about direct access to information also play a role in a museum's descriptive practice. Paul Marty, a professor whose research interests include museum informatics, notes that "It is possible that the functional convergence of digital libraries, archives, and museums has contributed to the changing expectations of all museum users, including museum visitors and professionals, about the information resources museums should provide online and in-house." Users, he contends, want museums to provide direct access to information in the same way as digital libraries do.[24]

SMITHSONIAN INSTITUTION: CROSS-COLLECTION SEARCHING

An example of a large-scale project to integrate description between libraries, archives, and museums is the Smithsonian Institution's Collections Search Center. Using data standards like MARC, Dublin Core, and VRA Core, a project team narrowed descriptive elements to thirty core data elements and created a system to extract data from library, archives, and museum databases. Once data from various systems is pulled into the single search center, items from multiple collections all pertaining to the same subject can be discovered at the same time, and connections once hidden from researchers can be exposed.[25]

The museum archivist is uniquely positioned to provide such direct access to contextual resources because the records held in museum archives are vital to a full understanding of museum objects. Museum archives contain records documenting the acquisition, care, exhibition, and study of museum objects, as well as the records of notable individuals and events that can shed light on myriad research topics. Museum archivists may encounter resistance to the idea that archival collections should be discoverable alongside object collections due to a perception that archival collections are not museum collections or that they are less valuable than object collections. However, to support the museum and its educational mandate, museum archivists should advocate for integrating the discovery of archival collections with museum object collections. Internal and external researchers studying museum objects will often find relevant resources in the museum archives but may not know to look there unless connections are created between the object collection and the archives collection. Many possibilities exist for linking the rich contextual information found in museum archives to other museum collections. One option is to bring collections together through search, allowing users to search archives, museum, and library collections at the same time. In a museum where archivists, librarians, and museum catalogers use separate databases, a system using crosswalks between them could be developed to allow information in all three segments to be searched concurrently

> **MUSEUM OF MODERN ART: EXHIBITION FILES**
>
> The Museum of Modern Art's Exhibition Files Project ties together online catalog records for exhibitions, artists, and museum objects with digitized content such as installation photographs, checklists, press releases, and exhibition catalogs. This linking allows users to see which artists and objects were represented in exhibitions, provides suggestions for related content, and allows users to view individual objects in exhibition views. The project also uses linked open data by linking artist names to descriptive records in Wikipedia and the Getty's Union List of Artist Names (ULAN).[27]

using a single search box, a strategy often referred to as a federated search. Creating this type of system would require deep collaboration between librarians, archivists, technologists, and those responsible for cataloging and describing museum objects. Even in museums where all three collections (library, archives, and museum objects) are described using a single system that has built-in functionality for cross-collection search, work will need to be done to create shared vocabularies and descriptive rules that will allow effective discovery across collections. For example, if the archives uses one version of a name, the library another, and the museum object collection yet another, no way will exist for a system to automatically understand that each variation of a name refers to the same individual without a concerted effort to link the names together, or for it to choose one authoritative version.

Museum archivists may also consider adding information from archival collections to museum object databases. For example, citations for archival materials could be added to museum object records. Conversely, mentions of museum object accession numbers could be noted in archival discovery tools and access systems.

Another option is linking information in different collections together using authority records following standards like the International Standard Archival Authority Record for Corporate Bodies, Persons, and Families, or ISAAR (CPF).[26] For example, if all of the objects acquired by a certain curator were indexed, records for those objects could be related to relevant archival materials through an authority record for the curator. Or, authority records for exhibitions could allow all materials regarding a single exhibition, including object records, exhibition catalogs, archival materials, and records of individuals related to the exhibition like the creators of objects, to be linked together.

The ideas and examples discussed here would be challenging to enact, as tools and workflows are far from standardized or widely implemented. However, linking information together could simplify the search for related materials, demonstrate the value of archival materials, and increase the profile of the museum archives as an integral part of the museum.

Managing Objects in the Archives

One topic likely to come up for museum archivists is managing the objects that invariably reside in museum archives. Although the term "record" often brings to mind formats like documents and audiovisual materials, the concept of *record* can be independent of format.[28] Archivists recognize that a record can be best understood in the context in which it was originally created and surrounded by other records created as a result of the same activity. This relationship between records is often referred to as the archival bond.[29] It follows that if an object is related to other materials through the archival bond, it can be considered a record and can appropriately be subject to archival management.

As a simple example, consider an institutional museum archives collection documenting a museum anniversary that includes a coffee mug emblazoned with a special design created to promote the anniversary. The collection also includes records of the development of the design listing the artist who created it and describing why the design is significant and how it relates to the museum's anniversary. The mug and the records are related by the archival bond—they both resulted from the same activity.[30]

Practically speaking, even if an object is a record and remains in the custody of the archives, it may be necessary to store it differently from other records. For instance, if a museum archives holds the collection of a soldier including papers, diaries, and a firearm, one would not want to store the firearm in a box with the papers and diaries. In this case, the firearm should be separated and stored appropriately. However, when an object is physically separated from the context of its collection, care should be taken to maintain the archival bond through description.

The care of objects can be challenging to archivists who may not be as experienced with storing and preserving objects as with storing other typical archival formats. However, museum archivists may be better suited to manage such materials than archivists working in other environments because museums and their staffs are well equipped when it comes to the storage and preservation of objects. Collaborating with museum colleagues on storage and preservation challenges is also a great way to showcase archives collections, promote understanding of archives functions, and demonstrate that archives collections should be treated with the same level of care and security as other collections at the museum.

Preservation

Museum archivists will have allies in their colleagues who already understand the importance of preservation strategies like proper storage conditions. On the other hand, storage, both physical and digital, is often highly sought after in the museum context, and archivists must advocate for the importance of the proper storage of their collections. To be effective advocates, museum archivists should understand the needs of their collections and be ready to use data to support these needs. Generally speaking, preservation can be divided into two areas: preservation management, which includes preservation planning and preventative care, and conservation, or treatment of damaged or at-risk items.

Preservation management ideally begins with a full collection assessment, wherein the entire collection is surveyed to assess extant conditions. Data about the collection, such as physical condition for analog records and at-risk media or file formats for born-digital records, should be recorded in a structured format. This data could be added to existing collections management databases, recorded manually as a simple spreadsheet or database, or recorded automatically for born-digital records using software such as drive mapping programs or file format identification tools. Although time consuming, gathering and analyzing this data to determine the most at-risk areas of a collection can provide effective justification for internal and external funding requests.

Preservation management also includes making sure appropriate storage conditions are in place and establishing procedures for handling, housing, and digital preservation.[31] For example, analog materials should be housed in appropriate containers, and users and archives staff should follow best practices for handling materials. Born-digital materials should have corresponding preservation metadata and ideally be preserved in a preservation system.[32] In the museum environment, creating a digital preservation program will likely require resolute advocacy skills and a collaborative mindset. Most museum departments create born-digital records, many of which, like object files and conservation treatment files, may be designated to reside permanently in their offices of origin and could be considered permanently active.

Museum archivists have the opportunity to develop beneficial relationships with in-house museum conservation staff, who may be available to advise on complicated or delicate treatment decisions and be able to refer archivists to appropriate treatment professionals as necessary.[33] Museum archivists can also make valuable contributions to their institutions in the area of preservation. For instance, as museums acquire a growing number of time-based media artworks, or other objects on media in various formats, they must grapple with issues of digital preservation.[34] Is it permissible to migrate artwork or other artifacts from at-risk media? What does a preservation format look like when dealing with a museum object? Having an archivist at the table when these issues are discussed benefits the institution and also the archivist, who could use the opportunity to raise awareness of the museum archives and the unique expertise of the museum archivist.

Further Reading

AIMS Work Group. *AIMS Born-Digital Collections: An Inter-Institutional Model for Stewardship*, 2012. https://dcs.library.virginia.edu/files/2013/02/AIMS_final_text.pdf.

Boles, Frank. *Selecting & Appraising Archives & Manuscripts*. Archival Fundamentals Series II. Chicago: Society of American Archivists, 2005.

Ritzenthaler, Mary Lynn. *Preserving Archives & Manuscripts*. 2nd ed. Archival Fundamentals Series II. Chicago: Society of American Archivists, 2010.

Santamaria, Daniel A. *Extensible Processing for Archives and Special Collections: Reducing Processing Backlogs*. Chicago: Neal-Schuman, 2015.

NOTES

1. For definitions of "appraisal" and related terms, see *Dictionary of Archives Terminology*, s.v. "appraisal," Society of American Archivists, https://dictionary.archivists.org/entry/appraisal.html, captured at https://perma.cc/DEJ5-U9LB. For a fundamental text on archives appraisal, see Frank Boles, *Selecting & Appraising Archives & Manuscripts*, Archival Fundamentals Series II (Chicago: Society of American Archivists, 2005).

2. See Deborah Wythe, "The Museum Context," in *Museum Archives: An Introduction*, ed. Deborah Wythe (Chicago: Society of American Archivists, 2004), 9–19, for a summary of typical museum organization and functions, institutional culture, and resulting records groups.

3. Sue McKemmish, "Placing Records Continuum Theory and Practice," *Archival Science* 1, no. 4 (2001): 333–59. Also, Frank Upward, "Structuring the Records Continuum Part One: Postcustodial Principles and Properties," *Archives and Manuscripts* 24, no. 2 (1996): 268–85; and Frank Upward, "Structuring the Records Continuum Part Two: Structuration Theory and Recordkeeping," *Archives and Manuscripts* 25, no. 1 (1997): 10–35. The term "noncustodial" is sometimes substituted for postcustodial. See Society of American Archivists, Dictionary of Archives Terminology, s.v. "noncustodial," https://dictionary.archivists.org/entry/noncustodial.html, captured at https://perma.cc/T8QW-NCKN.

4. Instead of addressing the content of individual records, functional analysis asks the archivist to begin appraisal by developing a full contextual understanding of the functions of an organization and the relative importance of those functions. The theory assumes the records created by the most important functions will be the most important to preserve. Functional analysis and macro-appraisal can be seen as requiring extensive research, data gathering, and analysis, which is time and cost prohibitive to archivists working at small, resource-starved institutions. However, this may not necessarily be the case. For example, university archivist Marcus Robyns argues that the "More Product, Less Process" (MPLP) approach championed by Mark Greene and Dennis Meissner can be applied to appraisal as well as to processing and outlines steps and methodologies, including example work plans, to using functional analysis as a lone arranger. Marcus Robyns, *Using Functional Analysis in Archival Appraisal: A Practical and Effective Alternative to Traditional Appraisal Methodologies* (Lanham, MD: Rowman & Littlefield, 2014).

5. Smithsonian Institution Archives, *Appraisal Methodology*, 1997–1998, https://siarchives.si.edu/sites/default/files/pdfs/SIA_Appraisal_Methodology_0.pdf, captured at https://perma.cc/9GEQ-H3WR.

6. For an example of a capstone policy, see National Archives and Records Administration, "White Paper on the Capstone Approach and Capstone GRS," April 2015, https://www.archives.gov/files/records-mgmt/email-management/final-capstone-white-paper.pdf, captured at https://perma.cc/3VVS-XWWA. For a museum example, see Cleveland Museum of Art, "Policy for Cleveland Museum of Art Records," 2014, http://files.archivists.org/groups/museum/standards//3.%20Records%20Management/CMA%20Records%20Policy.pdf, captured at https://perma.cc/A9KL-BQFY. For an example of a combination of the capstone and content appraisal approaches, see Museum of Modern Art, "MoMA Electronic Records Archive (MERA) Records Management Policy," 2016, http://files.archivists.org/groups/museum/standards//3.%20Records%20Management/MoMA-Archives_ElectronicRecords-Management-Policy.pdf, captured at https://perma.cc/PTE7-NNR3.

7. Helen Willa Samuels, "Who Controls the Past," *American Archivist* 49, no. 2 (1986): 115, https://doi.org/10.17723/aarc.49.2.t76m2130txw40746.

8. The Minnesota Historical Society used collection analysis as well as aspects of documentation strategy, macro-appraisal, and functional analysis to create a pragmatic framework that prioritizes records creators and outlines appropriate documentary levels based on business function—that is, some functions are more comprehensively documented than others. Mark A. Greene and Todd J. Daniels-Howell, "Documentation with an Attitude: A Pragmatist's Guide to the Selection and Acquisition of Modern Business Records," in *The Records of American Business*, ed. James M. O'Toole (Chicago: Society of American Archivists, 1997), 161–229.

9. For a helpful case study describing the application of the Minnesota Method to a university setting, see Tom Hyry, Diane Kaplan, and Christine Weideman, "'Though This Be Madness, yet There Is Method In't': Assessing the Value of Faculty Papers and Defining a Collecting Policy," *American Archivist* 65, no. 1 (2002): 56–69, https://doi.org/10.17723/aarc.65.1.c01107u676225hq3.

10. In archives, an accession is a group of related materials transferred to the archives at the same time. During the process of accessioning, the archivist assumes legal and physical custody of the materials, performs some level of description, assigns a unique identifier, may conduct a preservation assessment or carry out preservation activities, and typically begins assessing the future needs of the collection.

11. Erin Faulder, "Collecting Digital Manuscripts and Archives," in *Appraisal and Acquisition Strategies*, Trends in Archives Practice Series, ed. Michael Shallcross and Christopher J. Prom (Chicago: Society of American Archivists, 2016), 122–25. The transfer process will ideally include creating checksums and a file inventory noting file formats, sizes, and dates of modification and creation. Protocols for transferring born-digital records will likely flow from the method of acquisition, with transfers from external media, network-to-network transfers, and web-based transfers, for example, all having distinct workflows. For a discussion of transferring materials from external media, see Julianna Barrera-Gomez and Ricky Erway, *Walk This Way:*

Detailed Steps for Transferring Born-Digital Content from Media You Can Read In-house (Dublin, Ohio: OCLC Research, 2013), http://www.oclc.org/content/dam/research/publications/library/2013/2013-02.pdf, captured at https://perma.cc/85HC-GJLP. For a discussion of other scenarios, see AIMS Work Group, *AIMS Born-Digital Collections: An Inter-Institutional Model for Stewardship* (2012), https://dcs.library.virginia.edu/files/2013/02/AIMS_final_text.pdf, captured at https://perma.cc/43H4-D7XR.

12. Many attribute this approach to the influential article "More Product, Less Process," commonly referred to as MPLP (Mark A. Greene, and Dennis Meissner, "More Product, Less Process: Revamping Traditional Archival Processing," *American Archivist* 68, no. 2 (2005): 208–63, https://doi.org/10.17723/aarc.68.2.c741823776k65863). Others argue that MPLP is skewed toward manuscript repositories and that other types of archives had already approached arrangement and description in this way: see Carl Van Ness, "Much Ado about Paper Clips: 'More Product, Less Process' and the Modern Manuscript Repository," *American Archivist* 73, no. 1 (2010): 129–45, https://doi.org/10.17723/aarc.73.1.v17jn363512j545k.

13. Christine Weideman discusses setting minimal standards for processing, which are undertaken during the accessioning phase and include creating a catalog record and minimal description, usually at the box level, in "Accessioning as Processing," *American Archivist* 69, no. 2 (2006): 274–83, https://doi.org/10.17723/aarc.69.2.g270566u745j3815.

14. Daniel A. Santamaria, *Extensible Processing for Archives and Special Collections: Reducing Processing Backlogs* (Chicago: Neal-Schuman, an Imprint of the American Library Association, 2015), 15.

15. Deborah Wythe, "Description," in *Museum Archives: An Introduction*, ed. Deborah Wythe (Chicago: Society of American Archivists, 2004), 49.

16. Wythe, "Description," 43.

17. See Lisa M. Given and Lianne McTavish, "What's Old Is New Again: The Reconvergence of Libraries, Archives, and Museums in the Digital Age," *Library Quarterly* 80, no. 1 (2010): 7–32, for a discussion of convergence as it applies to the online environment.

18. For a discussion of how differences in descriptive practices make collaboration difficult, see Deanna Marcum, "Archives, Libraries, Museums: Coming Back Together?," *Information & Culture* 49, no. 1 (2014): 74–89.

19. Stephanie Allen et al., *Collective Wisdom: An Exploration of Library, Archives and Museum Cultures* (published on behalf of the Coalition to Advance Learning in Archives, Libraries and Museums by OCLC, 2017), 18, https://www.oclc.org/content/dam/research/publications/2017/collective-wisdom-white-paper.pdf, captured at https://perma.cc/SU3S-P8D5. See also Fiona Cameron, "Museum Collections, Documentation, and Shifting Knowledge Paradigms," in *Reinventing the Museum: The Evolving Conversation on the Paradigm Shift*, 2nd ed., ed., Gail Anderson (Lanham, MD: AltaMira Press, 2012), 226. For a summary of the many descriptive standards relevant to archivists, see Janet M. Bunde and Sibyl Schaefer, "Standards for Archival Description," in *Archival Arrangement and Description*, Trends in Archives Practice Series, ed. Christopher J. Prom and Thomas J. Frusciano (Chicago: Society of American Archivists, 2013), 12–85.

20. In some cases, museums do allow users direct access to materials. Certain museums maintain study rooms devoted to viewing items from the museum's object collection. Additionally, natural history museums often allow researchers direct access to specimens, often in storage areas; see chapter 13 for more information on this. For a discussion of the different standards, see Mary W. Elings and Gunter Waibel, "Metadata for All: Descriptive Standards and Metadata Sharing across Libraries, Archives and Museums," *First Monday* 12, no. 3 (2007), https://journals.uic.edu/ojs/index.php/fm/article/view/1628/1543, captured at https://perma.cc/6LGY-Z6RD. For a discussion of the relationship of archival descriptive practice to libraries and museums, see Kathleen Roe, *Arranging and Describing Archives and Manuscripts* (Chicago: Society of American Archivists, 2005) 25–27.

21. Emlyn Koster notes that this inward-looking culture was critiqued by some beginning in the early twentieth century, although it was not until the 1970s and 1980s that educators began to exert considerable influence over museums and their professional organizations. Emyln Koster, "The Relevant Museum: A Reflection on Sustainability," *Museum News* (May/June 2006). Cited from Anderson, ed., *Reinventing the Museum: The Evolving Conversation on the Paradigm Shift*, 202–11.

22. Stephen Weil, "From Being *about* Something to Being *for* Somebody: The Ongoing Transformation of the American Museum," *Daedalus* 128, no. 3 (1999): 229–58.

23. The American Alliance of Museums' "Core Standards for Museums" states that "The museum demonstrates a commitment to providing the public with physical and intellectual access to the museum and its resources." American Alliance of Museums, "Core Standards for Museums," https://www.aam-us.org/programs/ethics-standards-and-professional-practices/core-standards-for-museums, captured at https://perma.cc/S4VF-8PJQ.

24. Paul F. Marty, "Museum Websites and Museum Visitors: Digital Museum Resources and Their Use," *Museum Management and Curatorship* 23, no. 1 (2008): 83.

25. For a description of the project, see Ching-hsien Wang, "One Stop Search Centers," *Smithsonian Collections* (blog), March 21, 2016, http://si-siris.blogspot.com/2016/03/one-stop-search-centers.html, captured at https://perma.cc/62QD-VDFM. To view the search portal, visit http://collections.si.edu/search/, captured at https://perma.cc/E2G7-84X7. A draft of the data elements can be found at https://sirismm.si.edu/siris/EDAN_phase1_IndexMetadataModel_1.06.pdf, captured at https://perma.cc/M8N3-F37L.

26. International Council on Archives, "International Standard for Archival Authority Records for Corporate Bodies, Persons and Families," 2nd ed. (Subcommittee on Descriptive Standards, September 1, 2011), https://www.ica.org/en/isaar-cpf-international-standard-archival-authority-record-corporate-bodies-persons-and-families-2nd, captured at https://perma.cc/KYB7-5WN9. This standard is encoded using Encoded Archival Context for Corporate Bodies, Persons, and Families (EAC-CPF). Chapter 13 discusses how these records can link together related materials regarding scientific expeditions.

27. Jonathan Lill, "Putting It All Out There: The MoMa Exhibition History Project," *Museum Archivist* 27, no. 1 (2017): 1, https://www2.archivists.org/sites/all/files/MAS%20Newsletter%20Winter%202017_final.pdf, captured at https://perma.cc/NH4G-DY33.

28. Richard Pearce-Moses writes that "to the extent that records are defined in terms of their function rather than their characteristics, the definition is stretched to include many materials not normally understood to be a record; an artifact may function as a record, even though it falls outside the vernacular understanding of the definition." Richard Pearce-Moses, s.v. "record," *Glossary of Archival and Records Terminology*, https://www2.archivists.org/glossary/terms/r/record, captured at https://perma.cc/TA26-688T.

29 *Dictionary of Archives Terminology*, s.v. "archival bond," Society of American Archivists, https://dictionary.archivists.org/entry/archival-bond.html, captured at https://perma.cc/A54B-N443.

30 More complex examples and arguments for viewing certain objects as records best managed by archivists, as well as a discussion of how to determine when an object is functioning as a record, can be found in chapter 12.

31 See Erin O'Meara and Kate Stratton, "Digital Preservation Storage," in *Digital Preservation Essentials*, Trends in Archives Practice Series, ed. Christopher J. Prom (Chicago: Society of American Archivists, 2016), 78–125, for a detailed discussion of options and strategies for proper digital storage. For analog storage conditions, see Nelly Balloffet, Jenny Hille, and Judith A. Reed, *Preservation and Conservation for Libraries and Archives* (Chicago: American Library Association, 2005).

32 A detailed description of digital preservation is outside the scope of this publication. Many resources are available. For an overview, see Erin O'Meara and Kate Stratton, "Preserving Digital Objects," in *Digital Preservation Essentials*, 5–74.

33 The preservation section of this chapter is in large part summarized from Sarah R. Demb, "Preservation," in *Museum Archives: An Introduction*, ed. Deborah Wythe (Chicago: Society of American Archivists, 2004), 101–8, which provides more information about proper storage, handling, and preservation planning.

34 For an example of such a project, see Desiree Alexander et al., "Preserving and Emulating Digital Art Objects" (white paper report submitted to the National Endowment for Humanities, November 2015), https://hcommons.org/deposits/objects/hc:12634/datastreams/CONTENT/content captured at https://perma.cc/U3WM-B3JM.

6 ACQUISITION AND STEWARDSHIP OF MANUSCRIPT COLLECTIONS

Brad Bauer and Jennie Thomas

When the term "museum archives" appears in the professional literature of archivists, often what is meant is the institutional archives, which holds the body of records created by the parent institution in which an archivist works. However, museum archives may also include collections that originate outside of the museum, sometimes referred to as manuscript, special, or noninstitutional collections. Rather than documenting the operational activities of the museum, these collections might include a variety of records, such as the ledgers of a local business, correspondence files of a well-known artist, or field notebooks of an anthropologist.[1] Manuscript collections may be acquired as one component of a larger museum acquisition or solely by the museum archives; in either scenario, they are collected when aligned with the museum's mission, support research on existing object collections, or have value to the museum's public audience or research communities. This chapter will focus on the fundamental archival activities related to manuscript collections in a museum setting, such as the formulation of a collection development policy, appraisal and acquisition of collections, donor relations in the context of broader institutional collecting, and stewardship of collections.

Collection Development

The Collection Development Policy: How to Decide What to Collect and What Not to Collect

As described elsewhere in this publication, a policy that articulates which topics, materials, and formats are within the collecting scope of the museum archives is essential to the work of archival acquisition; this document is called a *collection development policy*.[2] Ideally, a collection development policy clearly identifies the benefits and intrinsic value of all materials—archival or otherwise—that support the core mission of the museum. It should also articulate priorities for collecting, which will support the museum archivist in building robust holdings through the acquisition of noninstitutional collections that are on par in fundamental value with all other collections at the museum.

Before formulating such a policy for the museum archives, the archivist should first consider if a separate policy is warranted for the archives, or if the museum's general collection policy is adequate. In some institutions, a stand-alone collection development policy for the museum's archival program may be necessary. However, given that both museum objects and archival materials may be donated or sold from the same sources and may arrive side by side as part of the same collection, a collection development policy that can be applied across the board can be an effective approach as well. Should the museum archivist opt for the latter, they should routinely weigh in on any amendments or updates to be made to the policy that address archival materials.[3]

A comprehensive collection development policy outlines priorities for the acquisition of manuscript collections, listing the topics and formats that the museum archives will, and will not, accept. It also may list the criteria used by the museum archivist in evaluating a collection for acquisition, including size, condition, and potential challenges to providing access, such as format and donor restrictions.[4] A comprehensive collection development policy can also assist in the rectification of gaps in a museum archives collection. For instance, a disparity in manuscript collection holdings documenting underrepresented artists might be identified. The collection development policy could then be updated to focus collecting in the gap area, after which another assessment would be made to determine acquisition progress. Establishing the scope of the museum archives' collection helps define it alongside those of the other acquiring departments at the institution, leveling the playing field and asserting it as one collection among all of the museum's collections and not one that stands apart. Proactive attempts to identify and fill gaps in museum archives collections through policy also help to raise the profile of the institution in the public eye and enhance overall the historical record and the research experience. The collection development policy is also an integral piece of the collections management policy, one of the five core documents necessary for museum accreditation by the American Alliance of Museums.[5]

The Value of Manuscript Collections to Museums

In some museums, archival collections may be deemed less valuable than museum objects due to a number of factors, such as the higher monetary value of some objects, for example, works of art, or strategic initiatives within the institution that focus on income-generating exhibitions and programming tied to high-profile objects, which tend not to be of the archival variety. The time it can take to find relevant materials in the museum archives can also be a factor in this perception. The information-seeking behavior of users of traditional museum collections management tools that focus description entirely on individual objects versus that of users of archival descriptive tools, such as finding aids that look at materials in the aggregate, can be very different—likewise, that of more inexperienced users solely schooled in a Google Images search environment. Even if an archival collection has a very good finding aid, it is not likely to describe each document at the item level, which is what some museum colleagues (curators, registrars) or inexperienced researchers prefer or expect. The immediate fulfillment that item-level description of museum objects can provide over aggregate archival descriptions (which may require further research to locate desired items) can make those objects seem more important simply because identifying and locating them is less time consuming. The daily work of museum archivists is to educate users in their descriptive tools—or to come up with more widely accessible means of description—to combat this perception.

Yet, the very thing that makes the perception of manuscript collections more intractable can provide unexpected benefits to curators who are tasked with designing exhibitions: context. Manuscript collections contain information regarding not only an individual object but its context as a whole. One of the curator's functions is to use objects to craft a narrative that helps museum visitors understand the significance or nature of an event, a time period, or a cultural phenomenon. Manuscript collections often contain complementary, ready-made narratives as a result of their documentation of daily activities, specific projects, and events. Additionally, manuscript collections have the potential to attract new researchers who may not have otherwise used the museum as a resource. This diversification of the museum's researcher base can elevate the archives' position within the organization by demonstrating the importance of the museum archives program to external as well as to internal users.

Appraisal: How to Evaluate Collections

Traditional archival appraisal strategies call on the archivist to evaluate manuscript materials for their informational and research value, as well as how complete or comprehensive the materials are in documenting their creator's life or events in which they participated, how relevant they are to their institution's collecting scope, their authenticity and integrity as records, and whether they require extensive conservation treatment or contain media that need to be reformatted for preservation and access.

When making appraisal decisions for manuscript collections in the museum setting, however, the archivist may be called upon to think more broadly about the possible uses of collections and how they might be relevant to the work of other museum colleagues. Rather than focusing solely on the scholarly or research potential in such collections, the museum archivist should also consider their potential use in exhibitions, educational programs, social media, and marketing. Documents

APPRAISAL OF MANUSCRIPT COLLECTIONS

When appraising a potential manuscript collection acquisition, the museum archivist could consider the following questions:
- Do the materials provide context for object collections?
- Do the materials contextualize the museum's history? Do they complement or expand on an institutional records collection?
- Do the materials have research or informational value? Is their content useful and significant to scholarly researchers and/or the general public?
- Could any of the materials be included in museum exhibitions? Do they provide context for any upcoming or existing exhibitions at the museum?
- Could the museum archives staff or institutional colleagues use the materials for teaching, programming, social media, or marketing?
- Can the museum afford the collection; not only in terms of the actual purchase price of the collection, but also the hidden costs of conservation, archival processing, and maintenance?
- Can the museum archives provide appropriate access? Does the archives have a public reading room with enough open hours to accommodate the anticipated research interest?
- Would the materials be more appropriately housed by another institution or in another geographical area?[6]

that might otherwise seem to have little informational value on their own could nevertheless have value as objects or be useful when featured in an exhibition or educational resource, illuminating and interpreting facets of a larger narrative.

During the process of negotiating an acquisition, the museum archivist seeks to do as thorough an archival appraisal as possible to ensure the materials fit the archives' collecting scope. This may occur by examination of the materials in person, or through review of an inventory or description of the materials that is detailed enough to enable sound decisions to be made from a distance. Museum archivists are often trained to think in terms of aggregated materials—such as a deep and extensive corpus of correspondence or a records series of documents in which a scholar can trace the evolution of a policy from idea to implementation—and are inclined to value completeness and depth within a given body of papers. Museum curators, however, are trained to view individual objects, including documents, as items around which to build a historical and social context that the object or document can help interpret and explain. For this reason, archivists in a museum setting should be attuned to the possible wider uses of archival materials that are offered when determining what to collect and skilled in demonstrating these uses to their colleagues.[7]

Acquisition

Having described the methods for determining whether materials offered for purchase or donation fit the scope of a museum archives' collection development policy, a question unique to the museum context remains: who is chiefly responsible for acquiring archival collections at the institution, the archivist, the curator, or other museum colleagues?

Acquisition Budgets

In many museums, as well as other archival repositories, collections may be acquired by donation or by purchase. For the museum archivist who acquires collections from noninstitutional sources, one of several budget scenarios may be in place: the archival acquisitions budget may be separate and overseen by the museum archivist, or archival purchases may be funded from a single institutional acquisitions budget meant to provide for the purchase of all items within the museum's broader collecting scope. In the latter case, the museum archivist must not only advocate for archival purchases but must do so alongside competing demands from other collections and curatorial departments. One way to regulate such competition would be through a collecting or acquisitions committee, comprised of staff from various departments who represent

WHEN ARCHIVES BECOME ARTIFACTS: THE ROLE OF MIXED COLLECTIONS IN A MUSEUM SETTING

In May 1939, Adolf Hess prepared to board a ship in Hamburg harbor, accompanied by his wife, Jette, and daughters, Vera and Ilse. The previous year, Hess had been arrested by the Nazi regime after the pogrom known as Kristallnacht, which targeted Jewish-owned businesses, synagogues, and other institutions, and he was imprisoned for a month at the Buchenwald concentration camp. He was released upon the condition that he leave Germany as soon as possible, and, as he and his family boarded the S.S. *St. Louis*, they looked ahead to the possibility of a new life in the United States, after first traveling to Cuba, the ship's destination. The fate of the *St. Louis* is well known: upon its attempts to dock in Havana harbor, the ship was turned back, with very few of its passengers having been allowed to disembark there. After a fruitless search for another port where they could land, including repeated attempts to be allowed access to the United States, the ship returned to Europe, where the remainder of its original 937 passengers landed in France. Of this number, over 250 were murdered in the Holocaust, as the Nazis eventually invaded and occupied the places where they found refuge outside of their homeland.

In the late 1990s, in anticipation of the 60th anniversary of the voyage of the *St. Louis*, the United States Holocaust Memorial Museum began to plan an exhibition to tell the story of this event. Museum curators sought out and received a variety of artifacts belonging to the families of victims and survivors, ranging from suitcases to photographs, postcards to ribbons, the hat worn by the captain of the ship, and pieces of silverware from its dining room. Yet, the most frequently obtained materials were documents and papers from the ship's passengers: travel documents, notes, diaries, letters, and other written evidence of their experiences which, when grouped together, resembled archival collections of family papers, evidence of their lived experience in documentary form.

One such collection consisted of the papers of the Hess family, donated by one of the daughters in 2000. The collection contains a variety of documents, such as records of Adolf Hess's service in the German Army during World War I, a boarding pass for the S.S. *St. Louis*, correspondence about attempts to secure visas, other travel documents such as passports, and records of the schooling that the daughters received after they were able to enter Cuba and settle there on a subsequent journey. As an archival collection, the documents sketch out biographical timelines unique to the various members of the Hess family. As artifacts, however, the individual items take on added significance, as prompts to tell wider stories about the shared experience of persecution, exile, and new beginnings as refugees in a foreign land. Adolf Hess's certificate of service in the German Army during World War I points to the efforts of many German Jews to demonstrate their patriotism with service to their homeland. School report cards of Hess's daughter Vera attest to the role of aid organizations that educated refugee children and provided job retraining courses for adults. The family's German passports—stamped with the bright red letter "J" for "Jew"—show the means by which a seemingly benign bureaucratic document was recast into an instrument of persecution.

These and similar documents have frequently been used in exhibitions at the United States Holocaust Memorial Museum, both in the initial temporary exhibition on the journey of the S.S. *St. Louis* and in subsequent exhibitions focused on related themes. While such documents, as component parts of archival collections, have been served to scores of students, historians, and other scholars in the museum's library and archival reading room, they have also, when temporarily removed from those collections and displayed in exhibits, served a different and widely varied audience of museum visitors, helping to illuminate and interpret larger historical trends, events, and phenomena.

FIGURE 6.1. Immigration papers for Adolf Hess, pertaining to his voyage on the S.S. *St. Louis* to Cuba in 1939. (HESS FAMILY PAPERS, 2000.130.2, UNITED STATES HOLOCAUST MEMORIAL MUSEUM, WASHINGTON, DC).

Acquisition and Stewardship of Manuscript Collections

different departmental roles and priorities—if this role is not already filled by the board of trustees or some other group—charged with collectively determining how funds are best allocated for purchases and other acquisition activities. The museum archivist should actively work to demonstrate to this group the importance of growing the museum's archival holdings through acquisitions in relation to the institution's overall mission and programming. Museum archivists with or without an acquisitions budget might also become well acquainted with development officers or similar staff within their museum to facilitate acquisition of noninstitutional collections and the resources to support them. These colleagues can assist in seeking grant funding or provide introductions to potential monetary donors who might fund the purchase of manuscript collections within specific targeted areas or who could finance the digitization, processing, or conservation of such collections.[8]

Archival Acquisition

In the case of institutional records, the archivist is always the point person for internal transfers, whereas acquisition of external collections will likely proceed differently and often must be acquired in collaboration with other museum colleagues. Such collaboration becomes especially crucial when collections contain a mixture of materials overseen by different departments at the museum, such as both manuscripts and objects, and it must be determined what staff will take responsibility for the acquisition, appraisal, and accessioning of the collection.

Donor Relations

Some donors come to the repository on their own, offering unsolicited collections that may or may not be within scope.[9] Donors might be sought out as well, and the museum archivist must be ready to cultivate relationships with individuals who may not have collections of their own, but are well placed to know of others who might—for instance, a researcher in the archives with a connection to an individual from whom the museum wishes to seek a donation. A museum archivist should be very familiar with the subject areas covered in their collections and look in a variety of places for potential acquisitions that might support research on those topics. They can do this by paying close attention to relevant news coverage, both local and national, including obituaries of individuals whose lives and activities intersected with subjects documented by the museum. They might attend social and cultural events related to the communities they are seeking to document, both to expand their network of contacts and learn more about those communities and their activities. They can read books, journal articles, and other sources of information about the topics they seek to document, noting the sources cited by their authors, especially when such authors conduct interviews with individuals or consult archival collections in private hands or otherwise not widely accessible.[10]

Once prospective sources of archival collections are identified, the next step is to determine how best to contact their owners. Some potential donors will be glad to be contacted by an archivist and to learn that a museum and its archives are interested in their life and career. Others may need to be introduced to the archivist by a friend or associate to establish credibility and build trust. This may be the case with high-profile donors in particular, who may require contact through their attorney, management agency, or others who conduct their business affairs; these individuals may be well positioned to know about the existence, nature, and scope of the donors' records as well.[11] In reaching out to a donor, the archivist should work with the best interests of the museum and its collections in mind, but also remember that they are asking the donor to part with something that may represent a significant portion of their life and legacy or that may consist of the last tangible connection they have with deceased loved ones.[12] In these particular cases, establishing a trusted relationship with a potential donor, or his or her heirs, may take years.

Thus, it may be helpful for the museum archivist to place themselves in the donor's shoes and to imagine what benefits a museum could potentially provide in addition to stewardship of their collection. Traditional benefits such as the potential for digitization and more widespread access to a donated collection, or tax deductions for charitable donations if the institution is a nonprofit, may be the same as those offered by archives that are not based in museums. However, given the higher visibility that many museums may have in comparison to more traditional archives, the museum archivist may

COLLABORATIVE ACQUISITION AND ACCESSION IN THE MUSEUM SETTING

A donor might offer a collection to a museum that contains three-dimensional art objects, original drawings, photographs, contracts, correspondence, business records, and published catalogs; such a range of items would require curators, registrars, and archivists to work collaboratively to determine the most appropriate institutional stewards for the materials. For some items, the decisions could be straightforward: art objects and drawings would be sent to the museum's fine art collection under the care of curatorial staff, while contracts, correspondence, and catalogs would be transferred to the museum archives. Some items, however, may fall into gray areas: for example, which department should accession a letter to the donor from a well-known photographer written on the verso of several of their art prints? Many factors should be weighed in making this determination, including how access will be provided, how the item fits with existing collections at the museum, and how the donor viewed the item, either as art or as document, as well as the appropriate collection development policy. These conversations might take place between stakeholders prior to acquisition, or at the museum's larger acquisitions meeting. Whatever the conclusion, the rationale for it should be fully documented so future staff are well informed, and the description produced should be cross-referenced in any separate systems.

No one-size-fits-all approach to acquisitions exists that can be applied to every type of museum, as specialization and division of labor will vary based upon the size of the institution and staff, its workflows, and other considerations. In some museums, the curators may typically meet with donors to review collections, negotiate terms of transfer, and handle the various steps of an acquisition, from the formulation of the deed of gift to the physical move of the materials to the museum; in others, the archivist may take the lead on any collections that contain archival elements. Larger institutions may even have independent, specialized staff who work individually on each facet of an acquisition. Thus, the differing collecting perspectives of the museum curator, who may be chiefly focused on the acquisition of objects, versus those of the museum archivist, who brings collection-based archival appraisal criteria to the process, should be well understood by any and all staff who may be handling negotiations to ensure fulfillment of the museum's collecting mission. Even though it may be challenging to do so at some institutions, museum archivists must advocate for their own expertise and collections, and position themselves to participate in the acquisition process. This will ensure that new acquisitions with archival components consist of materials that have informational and evidential value and adhere to the museum archives' collection development policy.

It is in the museum's best interest when museum archivists and curators cooperatively work together on acquisitions, sharing information about leads, contacts, and potential acquisitions, and figuring out who is best equipped to respond in a given situation. If a museum archivist independently brings in an acquisition, it is good practice for them to inform curators of materials within the collection that may be of interest, as the nature and subject of the materials may match a curator's area of specialization, or the materials could be of potential use in exhibitions or other museum programming. No opportunity to establish trust and build goodwill should be wasted, and the more a museum archivist builds constructive relationships with colleagues, the better positioned they may be when they need outside support for archival acquisitions. This kind of communication also raises the visibility of noninstitutional collections with colleagues within the museum overall.

Regardless of who is doing the work of acquisition, thorough records on the purchase or gift must be maintained. Donor files that contain email communications and other correspondence and inventories of materials serve this purpose. Actions may be tracked in a shared database or collections management system to ensure that efforts are not inadvertently duplicated. Likewise, future curators or archivists will be grateful to their predecessors for this documentation when they acquire subsequent accretions to an established collection and need background information about the initial acquisition.

have more tools at their disposal for building goodwill among prospective donors than their colleagues in other archival settings. The museum archivist may want to explore, with other museum departments, whether further benefits could be offered, such as lifetime museum membership, notification of the opening of new exhibitions, invitations to receptions and other special events, or receipt of publications produced by the museum. The archivist could also work with other departments to determine whether donor-specific public programs, educational offerings, or exhibitions could be held to reinforce the importance of the donation to the museum as a whole. The public visibility and reputation of a museum, including that of its exhibitions and collections, can also help convince donors that the museum's archives are a fitting repository for their collection. When a representative of a museum can express a sincere interest in the history of the donor and in preserving and making accessible the documentary evidence of their activities for decades if not centuries to come, and is able to frame that as ultimately beneficial to the donor, they will usually earn a respectful, if not enthusiastic, response.

Purchases

Some museum archives may be blessed with budgets that allow them to purchase collections. In these cases, the museum archivist may need to work one-on-one with an individual making a sale, a dealer or collector in a relevant subject area, or an auction house, where the museum archivist may be called upon to bid on a purchase. The two most essential points to consider in these situations are an appraisal of the materials for sale and their market value.

The museum archives can require an official appraisal of materials for sale. The American Society of Appraisers is a good source for accredited individuals who can authenticate that materials are what the seller claims and verify the market value of those materials.[13] The museum archives staff may also have the expertise to authenticate and estimate market value themselves. In these cases, the decision to purchase can be determined by available budget and an assessment against the collection development policy and any institutional collecting priorities. The museum archives may also wish to address and/or negotiate whether rights, if held by the seller, can be sold to the institution with the physical materials to widen the museum's ability to use the collections, not only for educational purposes but for revenue-generating projects and campaigns as well.

In the event that the museum archivist must bid on collections at auction, determining in advance what the institution feels is a fair price for them is imperative—this can often be determined by looking up the final sale price for similar items sold at previous auctions—as well as the limit of the institution's ability to purchase the materials. Due diligence must be done in advance: How reputable is the auction house? Does it authenticate materials itself prior to sale? What can be ascertained about the materials from the provenance and/or images provided through the auction catalog, and how certain can one be that the materials are what they claim to be? This way, if the museum archivist is bidding via phone or online, they have an idea of the price at which to start bidding (usually under what is considered fair market value unless the materials are highly prized) and, most important, when to stop. When attempting to purchase materials at auction, one must be willing to lose. In-person auctions add complexity to the purchase process and can involve one's ability to psychologically outwit competitors, to control one's physiological responses to the external stimuli of the moment, and to involve one's ability and willingness to take chances—particularly if one is attempting to purchase multiple lots, or groupings, of materials.

Process of Acquisition

Some museum archivists have the leeway to make appraisal and acquisition decisions independently, while others may need to obtain institutional approval by submitting proposed acquisitions to an acquisitions committee. Though this process may be rigorous, it is an opportunity for the museum archivist to introduce the materials to museum administration and emphasize their intrinsic value as well as their potential to support other collections and activities of the institution.

Once the proposed acquisition has been approved, the next step is to draft a deed of gift or purchase agreement, depending on how the collection will be acquired. Just as museums may have either a shared or a separate collection development policy governing acquisitions, so too may they have deeds of gift that are all-inclusive, governing all types of materials, or several types of deeds specific to individual types of materials.[14] If a museum uses one deed of gift form for all collections offered to it, the archivist should make certain it has been adapted to include issues relevant to archival, manuscript, and digital collections. Acknowledgment or thank-you letters should also be included with any gift agreement correspondence to facilitate the donor relationship.

Special Considerations for Deeds of Gift for Manuscript Collections

Information about intellectual property rights, which includes copyright and other elements such as trademarks and patents, should be included on the museum archives' deed of gift form. However, intellectual property rights are often not included on the museum's deed of gift form. For example, when an art object is donated, the museum is typically given the object's physical property, but the intellectual property rights for the artwork remain with the artist. In contrast, the archives' deed of gift form should provide the opportunity for the donor to retain such rights or transfer them to the museum as part of the donation, either in full or in part. Whenever possible, the transference of intellectual property rights will benefit those publishing from the collection as well as the institution, if it wishes to publish materials from such collections on the Internet, whether as part of online exhibitions or as a result of digitization of the materials to facilitate greater access.

Furthermore, donors of manuscript collections may ask for time-bound access restrictions on their gifted collections or limited access to certain types of materials. Temporary restrictions may be outlined in the deed of gift to protect the privacy of living persons who are documented in such materials, to ensure that the donor has first rights to using or publishing materials from their donated collection, or for other legitimate reasons. In regard to materials that are sensitive or restricted to protect third-party privacy, the deed of gift may also identify what steps the museum archives will take if such materials come to light during the processing of a collection.[15] Concerns such as these are not common with gifts of permanent collection objects.

Also in contrast to the museum's permanent collection objects, which are often only deaccessioned after much careful consideration and review by a panel made up of curators, senior administrators, or board members, deaccessioning archival materials is a much more frequent occurrence that is performed at the archivist's own discretion. Some collection contents might have been overlooked at the time of acquisition and are redundant, nonarchival, or simply outside of the museum's collecting scope, and the deed of gift can provide a mechanism enabling archivists to identify and dispose of duplicate or out-of-scope materials, greatly simplifying the processing of a collection.

Accessioning of Collections

With the acquisition approved, the next step is to transport the collection to the museum and accession it into the museum's holdings. The accession process can often highlight differences between museum and archival practice.

In most archival repositories, the accessioning of new materials is handled by an archivist who completes the required transfer paperwork or deed of gift, assigns a unique identifier such as a manuscript collection number to the collection, and creates an accession record along with either a fully developed catalog record or a collection-level record to be completed in full pending processing of the collection. Additional steps might include an analysis to determine conservation needs, an obsolescence assessment of born-digital or audiovisual formats, or the creation of a processing plan. During this work, the archival collection is viewed as an aggregate body of documents maintained as one unit according to the principle of provenance rather than treated separately based upon format, subject matter, or other identifying criteria.

For an accession at a museum archives, however, the registrar may play a more prominent role, responsible for many of the accessioning functions identified here in addition to tracking the movement of objects into and out of exhibitions or on loan to other institutions. While the work of a registrar in accessioning new collections can be a tremendous help to a museum archivist working with a large volume of incoming materials, it can also introduce elements to the process that are unfamiliar to archivists. Registrars tend to focus on accounting for the contents of an archival collection at the item-level and may wish to enumerate every document as they would when working with objects to ensure that nothing of value is lost or misplaced. Likewise, while many museum archivists have experience working with donors who place portions of their collections in the archives incrementally over long periods of time, with each successive accrual being added to the same existing collection, registrars who work with such collections may be more accustomed to describing and recording such incremental donations as independent accretions, which may or may not be linked to earlier ones. While this is a helpful process for determining and ensuring proper records of provenance and chain of custody, it can sometimes encumber the work of the archivist, who sees the value of these scattered documents in the aggregate, best arranged and described together as one unified collection. Likewise, the scholars, researchers, and other end users of archival collections will usually be most interested in viewing and using the collection as a complete body rather than as a series of accruals defined largely by the date when they were transferred to the museum archives.

Throughout the acquisition process, multiple opportunities arise when archivists, curators, and registrars can share their unique expertise and support each other's work. The museum's collection management system might be used to create records for archival collections; for example, if the registrar initially accessioned a collection at the item level, but then portions were deemed archival and transferred to the museum archives for further description and arrangement, the museum archivist should be able to use this data to construct a collection-level record that adequately describes the archival components of that collection. Or conversely, when dealing with a collection that will be split between the archives and another collection department, the museum archivist might first accession the collection as a whole, and then the registrar can identify the objects that need item-level accessioning. The accession records for those objects should then be connected to the collection-level record created by the archivist, resulting in a parent-child hierarchy that could be reflected in the archival finding aid or through other descriptive tools. Archivists, registrars, and curators can devise many variations on these practices that are uniquely suited to their particular museum and its collections, on an as-needed basis and as their descriptive systems and workflows allow. A combined collection management system, plus clear lines of communication, could allow for this sort of outside-of-the-box reimagining of workflows to allow procedures of both the museum and the archives staff to support each other's needs and requirements.

Conclusion

Despite differences in perspective and practice, archivists and their museum colleagues can work together toward their common goals, particularly when they understand the rationale behind differing practices and show flexibility in working out pragmatic solutions. The strengths of each profession can complement one another and contribute to the joint pursuit of acquiring, describing, preserving, and making accessible collections that fall within a museum's collecting scope. The museum archivist must leverage internal relationships and be a staunch advocate for manuscript collections and their value and use institution-wide, proving how important they are not only to the needs of external researchers but also to the institution itself, whether through the construction of an exhibition narrative, highlighting an anniversary through a social media campaign, teaching a specific skill through an educational program, or soliciting a donation from a local entrepreneur. By illustrating use and emphasizing value, these collections can become just as important to the museum, if not potentially more so, as a high-profile object.

Further Reading

Barnard, Megan, and Gabriela Redwine. "Module 15: Collecting Digital Manuscripts and Archives." In *Appraisal and Acquisition Strategies*, edited by Michael Shallcross and Christopher J. Prom. Trends in Archives Practice Series. Chicago: Society of American Archivists, 2016.

Buck, Rebecca A., and Jean Allman Gilmore, editors. *Museum Registration Methods*, 5th ed. Washington, DC: American Association of Museums, 2010.

Edwards, Phillip M. "Collection Development and Maintenance across Libraries, Archives, and

Museums: A Novel Collaborative Approach." *Library Resources & Technical Services* 48, no. 1 (2004): 26–33.

Given, Lisa M., and Lianne McTavish. "What's Old Is New Again: The Reconvergence of Libraries, Archives, and Museums in the Digital Age." *Library Quarterly* 80, no. 1 (2010): 7–32.

Klimaszewski, Cheryl. "Lumping (and Splitting) LAMs: The Story of Grouping Libraries, Archives, and Museums." *Canadian Journal of Information & Library Sciences* 39, nos. 3–4 (2015): 350–67.

NOTES

1. The *Dictionary of Archives Terminology* defines a manuscript collection as a collection of personal or family papers and notes that "although manuscript literally means handwritten, 'manuscript collection' is often used to include collections of mixed media in which unpublished materials predominate." *Dictionary of Archives Terminology*, s.v. "manuscript collection," Society of American Archivists, https://dictionary.archivists.org/entry/manuscript-collection.html, captured at https://perma.cc/WH4V-H9U3. Please also see chapters 8–13 of this publication for discussion of special formats and topical collections, including born-digital strategies.

2. In museums, this policy is often referred to as a *collections management policy*. According to the American Alliance of Museums (AAM), " . . . museums should create a collections management policy that outlines the scope of the museum's collection, explains how the museum cares for and makes collections available to the public, and clearly defines the roles of the parties responsible for managing the museum's collections." American Alliance of Museums, "Collections Management Policy," https://www.aam-us.org/programs/ethics-standards-and-professional-practices/collections-management-policy, captured at https://perma.cc/KQ9N-THW2. AAM also has a reference guide for developing a collections management policy. "Developing a Collections Management Policy," https://www.aam-us.org/wp-content/uploads/2017/12/Developing-a-CMP-2018.pdf, captured at https://perma.cc/ADS8-AQ7V. For background information on how to create a collection development policy for archives, see Faye Phillips, "Developing Collecting Policies for Manuscript Collections," *American Archivist* 47, no. 1 (1984): 30–42, https://doi.org/10.17723/aarc.47.1.x07k74g7331762q2.

3. The "Appraisal and Acquisition/Accession" portion of the "Standards and Best Practices Resource Guide" of the Society of American Archivists' Museum Archives Section is a resource for examples of collection development policies at https://www2.archivists.org/groups/museum-archives-section/2-appraisal-and-acquisitionaccession, captured at https://perma.cc/4SSV-CWUQ.

4. A collection development policy can also address the resources needed to acquire archival collections; for example, MoMA's "Manuscript Collections Development Policy" states that "expenses related to the arrangement, description and preservation of collections should be minimal or offset through donations, which will be solicited at the time of the gift or purchase of the related materials." See https://www.moma.org/research-and-learning/archives/about#manuscript-collections-development-policy, captured at https://perma.cc/X3FS-UUSY. For a discussion of the importance of integrating born-digital considerations into collections development policies, see Megan Barnard and Gabriela Redwine, "Collecting Digital Manuscripts and Archives," in *Appraisal and Acquisition Strategies*, Trends in Archives Practice Series, ed. Michael Shallcross and Christopher J. Prom (Chicago: Society of American Archivists, 2016).

5. The "Core Documents" portion of the Ethics, Standards, and Professional Practices of the American Alliance of Museums website outlines the five documents required of all accredited museums to codify and guide all decision-making and actions at https://www.aam-us.org/programs/ethics-standards-and-professional-practices/core-documents.

6. Furthermore, is a portion of the collection or a closely related collection already housed at another institution? If the collection is determined to be outside the museum archives' collecting scope, the museum archivist may want to consider alerting a more appropriate repository to the existence of the collection. For a discussion of cooperative collecting, see Cynthia K. Sauer, "Doing the Best We Can? The Use of Collection Development Policies and Cooperative Collecting at Manuscript Repositories," *American Archivist* 64, no. 2 (2001): 308–49, https://doi.org/10.17723/aarc.64.2.gj6771215231xm37.

7. For an example of how a seemingly archival document can be used as an object and vice-versa, within a museum setting, see Michael Jones, "From Personal to Public: Field Books, Museums, and the Opening of the Archives," *Archives and Records* 38, no. 1 (2017): 212–27. For a discussion of the materiality of archives and reflections on an exhibition using archival documents, see Peter Lester, "Of Mind and Matter: The Archive as Object," *Archives and Records* 39, no. 1 (2018): 4–20.

8. Fundraising topics are discussed in depth in chapter 14 of this publication.

9. For an exploration of unwanted gifts, see Sheila O'Hare and Andrew Smith, "Gifts Nobody Wants: The State of the Art in Dealing with Unwanted Donations," *Kansas Library Association College and University Libraries Section Proceedings* 1, no. 1 (2011), https://doi.org/10.4148/culs.v1i0.1363, captured at https://perma.cc/9KCM-9KXZ.

10. For a discussion of the importance of building relationships with donors of born-digital materials, see Geof Huth, "Appraising Digital Records," in *Appraisal and Acquisition Strategies*, 17–18.

11. In many cases, it can often be difficult to simply find a current address, telephone number, or email address that can be used to send an initial letter, greeting, or other expression of interest to the prospective donor, and these associates can be especially helpful in connecting the archivist with such a donor. For an overview of the literature on donor relations, see Dainan M. Skeem, "Donor Relations in the Twenty-First Century," *Journal of Western Archives* 9, no. 1 (2018), https://digitalcommons.usu.edu/westernarchives/vol9/iss1/9, captured at https://perma.cc/MKR7-D5AK. See also Aaron D. Purcell, *Donors and Archives: A Guidebook for Successful Programs* (Lanham, MD: Rowman & Littlefield, 2015).

12. For discussion addressing the emotional labor of archival work, see archivist Anna St. Onge's Association of Canadian Archivists presentation, "Already Enough Ghosts: The Invisibility of Emotional Labour in Archives," which illustrates the juxtaposition between the emotional impact of archival work and the expectation for archivists to maintain their objectivity and neutrality at http://hdl.handle.net/10315/31367. See also Megan Garbett-Styger, "Death, Dying and Archives: Learning to Work with Grieving and Dying Donors" (master's thesis, Western Washington University, 2014), 395, https://cedar.wwu.edu/cgi/viewcontent.cgi?referer=https://www.google.com/&httpsredir=1&article=1395&context=wwuet.

13 Search for an ASA-accredited appraiser by name, location, or expertise at ASA, "Find an Appraiser," https://www.appraisers.org/find-an-appraiser.

14 The "Appraisal and Acquisition/Accession" portion of the "Standards and Best Practices Resource Guide" of the Society of American Archivists' Museum Archives Section is a resource for examples of gift agreements at https://www2.archivists.org/groups/museum-archives-section/2-appraisal-and-acquisitionaccession. See also "A Guide to Deeds of Gift" from the Society of American Archivists at https://www2.archivists.org/publications/brochures/deeds-of-gift, captured at https://perma.cc/4LCS-ZWA2.

15 Additional information on donor and privacy restrictions as defined in deeds of gift is also provided in chapter 15 of this book.

7 PROVIDING ACCESS AND PROMOTING USE IN MUSEUM ARCHIVES

Lindsay Turley and Samantha Norling

One of the primary roles of a museum archivist is advocating for access to and use of archives by constituents, including institutional stakeholders, external researchers, and colleagues in the field. The museum archivist must identify access and use policies and procedures, select appropriate methods and tools for describing archival holdings and promoting discoverability, and implement outreach strategies that demonstrate the value of the archives program. Each of these activities presents opportunities for museum archivists to engage with stakeholders and users, whether through education or by activating archival collections for a variety of institutional and external uses.

Collections Access and Use Policy

A collections access and use policy should clearly identify guidelines for using the museum archives both on-site and remotely. It is often consistent with policies and procedures in place for research access to collections objects and must place access to these materials within the scope of the museum's overall mission.[1] Museum archivists should consider whether other documentation owned by the museum is made available to external researchers, such as object files managed by a registration or curatorial department. If it is, then the archivist should consult with the managing department to determine whether the archival access policies and procedures should align with or reference the department's existing access policies for its records. Additionally, archivists should keep in mind the difference between archival collections that have been processed and described to further the museum's public mission through research and those that have research value but are intended to serve administrative functions.

Depending on whether the museum considers archival collections part of its overall museum collection, these may be subject to the museum's collections management policy. A collections management policy outlines how the museum upholds its responsibility as a steward of cultural objects held in the public trust, including what the public's expectations should be for access and use; the archives may also have a separate policy.[2] A comprehensive collections access and use policy will go into more detail and provide guidelines for the museum archivist to exercise discretion, allowing for varying levels of research access based on the materials' fragility or sensitivity, the format or contents of the record, whether the collection has been formally processed, or whether a certain embargo period on access has passed. If a digital surrogate exists, it may be recommended as an alternative means of access to provide for the long-term care of the materials. A collections access and use policy will also set guidelines for physical access, such as determining the means by which audiences are granted access to museum archives and identifying patron handling guidelines while in the collections access area.[3] Examples of physical access guidelines include using pencil only for taking notes, wearing gloves and/or washing hands prior to handling, removing watches and bulky jewelry, and leaving food and beverages at home.

Security

Collection security is a high priority, and knowing exactly who is accessing the museum archives and documenting what they access are essential. When physically accessing archival materials on-site, external researchers should complete a researcher application that provides contact information, professional affiliation (when applicable), the materials they plan to access, the research purpose, and whether they are open to discussing their research with others. This personal and research-related information is not only important for security; these details can provide interesting insights as part of collection use statistics and help museum archivists better understand where staff time is being spent in assisting researchers (discussed in greater detail later in this chapter). In some cases, a museum may wish to verify the researcher's identity through government-issued identification and make a photocopy or scan to keep on file and retain and destroy according to the institution's relevant policy.[4]

Institutional resources may limit a museum archives' ability to implement specific security measures, but various techniques include limiting the amount of material allowed a researcher at any one time, requiring researchers to check all coats and bags, allowing only small notebooks at the research table, installing clearly visible security cameras, and physically monitoring the research room.[5] Museum archives might be housed in the same areas of the building as museum collections, requiring additional levels of security, such as only facilitating research appointments made in advance, identifying and paging all materials prior to a research visit, and requiring researchers to be accompanied as they move through the building.

For remote reference inquiries, the museum archivist does not need to consider the physical security of their archival holdings in the same way. However, they should decide if they need to implement safeguards against reproduction and download, and evaluate the materials they are sharing for confidentiality, privacy, or intellectual property concerns before making them available online or via email, as discussed later in the chapter.

Access to Unprocessed Holdings

Most museum archives hold at least a small backlog of unprocessed collections, and, even without the existence of finding aids or catalog records for the materials, researchers may know of them and request access to them. Security and confidentiality

FIGURE 7.1. The physical space where museums provide access to their archives may vary in size and capacity, but should abide by the guidelines suggested here. IMAGE COURTESY OF THE MUSEUM OF THE CITY OF NEW YORK, 2019.

are primary concerns when deciding whether to allow access to unprocessed materials, as determining if materials are missing from an unprocessed collection without a descriptive finding aid or container list is more difficult. While reviewing small portions of a collection for confidentiality concerns prior to research access might be possible, the museum archivist may not know whether the collection holds restricted materials in advance of processing. At the recommendation of the archivist, museum administration, or other governing body such as a collections committee, some museums may only allow the archives staff to access unprocessed archival collections, or they may restrict some materials to institutional staff. When considering access to unprocessed archival collections, a museum must weigh the benefits to scholarship in accordance with its mission against the risks to its security and the confidential nature of the materials.

Confidentiality and Privacy

The collections access and use policy should clearly identify what the museum considers confidential or sensitive information, state who is allowed what level of access to restricted materials, determine a schedule for how long the materials remain closed to both the public and to staff, and outline how access to the confidential materials will be controlled.[6] Restricted materials should be identified during processing and isolated or otherwise marked with a restrictions note based on the policy; suggestions for developing a considered restricted records strategy are outlined in chapter 15.[7] In some instances, museum archives may allow external researchers to access unprocessed collections with a higher level of staff oversight by signing a confidentiality agreement in which the researcher (internal or external) agrees not to take images or notes, or to disclose information from the restricted materials.

Copyright and Intellectual Property

Some museums address copyright and intellectual property in their collections access and use policy or may refer to a separate rights and reproductions policy. Regardless of how or where it is addressed, the museum archives should make clear its position on reproducing or publishing materials from its archival collections and provide the necessary forms to request permission to do so. Intellectual property is not always clear, especially in the case of unpublished original work, or if the creator has an active estate. If the museum has a rights and reproductions manager or legal counsel on staff, they can serve as an excellent resource when issues of copyright clearance arise.

This work extends to processing as well: every collection's finding aid should address copyright and intellectual property, making it clear when the museum does not hold the rights and in what cases the researcher will need to seek outside permission to reproduce or publish from the archives. When the archival collection is acquired from an external source, ideally this information is obtained from the donor or seller at the time the materials are accessioned and documented in the deed of gift. Museum archivists cannot assume that all users are well versed in the concept of "fair use," which provides that reproduction of copyrighted works for certain limited, educational purposes does not constitute copyright infringement.[8] A collections access and use policy can provide information on reliable resources for determining fair use, but should not make the judgment for the user or act in the role of clearing permissions for the researcher.

In recent years, museums and other cultural institutions have led the way in adopting the principles of open access (OA) when sharing collections content online, simplifying the often-complicated process researchers and other audiences go through to navigate copyright law and determine acceptable uses of materials. To this end, institutions are simplifying the copyright- and use-related language used in their online collections, adopting standardized licenses that make clear the specified or completely open uses that can be made of collections data and digital surrogates (image, video, audio, etc.) without having to obtain permission from a copyright holder.[9] Museum archivists are in a unique position to further the OA movement in museums by advocating for and participating in the adoption of the principles and practices of openness at their institution, adding archival collections to the scope of new or existing open access programs and, in the process, opening up archival materials to greater use and reuse than was previously possible.

IMAMUSEUM.ORG WEB ARCHIVE ONLINE COLLECTION

In 2017, the Indianapolis Museum of Art (IMA) launched a new campuswide brand, Newfields, of which the IMA was one component. In conjunction with the new brand, the IMA's existing website, imamuseum.org, was to be replaced by a completely new website, DiscoverNewfields.org. With the launch of this site, all pages previously available at imamuseum.org would redirect to the new homepage, effectively removing all existing pages from the Web. Anticipating both temporary and permanent loss of significant content from imamuseum.org—content that had been created over ten years of the site's active life and included multiple exhibition microsites and blogs—the IMA Archives stepped up to capture this born-digital content to ensure its preservation and provide continued access to both internal and external audiences.

The archivists used Webrecorder, a web archiving tool, to create a high-fidelity snapshot of almost all of the existing website prior to its retirement.[10] Preserving all captures in the WARC (Web ARChive) file format, Webrecorder also provides a simple public interface for each content collection that includes a description, a list of captured pages ("bookmarks") with accompanying metadata, and an integrated viewer for researchers to "play" the captured pages and experience the retired website as though it were live in their browser again.

Since the retirement of imamuseum.org, the web archive has become an invaluable resource for IMA staff to access content that has not yet been migrated to the new site, or that will not be re-created (e.g., past exhibition microsites and inactive blogs). Each collection within the web archive has been made publicly available, with copies of the WARC files preserved in the IMA Archives' digital repository.[11] The decision to make these web archives available to the public without restrictions or researcher registration requirements was informed by the museum's open access policy and in consideration of the public nature of this collection content during its active life, when it was freely available to all users on the web.

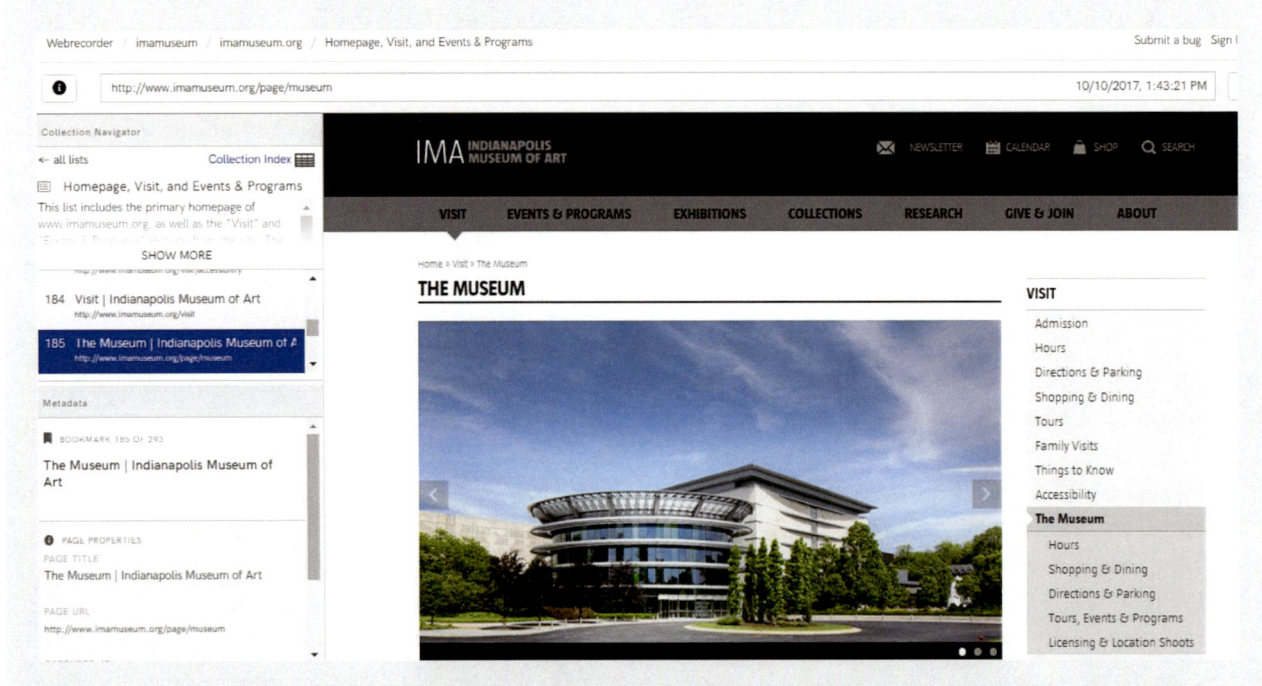

FIGURE 7.2. Screenshot of imamuseum.org page viewed in Webrecorder interface. Courtesy of the Indianapolis Museum of Art at Newfields.

Research Services and Fees

Not all institutions charge fees for research and duplication services because this poses an obstacle to access. However, museum archives may make the case that with limited budgets and staffing resources, minimal fees help sustain operations. Some institutions have found that processing and collecting fees are not worth the staff time, and, as a result, a repository may scan or photocopy a limited number of items, or allocate a certain amount of time per inquiry before applying any fees. A clear fee schedule should be identified so users understand how and when charges are applied, including instances when fees might be charged, such as for commercial films, and situations in which they are not, such as the nonprofit work of independent scholars. Some repositories also maintain lists of local freelance researchers to refer to long-distance researchers so that the institution is not further involved.

Discovery and Access Tools

Promoting the use of museum archives' collections, whether institutional records or special collections, begins with the creation of discovery tools for both individual collections (e.g., finding aids) and aggregated holdings of the museum archives (e.g., an online catalog). Institutions may find it helpful to cross-link discovery and access tools; for example, including a link to related archival digitized content or finding aid(s) from the online museum catalog so that researchers may utilize a single-entry point for accessing all institutional holdings. Archivists in repositories of all types will likely see a shift away from the traditional finding aid as born-digital records become more prevalent. The large quantity of born-digital records created by museums on an annual basis, coupled with the unique formats and access environments such as file servers and native applications will require museum archives to support new methods for facilitating discovery and providing access to these records. For example, researchers interested in governance correspondence may prefer to search through the contents of a past director's archived email account directly in a client application such as Outlook or through an email archiving application such as ePADD.[12] Access and discovery in either environment would more closely replicate the email records' original context, not limited by the traditional hierarchical finding aid, which could not fully represent the complex contents of this born-digital format.

Special Considerations for Museum Archives

Though many of these discovery and access tools are common across types of archival repositories, museum archivists should keep in mind considerations that can facilitate and encourage subsequent use by key audiences. Museum archivists who are more integrated with curatorial teams and activities within the institution might need to adapt archival descriptive standards to collection databases and management procedures designed primarily for museum standards, which are generally item-centric, as opposed to archival standards, which apply to large aggregates of hierarchical materials. In museum archives dedicated to institutional records, archivists can raise the profile of the archives externally, and its operational importance internally, by using descriptive tools to highlight connections between its holdings and other collections owned by the museum. Representing these connections in finding aids, inventories, catalog records, and metadata for digital objects can support and even directly lead to some common uses described in greater detail following, such as exhibitions with mixed archival and museum materials, marketing campaigns, and scholarship about the museum collections that draws on the archives' holdings to tell a more complete story.

Online Discovery and Access Tools

Ideally, the museum archives will have a presence on the museum's website where access and discovery tools can be made available as individual files or aggregated in a database for discovery across the archives' holdings. Sharing collection descriptions online and in accordance with professional standards opens additional avenues for discovery and subsequent use of the collections. Museum archives finding aids available in Encoded Archival Description (EAD) or Machine-Readable Cataloging (MARC) formats can be crawled and ingested by aggregators such as ArchiveGrid and WorldCat, where they can be discovered and explored among related archival and library holdings from around the world.[13] Many museums have robust digitization programs that provide online access to the digital surrogates of object-based collections. If digitized archival materials are not included in this online access portal, the museum archivist could advocate for the inclusion of archives within the same portal or for the creation of a companion online archives portal with functionality to support exploration across object and archives collections. For museum archives publishing digital surrogates online, digitized content and metadata shared through online portals can be aggregated in statewide or regional collection portals or in the Digital Public Library of America (DPLA) at the national level.[14]

Promoting Access and Use through Digitization

Increasingly, digitization activities have become an important vehicle for providing access and promoting use of archival collections, while also mitigating some of the preservation concerns that come with physical handling. Two keys for a successful digitization program within a museum archives are 1) tailoring the materials selected for digitization to align with institutional priorities and research requests; and 2) scaling digitization activities to the financial and staffing resources available.

Digitization Strategies

Materials selection and strategic project design are key to the success of digitization programs within museum archives. As is the case with all undertakings by museum archives, digitization projects should be designed with institutional priorities and current initiatives in mind. To support this alignment between the archives and other units within the museum, archivists managing these programs should identify cross-departmental initiatives where appropriate and leverage knowledge gathered during interactions with other departments to identify ways in which the archives can support priority projects. With knowledge of upcoming activities throughout the museum, such as exhibitions, public programs, or major fundraising campaigns, potential digitization projects can be prioritized to generate content that can be utilized during those events.

Pursuing digitization activities at a scale that makes sense for a repository is also key to the success of these efforts and can facilitate the integration of the digitization program with other access tools employed by the archives. Museum archivists must allot time for planning and weigh the costs of digitization in terms of staffing, equipment, and time against the available resources. As many museum archives may not have the resources to support large-scale digitization programs, incorporating smaller scale digitization-on-demand in response to specific reference inquiries might be a good place to start building capacity. Regardless of the approach to implementation, evaluating copyright and establishing standards for image capture and metadata creation are important at an early stage of the digitization workflow.[15] As discussed earlier, the collections access and use policy and other related policies and procedures should be in place to guide these decisions.

External Audiences and Use Cases

External audiences are defined as anyone who does not work within the museum and wishes to access the archives. This includes colleagues in the field, independent scholars and writers, students, professors, filmmakers, and the press, to name a few. How an institution serves external researchers will depend upon its staff resources and physical space. Some institutions may have reading/reference rooms with standard public hours, whereas others may require appointments to be made in advance. Remote inquiries and requests for appointments are most commonly received via email, though some individuals call, show up with no prior appointment, or contact an institution via postal mail. Policies for external research appointments should be made as clear as possible through the museum's website, an auto response for a standard email for research, and/or via a voicemail message. Preferences for receiving inquiries, how long a researcher should expect to wait for a response, and, if advance appointments are required, how far in advance researchers should schedule a visit should be indicated as well.

Most research in a museum archives has the goal of advancing scholarship on the topic, be it through publication, preparation of a lecture, organization of a program or exhibition, or instruction in the classroom.[16] The press may request archival materials either in support of a journalistic piece on the museum or its programming or in support of a topical piece not related to the museum. Filmmakers—both documentary and commercial—may also request access to archival materials to conduct research to establish context for a factual piece or to verify information to accurately set and depict a fictional piece. Documentary producers often include archival photos, documents, and film in their productions as well. Keeping statistics on requests for permission to use archival materials is an additional way of tracking collection use.

Colleagues from other museums often visit in preparation for an exhibition or for collections-based research. They may wish to request a loan of original materials from the archives or a facsimile to include in an upcoming exhibition or the accompanying catalog. They may also wish to conduct research in support of an exhibition, but do not plan to include any of the original physical materials from the museum archives in it.

Outreach Strategies

Many opportunities exist to activate the museum archives' holdings for both internal audiences, such as colleagues and board members, and for a general external audience. Outreach to external audiences can take many forms, such as public exhibitions and publications, as well as targeted programs including tours, archivist talks, and collaborations with local schools and universities to enrich student learning.

Exhibitions and Publications

Within the museum environment, the most prevalent way of engaging with the public is through exhibitions—whether on-site at the museum's physical location, by lending materials to other cultural institutions, or through digital exhibitions hosted online. Archival materials can be used to support and provide context within broader thematic exhibitions on a particular person or organization, historical event(s), topic, artistic genres/movements, and so on. Significant objects in a museum's collection are often regularly displayed, and archival materials from previous exhibitions of the object can demonstrate how scholarship has evolved on a specific topic. Exhibitions composed entirely of archival materials may focus on the history of the institution or on a department or program over the years. As mentioned earlier, museum archives may also include special collections acquired by the museum, in addition to the records generated by it, which provide a wide range of thematic, monographic, and visual exhibition materials depending on the focus of the museum.

The museum can publish catalogs to support exhibitions, often drawing even more heavily on archival materials than exhibitions might to further scholarship. Archival materials are often published in texts independent of exhibitions—for example, in institutional histories—or an author may turn to archival materials to interpret an artist's original intentions, which might not have been made publicly available at the time the work was created or first exhibited, to enhance contemporary understanding of the work.

Programs and Special Events

Conducting a tour of the archival facilities and sharing select highlights from the collections is an excellent way to increase visibility. The museum can market these as group tours, offer them to members at special events, or direct them to donors and museum trustees, as well as to the general public through open house days. Many museums find a successful engagement tactic is to provide tangible connections to the institution's history by sharing archival materials that shed light on early leaders' and curators' acquisition decisions that fundamentally shaped the trajectory of the museum.

In addition to programming such as tours hosted and organized by the archives, museum archivists can partner with their public programs department to support a variety of programming, ranging from curator-led tours to panels and symposiums. Also, including images of the materials in accompanying visual presentations or behind-the-scenes tours provides another vehicle for bringing the museum archives into the public eye.

Merchandising, Social Media, and Publicity

Almost every museum has a museum shop that, in addition to a wide selection of books and merchandise related to temporary exhibitions, also includes a selection of merchandise featuring objects from the collection. Archival materials and photographs can provide a variety of content for licensing and merchandise. However, the monetization and commercialization of museum archives holdings should be approached cautiously, with a full assessment of any cultural sensitivity or copyright issues that may arise from selecting certain items for this use.[17]

Social media platforms and blogs are a great showcase for archival materials in support of internal programming, tie-ins to current events, and celebrations of anniversaries, holidays, and special interest days. Depending on its role in relation to marketing and outreach, the museum archives may even have a dedicated social media platform(s) to represent the museum publicly. Social media is an excellent way to share unique items from the museum archives that may not have many opportunities for display. Throwback Thursdays (#TBT), Flashback Fridays (#FBF), and special days such as Ask An Archivist Day (#AskAnArchivist) provide regular opportunities for sharing archival materials via social media.[18]

With merchandising and social media, museum archivists must make sure both shop and social media personnel understand that they are responsible for confirming copyright status and securing any necessary permissions. Staff often need a reminder that just because the museum physically owns the item, it doesn't always own the content. In addition to these outreach strategies, museum archivists should not underestimate the benefits of traditional publicity methods. Issuing a press release to announce a grant-funded project, a new acquisition, or the availability of a recently processed collection can garner attention for the repository and reach new audiences as well.

Internal Audiences and Use Cases

Many users of archival collections that preserve the organization's records within a museum setting and will be museum staff, executives, and other internal stakeholders, such as trustees. Procedures for contacting archives staff should be established and communicated to these user groups on a regular basis, but museum archivists should anticipate inquiries coming up in more ad hoc ways, such as during meetings or even chance encounters in the hallway. A museum archives benefits when sufficient staff resources allow for timely responses to reference inquiries of all types, as every reference interaction with institutional users has the potential to demonstrate the value of the archival collections and archives staff in supporting a wide variety of institutional needs originating from all departments, administration, and governing bodies.

Every department within the museum can benefit from the work of the museum archives. Curatorial and registration departments may seek archival materials to develop exhibition content, to include in an exhibit, to interpret context, or to address a historical institutional topic, as well as to

---

MUSEUM OF THE CITY OF NEW YORK "I SPY NEW YORK" CAMP: CAPTURING THE CITY THROUGH THE CAMERA

This educational program at the Museum of the City of New York was offered to students ages seven through nine, exposing them to the museum's renowned photographic archives while they met with staff behind the scenes to learn about the collection. Students worked under the direction of a professional photographer to photograph major elements of New York City, including its buildings, parks, and people, which are prominently documented in the museum's archives from the late nineteenth century to the present. The program offered a behind-the-scenes view of how photographic archives document the city and are used to support the museum's mission through its exhibitions programming. Student activities included:

- visiting the photographic archives to learn about the history of photography through different photographic media;
- seeing a variety of city images and subjects documented by the collection;
- learning how to use a professional digital camera;
- taking field trips to Central Park, Battery Park, the Brooklyn Bridge, and other iconic New York City sites;
- visiting galleries and participating in scavenger hunts to look at photographs on view;
- looking at cyanotype prints in the photographic archives, then making their own;
- meeting museum professionals to learn about behind-the-scenes operations; and
- editing and printing a final photograph for inclusion in a culminating exhibition.

manage collections in regard to provenance, exhibition history, or donor and collector information. Education and program departments may seek materials to support docent-led tours and presentations or to create educational materials such as brochures, videos, or web content. Marketing and publicity personnel may utilize archives to commemorate anniversaries or special events in the museum's history, or to enhance its social media platforms. Development and finance can draw on archival materials to develop affiliate group activities, cultivate historical donor relationships, and bolster fundraising and capital campaigns. Administration and governing bodies can reference historic strategic plans, missions, and major initiatives, as well as meeting minutes, agendas, and materials related to major decisions. Facilities and grounds can refer to records pertaining to land use and architectural documentation informing renovations, additions, and current building operations, especially as museums continue to bring aging physical plants up to current museum environmental standards.

Demonstrating the Value of Museum Archives

Archivist and information science educator Elizabeth Yakel put it best when she said, "Education is a continuous, cumulative, exhausting, and rewarding process. . . . All other achievements, indeed the strength of the entire program, hinge on instructing the institution's employees and managers about the potential role and benefits of an archives."[19] To this end, "inreach," or outreach to internal audiences, can take many forms, and the museum archivist should be strategic in utilizing knowledge of priorities and activities of museum departments and user groups to communicate how the archives can provide support to specific initiatives. This approach allows a museum archivist to increase the internal user base and, by extension, the relevance and recognition of the program within the organization. Complementary to this approach, a museum archivist should consider regular education of staff and administrators as the greatest form of inreach, whether it be by scheduled training sessions or more informal meetings or in conversations where appropriate.

Balancing Outreach with Inreach

Balancing outreach and inreach can be challenging for museum archivists. Whenever possible, a museum archivist should look for opportunities to reach both internal and external users of the archives with outreach initiatives. For example, if the archivist has created a pop-up display of archival materials for a visiting group, an email could be sent out to staff to invite them to view the materials before or after the group's visit. Conversely, consider sharing a post on social media for external audiences about a visit of long-time staff to the museum archives to assist in identifying historical photographs—this reaches the staff who came into the archives, but the social media post also gives a behind-the-scenes look at the archives, its holdings, and the work that goes into making archival materials accessible.

Capturing Statistics and Reporting

Capturing reference, collection development, and use statistics is an important component to the successful management of any archives program and becomes even more important for museum archives needing to continuously demonstrate—in quantifiable terms—the service provided and value brought to the institution. Methods for gathering these statistics can vary, but they should be well documented and communicated to all staff and volunteers who might field an inquiry or carry out activities documented through metrics. Statistics can be captured in a variety of ways: spreadsheets, forms, and reference modules within archives management programs are just a few possibilities.

Managers of museum archives should develop the tracking tools with the needs and priorities of the institution in mind, being mindful to capture those statistics that are most meaningful to museum administration. Types of statistics and specific pieces of information that might be captured include:

- Reference Statistics and User Information
    - Researcher information (name, contact information, whether public, staff, or other affiliation of note)
    - Method of inquiry (telephone, email, in person, etc.)
    - Topic of inquiry (to inform processing and collecting priorities, the archives should develop a fixed list of topics both

representative of the archival collections and important to the institution, and to categorize reference inquiries into those set topics as part of the captured reference statistics)
    - Time spent assisting patrons
- Use and Outreach Statistics
    - Internal and external research visits (who, when, research topics, collection[s] used)
    - Number and types of reproduction requests, including any earnings from image preparation or use fees
    - Attendance at exhibitions and programs put on by the museum archives
    - Interactions/followers on the museum archives' social media posts or accounts
    - Number and kind of publications employing archival collections (articles, books, documentaries, exhibitions, websites)

These and other statistics can be compiled throughout set periods of time, such as a fiscal or calendar year. At the end of each time period, these statistics can be communicated through a report to managers and museum administration. Some museums may incorporate these statistics into a museum-wide annual report or member magazine/newsletter. Regardless of how these statistics are communicated to stakeholders, they should be captured consistently year to year and evaluated in similar ways with each cycle so that trends and changes in researcher interest, use of the museum archives, collections growth, and other areas can then be evaluated. When gathered and evaluated consistently over a period, statistics can inform important decisions such as those regarding processing priorities, setting public hours, staffing and space allocation, and budgeting, to name a few. The museum archivist should also advocate for inclusion of these statistics in annual reports and other public-facing materials.

Conclusion

The most effective way to gain support for a museum archives program is to demonstrate that the collections are significantly accessed and are actively contributing to institutional priorities. Museum archivists open dialogue with their constituents, promote the archives program, and encourage greater use of collections both internally and externally; this is best done when supported by access and use procedures that are easy to follow for archives staff, other museum departments, and a variety of external users. Greater access to the museum archives increases opportunities to include its collections in exhibitions, public programs, digitization projects, marketing and social media, and inreach and outreach activities. Supporting these activities will cement the value of the museum archives to the institution and make it possible for the archivist to drive initiatives that center around its program to further promote use of the collections.

Further Reading

American Library Association. *ACRL/RBMS Guidelines Regarding Security and Theft in Special Collections.* October 5, 2009. http://www.ala.org/acrl/standards/security_theft, captured at https://perma.cc/H2SA-K25K.

Bryant, Megan P., Cherie C. Chen, Kenneth D. Crews, John ffrench, Walter G. Lehmann, Naomi Leibowitz, Melissa Levine, Sofía Galarza Liu, Michelle Gallagher Roberts, Nancy Sims, Deborah Wythe, and Anne M. Young. *Rights and Reproductions: The Handbook for Cultural Institutions*, 2nd ed., edited by Anne M. Young. Lanham, MD: Rowman & Littlefield, 2019.

College Art Association. *Code of Best Practices in Fair Use for the Visual Arts.* February 2015. http://www.collegeart.org/pdf/fair-use/best-practices-fair-use-visual-arts.pdf, captured at https://perma.cc/U6FH-PRA8.

Lacher-Feldman, Jessica. *Exhibits in Archives and Special Collections Libraries.* Chicago: Society of American Archivists, 2013.

Miller, Steven J. *Metadata for Digital Collections: A How-To-Do It Manual.* New York: ALA Neal-Schuman, 2011.

Theimer, Kate, ed. *Outreach: Innovative Practices for Archives and Special Collections*, no. 2. Lanham: Rowman & Littlefield, 2014.

NOTES

1. The Museum Archives Section of the Society of American Archivists has created a "Standards and Best Practices Resource Guide," which includes examples of policies and forms; the policies of comparable institutions provide a starting point for drafting or updating access and use guidelines. Society of American Archivists, "Museum Archives Section," https://www2.archivists.org/groups/museum-archives-section, captured at https://perma.cc/Q4GZ-BTUU.

2. For more information on museum collections management policies, see American Alliance of Museums, *Alliance Reference Guide: Developing a Collections Management Policy* (Arlington, VA: American Alliance of Museums, 2012).

3. While some museum archives may have dedicated research room staff and public research hours, others with limited staff and physical space for hosting research appointments may need to prioritize appointments in accordance with their museum's mission.

4. Some museums may find it easier to track this information in a searchable database in the event irregularities with the accessed materials are noted later. The Rare Books and Manuscripts Section (RBMS) of the Association of College and Research Libraries (ACRL) recommends permanent retention of researcher registration and circulation records, with access restricted to these records due to privacy and confidentiality concerns. Full RBMS recommendations on security policies can be found in the "ACRL/RBMS Guidelines Regarding Security and Theft in Special Collections" at http://www.ala.org/acrl/standards/security_theft.

5. Researchers may be observed by physically maintaining a clear line of sight to the researcher and archival materials or continuously walking through the research room. Only as many researchers as staff can adequately monitor at one time should be allowed, and the research room should never be left unstaffed.

6. Francis X. Blouin Jr. and William G. Rosenberg, *Processing the Past* (New York: Oxford University Press, 2011), 163–64.

7. Gregory S. Hunter, *Developing and Maintaining Practical Archives*, 2nd ed. (New York: Neal-Schuman Publishers, Inc., 2003), 213–15.

8. Some researchers mistakenly think that if they are publishing in the name of a nonprofit or educational entity, the work falls under fair use, when this is not always the case. For more information, see Peter B. Hirtle, Emily Hudson, and Andrew T. Kenyon, *Copyright and Cultural Institutions: Guidelines for Digitization for U.S. Libraries, Archives, and Museums* (Ithaca, NY: Cornell University Library, 2009).

9. Common licenses utilized by museums and other cultural institutions with open access programs are Creative Commons (https://creativecommons.org/) and RightsStatements.org (https://rightsstatements.org/en/). A detailed examination of these licenses, with examples of open access implementations in cultural organizations, can be found in Anne M. Young, ed., *Rights and Reproductions: The Handbook for Cultural Institutions*, 2nd ed. (Lanham, MD: Rowman & Littlefield, 2019).

10. Since this project was undertaken, the Webrecorder project has been renamed Conifer. See https://conifer.rhizome.org.

11. Conifer, "Indianapolis Museum of Art at Newfields Web Archives," https://conifer.rhizome.org/imamuseum.

12. "ePADD is free and open source software developed by Stanford University's Special Collections & University Archives that supports the appraisal, processing, preservation, discovery, and delivery of historical email archives," Stanford Libraries, "ePADD," https://library.stanford.edu/projects/epadd, captured at https://perma.cc/ZZF3-75JZ.

13. For additional information, visit the ArchiveGrid (https://beta.worldcat.org/archivegrid) and WorldCat (http://www.worldcat.org) websites.

14. DPLA (dp.la) has established a network of service hubs that are geographically based within a specific state or region (e.g., Kentucky Digital Library and Mountain West Digital Library). These hubs provide more local access points for contributing digital collections metadata to DPLA for increased access and use.

15. Copyright is a complex topic covered in detail in many excellent, comprehensive resources that focus on its implications in a cultural heritage context. Of note is *Rights and Reproductions: The Handbook for Cultural Institutions* (Arlington, VA: American Alliance of Museums, 2015), as well as the *Code of Best Practices for Fair Use in the Visual Arts* (New York: College Art Association, 2015).

16. The collections access and use policy should provide guidance to researchers on how to request permission for use—be it direct duplication or publishing information—and outline how to formulate correct citations.

17. In recent years, examinations of the colonial roots of museums and museum collections have included valid criticisms of the various ways in which museums exploit other cultures to shape and support their community's dominant narrative. Alice Procter covers this history in detail in her book, *The Whole Picture: The Colonial Story of the Art in Our Museums & Why We Need to Talk about It* (London: Cassell, 2020).

18. Society of American Archivists, "#AskAnArchivistDay—October 3 2018," https://www2.archivists.org/initiatives/askanarchivist-day, captured at https://perma.cc/CV4V-346G.

19. Elizabeth Yakel, "Institutionalizing an Archives: Developing Historical Records Programs in Organizations," *American Archivist* 52, no. 2 (1989): 204, https://doi.org/10.17723/aarc.52.2.x52q3m88264v522h.

PART II

8 IN WITH THE OLD, IN WITH THE NEW: ARCHIVAL PROCESSES FOR AUDIOVISUAL ASSETS AND RECORDS

Seth Anderson and Rebecca Chandler

The average American spends approximately ten hours of their day in front of a screen.[1] Screens are now part of everyday life, and the audiovisual media they display is a key contributor to their popularity. In social media, phone apps, streaming video, or online advertisements, media is unavoidable and consumption is increasing.[2] The primacy of "screen time" has impacted museums as well. Phones and monitors are now a ubiquitous part of the museum visit. They guide visitors through galleries with audio soundtracks, provide dynamic displays, and even enhance visits through augmented interactive apps.

Archives are doing their best to respond to a growing emphasis on media in their institutions and collections. OCLC's 2010 survey of special collections and archives, "Taking Our Pulse," found that "visual and audiovisual materials (such as photographs, video, and audio) are the most frequently collected born-digital formats."[3] Collection is inevitably followed by expectations of access.[4] In a museum, this may be the education department asking for footage from old television programs, curators seeking recordings of past performances, or a user looking for oral histories. Whatever the request, archival media is in demand. Yet, a stark contrast often exists between the popularity of audiovisual records and the archives' ability to provide access. Rapid changes in audiovisual technology and production practice make it difficult to keep up and ensure materials are collected, preserved, and accessible. Physical materials sit on shelves and await digitization, while born-digital records are produced at increasing rates, whether on high-end cameras or iPhones.[5]

These developments challenge existing methods of managing and preserving audiovisual records. Museum archives can no longer be passive in their approach, waiting for deposit of fragile analog and pervasive digital audiovisual materials. This chapter explores the changing digital landscape of audiovisual records and advocates for change: change that meets the needs of increasingly media-savvy museums and establishes the museum archives as central to the longevity of audiovisual records as early as possible.

Assets and Records

In response to the mobile and social Internet, museums now seek opportunities to engage and connect with patrons. Museums compete with many other daily distractions like the news, email, and social media, and they must find ways to stand out and maintain an ongoing relationship with users beyond the traditional visitor experience.[6] Following the lead of industry, many have adopted integrated media strategies: unified media outputs that align with, or are incorporated into, exhibitions, marketing, educational programming, and other activities.[7] Examples include direct engagement programming like the Museum of Modern Art's "Ask MoMA" live Q&A videos; online exhibitions or "events" like the Los Angeles County Museum of Art's interactive mobile phone series, Cell Phone Stories; and enhanced museum experiences through apps like the Hirshhorn Eye (or Hi) app.[8] Audiovisual media are at the core of these activities and thus have an unavoidable impact on a museum archives' approach to collection, preservation, and access of audio and video records.

Use of audio and video within the museum is not new. Projections and screens have been incorporated in exhibits and programming for years. What has changed is the life cycle of audiovisual records. The cost or lifespan of a physical medium no longer constrains the creation or use of a recording. Now, digital audio and video can be generated quickly and at low cost. Materials are easy to retrieve and repurpose for new productions. If managed effectively, the useful lifespan of a digital recording may never end.

This corresponds to a shift in the classification of audiovisual materials from records to media assets. An asset, by definition, is not remarkably different from a record, but it is perceived as something distinct from the materials in an archives. A digital media asset is immediate and of use to the activities of the museum. By contrast, museum staff often see digital records as being at the end of their useful life, stored away in the museum archives, and potentially difficult to access. This misconception provokes the reluctance to transfer materials to the archives for fear they will no longer be as readily accessible as "assets." Regardless of the classification, archival principles remain applicable to all audiovisual materials, whether they are considered assets, records, or both. This is especially true of audiovisual materials whose unique preservation and access needs make them susceptible to obsolescence, degradation, and loss. In response, the museum archives must reposition its services to support audiovisual materials as both assets and records.

A Service-Oriented Approach

Responding to changes in audiovisual creation and use requires a reassessment of the museum archives' relationship to the institution. The archives exists within a broader audiovisual ecosystem, which incorporates institutional policy and procedure, software and hardware infrastructure, and staff members to support production, management, and storage. An ideal system is designed to support best practices as early as possible and ensure the long-term availability of records and assets whether they end up in the archives or in other systems throughout the museum.

Unfortunately, this is not always the case; too often gaps or breakdowns occur in the process, which introduce common risks to the longevity of audiovisual materials. This is not the fault of any technology, department, or individual within the museum, as preservation is not often their responsibility or area of expertise. It is instead the result of a lack of focus on the long-term value of these materials as records or a disproportionate focus on their immediate use as assets. Too often, media assets are treated as temporary goods.

When faced with the challenge of properly managing an audiovisual record or asset, a museum's infrastructure and resources may simply be ill equipped and unprepared. In the life cycle of an audiovisual record, this can lead to loss, damage, lack of metadata, and improper use.[9] As archivist Christopher Prom points out, "an authentic record does not preserve itself, and even the best-intentioned records creators often lack the resources or expertise to act

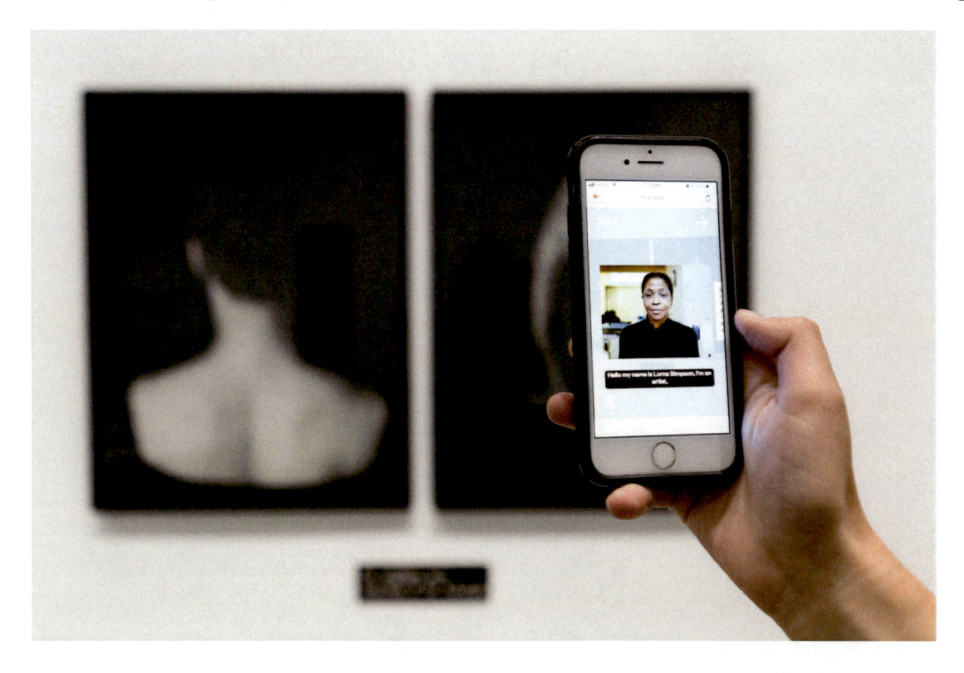

FIGURE 8.1. Mobile applications, like the Hirshhorn Eye, are among the drivers of an increase in multimedia production at many museums. IMAGE COURTESY HIRSHHORN MUSEUM AND SCULPTURE GARDEN. PHOTOGRAPHY BY ERIN SCHAFF.

as permanent custodians for non-current records. Nor can we rely on those who provide the service of temporarily storing and transmitting records."[10]

In response, the museum archives must assume responsibility for the caretaking of audio and video at all points in the records/asset life cycle. This does not necessarily mean it must acquire every recording and support all systems involved in production or use. Instead, the archives acts as a unifying service, filling in gaps in policy, staff support, and, in some cases, technology. Such a service-oriented approach should be responsive to:

- **The needs of the institution.** What types of audiovisual materials does the museum create, and how does it utilize them in its programming? What are the expectations of staff with regard to accessibility and reuse?
- **The characteristics of digital audiovisual materials.** What formats support the needs of the museum and users? What metadata is essential for both immediate use and long-term accessibility?
- **The capabilities of relevant departments and technologies.** What systems (technological and procedural) are in place to support the museum's audiovisual materials? How can these be repurposed for preservation or access? What existing expertise can the museum archives build on to introduce or improve preservation actions within existing organizational frameworks?

An effective response may require services beyond traditional activities for records management and access, but this broader role for the museum archives is not simply a means to an end. It also provides a compelling case for ongoing support.

The Digital Curation Sustainability Model ties the value of digital assets, like audiovisual records, directly to the preservation activities that maintain them. Without a sustainable investment in digital curation, an institution is unable to realize the current or future value of its assets.[11] Assuming a comprehensive and proactive approach to the needs of audiovisual materials as both assets and records positions the museum archives as an essential service to both users and museum operations, strengthening the case for increasing resources and opening new opportunities for collaboration throughout the museum.

Planning for AV

To respond to the current needs of audiovisual materials and their users, it is best to start from scratch by assessing current institutional practice as it pertains to their creation and use, and updating archival policy as needed. In outlining best practices for managing audiovisual materials, the following sections provide guidance at all points in the records and asset management life cycle. As no two museums are alike, these recommendations are not prescriptive and should be adapted to the context of the reader's institution.

Collection Development Policy

An outdated collection development policy is often too slow to respond to current demands for preservation and access of media assets. The appearance of new media types for emerging internet platforms (e.g., social media, podcasts, live streams) and changing exhibition practices require consistent response through archival policy. Updates to policy should also address the reusability of digital media by defining a role for the museum archives in the management and, if necessary, preservation of assets and materials better suited for production than research. These may include materials outside the scope of previous policy, such as uncut audio and video footage, digital production software project files, and multiplatform media assets. The collection development policy must be responsive to these factors, but also remain within the bounds of the archives' and the museum's resource capacity. It must strike a delicate balance between collecting what stakeholders deem valuable in the short term and what will truly be useful for future production and research.[12]

Proactive Collection

Timelines for transfer of physical audiovisual materials to the museum archives are often adopted for born-digital materials, placing years between their creation and preservation. Waiting years to acquire these materials introduces risk—as digital formats and digital storage are often volatile and short-lived—and relies on records creators to perform records management actions they are ill equipped to support. For this reason, collection of born-digital audiovisual materials should not be periodic, but rather a routine element of existing production workflows. The museum archives should define shorter retention and transfer timelines to protect vulnerable digital audiovisual collections and secure necessary metadata and contextual information in a timely manner.

File Tiers

Target File Tiers

Potential uses for digital audiovisual materials in a museum are limitless; certain file formats will not work well for all of them. For example, a high-resolution file selected for projection in an exhibition would not also be suitable as an online access copy due to the challenges of streaming large, high-quality audio and video. Target file formats should correspond to their anticipated use case. In many cases, two or three tiers of files are necessary.

These tiers are typically known as the preservation master file, the access master file, and the access copy file. The preservation master file is a high-resolution file created from the digitization of a physical source asset generated during production or selected during collection. It acts as the digital surrogate for the physical original object.[13] Sometimes referred to as the mezzanine copy, the access master file is a medium-sized file small enough to be easily handled by most computer and editing systems but of a high enough resolution to be a quality source for creating most derivatives and for editing into new digital content. Access masters can be stored online or nearline depending on the expected frequency and method of access.[14] The access copy is a low-resolution file that can be distributed over the Internet or maintained on some other platform used for frequent or easily obtainable listening/viewing, such as the museum's asset or web content management system. An access copy can be regenerated from the preservation master or access master when needed and does not require the application of long-term digital preservation efforts.[15]

Metadata

The longevity of any audiovisual object is often attributable to the quality of metadata captured throughout its lifespan. Complex technical characteristics and intricate relationships of files call for careful planning of schema, metadata collection, and maintenance procedures to ensure that quality information is captured. Adopting a standard in whole or in part can make metadata creation or capture much easier. Those typically used or referenced for audiovisual materials include PBCore, reVTMD, AES 57, and PREMIS.[16] These standards include properties that correspond to the technical and structural characteristics of analog and digital audiovisual materials, but should be supplemented by other standards for descriptive, rights, and administrative metadata, such as Dublin Core, METS, and EAD, as well as homegrown properties—including exhibition information, identification of collection materials, and event details—that capture institutional context.[17]

Acquiring AV

Collection of Born-Digital AV

A comprehensive collection development policy and plans for acquisition of audiovisual materials are useful tools for collection of born-digital materials, but responding to the scale of audiovisual files in museums will always be a challenge. The proliferation of audiovisual materials within museums complicates typical practices of submission or retrieval. Instead of depending on a few reliable sources within the museum, the archives must identify the many departments or individuals with born-digital video or audio materials tucked away among their records and make strategic decisions to ensure quality assets are collected for preservation and access.

Locating Collections

Finding born-digital audio and video materials in the museum is not always straightforward. The availability of numerous storage locations and mechanisms (e.g., hard drives, network storage, personal computers, removable media, etc.) results in widely dispersed pockets of audiovisual files throughout the institution. These may be buried in folder hierarchies or hidden away on a hard drive in someone's cubicle, a closet, or elsewhere. Determining where to look and knowing what to look for requires institutional knowledge, collaboration with relevant staff, and diligence. Consider the following factors when unearthing born-digital collections:

- Source departments or individuals. Who produces audiovisual materials (e.g., digital media, marketing, audiovisual support departments)? Who receives or collects them for use in their research or programming (e.g., education, curatorial, special events)? Is production outsourced? If so, are these materials available for collection?
- Related procedures. What workflows exist for production, delivery, and use of the audiovisual assets? Do outdated or ad hoc procedures exist that should be addressed? What systems and storage mechanisms are commonly used?

These details reveal the full life cycle of an audiovisual record and should illustrate where materials are kept and who engages with them. They also uncover procedural gaps where the museum archives can provide guidance or services, paving the way for better management of these files. Revealing the complex system of audiovisual management within the museum provides the basis for targeted engagement with stakeholders and systems for the introduction of preservation activities.

Selection of Digital AV

Variations in production practice over time and an absence of (or failure to adhere to) existing guidelines often lead to file formats of varying quality, size, and complexity. Not every asset will be available as a high-resolution master that meets preferred format

MAKING COLLECTION ROUTINE

Challenge

A museum generates livestreaming video of public programs to YouTube throughout the year, featuring conversations with artists and scholars, panel discussions, and speeches from special events. The AV unit produces these videos with a system that supports live editing of multiple camera angles: the stage and close-ups of participants. For each event, the AV unit saves the following: a master edit with synchronized audio, a mixed master audio track combining each microphone feed, and high-resolution copies of each video camera's output.

Museum staff would prefer routine access to these materials for use in promotional media and other multimedia products, but currently can only receive these materials upon request to the AV unit. The archives would like to collect these recordings, but corresponding procedures have not been implemented since the AV unit began using the livestreaming system.

Points to Consider

- What systems are in place to support collection and access?
- What elements of the production should be collected?
- Do the files generated during special events align with the archives' format specification? What formats would staff require for access or reuse?

Solution

Working with the AV unit, the museum archives identifies a procedure for transfer and normalization of special event recordings to various systems throughout the museum to support preservation and access. The AV unit configures its production system to generate high-resolution preservation files, access masters, and access copies that adhere to the archives' format specification. This output is limited to the master edit of the event and the mixed audio master. Individual camera angles are not retained, as the archives' assessment determined footage useful for research and production would be contained in the edited output of the event.

These files are saved in a new folder on the storage network that is monitored by the museum's digital asset management systems (DAMS) and the archives' preservation system. When new files are added to this watch folder, an automated workflow is started that ingests the access materials into the DAMS where staff can access them. Preservation and access copies are ingested into the digital repository.

The AV unit also exports event and production metadata from its system and forwards these to the archives for import into the preservation system.

specifications. Very often, materials will be available in different forms (e.g., final versions, alternate edits, raw footage, outtakes, etc.) and formats according to their distribution platform or use. Determining which files to collect among these many options must balance the value of the recorded content (as defined by the collection development policy) and the quality of materials on hand. The museum archives must be careful to identify and select the best available version for use as preservation or access masters, or those files that can be transcoded to conform to existing format specifications.

When engaging with a diverse collection, the museum archivist should prioritize formats that are open, well supported, and documented, as these are better suited for long-term preservation. In cases where no preferable formats are available, they should select files with higher values in the bit rate and bit depth (video and audio files), chroma sub-sampling (video), frame size (video), and sampling rate (audio). Larger values in these file properties indicate a greater amount of encoded information captured in the audio and video.[18] To save on storage requirements and simplify collection management, the archivist should avoid keeping numerous access copies in addition to the master format. Access copies can be generated as needed from master copies in the future.[19]

Digitization of Physical AV

The contents of physical audiovisual materials are often seen as a treasure trove for research and museum programming. They are increasingly in demand as museums look to illustrate their historical importance and engage visitors with evocative footage of the past. Yet, these recordings are often inaccessible for these purposes due to their age and the cost of digitization. Unfortunately, these materials also face multiple risk factors that will render them partly or completely inaccessible in a relatively short period of time, even for digitization. The plastics, metals, dyes, and other chemical materials used in their creation are inherently unstable and reactive to their environment.[20]

Experts estimate that archives have until approximately 2028 to digitize magnetic media before it is lost.[21] To ensure the contents of physical materials remain viable and accessible in the future, the content held on obsolescing and degrading media must be reformatted, that is, migrated from its current format to another. For arguably all content held on legacy physical media, digitization is the reformatting required to preserve and make these holdings accessible.

Approaches to Digitization

When embarking on a legacy audiovisual digitization initiative, the museum archivist faces a decision: should digitization work be done in-house, outsourced, or insourced? Not all options are available to every archives, and each option has its own requirements to consider.

- **In-house digitization.** Does the archives or museum have necessary digitization technology in-house? How much would it cost to create and maintain a workstation? Does staff have appropriate expertise to address the formats in the museum's collection? Is the workstation(s) capable of the throughput necessary to digitize all at-risk legacy AV assets prior to their loss to degradation?
- **Outsourced digitization.** How does this cost compare to in-house digitization? Can a vendor be trusted with valuable and fragile materials? What is the trade-off between efficiency and quality control? What cost increases can be anticipated as obsolescence and degradation increase?
- **Insourced digitization.** Can the museum provide suitable space for the vendor to set up and operate digitization equipment? Does the sensitivity of the materials merit the additional overhead of an on-site operator?

These options do not present an all-or-nothing scenario. A museum archivist may decide to digitize certain formats in-house, while sending more specialized formats to vendors. Any combination of these solutions is certainly acceptable; the archivist must decide based on their own collections' requirements.

Approaches to Quality Control

A digitization project does not end with the delivery of files to the museum archives. Whether an in-house or outsourced approach is selected, the archives must perform quality control checks on the deliverables to ensure its standards have been met. Quality control checks can be divided into two categories: quantitative and qualitative.[22]

It is also worthwhile to compare the differences between the preservation master, the mezzanine copy, and the access copy for a given original item. Differences are unavoidable, as these tiers are by nature of differing quality, but the archivist must determine if they are within acceptable the range of acceptable quality.

Quality Control Documentation, Communication, and Rework

The museum archivist should document questions or issues when they arise and alert the operator. Open communication with the vendor is key; not all identified issues may result in rework. If rework is required, be sure to put the new deliverables through the same quality control process.

FIGURE 8.2. Proper housings and storage conditions significantly extend the lifespan of film and video materials.
PHOTOGRAPH COURTESY GREGORY RAML AND AMERICAN MUSEUM OF NATURAL HISTORY LIBRARY.

SELECTING SOURCE MATERIALS

Challenge

A museum archives contains all fifteen episodes of a short-lived television program produced by the museum in the 1950s. A cultural critic of the era hosted this educational series, which features interviews with experts in the field and former members of the museum staff. The series is of great interest to users but has been unavailable for access because the archives' U-matic videotape player is no longer operational. The archives would like to create digital copies of each episode for preservation and access.

The archives holds two copies of each episode on different formats. The original copies are 16mm kinescopes, a direct-to-film recording of the live broadcast, and they have rarely been accessed since their recording. They were previously processed and rehoused in archival canisters and have been stored under ideal conditions.

The second copy is on three-quarter-inch U-matic cassette tapes. These transfers were created from the film originals via telecine during the rehousing process and were intended for production use in a retrospective about the museum. The tapes were subsequently transferred to the archives and served as access copies for many years. The tapes are in good condition, but the image quality is mediocre as a result of degradation and frequent use in the reading room.

Points of Consideration

- How will these materials be used? For research only? For production?
- Could handling and/or digitization damage the original materials?
- How do the costs of film and video digitization compare?

Solution

Despite the lower-quality image, the museum archives selects the U-Matic tapes as a suitable source for digitization of the television series. Because these digital copies will only be used for streaming online and in the reading room, the lower-quality image will not detract from users' ability to understand the various interviews and discussions presented in the series. The potential for damage and the high cost of film transfers ruled out the use of the film originals.

Preserving AV

Preservation of Physical AV

As discussed earlier in this chapter, digitization is the required course of action to preserve most physical legacy AV materials. Until digitization is possible, storing media in appropriate environments may help ensure their viability for the near term. All audiovisual formats benefit from cooler and drier conditions to help slow the onset of issues such as soft binder syndrome and vinegar syndrome. It is acceptable to store magnetic media at cool temperatures approaching room temperature, but film should ideally be stored in cold or frozen conditions to extend its life.[23]

Preservation of Digital AV

Preservation of digital audiovisual materials should incorporate standard best practices for preservation of any digital information as outlined in the Open Archival Information System (OAIS) standard, as well as related standards and best practice specifications (e.g., ISO 16363, NDSA's Levels of Digital Preservation).[24] The policy and actions specified by these resources are essential to ensuring the integrity and longevity of audiovisual materials.

Storage

Storage of audiovisual materials should utilize appropriate digital storage formats based on storage size, the type of file being preserved, and an estimated frequency of access. At minimum, the museum archives should keep two copies of preservation masters and one access master copy. Access copies may be kept in preservation storage or created as needed from preservation or access master copies.

File Fixity

Periodic audits of file fixity should be a primary component of any audiovisual preservation plan. However, fixity checks are often conducted at the file level, encompassing the entire structure and contents of an audiovisual file (e.g., wrapper, media streams, embedded metadata). These results may be misleading, as the cause of the failure may be isolated to a specific component of the audio or video file. A useful alternative to file-level checksums is the practice of generating intrafile checksums for fixity validation.[25]

Data Migration

As with physical audiovisual formats, some digital file types may not be suitable for long-term preservation or use and must be reformatted to facilitate ongoing preservation and access of recorded information. Migration pathways should limit alteration as much as possible. Where possible, the archivist should isolate migration to individual parts of a file, through transcoding (the transformation of an audio or video stream's codec) or transwrapping (the reformatting of the file's wrapper or container format).[26] For example, in changing a Quicktime-wrapped file to the MXF wrapper, the video and audio data should not be transcoded within the wrapper.[27]

Accessing AV

Meeting expectations for access to audiovisual materials can be a challenge for museum archives. A quick search on Google or YouTube returns hundreds, if not thousands, of multimedia resources available at the click of a mouse. Expecting the same of archives takes for granted the technical, legal, and ethical constraints on providing access. While an archives may not be able compete with the convenience of the Web, it must still establish services that support user needs to the best of its abilities.

Access Services

Access does not have to be one-size-fits-all for the various groups the museum archives supports and the assorted collections it manages. Access services can be tailored to the specific needs of different user groups, and appropriate access tools and support services (e.g., research guidance, levels of description, staff oversight, etc.) can be implemented accordingly. For example, the user who accesses audiovisual materials in the reading room may not need detailed, granular metadata (although it does often help) about an audiovisual collection as they will establish context from finding aids, research of related collections, and support from museum archives staff. By contrast, a staff user may require more contextual and descriptive information and better features for navigating to specific points in time-based media, to help them pinpoint footage that fits their topic.

For each type of access service provided by the museum's archives, the archivist should specify the availability of materials according to rights and permissions, the corresponding access technology, and the metadata required to support interpretation or reuse. If resources are a constraint, they can use service levels to set and manage expectations. Users will always expect the most convenient and broadest access; the archives is responsible for finding the correct balance between their expectations and reality.

Technology Selection

Determining the right technology to use is often the biggest hurdle to access. A sleek and convenient tool to distribute streaming media far and wide may be preferred or expected, but in shaping access for a service-oriented approach, the focus must be on the requirements of the museum, the collection, and the user.

Access and Rights Management

Access technologies should provide appropriate controls to manage and restrict access according to archival policy and institutional rules, rights and permissions constraints, and the type of access provided. This is especially important for management of the underlying rights of audiovisual materials. In addition to the rights considerations of a completed production, the copyright status of incorporated materials—performers and audience members; incidental or performed music; works of art; licensed video or audio footage—must also be accounted for.[28] Access controls such as location restrictions, time limits, and high-security streaming protocols are useful features to control where and how users access archival media.

Metadata

The archivist should look for systems that can support the broader needs of archival description. Production-oriented systems do not always provide comprehensive metadata support and can limit the scope of metadata available about collections. Systems that support comprehensive descriptive schema, generate useful provenance and/or preservation metadata, and export metadata in useful formats or exchange it with preservation systems should be prioritized.

Navigation

The time-based component of audiovisual materials sets them apart from other collection materials in the museum archives. Navigating large collections of audiovisual materials with varying durations is a challenge to users, who don't have unlimited time or patience to locate a relevant segment. Whether for research or production, users prefer granular access to segments within a video or audio recording, allowing them to navigate to points within the recording instead of viewing the entire piece.[29] Functions like time-based annotation or tagging to support search and navigation at the segment level, as opposed to the item level, can significantly impact the usefulness and efficiency of access systems.

Existing Systems

Many museums utilize digital asset management systems, content management systems, and enterprise video hosting services that offer useful services for internal staff access, authenticated streaming distribution, and sophisticated navigation tools. Building archival services into existing museum systems may limit the cost of implementation and leverage existing capacity to provide access. It also provides another opportunity to further integrate the archives into routine operations and again to emphasize its importance to the mission of the museum.

Conclusion

The complexity and demands of audiovisual materials can seem overwhelming. The challenges of both digital and analog formats—obsolescence, systems support, increasing scale, growing demand for access—are urgent and in need of solutions. Action, sooner rather than later, is essential. Media's importance to both users and museum operations will only increase in the years to come. The museum archives must carve out a central role in the life cycle of audiovisual materials, as assets as well as records, to ensure these resources remain available.

Further Reading

Brylawski, Sam, Maya Lerman, Robin Pike, and Kathlin Smith, editors. *ARSC Guide to Audio Preservation*. Eugene, OR: Association for Recorded Sound Collections, 2015. https://www.clir.org/pubs/reports/pub164/, captured at https://perma.cc/M4WL-7VJL.

Cocciolo, Anthony. *Moving Image and Sound Collections for Archivists*. Chicago: Society of American Archivists, 2017.

The FADGI Audio-Visual Working Group. "Creating and Archiving Born Digital Video." Washington, DC: Federal Agencies Digitization Guidelines Initiative, 2014. http://www.digitizationguidelines.gov/guidelines/video_bornDigital.html, captured at https://perma.cc/B3V6-VUJ2.

Lacinak, Chris. *Guide to Developing a Request for Proposal for the Digitization of Video (and More)*. New York: AVPreserve, 2013. http://www.avpreserve.com/wp-content/uploads/2013/10/AVPS_Digitization_RFP_Guide.pdf, captured at https://perma.cc/EDQ9-QTZE.

Schüller, Dietrich, and Albrecht Häfner, editors. *Handling and Storage of Audio and Video Carriers*. International Association of Sound and Audiovisual Archives, 2014. http://www.iasa-web.org/tc05/handling-storage-audio-video-carriers, captured at https://perma.cc/5KWF-5KBC.

NOTES

1. The Nielsen Company, "The Nielsen Total Audience Report," Q1 2016, http://www.nielsen.com/content/dam/corporate/us/en/reports-downloads/2016-reports/total-audience-report-q1-2016.pdf, captured at https://perma.cc/TY32-6TDM.

2. The Nielsen Company, "Video 360 2017 Report Highlights," 2017, http://www.nielsen.com/content/dam/corporate/us/en/reports-downloads/2017-reports/nielsen-video-360-highlights-2017.pdf, captured at https://perma.cc/RC5U-4RDE.

3. Jackie M. Dooley and Katherine Luce, "Taking Our Pulse: The OCLC Research Survey of Special Collections and Archives" (Dublin, OH: OCLC Research, 2010), 59, http://www.oclc.org/content/dam/research/publications/library/2010/2010-11.pdf, captured at https://perma.cc/S7DZ-MD3W.

4. Dooley and Luce, "Taking Our Pulse," 37.

5. While physical AV materials are typically called "analog" in the vernacular, the reality is that they can be analog or digital. An example of a physical, digital AV asset is a DAT or MiniDV tape.

6. Debbie Fellman et al., "The Getty Museum Integrated Marketing and Communications Plan," The Getty Museum, http://richard-hooker.com/pdf/getty_plan/getty_plan.pdf, captured at https://perma.cc/8R7V-YZ3X.

7. Jasper Visser, "Integrated Media Strategies for Museums," *The Museum of the Future* (blog), May 29, 2011, https://themuseumofthefuture.com/2011/05/29/integrated-media-strategies-for-museums, captured at https://perma.cc/CD8P-FDNR.

8. Museum of Modern Art, "Ask MoMA—Live Q&As," YouTube, https://www.youtube.com/playlist?list=PLfYVzk0sNiGEmRqIcaaGBC-Hs3fPCmiID, captured at https://perma.cc/GE5D-CDWZ; "Cell Phone Stories, About," https://cellphonestories.wordpress.com/about, captured at https://perma.cc/27QC-AV96; "Hirshhorn Launches New Generation of Museum Mobile Video Guide" (press release), Hirshhorn Museum and Sculpture Garden, June 27, 2018, https://www.si.edu/newsdesk/releases/hirshhorn-launches-new-generation-museum-mobile-video-guide, captured at https://perma.cc/AA6K-ZACT.

9. Kara Van Malssen, "Planning Beyond Digitization: Digital Preservation of Audiovisual Collections," in *Caring for Invisible Assets: On Preservation of Digital AV Collections*, ed. Annemieke de Jong (Hilversum, Netherlands: Netherlands Institute for Sound and Vision, 2011), 74–75.

10. Christopher Prom, "Making Digital Curation a Systematic Institutional Function," *The International Journal of Digital Curation* 6, no. 1 (2011): 140.

11. Neil Grindley, "The Digital Curation Sustainability Model (DCSM)," February 2015, 18. 4C Project.

12. Federal Agencies Digital Guidelines Initiative (FADGI), "Creating and Archiving Born Digital Video" (2016), 13. See chapter 3 of this publication for a discussion of museum archives' collection development policies.

13. The preservation master is used as the source for migration to future preservation formats. These should be infrequently accessed except for the generation of high-resolution derivatives and for ongoing digital preservation activities. As such, offline or data tape storage can be considered.

14. The access master file is an optional middle tier that is useful when a strong use-case exists for editing or broadcasting, or when the preservation masters are so large or specialized that they are challenging to work with on a routine basis. Selected access master formats should be compatible with the museum's production systems to avoid the need to transcode additional copies.

15. For further information on selecting target file formats, please consult the following resources: Kevin Bradley, ed., *Guidelines on the Production and Preservation of Digital Audio Objects* (South Africa: International Association of Sound and Audiovisual Archives, 2009), https://www.iasa-web.org/tc04/audio-preservation, captured at https://perma.cc/D965-YJ34; and Carl Fleischhauer and Kevin Bradley, eds., *Guidelines for the Preservation of Video Recordings* (London: International Association of Sound and Audiovisual Archives, 2018), https://www.iasa-web.org/tc06/guidelines-preservation-video-recordings, captured at https://perma.cc/NA8P-TW4S.

16. Public Broadcasting Metadata Dictionary Project, "PBCore 2.1," http://pbcore.org, captured at https://perma.cc/4BYQ-GTBP; "AVI MetaEdit & ReVTMD," AVP, https://www.weareavp.com/products/avi-metaedit-revtmd/, captured at https://perma.cc/LWX5-TGVE; Audio Engineering Society, "AES57-2011 (r2017) AES Standard for Audio Metadata—Audio Object Structures for Preservation and Restoration," April 29, 2017, http://www.aes.org/publications/standards/search.cfm?docID=84, captured at https://perma.cc/2693-5CBL; Library of Congress, PREMIS Editorial Committee, "PREMIS Data Dictionary for Preservation Metadata Version 3.0," June 2015, https://www.loc.gov/standards/premis, captured at https://perma.cc/3U38-TS3S.

17. When collecting metadata, the archivist should not overlook valuable metadata sources throughout the museum. Collection management systems (e.g., the Museum System, Past Perfect, etc.) often contain useful contextual details about items, exhibitions, or events featured in audiovisual productions. Project management tools (e.g., JIRA, Basecamp, Trello) may contain useful information about the production process that can inform selection and future use.

18. FADGI, "Creating and Archiving Born Digital Video," 7–10.

19. FADGI, "Creating and Archiving Born Digital Video," 13.

20. Dr. Michele Edge, "The Deterioration of Polymers in Audio-Visual Materials," IASA Technical Coordinating Committee, https://www.iasa-web.org/deterioration-polymers, captured at https://perma.cc/9DY8-Y8D3.

21. The Library of Congress, "The Library of Congress National Recording Preservation Plan," https://www.loc.gov/programs/static/national-recording-preservation-plan/publications-and-reports/documents/NRPPLANCLIRpdfpub156.pdf, captured at https://perma.cc/3NHV-Z9PV.

22. Quantitative checks are based on an easily definable logic and can be awarded a pass or fail—there are no gray areas here. For example, if an archives specified that all audio preservation masters would have a particular sample rate, all corresponding deliverables must have that sample rate to pass. Many quantitative checks can be automated using software applications, as the logic is straightforward and easily checked. Qualitative checks are based on subjective human judgments as to the quality of a deliverable. They require playback of a given file to determine whether or not it meets expectations. When working with archival AV materials, a wide variety of qualities may be acceptable based on the original equipment used to make the recording, the format, the age of the item, the professional or amateur nature of the recording, and so on. A poor original recording will never result in a pristine digital surrogate. However, certain possible errors may stand out to someone performing quality control checks and should be brought to the attention of the operator.

23. As outlined in ISO 18934:2011, Imaging materials—Multiple media archives—Storage environment, the ideal temperature range for magnetic, optical, and motion picture media is in the range of -4°F to 60°F, depending on the materiality of the format, and at a relative humidity between 30% and 50%. This is a fairly large range that can be difficult to conform to in

mixed media collections. Cool storage—32°F–46°F at 30%–50% relative humidity—is identified as "Good" or "Very Good" for all media materials studied in ISO 18934. International Organization for Standardization, "ISO 18934 Imaging materials—Multiple media archives—Storage environment," https://www.iso.org/standard/55518.html, captured at https://perma.cc/J84B-7FT4.

24 Consultative Committee for Space Data Systems, "Reference Model for an Open Archival Information System (OAIS)," (Washington, DC: CCSDS Secretariat, June 2002); Consultative Committee for Space Data Systems, "Audit and Certification of Trustworthy Digital Repositories" (Washington, DC: CCSDS Secretariat, September 2011); Morgan Phillips et al., "The NDSA Levels of Digital Preservation: An Explanation and Uses" (Washington, DC: National Digital Stewardship Alliance, 2013).

25 Intrafile checksums are generated for the encoded audio or video information within the file, excluding the embedded metadata and other container information. This allows for changes to the embedded metadata without altering the checksum values of the media streams. In addition to corresponding external metadata records, checksum values can even be added to the file's embedded metadata for storage. Dave Rice, "Reconsidering the Checksum for Audiovisual Preservation: Detecting Digital Change in Audiovisual Data with Decoders and Checksums," *IASA Journal*, no. 39 (June 2012), https://www.iasa-web.org/sites/default/files/iasa-journal-39-part8.pdf, captured at https://perma.cc/6XSG-ABAE.

26 FADGI, "Creating and Archiving Born Digital Video," 15–16.

27 Migration plans must also address relevant technical characteristics of audiovisual files to maintain a consistent level of quality and integrity. Chroma sampling, frame rates, and bit depth should remain at the same value throughout migration. Compression in preservation masters is to be avoided. If required for storage considerations or institutional needs, mathematically lossless (e.g., FLAC, FFV1), not visually lossless, or "lossy," compression formats (e.g., H.264, MP3) should be used. Mathematically lossless formats retain original data values and lower file sizes without a subsequent loss of quality. By contrast, lossy compression algorithms permanently remove data values from the encoded media and can result in loss of image and audio quality. Chris Lacinak, "A Primer on Codecs for Moving Image and Sound Archives & 10 Recommendations for Codec Selection and Management" (New York: AVPreserve, 2010), 4, https://www.avpreserve.com/wp-content/uploads/2010/04/AVPS_Codec_Primer.pdf, captured at https://perma.cc/LUM6-XUJX.

28 Brandon Butler, "Audio Preservation: The Legal Context," in *ARSC Guide to Audio Preservation*, ed. Sam Brylawski et al. (Eugene, OR: Association for Recorded Sound Collections, 2015), 155.

29 Richard Wright, "Preserving Moving Pictures and Sound," *DPC Technology Watch Series* (United Kingdom: Digital Preservation Coalition, 2012), 19, http://dx.doi.org/10.7207/twr12-01, captured at https://perma.cc/5HEE-FVRY.

9 ORAL HISTORY: A PRIMER FOR CREATION, OUTREACH, AND ADVOCACY

Ellen Brooks and Megan Schwenke

The Oral History Association defines oral history as a "field of study and a method of gathering, preserving, and interpreting the voices and memories of people, communities, and participants in past events."[1] Oral history interviews can be conducted by a museum archives, or on behalf of it; they can also make their way into the holdings of a museum archives as part of a manuscript collection.[2] The interviews may focus on a certain collecting area of the museum, provide interpretation and context for museum collection objects or themes, illustrate the institution's own history, or combine parts from all of these. Conducting oral histories is becoming a common way for museums to include previously overlooked people and perspectives in the historical narrative.[3] This chapter proposes that oral history should be a component of a successful museum archives, arguing that maintaining an oral history program positions it as an important institutional resource, strengthens collection development, raises the profile of the archives within the museum and the larger community, and allows it to enhance its overall contribution to the museum's interpretative mission. The chapter also outlines best practices for conducting oral history for museum archivists.

The Value of Oral History to Museum Archives

As evidenced throughout this publication, museum archivists often juggle competing demands with limited time and resources. Given the significant work required to properly research and prepare for a single oral history interview, let alone initiate a program with multiple interviews, why might a museum archivist undertake this work? The following section seeks to illustrate the myriad benefits oral history can bring to a museum archives, from collection development, to community building, to advocacy for the archives as well as for the museum.

Collection Development

Museum archivists undertaking oral history projects must strike a balance between collection development and resource management, considering available funds and resources as well as the museum's and the archives' missions and audiences. Subjects in the archives collection or museum collection that would most benefit from the texture and contextual enhancements that oral history can provide should also be identified. In some cases, oral history may be the best or only way for the museum to amass documentation on a particular community or topic. When museums cannot collect materials or materials do not exist, oral history provides an opportunity to ensure that otherwise underrepresented stories can be told.[4] In 2014, the Wisconsin Veterans Museum (WVM) undertook an initiative to incorporate the story of the Hmong community into its Vietnam War narrative and exhibit. The majority of Hmong who made their way to the United States during that era were refugees who had fled their homes, crossed borders, and lived in refugee camps for years. As a result, members of these Hmong communities have very little in terms of materials or artifacts. To tell their story, the museum relied almost exclusively on Hmong oral histories and, consequently, the expertise and knowledge of the museum archivist conducting the interviews. Through her work connecting with and conducting interviews with members of the Hmong community, one of the museum's archivists became the institutional expert on Hmong culture and history and subsequently worked directly with colleagues to determine how the Hmong narrative could best be interwoven into an existing Vietnam War exhibit. Her responsibility was to ensure that the objectives and expectations of both the Hmong community and the museum were identified and honored throughout the project. She also played a role in identifying objects belonging to the Hmong narrators and their communities that might be contributed to the museum's collection to increase the impact the museum could have in telling the story of Hmong soldiers during this era.[5] In this circumstance, oral history, with a museum archivist in charge, played an invaluable and primary role in collection development and interpretation for the museum and the museum archives.

Museum archivists are often aware of gaps in time or subjects in their institutional records from their own experiences working with the collections; additionally, users might point these out, or they might be uncovered in processing or reference work. Targeted oral history interviews can bridge these gaps and also enhance and contextualize existing collections. For example, many museums with institutional archives undertake interviews with

---

THE VALUE OF COLLECTING ORAL HISTORY IN A MUSEUM SETTING

The slogan at the Wisconsin Veterans Museum (WVM) is "Every veteran is a story," and the mission of the staff is to collect and preserve materials from veterans and to utilize them in engaging and educating the public. The museum's collection contains many items, but the most exciting museum objects and archival items are those with good stories behind them: stories help put a human face on military service and connect civilians to veterans. Gathering such stories often depends on oral history interviews because they capture the experience of veterans in their own words. This unique centering of narrator agency leads to valuable diversity in perspectives and allows the museum to present a well-rounded, complex narrative. This is evidenced in an interview with Laura Naylor of the Army National Guard:

> When I talk about Iraq, I try to do it nonbiasedly, and I try to give you the down and dirty. I try and tell you the good and the bad. . . . But then you need to talk to other soldiers who loved being over there, and who fought a good fight, and who feel like they came away with doing something really good. And then you can talk to the soldiers who were the post office workers, and they sat in the post office all day and were bored out of their minds. And so the one thing I would tell you is talk to more soldiers if you really want to know a lot about it. But to sum it up, I would say that it's a very versatile war. There's a lot of different things going on all at once and every story is very original. You just have to hear different perspectives, and not get stuck in one place.[6]

Most people, civilians and veterans alike, may approach WVM with preconceived ideas about what it means to serve in the military and what war is. Museum staff aims not to dispel those notions necessarily, but to offer multiple alternatives and encourage visitors to expand their way of thinking. Presenting the firsthand experience of veterans in their own words via oral history is an extremely effective way to accomplish that objective.

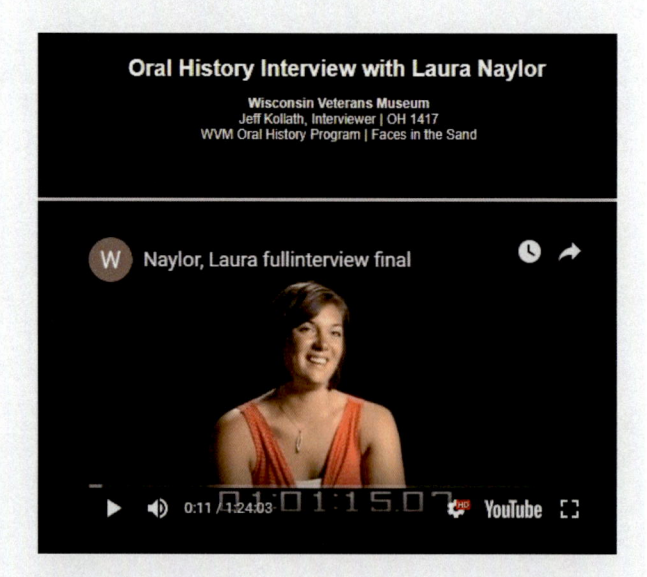

FIGURE 9.1. Still image from Wisconsin Veterans Museum's interview with Laura Naylor, viewed online via the OHMS Viewer; OHMS is discussed later in this chapter. COURTESY OF THE WISCONSIN VETERANS MUSEUM.

FIGURE 9.2. Ellen Brooks and Seethong Yang interview Hmong veteran Nao Tou Lor for the *Secret War in Laos* exhibit, November 14, 2014. COURTESY OF THE WISCONSIN VETERANS MUSEUM.

long-time staff, former or present, and create oral history programs to strengthen the existing body of records on their history.[7] The Craft and Folk Art Museum's (CAFAM) Oral History Project includes close to sixty hours of interviews and corresponding transcriptions with former staff and board members active during the Los Angeles institution's first thirty years. The museum's former librarian conducted the interviews to capture behind-the-scenes stories of CAFAM, now available at the University of California, Los Angeles Library's Center for Oral History Research.[8]

Raising Visibility

Oral history often garners attention and interest from all types of constituents and has the potential to raise the profile of the museum archives in the larger community. Seeking out narrators with diverse backgrounds external to the institution enables museum archives staff to develop new relationships with different groups, some of which they may not have had ready access to. For example, scholar John Kuo Wei Tchen's work explores the development of the "Dialogic Museum," "a work process where documentation, meaning, and representation are acknowledged to be co-developed with those whom the history is of, for, and about."[9] Working with community groups and sharing authority over the historical narratives presented in museums can engage local partners and populations, creating sustainable interest and investment in the museum. Additionally, oral history can be a useful tool for connecting with local organizations, as it is easily shared and lends itself to partnerships in creative projects. A museum archives might partner with a local radio station to air interview recordings or audio vignettes that include oral history.[10] Museum archives can also work with nearby libraries or schools to showcase interviews through shared programming and events; such collaborations can mutually benefit both partners by broadening outreach capacity.

An institutional oral history program can act as "in-reach" and increase the visibility of the museum archives internally, especially in large museums. This can involve staff directly in a historical project spearheaded by the museum archives, raising its profile among museum colleagues and investing them in its success. Selecting narrators across the museum's ranks, from front-line workers to preparators to curators, demonstrates to all staff that their experiences and memories are a valued and valuable part of the institution's history. Long-time donors, particularly those interested in the museum's history, can be excellent choices for narrators of institutional oral history programs in addition to staff members. They will have their own unique perspective on the museum's history, and these individuals are often pleased to be asked to be interviewed. The experience allows them to share stories and memories important to them, and the knowledge that these insights will be preserved for the long term makes it all the more significant.[11] Creating these positive experiences, and capitalizing on the overall popularity of oral history, can build or strengthen relationships with potential funders and individuals who then become valuable stakeholders in the work of the museum archives.

Oral History-Based Interpretation

One of the most popular ways of using oral history in the museum context is to include interview recordings in an exhibition space. This can be done in many ways, including listening kiosks, user-launched audio and video screens, or recordings played aloud in galleries.[12] Some institutions layer additional technology onto their oral history recordings: in 2017, the Illinois Holocaust Museum's Take a Stand Center opened an interactive experience in which visitors could dialogue with Holocaust survivors through three-dimensional holograms and custom interactive voice technology.[13] However, museums do not require expansive budgets and access to a high level of technology to successfully incorporate oral history into exhibitions; it can be done as simply as including quotes from interview transcripts in a gallery label. The key is to allow the content of interviews to guide exhibition design.[14] Thus, museum archivists have the opportunity to think beyond an interview's potential for use in the reading room to how it might be contextualized within galleries and programs over time; this role in interpretation may set them apart from archivists in other contexts.

In addition to contributing to interpretation, oral history can open new avenues of access. Audio-driven walking tours and place-based audio projects are gaining popularity; these tours are a natural extension of the traditional audio guides many museums offer, and oral history works well with projects that take museum content outside of the physical gallery space.[15] Designing something outdoors or place-based may not work for all institutions, however, and likewise, not all potential users are able to visit museums in person. Making oral history available via the archives' or museum's website is another way to expand the reach of collections and open up new opportunities for engagement that do not require users to leave their homes. In September 2015, the Harvard Art Museums partnered with StoryCorps and National Grid to record conversations about the artist Corita Kent to extend the reach of the exhibition *Corita Kent and the Language of Pop*. The project recorded more than

ORAL HISTORY AND THE WEB

Traditionally, users access oral history interviews via recordings in an archives reading room, and, when a transcript is available, often make primary use of it, foregoing listening to the associated interview at all. While working with a written document provides an ease, it cannot convey the texture and meaning in a narrator's voice, tone, and inflection.[16] Institutions are now leveraging digital technology to provide oral history interview recordings alongside their transcripts on the web, expanding and improving the quality of access for users while increasing exposure of and engagement with oral history projects within the organization and the larger community.

Brooklyn Historical Society (BHS) maintains a growing collection of oral history interviews, over 1,200 and counting, conducted by BHS staff as well as donated by independent oral historians and organizations. BHS began to digitize, catalog, and describe its legacy oral history collections, as well as two additional donated collections, in 2015. This work culminated in the creation of an Oral History Portal to allow users to interface directly with the audio recordings and transcripts.[17] The portal utilizes the Oral History Metadata Synchronizer (OMHS), a tool developed by the University of Kentucky Libraries, which enables playback of audio or video files alongside time-synced, text searchable transcripts and/or indexes.[18] Working with OHMS and with metadata imported into WordPress, the BHS portal allows users to watch or listen to interviews and to search names and keywords within individual interviews as well as across interviews in multiple collections.

The effort has had many benefits. The infrastructure developed for the portal functioned as a pilot for collections access at BHS and can be reused and scaled for additional oral history holdings and any other time-based media in the collections. The completed project was rolled out at a meeting of the society's board and at several professional conferences to significant excitement, raising the visibility of the oral history collection to the institution's administration, archives and oral history professionals, and the general public. The portal has also raised the profile of BHS in the community: Muslims in Brooklyn, a new oral history project, has increased awareness of the work of BHS and serves as an opportunity for the staff to seek collections documenting Muslim communities beyond the interviews.[19]

twelve hours of interviews over three days, showcasing the stories of thirty-five individual participants. Several are available via the museums' website, supplying additional context to Kent's art as well as her impact as an artist and individual. The project also provided unique supplementary content not available in the museum, offering remote access to the exhibition and its subject.[20]

Best Practices for the Museum Archivist

Museum archivists should approach oral history projects with preparation and respect for the process. Carrying out oral history well, which means obtaining quality content in an interview and collaborating respectfully with narrators and partners, requires extensive planning. Fortunately, many resources are available to help archivists understand what oral history is and how it is best practiced. Rather than duplicate that information here, the following list details key questions for the museum archivist to consider when exploring the feasibility of an oral history interview or project, as well as steps to take in developing one.[21] Ideally, the museum archivist should record answers to these questions in a master planning document; a brief version of such a document can be used to introduce the project to stakeholders, and a detailed version should be kept accessible for project staff for reference.[22]

Planning the Interview

Why Is the Museum Archives Doing this Project/Interview?

First, the museum archivist should consider the impetus to do oral history: who or what are the drivers for the project? Will the interview(s) complement an archival collection or a museum collection object? Will the narrator(s) and/or subjects covered fill a gap in collection holdings? Must the interview be completed and made available within a timeline, such as an institutional anniversary or celebration? How might the project support the museum's mission, directly or indirectly?

What Is the Desired Final Result or Product?

Oral history has many potential applications within the museum context: Will the interview(s) be part of a website, an exhibition, or a publication, either produced by the museum archives alone or by its parent institution in tandem? Will the interview(s) result in a new archival accession? Could the interview(s) be utilized by noninterpretative staff such as the museum's communications or development departments to promote the institution or the archives specifically?

Who or What Is the Focus?

Interview narrators might include community members, veterans, or immigrant groups related to a museum initiative or collection object, and subjects could span museum history and/or the achievements of its staff, or a specific event, industry, or other topic. Determining the focus will aid in narrator selection, along with drafting interview questions and/or topic areas to cover.

How Will Narrators Be Selected? How Will They Be Contacted?

Consult with museum colleagues; they may know narrators who fit the project focus as well as maintain relationships that can result in an introduction. For institutional oral history projects, it may be worthwhile to consult with colleagues in the development department specifically to identify supporters or donors to include on the project's list of potential narrators. Once contact has been made with a narrator, if possible, arrange a phone call or in-person meeting for a pre-interview to share the goals of the project, to review logistics like desired length of interview and potential location, and, of course, to secure their agreement to be interviewed. A pre-interview call or meeting is also a great opportunity to build rapport between interviewer and narrator.

Who Will Conduct the Oral History Interview(s)?

All interviewers, if not already trained, should seek out and educate themselves on oral history guidelines before sitting down to conduct an interview.[23] Developing skills should be exercised by conducting practice interviews prior to officially meeting with a narrator and starting to record.

If other museum staff or volunteers will conduct interviews, the museum archivist should take an active role in the planning and preparation for them, ensuring that the final product will be suitable for accession into the archives. This also provides an opportunity for the museum archivist to share oral history expertise with colleagues; it is a chance to take a teaching role and might include sharing release form templates, instructing on interviewing techniques, and/or providing access to interviews from archival collections as samples.

How Should the Interviewer Prepare?

Preparation signals to the narrator that the interviewer respects their time and experience. To research events and topics intended for inclusion in the interview, as well as narrators, the interviewer should leverage information at hand and consult related archival collections, research materials, and objects available in the museum archives and in the larger institution. Museum colleagues such as curators or administrators may also know the narrator well and have potential questions to contribute.

How Will the Interview(s) Be Recorded?

Recording equipment is a significant component of oral history projects and should not be left as an afterthought. The selection of audio or video recording equipment should take into account institutional resources, project goals, technical acumen, narrator comfort, and storage and access of final interview files.[24] Oral history depends on audio, and thus use of quality audio equipment should be the number-one priority. If obtaining and preserving quality audio is not a challenge for the project and the museum archives, video could be pursued as well.[25]

When selecting AV equipment, the museum archivist overseeing an oral history project might utilize existing museum resources: Does the IT department have recording equipment that could be borrowed to record interviews? If the museum has a videographer on staff, would they be willing to record the interview for the archives, perhaps with the option to use footage in other institutional film projects as a potential added incentive?

How Will Permission to Record and Share the Interview(s) Be Secured?

Obtaining a signed legal release form from the narrator is imperative.[26] Early consideration of potential applications of the final interview(s) as already discussed come into play here; these should be detailed in the release form and thoroughly explained to the narrator so they fully understand and are comfortable with the possible future uses of their interview. Consulting with museum counsel to review and approve the language in narrator releases prior to beginning an interview or program is recommended. The archivist should decide at what point in the process the narrator and interviewer will sign the release forms and keep that consistent across interviews.

What Metadata Needs to Be Recorded?

Establishing what type of data need to be collected for every oral history interview before any interviewing is done is important. Descriptive, administrative, and technical metadata will all prove vital in the arrangement and description process, and it must be captured as soon as possible, ideally before or immediately after an interview.[27]

Conducting the Interview

Where Will the Interview(s) Be Recorded?

Various settings could work as an interview site: the museum archives, a museum gallery near a related object, or a narrator's home are all possibilities, but most important is a quiet space with limited distractions. If the interview will be recorded on video as one in a series, the interviewer should consider using the same space and setup throughout to maintain a consistent look, feel, and audio quality.

How Will Future Audiences Be Accounted For?

That which may be obvious to the interviewer and narrator during the interview may not be evident to future users, especially in audio-only recordings and in most transcriptions. If possible, any visual materials referenced in the interview should be explained. The interviewer should ask the narrator to explain any jargon used and pose follow-up questions on complex subjects that may be unfamiliar to listeners. Future users cannot simply look at an oral history file, or the physical media that it resides on, and know what it contains. The interviewer must take thorough notes, during and/or immediately after the interview, that can be translated into descriptive metadata.

After the Interview

What Paperwork/Project Documentation Will Be Preserved?

Project planning documentation, questions/topics list, research materials, and any additional notes gathered by the interviewer and/or museum archives staff should be preserved as records of the oral history project. Signed legal release forms should be kept in close proximity to recordings in storage systems, digital or otherwise, for easy reference.

How Will Each Interview Be Processed for Preservation and Access?

The interviewer should write a summary of the interview immediately following the recording, including key subjects discussed and topics covered, as well as any important information about the structure of the interview and the quality of the recording. This draft text can serve as a placeholder until a more formal abstract is written. A full transcript can be created in-house, or this work can be outsourced to a transcription service, with or without indexing. The narrator then might review the final transcript for any corrections or clarifications. In addition to the transcript, index, and/or abstract, the metadata recorded during and after the interview should be organized in the museum archives' content management system. What metadata should be front-facing and what, if any, should be for internal use only will need to be determined.

How Will the Museum Archives Work with the Narrator(s)/Community to Make the Oral History Interview(s) Accessible?

Discovery tools describing the interview should be created to make it findable by users as appropriate, as well as consideration given to whether the recording will be accessed on-site or remotely. The archives should strive to work with its community, not just for it, whenever possible, consulting with community members such as visitors, local leaders, and friends groups along with the people represented in the oral history project: what are their expectations for access to these materials? Museum colleagues can be consulted as well: Could the interview be linked to related objects or exhibitions in the museum's collections database or digital asset management systems? Might it be integrated into upcoming programming or new outreach initiatives, originated by the archives or by the museum, or in tandem? With the help of the museum's communications department, the archivist can consider issuing a press release to publicize the final product. By staying in touch with narrators, the archivist can alert them to outreach activities as they take place so they may participate if they wish.

Conclusion

Oral history projects both execute and expand upon a museum's and its archives' mission to develop and interpret its holdings. For museum archivists who steward oral history interviews in their collections or are thinking about starting an oral history program, this work can fill in gaps in collection holdings and promote the archives program both inside and outside the institution.

Further Reading

Ameri, Anan. "Case Study: Why Oral History Matters: The Experience of the Arab American National Museum." In *Oral History in the Digital Age*, edited by Doug Boyd, Steve Cohen, Brad Rakerd, and Dean Rehberger. Washington, DC: Institute of Museum and Library Services, 2012. http://ohda.matrix.msu.edu/2012/06/arab-american-national-museum, captured at https://perma.cc/6DVX-S3XV.

Frisch, Michael. *A Shared Authority: Essays on the Craft and Meaning of Oral and Public History.* Albany: SUNY Press. 1991.

Oral History Association, "Archiving Oral History: Manual of Best Practices." https://www.oralhistory.org/archives-principles-and-best-practices-complete-manual, captured at https://perma.cc/22SU-J9PY.

Oral History Association, "Principles and Best Practices for Oral History," https://www.oralhistory.org/principles-and-best-practices-revised-2018, captured at https://perma.cc/SN28-28LP.

Oral History Association, "Remote Interviewing Resources." https://www.oralhistory.org

/remote-interviewing-resources, captured at https://perma.cc/J9MZ-RC6G.

Perks, Robert, and Alistair Thomson. *The Oral History Reader*. 2nd ed. New York: Routledge, 2006. Chapters 32 and 33 are particularly relevant to the discussion of the intersection of oral history, archives, and museums.

United States Holocaust Memorial Museum. "Oral History Interview Guidelines." https://www.ushmm.org/m/pdfs/20121003-oral-history-interview-guide.pdf, captured at https://perma.cc/HK83-ECQ4.

NOTES

1. Oral History Association, "Oral History: Defined," http://www.oralhistory.org/about/do-oral-history, captured at https://perma.cc/9C7Z-32R8. Museum archives might expand on this definition to further describe their oral history interviews; for example, the Wisconsin Veterans Museum (WVM) stipulates that oral history recordings in the collection include a narrator and an interviewer who have agreed to record a conversation that will be publicly accessible and used as a primary historical source; see https://wisvetsmuseum.com/oral-histories, captured at https://perma.cc/4N8J-4C99.

2. See chapter 6 of this publication for further discussion on manuscript collections in museum archives.

3. Within the field of oral history, practitioners are seeking to challenge, and in some cases to replace, narratives of white supremacy and settler colonialism by making an effort to collect interviews with marginalized people and communities, including Indigenous and tribal representation. For more discussion and resources, see Columbia University Oral History Master of Arts, "Oral History, Indigenous Oral Histories, and Decolonization," http://oralhistory.columbia.edu/blog-posts/people/oral-history-projects-that-challenge-white-supremacy-tww54, captured at https://perma.cc/P5CA-L4NS.

4. "Oral History, then, offers the opportunity to balance an archival collection by extending documentation to groups or individuals not normally possessed of papers or who are outside the purview of most collecting agencies." James E. Fogerty, "Filling the Gap: Oral History in the Archives," *American Archivist* 46, no. 2 (1983): 155, https://doi.org/10.17723/aarc.46.2.r775717748477g34, by way of Jessica Wagner Webster, "'Filling the Gaps': Oral Histories and Undocumented Populations in *American Archivist*, 1938–2001," *American Archivist* 79, no. 2 (2016), 254–82, https://doi.org/10.17723/0360-9081-79.2.254.

5. The Oral History Association defines the narrator in an oral history interview as "a person being interviewed during an oral history recording. While there are many possible terms, including interviewee or chronicler, . . . our Core Principles and Practices uses the term narrator exclusively. We do this as an acknowledgment that the people we interview have agency and are not merely 'living human subjects.'" See http://www.oralhistory.org/narrator, captured at https://perma.cc/F359-HTAA.

6. Oral history interview with Laura Naylor, 2008. Copyright Wisconsin Veterans Museum.

7. A number of museums have established institutional oral history initiatives: SFMoMA, http://bancroft.berkeley.edu/ROHO/projects/sfmoma/index.html, captured at https://perma.cc/X9JK-DYKQ; Smithsonian Institution Archives, http://siarchivessi.edu/research/oralvidhistory_intro.html, captured at https://perma.cc/CFC2-TU72; MoMA, https://www.moma.org/research-and-learning/archives/oral-history#institutional-oral-history-program, captured at https://perma.cc/CMX9-L8NSl; the Metropolitan Museum of Art, https://www.libmma.org/digital_files/archives/Oral_Histories.pdf, captured at https://perma.cc/2QQ8-4TSM; and Britain's Natural History Museum, http://www.nhm.ac.uk/research-curation/science-facilities/cahr/projects-partnerships/museum-lives/index.html, captured at https://perma.cc/DNS6-436G.

8. See UCLA Library's Center for Oral History Research CAFAM Oral History Project page for more information at http://oralhistory.library.ucla.edu/viewItem.do?ark=21198/zz00096tgk&title=%2520Craft%2520and%2520Folk%2520Art%2520Museum%2520Oral%2520History%2520Project, captured at https://perma.cc/L7GD-EADJ.

9. Linda Shopes discusses Tchen's work at the Museum of Chinese in America in "The Museum of Chinese in America: Continuity and Change," Mid-Atlantic Regional Center for the Humanities (2017), https://march.rutgers.edu/the-museum-of-chinese-in-america-continuity-and-change, captured at https://perma.cc/3WEE-Q3GL. Additional examples of dialogic community memory work in a museum setting can be found via "Open House: If These Walls Could Talk" at the Minnesota History Center, https://www.mnhs.org/exhibits/openhouse, captured at https://perma.cc/4QMG-T5K2, and The Legacy Project from the Weeksville Heritage Center, https://www.weeksvillesociety.org/the-legacy-project, captured at https://perma.cc/K99G-HXSF.

10. For an example of this type of collaboration, visit the webpage for the collection, "Wisconsin in the First World War" on the Wisconsin Life series, published by Wisconsin Public Radio. Many of these audio vignettes use oral history recordings and were published in collaboration with the Wisconsin Veterans Museum Oral History Program, https://www.wisconsinlife.org/series/wisconsin-in-the-first-world-war, captured at https://perma.cc/2BN7-SP2Y.

11. Educator Hope Jensen Leichter and museum professional Michael Spock point out additional benefits to the narrator: " . . . the act of constructing and telling a story is itself a learning experience. Not only does it make the memory of the experience move vivid and lasting, but telling a story offers a self-reflective opportunity to make sense of and understand events—to place them in the context of one's life and beliefs." Hope J. Leichter and Michael Spock, "Learning from Ourselves: Pivotal Stories of Museum Professionals," in *Bridges to Understanding Children's Museums*, ed. Nina R. Gibans, 66–80 (Cleveland: Children's Museums: Bridges to the Future Project, 1999).

12. Modes of presentation for oral history in museum exhibitions is an ongoing topic of discussion; see Amanda Tewes, "Curating Oral History in a Museum Setting," *Berkeley Library Update* (blog) https://update.lib.berkeley.edu/2018/07/31/curating-oral-history-in-a-museum-setting, captured at https://perma.cc/W6DT-Y47B.

13. Visit the website for the Illinois Holocaust Museum's Take a Stand Center to see more on the exhibition at https://www.ilholocaustmuseum.org/tas, captured at https://perma.cc/8HU3-L8CM, and for information about the technology behind it, read Zoe Mutter's case study, "Living History" on the *AV Magazine* website, https://www.avinteractive.com/case-studies/living-history-10-12-2018/?fbclid=IwAR1PHuhYjbDvf9Q2FAB-xZ5uRJUO-9gt8MC7ep_U7CoS3OHZIxL4ETA2bv0, captured at https://perma.cc/MGG4-WTM4.

14. For further reading on examples of oral history in museum exhibitions, and the challenges therein, see Sarah Zenaida Gould, "Challenges in Exhibiting Oral History," in the *Oral History Review* (blog), March 4, 2016, https://blog.oup.com/2016/03/exhibiting-oral-history, captured at https://perma.cc/74KB-SAW9.

15. See Simon Bradley, "History to Go: Oral History, Audiowalks and Mobile Media," *Oral History* 40, no. 1 (2012): 99–110; several "sound walks" projects incorporating oral history sponsored by the Museum of London are discussed.

16. For more on this topic, see Steven High, "Telling Stories: A Reflection on Oral History and New Media," *Oral History* (Spring 2010): 101–12; and Stacey Zembrzycki, "Bringing Stories to Life: Using New Media to Disseminate and Critically Engage with Oral History Interviews," *Oral History* (Spring 2013): 98–107.

17. Brooklyn Historical Society's Oral History Portal can be found at http://www.brooklynhistory.org/library/oralhistory, captured at https://perma.cc/67MC-PD3V; its creation was funded by the New York Community Trust, while the initial digitization, cataloging, and description effort was funded by a grant from the National Historical Public Records Commission. Julie I. May, formerly the managing director of the Library and Archives at BHS and codirector of the portal project, generously provided background for this section.

18. OHMS is an open-source tool developed by the Louie B. Nunn Center at the University of Kentucky and an extremely useful resource for getting oral history or any time-based media online, http://www.oralhistoryonline.org, captured at https://perma.cc/FXF2-JTFH. See the "Partners" page for a number of organizations utilizing OHMS and links to the tool in action.

19. For more on the Muslims in Brooklyn project, see Brooklyn Public Library, "Muslims in Brooklyn," http://brooklynhistory.org/projects/muslimsinbrooklyn, captured at https://perma.cc/A695-4ZCP.

20. For more detail, and interviews, see Harvard Art Museums, "StoryCorps and Corita Kent," https://www.harvardartmuseums.org/tour/storycorps-and-corita-kent, captured at https://perma.cc/6MTF-XCU9. Accessibility for all museum users is an important consideration when incorporating oral history into exhibitions and programming; Brad Rakerd, professor of Communicative Sciences and Disorders, makes several suggestions on how to improve access for users with hearing loss in galleries as well as in the reading room, including improving overall audio quality of recordings, providing cues to visual speech such as contextualizing images, and allowing users the option to control the progress and speed of the recording. See Brad Rakerd, "On Making Oral Histories More Accessible to Persons with Hearing Loss," *Oral History Review* 40, no. 1 (2013): 67–74.

21. Many of these questions come from Dana Gerber-Margie, Troy Reeves, and Ellen Brooks, "Guidelines and Recommendations for Oral History Projects" (2017), Recollection Wisconsin, http://recollectionwisconsin.org/wp-content/uploads/2016/06/WIOralHistory_Part1_Questions.pdf, captured at https://perma.cc/Z47S-Z7NQ.

22. See additional resources on oral history project planning in Douglas A. Boyd, "Designing an Oral History Project: Initial Questions to Ask Yourself," and Marsha MacDowell, "Project Planning and Management," both in Institute of Museum and Library Services, *Oral History in the Digital Age* (blog), 2012, at http://ohda.matrix.msu.edu/2012/06/designing-an-oral-history-project and http://ohda.matrix.msu.edu/2012/06/project-planning-and-management, captured at https://perma.cc/HAG5-D799 and https://perma.cc/9EDG-WTBE, respectively.

23. Extensive resources for conducting oral history interviews are available through the Oral History Association at http://www.oralhistory.org, captured at https://perma.cc/DR5Q-5NBM, as well as the Oral History Section of the Society of American Archivists at https://www2.archivists.org/groups/oral-history-section, captured at https://perma.cc/Z8FD-VZXA.

24. Much debate has taken place over the use of audio or video in oral history recordings; for a primer, see Joanna Hay, "Case Study: Using Video in Oral History—Learning from One Woman's Experiences," Institute of Museum and Library Services, *Oral History in the Digital Age* (blog), 2012, http://ohda.matrix.msu.edu/2012/06/using-video-in-oral-history, captured at https://perma.cc/VZ3Y-RGK5.

25. For resources discussing file naming conventions, tools to aid with data integrity, and websites that offer comparisons of digital recorders, see *Oral History in the Digital Age* (blog), http://www.oralhistory.org/oral-history-in-the-digital-age/, captured at https://perma.cc/3VX4-MM4B. The preceding chapter in this publication, which addresses audiovisual records, also considers elements of this topic.

26. For examples of oral history narrator release forms, see the Society of American Archivists Museum Archives Section's Standards and Best Practices Working Group's Resource Guide at https://www2.archivists.org/groups/museum-archives-section/2-appraisal-and-acquisitionaccession, captured at https://perma.cc/9KU2-TUGN.

27. For more information on metadata and oral history, see Elinor A. Maze, "Metadata: Best Practices for Oral History Access and Preservation," in Institute of Museum and Library Services, *Oral History in the Digital Age* (blog), 2012, http://ohda.matrix.msu.edu/2012/06/metadata captured at https://perma.cc/UR9Z-H98S.

10 PHOTOGRAPHS: THE HEART OF THE MUSEUM ARCHIVES

Madeleine Thompson

Photographs are among the most cherished items in many archival collections. In the museum setting, staff from curators to fundraisers rely upon them, and they are among the items most frequently requested by users. They may be prized for their informational, aesthetic, and sometimes even financial value. Photographs are often called upon to pump life into history's veins, and it would be hard to find museum archivists without beloved photographs in their care. At the same time, managing and preserving photographs can present challenges—in part because often many players in a museum setting feel strongly about them and in part because of the steady beat of their preservation requirements.

Previous writing on photographs in the museum setting emphasizes these two principles—that photographs hold extensive value and that caring for them can pose challenges—and they remain true today.[1] Since earlier writing on the subject, however, the rise of digital photography has changed things dramatically. Since the 1990s, digital has taken root as the primary photography format, and museum archives now face nearly three decades' worth of digital photography to manage. Additionally, there is a lot of it: digital technology has resulted in an exponential increase in the volume of photographs. In 2019, the US National Archives' Still Pictures Unit found that while it took the unit fifty years to accumulate 14 million analog images, it acquired 4.1 million digital images in about ten years.[2] Furthermore, where analog photographs present particular preservation requirements, digital photographs come with perhaps even greater complexities surrounding their management and care.

Given the value of photographs to museum staff and users, being informed about caring for digital photographs in their collections is important for museum archivists. After a brief review of the kinds of photographs typically found in the museum setting, this chapter turns toward a discussion of how museum archivists can best operate within their institutional context to manage photographs effectively. The chapter's remaining sections consider the archival fundamentals—appraisal, description, access and use, and preservation—in the context of digital photography. These sections are meant to be informative, not prescriptive, and they raise considerations for museum archivists at institutions of all sizes as they work to preserve the photographs in their care.[3]

Photographic Records in the Museum Setting[4]

Among the most common types of photographs in the museum setting are those documenting the object collections. In many cases, these photographs serve as surrogates for the objects themselves and are thus heavily consulted by curatorial departments and may be managed by them as well. Photographs can document all phases of an object's life cycle, from creation to acquisition to conservation treatments to exhibition, and they may even be retained after an object has been deaccessioned. An object may be featured on its own in a photograph or in the context of an installation or exhibition. Other contextual photographs might show an object *in situ* during an archaeological expedition or an artwork hanging in a collector's home. In addition to their value to curatorial staff, these photographs of objects in context are of distinct interest to scholarly researchers.

Similarly, photographs documenting a museum's history—its exterior and interior spaces; its staff, trustees, and visitors; its activities—can be vital to both users and staff seeking to understand or promote a museum's legacy. Photographs of museum buildings may reveal changes in their appearance or use over time. Gallery shots can show which items were displayed and where; they can also offer important insight into the evolution of exhibition design. Images of staff and trustees may be valuable not only as documentation of a museum's history but also as the precious treasures of a family's history. Views of visitors may provide demographic and cultural information or suggest which exhibitions or installations were particularly popular. As a result of the ephemeral nature of special events and educational programs, images of these and other activities may offer information and context not captured in textual records.

Photographs created by curatorial and conservation staff for research purposes are another common type of photographic record in the museum setting. Staff members may use photographs to document objects both inside and outside of a museum's collection; often these photographs are associated with textual documentation and publications. As with all archival records, these research images may have a value beyond their original purpose. A photograph taken to show an object being excavated during an archaeological expedition, for example, may also reveal important details surrounding the history and culture of the dig, including staff responsibilities and interactions with local peoples.

Finally, many art museums have curatorial departments dedicated to collecting photography. Beyond this, museum archives may hold other examples of photography as works of art, particularly within special collections.[5] Many have written on the relationship between photography as documentary record and photography as art, and artists themselves also play with this relationship in their works.[6] Museum archivists will find discussing this subject further with their curatorial colleagues useful—not to mention interesting—both in theory and in the context of whether a photograph's value as documentary record or art impacts decisions made within the institution regarding its care.

FIGURE 10.1. Gallery shots can show which items were displayed and where; they can also offer important insight into the evolution of exhibition design. GALLERY IX, X 9TH ANNUAL EXHIBITION OF WORK BY CLEVELAND ARTISTS AND CRAFTSMEN, 1927, NEGATIVE NUMBER 7498, CLEVELAND MUSEUM OF ART ARCHIVES.

PHOTOGRAPHS IN "LIVING MUSEUMS"

For archives of "living museums"—as zoos and botanical gardens are sometimes considered—the most common images are not of inanimate objects but of living or once living animals and plants. At the Wildlife Conservation Society Archives, headquartered at WCS's Bronx Zoo, images of bears, crocodiles, pelicans, and the thousands of other animals that have inhabited the zoo dominate the historical photograph collection. Taken by WCS's staff photographer—a position that has existed nearly since the zoo's opening in 1899—these images were often created for educational purposes, to provide audiences from schoolchildren to scientists with photographic representations of animals. Today, they continue to hold an educational value, giving scholars and others interested in the histories of zoos and animals a look into which species once lived at the zoo. Some of these animals have since gone extinct, including the Barbary lion and the thylacine (also known as the Tasmanian tiger), and little other photographic documentation of them exists. Photographs in the collection also show zoo animals in their exhibits and interacting with keepers and visitors; as such, they offer valuable documentation for those studying the care and treatment of animals over time. Further still, some of the images of animals function in ways almost similar to images of former staff. These images—like this photograph of Sultan, a Barbary lion who was one of the first inhabitants of the zoo's Lion House—can be poignant memorials to individuals that spent their lives at the Bronx Zoo and were known and beloved by staff and visitors from near and far.

FIGURE 10.2. Photographs in "living museums" preserve living and once-living plants and animals, like Sultan, one of the earliest inhabitants of the Bronx Zoo's Lion House, pictured here in 1903. © WILDLIFE CONSERVATION SOCIETY.

Working within the Institutional Context

Photographs may be created, collected, and used by a variety of museum departments, from curatorial and conservation staff members to those in public relations and development. Many museum staff outside of the archives rely on historical images for everything from research to promoting the institution. Additionally, photographs—and particularly of museum objects and exhibits—can have a much longer period of use by museum staff than textual records.

The dispersal of photographs among different departments within a museum can create complexities. Discussions about the management of photographs may also need to be approached with sensitivity, as departments sometimes have strong feelings of ownership toward their holdings and particularly toward photographs. That said, dispersed collections create terrific possibilities for collaboration. Museum archivists may seek out opportunities to work with other departments to increase efficiency, facilitate discovery, develop exhibitions, and consult on preservation methods. At a minimum, it is beneficial for museum archivists to understand other departments' holdings as well as how access and licensing requests regarding these holdings are handled. Collections management systems can serve as tools to address the challenge of photographic materials dispersed across various departments. They allow museums to associate photographs held by the archives with related ones held by other departments or to bring together virtually, for instance, textual records held by the archives with related photographs held by another department.

Depending on collection policies, museum archivists may engage with a variety of other museum staff in regard to record creation and management.[7] Perhaps most important is the museum's photographer—or photography staff, in the case of larger institutions. Professional photographers tend to devote considerable effort toward managing their output, and they are often knowledgeable about both the technical complexities behind digital photography as well as the tools available for managing digital photographs. At the same time, they may not be considering the long-term preservation of their work. Museum archivists should develop relationships with photography department staff to collaborate on image management policies and practices that serve not only the immediate production goals of photography staff but also the preservation goals of the museum archives. These policies and practices might address such issues as

- whether all of the photography department's images will be transferred to the museum archives, or whether that department will do some form of appraisal before transfer;
- how photographs will be transferred (for example, by hard drives, the network, the cloud) and how often;
- what file naming conventions will be used;
- what embedded metadata can be easily and efficiently added by the photographer at the time of capture or during image processing and editing. The section on description later in this chapter includes more information about embedded metadata.

If an institution relies on outside photographers whose work will eventually be transferred to the museum archives, the museum archivist could similarly discuss policies and practices with the staff members managing these photographers. Understanding the rights outlined in contracts with outside photographers is also important for museum archivists, and it is essential that a system is in place for documenting these rights. For instance, a copy of the contract could be stored with the outside photographer's image files or, better yet, the rights terms could also be embedded in the files. This obviates the need to attempt to track down rights information when the photographs are transferred to the museum archives and when this information will be more difficult to find.[8]

In some museums that have digital asset management systems (DAMS), the museum archives manages the system. Its administrator is a museum archives staff member, and the system operates with archival preservation, or at least access to archival materials, in mind. However, in other museums with DAMS, the system lies outside the museum archives. A marketing or photography department might administer it, for instance, and its content—such as a staff photographer's work—is ingested and made accessible soon after its creation. Staff in such departments as communications, marketing, and development typically rely upon this content.

In these cases, the system may be designed around access but not preservation.[9] Although differences can arise between museum archivists and DAMS administrators who operate outside the museum archives, they are best approached through communication and relationship building.[10] Ideally, museum archivists and DAMS administrators can work together to understand how their respective goals overlap and differ, and they can develop collaborative practices that allow users ready access to digital content while also providing for the preservation needs of that content.

Types of Photographs

Photographs range widely by type, from early daguerreotypes to today's born-digital photographs. With these variations also comes a wide range of good practices for their management and preservation. Because museum archives may hold many different types of photographs among their collections, familiarity with these practices and how they differ by type of photograph is important for the museum archivist. The broad category of analog photographs varies significantly, depending on whether the photograph is a positive or a negative and on the nature of its support material. Several excellent resources for identifying the different types of analog photographs and describing preservation methods are available. See the Further Reading section at the end of this chapter for more on this.[11]

The remainder of this chapter will consider the management and care of digital photographs, which have become increasingly common in archives over the past two decades. The sections following consider archival fundamentals in the context of digital photographs, both digitized and born-digital images.[12]

Appraisal

Defining a clear collection development policy—the basis for sound appraisal decisions—is especially important for photograph collections and even more so for digital photographs. Two key reasons for this exist. The first is the exponential increase in volume created by digital technology. In the past, analog photographers might shoot a handful of images of a museum event and perhaps only print or retain a selection of those; digital photographers at a museum event today might shoot hundreds of images within just a few minutes and retain all of them. Compounding this volume is the ready accessibility of digital photography. Anyone with a smartphone today has not only a digital camera always at the ready, but also digital storage for their images and various means of sharing them. Setting limits in a collection development policy that considers how time and expenses will best be prioritized allows a museum archives to ride—rather than be inundated by—the ever-rising wave of digital photography.

The second reason for taking particular care with appraisal when it comes to digital photographs is their need for identification. Photographs present a particular challenge because, unless they have been individually annotated before they reach the museum archives, they will require some identification. Without an identifiable photographer or subject, a photograph may be essentially inaccessible or unusable. The work of identification can be fun—trying to identify photographers as well as staff, former exhibits, and objects in a photograph can call on museum archivists' great detective skills—but it can also be very labor intensive. Where the need for identification is true of all photographs, both analog and digital, the volume of digital photography can multiply this work. Some museum archives have successfully turned this challenge into an opportunity by crowdsourcing the identification process. See "Engaging the Community through Photo Identification" for more on this.

Additionally, the ability to give file names to and embed metadata within digital photographs can make identification of digital photographs easier than that of their analog counterparts. For this reason, museum archives might take into account how much of this descriptive metadata is present before accepting digital photograph collections. As "Working within the Institutional Context" discussed, working directly with records creators can help to facilitate this. Among a museum archivist's major difficulties can be encountering a digital folder titled "Gallery Photos" with hundreds of files simply labeled "IMG_0001, IMG_0002, IMG_0003 . . ." and no accompanying descriptive metadata.

Requiring that digital photographs enter the museum archives with some descriptive metadata is an important means of ensuring that these items are discoverable; likewise, requiring some form of rights metadata is essential to ensuring that these items are accessible and usable. Take, for example, a museum archivist appraising the collection of a scientist featured in a temporary museum exhibit that includes digital photographs with no rights metadata. Given the ease with which digital images can be shared, how can this archivist confirm the provenance of these photographs—that they weren't shared with the collection's creator by a colleague, or even that they weren't downloaded from the Internet? Even with confirmation that the collection's creator took the photographs, the museum archivist should still be clear on the rights afforded to the museum archives—through, for example, the institution's intellectual property policy or a gift agreement—for making these photographs accessible and usable. These are considerations for any type of record, but the fact that photographs are often a museum archives' most reproduced and licensed items intensifies the need for caution. A museum archivist who is certain that the archives does not hold the rights to a collection of digital images might decide against choosing to accession them.[13]

Beyond qualitative appraisal decisions, museum archivists may choose to apply quantitative appraisal methods to digital photographs. Quantitative appraisal may be especially useful in cases where a museum archivist encounters many similar images of the same subject, such as gallery installation images of a single exhibition. Ideally, some sort of visual assessment will determine the best or most representative images. However, museum archivists overwhelmed with several terabytes' worth of photo sets composed of very similar images of the same subject may wish to employ some form of quantitative appraisal to select only the images that they can reasonably manage to describe, make accessible, and preserve.[14]

Description

Even more than textual records, photographs that are not described or contextualized risk losing their informational value. Without the proper forms of description, they may become undiscoverable by museum archives staff and users as well as unusable for reproduction and licensing purposes. This is why photographs should ideally receive some item-level description. With analog photography, a museum archivist might write some description—perhaps the photographer's name, a descriptive title, a date, an identifier, and the source collection—on the housing of the photograph or set of photographs, perhaps an envelope. In the digital realm, these details and more can be embedded within the header of an image file itself so that it can accompany the file regardless of its location.

Two forms of embedded metadata for digital photographs exist: technical and descriptive.[15] Whereas the camera automatically captures technical metadata, descriptive metadata can require some manual data entry—although even descriptive metadata can be automated to some extent through the camera settings as well as through image processing software.[16] Of course, attempting to describe a collection of tens of thousands of photographs at the item level could take museum archivists their entire careers. Making the work manageable will involve decisions about how much descriptive information each collection requires; and a museum archivist might consider how current museum priorities and initiatives could inform those decisions. Making the work manageable will also likely involve the use of metadata templates so that the same information can be applied across an entire folder, series, or collection. A very minimal processing approach would be to apply the same

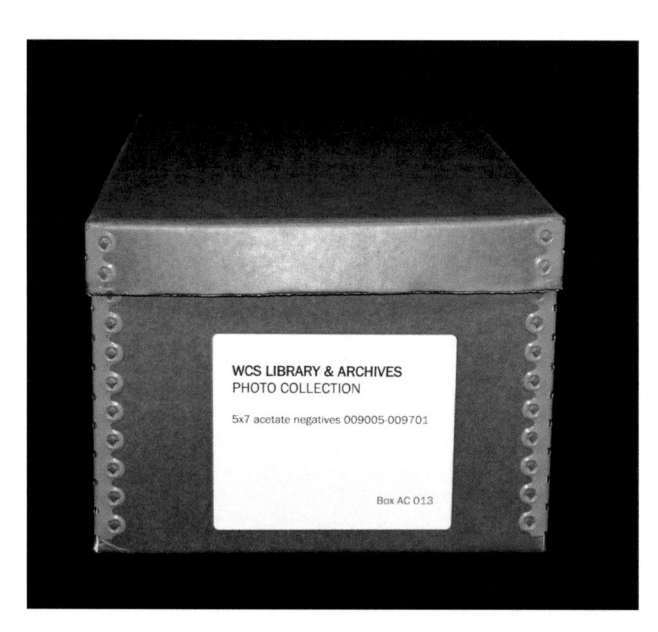

FIGURE 10.3. This box of approximately 400 negatives represents all the 4x5 negatives created by the staff photographer at the author's institution in the first six months of 1941. If the current staff photographer were to print her digital photos today, she would fill one of these boxes within two weeks on average. PHOTO BY THE AUTHOR.

basic descriptive information—the name of an exhibition, for example—to each photograph file in the collection. As with all processing, these decisions will differ for each museum archives and possibly for each collection within that archives.

Compared to the museum archivist's work with analog photographs, the ability to apply the same metadata to a large volume of digital photographs through a template speeds up the description process. At the same time, while applying the description is easily automated, acquiring the information that will comprise that description—information, for instance, about a photograph's content and creator—can still be labor intensive. Additionally, while technical metadata may record when and where a photograph was taken, the accuracy of this information relies on the camera's settings to be configured properly. For these reasons, museum archivists must work with photographers as closely as possible to aid in the description process. This work may take various forms, from acquiring information at the time of accession to working directly with photographers to consider how recording descriptive information could be incorporated into their

ENGAGING THE COMMUNITY THROUGH PHOTO IDENTIFICATION

Photo identification can be difficult and time consuming for museum archives staff, so many archives benefit from reaching outside their own walls for help. The San Diego Air and Space Museum Archives, for instance, relied on the online community to assist in photo identification. Using an API, they gathered tags and comments created by the public in a photo-sharing service and stored them in the photographs' catalog records. In another example, though this is a special collection in a museum and not a typical museum archives, the Teenie Harris Archive's approach to photo identification may also serve as a model for museum archivists. Part of the Carnegie Museum of Art, the Teenie Harris Archive has worked with local community members to help identify the people, places, and events captured by the famed photographer of Pittsburgh's Black community. This community outreach has taken many forms, from online requests to oral history events held in libraries, churches, retirement centers, and other community spaces. Additionally, during exhibitions of the archive, the museum has offered cards for visitors to contribute information about the images on display. The details gathered in all of these settings have in turn been used to create catalog records for the photographs. In these cases and others, the archives not only benefited from help with identification, it also helped to engage broader communities in these collections.

FIGURE 10.4. Staff of the Teenie Harris Archive relied on community involvement in identifying the people, places, and events captured by the photographer, Charles "Teenie" Harris. Dolores Stanton and Eleanor Hughes Griffin standing in front of George Harris's confectionery store, 2121 Wylie Avenue, Hill District, July 1937. © CARNEGIE MUSEUM OF ART, CHARLES "TEENIE" HARRIS ARCHIVE.

workflow. Regardless of the source of this information, it is also important that museum archivists document that source within their metadata.[17]

Access and Use

Museum archives seeking to provide online access to digital materials have a range of options available to them. These options vary not only in features but also in price and in the technological knowledge required to implement and maintain them. On one end of the spectrum are museum archives using free photo-sharing services to make their digital images publicly accessible; on the other end are museum archives with custom-built digital repositories created and maintained by in-house staff. Some museum archives rely on commercially available digital asset management systems, while others use open-source software for online access to their collections.[18] Depending on the needs of a museum archives in providing digital access, the following questions should be considered:

- What file types can be ingested into the system?
- How flexible is the system in terms of metadata? What element sets does it support? Can local elements be added?
- Does the system strip embedded metadata from files upon ingest?
- Can images be watermarked?
- What are the options for accessing files? Can they be downloaded? At what resolution?
- How is the system backed up?
- Can files and metadata be extracted from the system should the museum archives choose to move to a different one?
- Will the system integrate with other museum systems, including digital asset management systems, collection management systems, and web content management systems?
- If a vendor is involved, what technical support services do they offer?
- Will the museum archives have the necessary funding and resources to maintain, and possibly expand, the system in the foreseeable future?

Beyond determining methods of digital access, museum archives must understand their rights to make photographs publicly accessible and, when applicable, to license them. This is true for all archival materials but especially photographs because of the frequency with which they are accessed and licensed. Photographs created by and for the museum are often museum property, but museum archivists should be clear on their institution's intellectual property policy. Additionally, photographs of works of art may involve several layers of copyright, and this may be further complicated when photographs show subjects loaned by another museum. Ultimately, when in doubt, museum archivists should seek out their museum's legal counsel to ensure that they are following copyright law. It bears repeating that the highly shareable nature of digital photographs intensifies the obligation museum archivists have to confirm their provenance before they make them accessible online and especially before they are licensed.[19] Museum archives with images of visitors in their collections that license those images for commercial purposes should also be aware of the legalities surrounding model releases.

Aside from legal concerns, museum archives should consider other reasons that images may require some level of restriction. For instance, as museum archivists Bernadette Callery and Deborah Wythe, authors of the chapter on photographs in *Museum Archives: An Introduction* (2004), point out, archaeological and anthropological collections "often include images of sacred sites and objects that might best be covered by some level of restriction. Views of archaeological sites can provide information that would lead illegal pot hunters to protected areas. Some building photographs could compromise museum security if released."[20] Even if the photograph does not appear to provide enough context to reveal a location, digital photographs taken with a camera equipped with geotagging may have location information embedded within their metadata.

In short, museum archivists may have significant research to do before making photographs accessible online or before licensing them, if they choose to do this. However, for photographs not restricted by laws or policies, it almost goes without saying today that the benefits of increasing public access can well outweigh the effort. Depending on a museum archives' priorities and policies, it may choose to provide open access to online collections of photographs or to require licensing agreements and fees for particular types of use. Museum archives that do license digital images benefit from clear and efficient practices for the management of agreements and funds as well as from coordination with others in the museum who may fulfill rights and reproduction requests.

Preservation

Photographs are subject to the same preservation concerns as other born-digital records, and typical born-digital preservation actions apply to them. In the context of photographs, one particular preservation factor deserves further discussion: format. The Library of Congress's current Recommended Formats Statement designates the TIFF as the file format most highly recommended for digital images.[21] Archives tend to prefer TIFF files as a sort of digital archival "master" because of their ability to preserve lossless images.[22] At the same time, many professional photographers shoot in a raw format, and raw images are sometimes considered digital "negatives."[23] Museum archives that choose to retain raw images are advised to migrate these images out of the proprietary formats in which they are shot to DNG. Created by Adobe Systems to support image preservation, DNG (or Digital Negative format) is a standardized, openly documented format.

Conclusion

This chapter's title distinguishes photographs as the heart of the museum archives. Through photographs, a museum's collections, spaces, visitors, and other subjects flow from decade to decade. Photographs can be powerful emotional cues both for museum archivists and other museum staff as well as for researchers and visitors. While we may tend to romanticize analog photographs—the physical beauty of ambrotypes, gelatin silver prints, Kodachrome slides—we know, of course, that the digital photographs are potent markers of the museum history of tomorrow. With diligent, rhythmic care from museum archivists, they will continue to carry the lifeblood of the museum long into the future.[24]

Further Reading

Federal Agencies Digital Guidelines Initiative. *Technical Guidelines for Digitizing Cultural Heritage Materials: Creation of Raster Image Files.* 2016. http://www.digitizationguidelines.gov/guidelines/FADGI%20Federal%20%20Agencies%20Digital%20Guidelines%20Initiative-2016%20Final_rev1.pdf, captured at https://perma.cc/DR59-ZLQ6.

Frey, Franziska et al. *AIC Guide to Digital Photography and Conservation Documentation.* 2nd ed. Washington, DC: American Institute for Conservation of Historic and Artistic Works, 2011.

Journal of Digital Media Management. Birmingham, AL: Henry Stewart Publications, 2012–present.

Library of Congress. "Recommended Formats Statement for Still Images." Library of Congress Preservation Resources. https://www.loc.gov/preservation/resources/rfs/stillimg.html, captured at https://perma.cc/8FLC-VGCC.

Ritzenthaler, Mary Lynn, and Diane L. Vogt-O'Connor. *Photographs: Archival Care and Management.* Chicago: Society of American Archivists, 2006.

NOTES

1. See Bernadette Callery and Deborah Wythe, "Photographs," in *Museum Archives: An Introduction*, 2nd ed., ed. Deborah Wythe (Chicago: Society of American Archivists, 2004), 123–40.

2. Billy Wade (supervising archivist, National Archives and Records Administration Special Media Records Division Still Picture Branch), email to the author, February 11, 2020.

3. While this chapter is directed at museum archivists, much of its content, particularly the sections on fundamentals, is applicable to all archivists working with photographs.

4. Callery and Wythe's "Photographs" has an excellent discussion of this subject under "Types of Photographs and Photographic Collections," and this section relies heavily on that text (pp. 123–27).

5. In addition to the photograph types discussed here—those created in the course of a museum's everyday business, or those collected by a photography department—are images often grouped under the term "special collections" (as defined in chapter 6). These are photographs that have been taken by someone outside of the museum's staff, although, ideally, they relate to the museum's mission or collecting policy. Often, they have been taken or collected by constituents with some connection to the museum, such as local affiliated professionals or amateur groups or even frequent visitors. For some museum archives, these photographs can be important resources that

offer a diverse perspective, and they may constitute a major portion of their holdings. It is also worth noting that while accepting donations of special collections can be tempting—and, in many cases, wholly appropriate—museum archivists should balance the potential usefulness of these collections against the archives' ability to provide for their sustained care alongside the other photographic records managed by the archives.

6 For some examples of artists, see MoMA Learning, "The Photographic Record," https://www.moma.org/learn/moma_learning/themes/photography/the-photographic-record, captured at https://perma.cc/G8GM-ZPB9. Beyond the question of photography as art versus document, it is also important to keep in mind that photography as art has been embraced in the fine arts world only in relatively recent times. Although photography departments have existed at some modern art museums since the early twentieth century, the Los Angeles County Museum of Art, for instance, established its photography department in 1983, and the Metropolitan Museum of Art did not establish its Department of Photography as an independent curatorial department until 1992.

7 When working with photographs that will eventually be transferred to the archives, museum archivists do well to take the approach of the embedded archivist. Although the term is often used in conjunction with educational outreach, the embedded archivist has also gained traction as a role that archivists play more generally within institutions. (See Geof Huth, "Appraising Digital Records," in *Appraisal and Acquisition Strategies*, Trends in Archives Practice Series, ed. Michael J. Shallcross and Christopher J. Prom [Chicago: Society of American Archivists, 2016], module 14.) With the rise of born-digital materials in archives has come the need for archivists to develop relationships with records creators at the time of creation. As much as some museum archivists may want to wait for records to come to them—or, maybe more realistic and less desirable, wait for the call to come clear out a departed staff member's office—many today are actively engaging with records creators not just at the point of accession, but much earlier in the records' life cycle, while they are still active records. Understanding how active records are created, stored, backed up, accessed, and shared can be vital for museum archivists as they seek to preserve these records. In turn, museum archivists are playing increasingly significant roles in guiding the management practices surrounding active records in all formats.

8 For more on this subject, see Brian Keough and Mark Wolfe, "Moving the Archivist Closer to the Creator: Implementing Integrated Archival Policies for Born Digital Photography at Colleges and Universities," *Journal of Archival Organization* 10, no. 1 (2012): 69–83, https://doi.org/10.1080/15332748.2012.681266.

9 In addition to the fact that some DAM systems may not facilitate common digital preservation actions, DAM systems outside the archives may also diverge from software designed for archives in other ways. For instance, they may not allow for metadata schemas standard to archives, or they may not allow for images to be understood in context.

10 In "When Archivists and Digital Asset Managers Collide: Tensions and Ways Forward," Anthony Cocciolo explores these differences in more depth. As he points out, problems can arise between archivists and DAM system administrators who operate outside of the archives, particularly when DAM systems that lack archival features are mistakenly considered by others within the institution as its digital archives. He notes that these problems can be exacerbated when these DAM systems—justified by their usefulness in the creation of materials aimed at revenue generating—receive more attention and funding than digital preservation efforts within the archives. Ultimately, Cocciolo advocates for better communication and relationship building between these positions. See *American Archivist* 79, no. 1 (2016): 121–36, https://doi.org/10.17723/0360-9081.79.1.121.

11 In addition to the publications listed in the Further Reading section, other excellent sources for learning more about analog photographs include the Image Permanence Institute (IPI), which has published several books, reports, and other guides to the preservation of various types of photographs, both analog and digital; the National Park Service's Conserve O Gram series, which includes a subseries on photographs that covers, among other subjects, cold storage for photograph collections; and the Northeast Document Conservation Center (NEDCC), which offers its Preservation Leaflets online, including number 5, devoted to analog photograph types and their preservation.

12 Although it is beyond this chapter's scope to discuss digitization workflows in detail, a few points should be reviewed. Museum archives engaged in still-image digitization must determine whether they will digitize in-house or contract with an outside party. The major factors influencing this decision are staffing capabilities, equipment, and funding. This decision may also change on a project basis; a museum archives may have equipment capable of digitizing photographs and other flat items but not bound books or oversize materials. Because scanning is fairly straightforward work, it can be an excellent activity for volunteers. However, because it can be tedious, it is recommended that it not be a day-long activity for a single individual, and museum archivists working with volunteers should always factor in quality review time. For museum archives that choose not to digitize in-house, many vendor options exist. Additionally, museum archives seeking to digitize should consider whether consortial options or mobile digitization services are available to them. Regardless of who performs the digitization, museum archivists should be familiar with digital imaging standards. The Federal Agencies Digital Guidelines Initiative's *Technical Guidelines for Digitizing Cultural Heritage Materials: Creation of Raster Files* outlines recommended digitization practices and guidelines based on the shared best practices of FADGI's Still Image Working Group, a collaborative effort to develop common sustainable digitization practices for still-image materials in cultural heritage institutions. In addition to such technical factors as recommended resolution and bit depth, these guidelines cover all aspects of digitization projects, from equipment to storage.

13 Museum archivists may make other qualitative appraisal decisions regarding digital photographs that mirror the decisions traditionally made in appraising analog materials. These decisions range from whether the photographs' subjects fit within the museum archives' collecting scope to whether the photographs' condition—and in the case of digital, their file format is one aspect of condition—bears upon the museum archives' commitment to preserving them. Archivists may also attempt to weed duplicates from their accessions, and several software options are available for identifying duplicate digital images. Museums with photography departments that distribute digital images may find that multiple staff members have saved the same images from the photography department. If the museum archives is collecting photographs directly from the photography department, it may decide not to maintain all the duplicates that have been distributed to other staff and saved among their files, and some method of deduplication will be necessary.

14 As part of its National Digital Stewardship Residency Project, Johns Hopkins University's Sheridan Library carried out qualitative appraisal using a sampling script. For more on this, see Elizabeth England, "Automating Digital Archival Processing at Johns Hopkins University," *The Signal*, https://blogs.loc.gov/thesignal/2017/05/automating-digital-archival-processing-at-johns-hopkins-university, captured at https://perma.cc/F8J8-SY48.

15. The EXIF (Exchangeable Image File) format contains technical metadata. The EXIF standard is maintained by JEITA (Japan Electronics and Information Technology Industries Association). For an overview of EXIF, see "Exif Exchangeable Image File Format," Sustainability of Digital Formats: Planning for Library of Congress Collections, https://www.loc.gov/preservation/digital/formats/fdd/fdd000146.shtml, captured at https://perma.cc/NP2H-7ELR.

    When a digital image is created, the capture device—that is, the camera—automatically records technical information and embeds this within the image as EXIF data. Among other details, these data may include the camera's make, model, and settings, as well as the image's pixel size and its date, time, and location of capture.

16. Descriptive information is typically embedded in the image as IPTC data. Developed by the International Press Telecommunications Council, the IPTC Photo Metadata Standard has become the most widely used standard to describe photos. See "Photo Metadata," IPTC, https://iptc.org/standards/photo-metadata, captured at https://perma.cc/DRZ2-N2U6. Although IPTC is commonly referred to as descriptive metadata, it includes fields for recording not only information about an image's content, but also administrative information (including who took the image, and where and when it was taken) as well as rights information.

    EXIF and IPTC metadata can be viewed through various ways, including through camera settings, some computer operating systems, and internet browser extensions. Embedded metadata may also be viewed as well as edited using image processing software, and some software includes templates that allow users to apply IPTC metadata to image files on an individual or bulk level. These products also integrate with scripting tools that can aid in the process of recording metadata; one script, for example, will copy an image's filename to its IPTC Title field. This tool and others can be found at "Filename 2 Title: How to Automate," Controlled Vocabulary, https://www.controlledvocabulary.com/imagedatabases/filename2title.html, captured at https://perma.cc/2R3G-AGSH.

17. Indeed, along with metadata embedded at the file level, museum archives should consider adopting further metadata standards to record other information about a digital photograph, such as additional administrative, rights, structural, and preservation metadata. Often, fields within the embedded metadata are interoperable with other common metadata standards. For instance, five fields in the current IPTC Core are interoperable with the commonly used metadata standard Dublin Core. These are Title, Subject/Keywords, Creator, Rights/Copyright Notice, and Description. Tools are also available for extracting embedded metadata to be repurposed for use with these other standards. See, for example, the Embedded Metadata Extraction Tool (EMET) developed by Artstor, https://sourceforge.net/projects/emet, captured at https://perma.cc/7LGW-466M.

    Since IPTC does not document hierarchical information or relationships between related items, relying on additional metadata standards such as the Metadata Encoding and Transmission Standard (METS) and Dublin Core is especially important for describing a digital photograph's relationship to other photographs in the same collection or series.

18. Further still, many museum archives make their materials available through consortial platforms, from local or specialty groups to the Digital Public Library of America.

19. Museum archives with strong holdings in special collections photographs or other photographs not created by museum staff may also find it useful to consult the Library of Congress's Rights and Restrictions Information database, https://www.loc.gov/rr/print/res, captured at https://perma.cc/RSL3-ZULB. Additional data can be found in New York Public Library's Photographers' Identities Catalog, https://pic.nypl.org/, captured https://perma.cc/VA32-3R6N.

20. Callery and Wythe, "Photographs," 136.

21. The statement identifies the formats that will "best meet the needs of all concerned, maximizing the chances for survival and continued accessibility of creative content well into the future." The recommended formats, in order of preference, are TIFF, JPEG2000, PNG, JPEG/JFIF, Digital Negative DNG, BMP, and GIF. See "Recommended Formats Statement," Library of Congress Preservation Resources, https://www.loc.gov/preservation/resources/rfs, captured at https://perma.cc/8FLC-VGCC.

22. That is, as opposed to JPEGs, which are lossy and thus may lose image quality as they are edited or resaved.

23. Shooting in a raw format defers processing until it is rendered in a desktop software, allowing photographers to make precise adjustments before the image is converted to a TIFF or other format.

24. The author wishes to acknowledge the contributions of Kelli Bogan and the editors of this book, who provided useful comments and recommendations on this chapter. She also wishes to thank the staff photographer at her own institution, Julie Larsen Maher, who has been a model partner in ensuring the preservation of the current photographic record.

11 COLLECTING AND STEWARDING THE BUILT ENVIRONMENT

Rachel Chatalbash and Suzanne Noruschat

Museum architecture is an important element of the museum experience.[1] Many museums have commissioned well-known architects to construct their buildings, and some of the most renowned museum designs since the beginning of the twentieth century include Frank Lloyd Wright's Solomon R. Guggenheim Museum (1959), Louis Kahn's Kimbell Art Museum (1972), and I. M. Pei's East Wing of the National Gallery (1978). These singular museum projects have helped give rise to the "starchitect"—a well-known architect with celebrity status—and the public often visits museums to view the building itself as much as to see the museum's collections and exhibitions.[2] Managing, preserving, and providing access to the records of the museum building is often the responsibility of the museum archivist.[3]

In most museum archives, these records are, first and foremost, used to maintain and preserve a museum building and its grounds. The drawings in the museum archives are used to support current operations and provide technical information to caretakers and conservators. Thus, museum staff and architects commissioned by a museum to conserve or renovate a museum may be major users of a museum archives' architectural collections.

These architectural records are also essential for historical research, especially when they document famous architects and buildings. When an architect is hired to design a museum, the museum typically retains a set of architectural plans documenting the construction, from early sketches to as-built drawings. Additionally, a museum archives might contain correspondence between museum officials and an architect, construction drawings, specifications, samples, photo and video documentation of the building process, and models. These architectural materials, which this chapter will review in detail, are fertile ground not only for researchers trying to understand a particular structure, but also for those researching aspects of an architect's oeuvre or biography. The museum building has itself become an object in the museum's collection, worthy of study and conservation.[4]

Some museum archives may collect architectural materials beyond those of the museum building. For example, a historical society might undertake regional collecting, documenting architecture and the work of architects in its area; a museum that specializes in a particular subject area might collect architectural materials relating to that topic. Others might collect architectural materials documenting additional works by the architect who designed their museum building.

The architectural materials held by museum archives provide insight into the buildings that house and display much of our nation's cultural heritage; it is therefore essential that a publication on museum archives include a chapter on architectural materials. Museum archivists must understand the typical composition of architectural records and the possible methods for their stewardship. This chapter will outline guidelines for collection development and acquisition, appraisal considerations, arrangement and description, and the housing of architectural materials in a museum archives context. Managing architectural records can be challenging—paper drawings can be large and cumbersome, reading plans can be difficult for a nonexpert, and the preservation of the proprietary digital formats so common in the architectural field can be an obstacle. This chapter will present strategies for managing architectural materials and address their many potential uses in the museum setting. Proper management of architectural materials strengthens and demonstrates the practical value of the museum archives to an institution's administration and to the general public.

Types of Records

Architectural records pose unique challenges to museum archivists who are unaccustomed to working with them. Architectural records can comprise an especially wide range of material types—textual, graphic, audiovisual, three-dimensional—many of which require special handling, storage solutions, and descriptive standards. Moreover, such collections tend to include many specialized technical documents whose significance might not be readily apparent to those unfamiliar with business and design practices at architectural firms. However, some regularity exists in the types of documents an archivist is likely to encounter, and acquiring a general familiarity with these document types will ease the process of appraising, arranging, describing, and providing access to architectural materials.

Drawings and the Phases of Design

Drawings are often among the most voluminous records created for building projects. They convey how the design of a structure or landscape evolved and technical and physical details about how that structure or landscape was constructed. Thus,

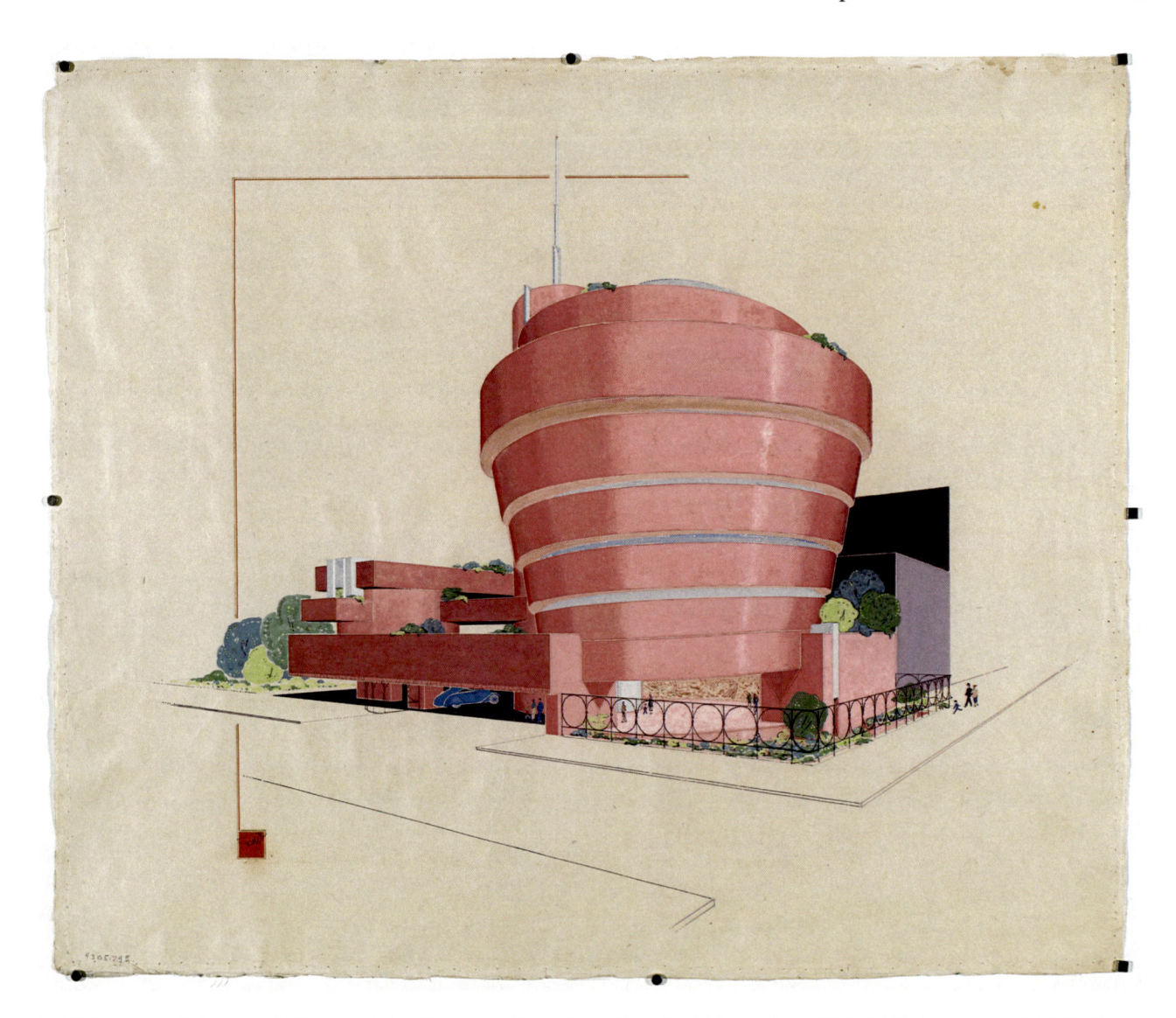

FIGURE 11.1. Solomon R. Guggenheim Museum (New York, New York) [drawing 4305.745]. Copyright © 2022 Frank Lloyd Wright Foundation, Scottsdale, AZ. All rights reserved. The Frank Lloyd Wright Foundation Archives (The Museum of Modern Art | Avery Architectural & Fine Arts Library, Columbia University, New York).

106   Rachel Chatalbash and Suzanne Noruschat

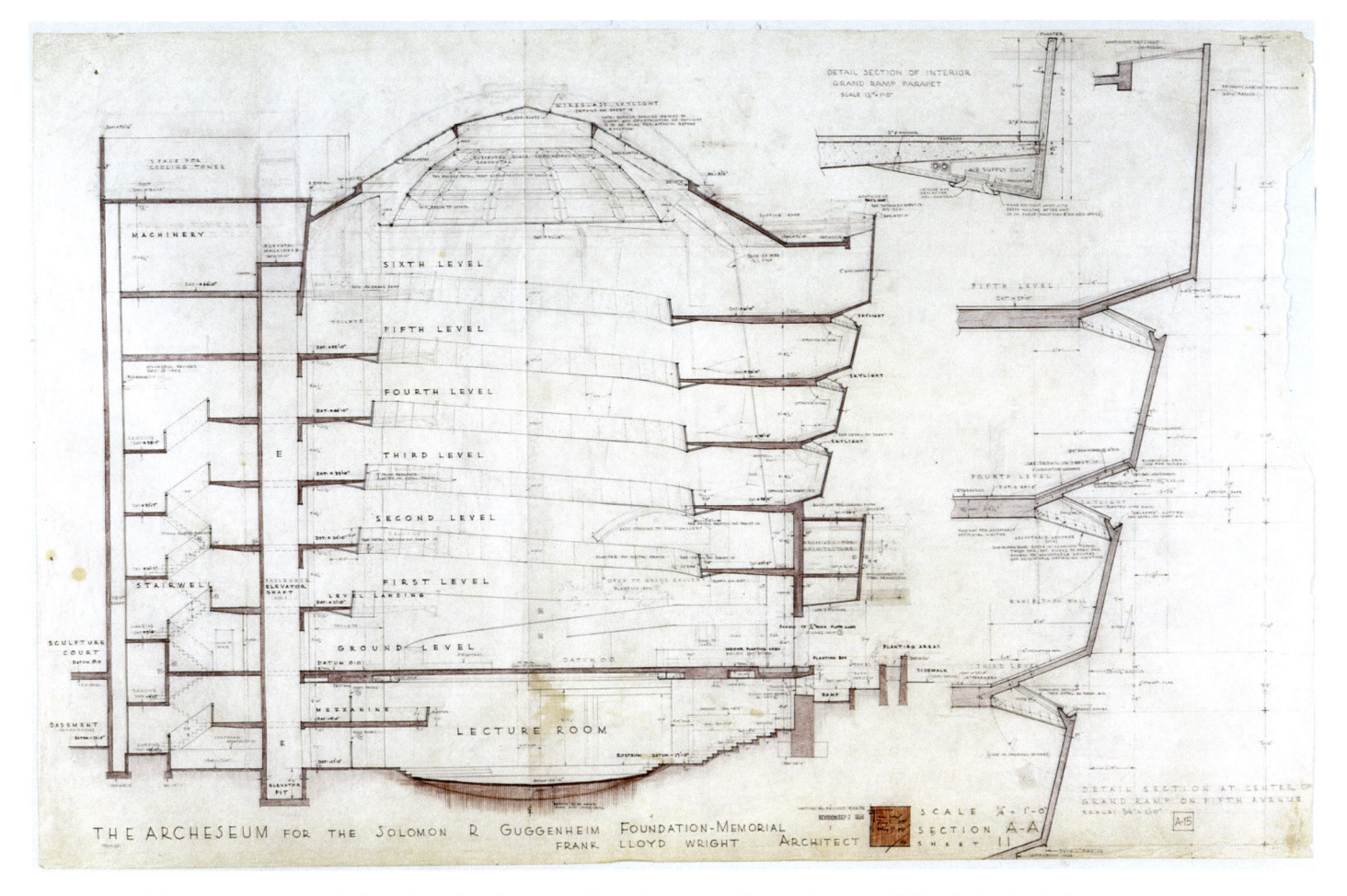

FIGURE 11.2. Solomon R. Guggenheim Museum (New York, New York) [drawing 4305.451]. © 2022 Frank Lloyd Wright Foundation, Scottsdale, AZ. All rights reserved. The Frank Lloyd Wright Foundation Archives (The Museum of Modern Art | Avery Architectural & Fine Arts Library, Columbia University, New York).

drawings are important records for those seeking to understand a project's design history and development and for those wishing to perform maintenance and conservation.

Architectural designs tend to proceed through a series of phases, each of which yields a different drawing type. For example, two drawings from Frank Lloyd Wright's studio demonstrate different phases of the design and planning of the Guggenheim Museum—the first, a presentation rendering, and the second, a section drawing.

At the beginning, as an architect and a client are working out initial ideas for the project, the architect will make a series of conceptual drawings and sketches. Further details are provided in the next phase of design development drawings. When the architectural firm is ready to seek permits and bids from contractors who will construct the building, sets of construction or working drawings are prepared. These are drawn to scale and provide the necessary details and measurements that will allow contractors and subcontractors to carry out the design, although construction drawings may be altered and annotated along the way if changes are made. It became common during the twentieth century for construction drawings to be arranged and labeled systematically, with letter abbreviations indicating drawing type—"E" for electrical, "L" for landscape, "P" for plumbing—and sheets numbered sequentially.[5]

Construction records for major architectural projects such as museum buildings tend to include many different types of drawings: site plans, landscape designs, excavation diagrams, and various detail drawings, floor plans, elevations, and sections. Museum archivists might also expect to encounter large numbers of shop drawings, which detail finishes or specialized construction work undertaken and prepared by subcontractors, as well as presentation renderings, which are visual materials—usually highly polished, colorful perspectives—that the architect prepares to convey the design concept to

Collecting and Stewarding the Built Environment

audiences of note, such as museum trustees. Other categories of drawings are "as-built" or "record" documents, which show the work as finally constructed and thus constitute valuable resources for renovation and restoration projects. Along with drawings, museum architects often use three-dimensional models to present their design concept to their clients and for structural experimentation and testing during the design process.

Photographs and Other Documentation of the Design and Construction Process

While drawings and models are often thought of as the primary design deliverables of architectural firms, a host of other documents are created or accumulated during the design and construction process. Photographs, for instance, are often taken to document the site, the progress of the building's construction, and the project's final form upon its completion. Occasionally, audiovisual recordings may be used to capture images of the project or the voices of those involved with its planning. Architectural project files might also contain textual documents: correspondence between designer and client, communication between architectural firms and planning departments, and communication with contractors. They may also include other information collected during the course of design and construction, such as equipment manuals and operating instructions from manufacturers, product catalogs, and material samples. Finally, written legal and technical documents are components of most architectural archives. Along with contracts, museum archivists will likely find specifications in their institution's construction files, which provide written instructions and technical details for the builder.

For many years, most architectural firms have been creating these documents electronically. Museum archivists who are acquiring records of more recent building projects should therefore expect at least some materials in digital formats. Correspondence, reports, photographs, and standardized documents like specifications may be transferred to the archives, not on paper or as printouts, but as digital files, likely in standard file formats like PDF, JPEG, and PST. Drawings and models, too, may be acquired as born-digital records generated with computer-aided design (CAD) and/or building information modeling (BIM) software.[6]

The challenges of and steps for appraising, preserving, arranging, describing, and providing access to digital design records are discussed next, along with recommendations and procedures for processing, storing, and sharing physical materials.

Appraisal

If a museum's archives is just beginning to collect the records of its built environment, the archivist should survey and gather building documentation. A significant amount of architectural materials may be dispersed throughout the museum, especially if a museum building has existed for many years prior to the museum archivist's collecting efforts. The materials may reside in offices, a facilities building management system, or even exhibition files if gallery spaces are reconfigured for exhibitions. The museum archivist should make every effort to identify architectural materials throughout the institution, recording information such as location, format, condition, quantity, and subject matter. In this initial survey, materials may be described in depth or in more general terms; the point is to gather as much information about the records as needed to make informed collecting and appraisal decisions.

During a survey, the museum archivist may discover that certain departments, such as facilities, are accustomed to using historical drawings for internal purposes. It is important to remember that the job of the museum archivist is to collect as complete of a picture as possible of the built environment. Strategies such as reproducing drawings for departments, while the museum archives manages the originals, can be employed to gain the cooperation and trust of those using architectural records for their everyday work.

As more work is completed on a building in the form of renovations or additions, new architectural records will be created. Therefore, the acquisition of a museum's architectural records will always be ongoing. Building records should be part of every museum archives' records management program so that new materials are automatically transferred to the museum archives at the end of every building project.

The museum archives may not be the only repository in a museum collecting and providing access to architectural materials. A museum's curatorial departments may also collect in this area, and, if they do, the materials in that collection fall outside of the museum archivist's scope of duty. Defining the collecting policies of each department so as not to compete for architectural materials will be useful. For example, a museum's archives might limit its collecting to its building and associated architects, while the museum's curatorial departments might decide to collect more broadly around other subject areas.

As chapter 6 has outlined, no single strategy exists for appraising archival materials. However, because architectural records can be voluminous, appraisal is a key step to sound archival management and may make the difference between a well-organized, easily accessible collection and one that is unwieldy and difficult to navigate. As explained, architectural materials are likely to be dispersed in different museum offices, and, to maintain *respect des fonds*, the inclination might be to keep the materials separated and associated with their originating office. However, as museum archivist Maygene Daniels explains in the second edition of *Museum Archives: An Introduction*, gathering building-related documents in a single record group as far as possible is best "for practical efficiency," preserving in the central archives records of long-term value, such as a master set of construction drawings.[7] The museum archives could receive multiple copies of construction drawings, along with preliminary sketches, design development and shop drawings, and a host of other documents—contracts, specifications, memoranda, notes, receipts, brochures, and reports—that could have come to the museum during the planning and construction phases, or after the building was completed. Such an array of records could prove difficult to appraise with confidence and certainty.

During the process of archiving architectural records, questions may arise about which drawings to retain along with the master set of construction drawings and which written documents are most essential. Due to the museum archives' focus on preservation of the museum building, the museum archivist may be inclined to keep more extensive documentation of the building, such as documentation of minor changes to drawings or other specifications.

Because appraisal decisions can depend on context—institutional goals and objectives, researcher needs, institutional resources, among other factors—no definitive and universal standard exists for institutions to follow when appraising architectural records. Fortunately, some general guidelines have been proposed. In their book *Architectural Records: Managing Design and Construction Records*, Waverly Lowell and Tawny Nelb provide an appraisal grid that ranks documents on a scale of high ("permanent") to low ("destroy or transfer") priority, identifying as permanent those materials most likely to convey valuable information that endures over time and therefore should be retained in the archives.[8] The appraisal grid is a useful guideline to refer to when making appraisal decisions as it is based on a consideration of which types of documents offer the greatest insight into the building's most significant formal and structural properties, as well as into the intentions, ideas, and events informing its design and construction. Preliminary sketches, for instance, provide insight into the initial concept for the building project, while the final record set shows the fleshed out, and usually altered, design when construction was initiated, enabling understanding of the project's evolution and development. The final record set also, if complete, offers a comprehensive overview of the building's important components and systems, precluding the necessity of retaining many additional and perhaps redundant plans and drawing sets. Decisions about appraisal, however, should not be guided by too rigid a formula or laundry list, but rather by an understanding of which extant records best document the significant features and unique history of the museum building. Each design develops in its own way, and many museums possess particularly distinctive characteristics or innovations in design that museum archivists will want to document, if possible. Significant documentation can potentially be found in correspondence, reports, product samples, construction photographs, shop drawings, and models as well.

While the same general appraisal guidelines and recommendations exist for born-digital design records as they do for analog materials, appraisal of born-digital files poses several challenges that museum archivists should be aware of if acquiring such materials. First, as is the case with many born-digital acquisitions from donors, file naming within architectural firms can be idiosyncratic, and it can be difficult to decipher the content of records by examining file names alone. Fortunately, design management software is leading to better file organization in firms, and standard file types—PDF, JPEG, DOCX—that are relatively easy to transfer and preserve are among the common formats used for project documents.

The second challenge to appraisal posed by born-digital content is also, fortunately, surmountable with available tools. In recent years, virtually all design work performed in architectural firms has been done with proprietary software and, as yet, few archives and libraries have access to software that would enable them to open and view files in their original environment. In time, a software library providing fair-use access to the most common software used by design firms might be established.[9] For now, however, free readers allow repositories to examine contents at low cost, albeit with some loss of data.[10] Repositories able to acquire design software can also work on their own to seek and secure the free or discounted educational licenses often available for museums that are part of a university and occasionally for nonaffiliated nonprofit organizations.

Common file extensions for the most widely used software are DWG (AutoCAD) and RTE/RVT (Revit), and some drawings could even come to archives having already been migrated to PDF or to PDF/E.[11] Whatever format is encountered during the appraisal phase, it is important before working with any files to ensure that preservation measures are taken according to digital preservation standards, which specify procedures for storing, copying, auditing, and documenting digital materials.[12]

Collection Management and Preservation

Among the variety of records comprising architectural archives, the most challenging to physically manage and store are drawings and models. Both are usually large in scale, troublesome to move, and rarely in perfect physical condition after being handled repeatedly during their lives as working documents.[13] Moreover, because of the reproduction processes historically used to produce and copy drawings, certain types of architectural prints, such as diazotypes, are light sensitive and prone to fading as well as to discoloring other drawings with which they come into contact.[14] Ensuring that drawings and models are housed properly is key to protecting and managing these records efficiently.

Generally, architectural drawings are stored in three common ways: in flat-file cabinets, in archival tubes or racks that hold rolls, and in acid-free folders placed in archival document containers. Decisions about which storage options to employ will largely depend on drawings' sizes, their state and condition when they come to the archives (flat, rolled, or folded), their use requirements, and the availability of storage options. Ideally, large drawings should be placed in flat-file drawers sized to accommodate them. Within each drawer, drawings should be placed in large acid-free folders and not packed too densely. If an adequate amount of flat-file storage is unavailable, or if drawings are already rolled and cannot be flattened, a good alternative is to store them in archival tubes, wrapping them around an acid-free cardboard core and covering the roll with archival paper. Small-scale drawings and sketches, and large prints and shop drawings that come to the archives already folded, can be housed in any appropriately sized archival container in which they will fit comfortably. Whichever methods of storage are employed, ensuring that off-gassing prints are separated from other drawings and that the general conditions in the storage space are within acceptable ranges for temperature, humidity, light, and other environmental factors are important.

Conservators at the museum may provide guidance about the storage environment and which storage solutions are optimal given the use requirements and conditions of drawings and other materials. Conservators may also be consulted when treatment and custom housing are needed. Some of the common issues requiring the intervention of a conservator are tears and brittleness that make the handling of drawings difficult, the presence of mold, and substances used by the architect, such as adhesives, that have broken down over time and damaged the surface of drawings. If the museum archives acquires architectural models, which often are damaged and fragile, help may be needed not only with repair, but with designing and building custom containers in which to store the objects safely.

As mentioned in the section on appraisal, acquisition of born-digital records also necessitates preservation protocols. To ensure that any digital files acquired are properly and safely preserved, museum archivists should store the files according to digital preservation standards, following the same procedures for design records as for any other digital materials, including saving multiple copies on secure servers and drives, running checksums to monitor the integrity of files, and creating documentation about the files and formats that have been acquired. Beyond these steps, one might take further measures to ensure that design data generated with proprietary software remain accessible in the long term. These might include migrating files to standard formats, such as STEP for CAD and IFC for BIM.[15] Another method is use of emulation or visualization technologies to retain access to the original version of the design software that created the files. Digital collections or IT staff can be a valuable source of information and support to help the museum archivist explore the extent of possible preservation strategies.

Arrangement and Description

Arrangement and description are not significantly different for architectural records than for other archival materials. "Just as other archival materials are managed primarily at the series level," Maygene Daniels notes, "architectural documents too should be understood and described as related groups of materials using the established tools of archival practice."[16] As mentioned previously, building-related records likely will come to the institutional archives from several museum offices, and the culling together of these materials into a single record group is the most efficient way to describe the collection and facilitate access as well.

In recent years, repositories that collect architectural records have tended to follow the arrangement and description guidelines outlined in Kelcy Shepherd and Waverly Lowell's *Standard Series for Architecture and Landscape Design Records: A Tool for the Arrangement and Description of Archival Collections*.[17] Although principally intended for processing large volumes of records acquired when architects and firms donate materials for multiple projects or their entire office holdings, the *Standard Series* can serve as a useful guide for arranging and describing architectural records on a more limited scale as well. In particular, the *Standard Series* helps when the original order of materials is indeterminate, such as might easily occur when gathering documents from different offices into a single collection. The *Standard Series* provides a general structure—a hierarchical series and subseries arrangement—based on the main functional areas of architectural practice (a series for personal papers, professional papers, faculty papers, office records, project records, and art and artifacts) and on the record types or specific activities that occur within these larger functions (at the subseries level). While every series may not be relevant within a museum archives (for instance, personal and faculty papers are not likely collected from the architect), architectural drawings and other types of design documents can be arranged and described according to the guidelines outlined for project records, using the terminology Shepherd and Lowell recommend.

COLLECTION: MUSEUM BUILDING PROJECT RECORDS

1. Correspondence
2. Contracts
3. Drawings
   A. Sketches
   B. Plans
   C. Elevations
   D. Presentation renderings
   E. CAD files
4. Models
5. Photographs
   A. Site
   B. Construction
   C. Completed project
6. Reports
7. Specifications

Other unique series or subseries examples include building proposals, samples, fixtures, and furniture.[18]

If the archives was also to acquire documentation about the building's architect(s), the professional papers series could perhaps be adapted to include general architect- or firm-related information such as awards, writings, photographs, and reference files.

Depending on the volume and types of records and the purposes these records will serve, museum archivists will need to assess the appropriate level of processing and description required. A small volume of materials may not warrant use of the *Standard Series* arrangement, and retaining original order may be preferable in cases when this is possible. Rather than describing all materials in aggregate, as is the case in the *Standard Series*, describing at the item level may be preferable for the purpose of facilitating quick access to specific documents—such as construction drawings needed for repair or renovation work. As Daniels prescribes, item-level description for construction drawings would include information usually provided in each drawing's title block, such as its alphanumeric designation, title, and latest revision date, as well as other information that could possibly be useful for swift identification, such the scale and size of the drawing, and perhaps its medium.[19] The museum's facilities office and curators may be helpful in determining which building records could prove essential for renovation projects or exhibitions, but museum archivists should always balance and weigh the need for detailed item-level description that is typical of cataloging works of art against the practice within the archival profession of arranging and describing materials in aggregate.

Reference and Access

Both internal and external researchers use architectural materials. To provide access to architectural materials, museum archivists will want to ensure that their reading room guidelines can accommodate oversized materials including architectural plans and models. They will also need to decide how to address certain records the museum may not wish to share with the public, such as those detailing security systems or collection storage areas. The museum may also establish a policy through which historical building records are made available, but newer records of a building are not, drawing a distinction between operational buildings and historical sites available for anyone to study. Such access policies should be approved at the highest possible administrative level with the goal of providing more access and discovery points rather than closing collections down.

Providing access to digital design materials will require decisions about the means for sharing such records both within the institution and with outside researchers.[20] For example, providing access to materials in nonstandard formats, such as CAD and BIM drawings and models created with proprietary software, is more complicated, and, in time, best practices and standards will likely be developed to manage access to these kinds of complex materials. For now, however, a few viable options can be employed. As mentioned earlier in the sections on appraisal, collection management, and preservation, migration to PDF, STEP, or another open format is one way to access content, albeit it with some data loss. Using a free reader is another low-cost option for repositories wishing to provide access to CAD and BIM documents, although these readers also require a tradeoff in terms of informational content. If the concern is to view records in their native software environment with full functionality and information intact, acquiring and preserving the ability to use original software is the best strategy to explore. Each of these options for managing access to CAD/BIM files will likely require new competencies from archivists, such as familiarity with file formats, an understanding of the purposes of different design software platforms, and perhaps training in how to operate software programs, even if only at a very basic level.

The possibilities for providing access to architectural materials extend far beyond the reading room. Architectural materials lend themselves well to in-museum exhibitions and publications. They can be used to create films and programs documenting museum buildings while also providing opportunities for others, especially students, to construct replica building models as part of their course of study. They also offer marketing opportunities: drawings of famous buildings are often sought after for museum merchandising. This may be as simple as reprinting a drawing of a museum building on a tote bag or as complex as commissioning a designer to create a jewelry line inspired by the form of the museum, as the Yale Center for British Art did for its Louis Kahn–designed building in 2017 and 2018.[21]

The museum may not own copyright for the drawings in its collection unless it was transferred as part of the architect's contract with the museum. For example, even though the Yale Center for British Art's Institutional Archives owns copies of Kahn's plans for its museum building, copyright for them is held by the Architectural Archives at the University of Pennsylvania, which stewards Kahn's entire collection. So, while a museum archivist may be able to provide access to an architectural collection, as with many other types of collections in the archives, the institution and researchers may not be able to use the collection's records without permission from the architect, firm, or license holder. Seeking permissions for architectural drawings for which a museum doesn't hold copyright is worthwhile, as reproducing them for educational and marketing purposes often yields compelling results.

Collection Development

This chapter has largely focused on the management of architectural materials that document the design and construction of a single museum building. While the majority of museum archives limit their collecting only to the museum site, some may wish to document architectural projects beyond their own institution. Areas of collecting could include materials on other projects by the architectural firm that designed the museum building, or on work designed by others in the geographical area. Far too few institutions have committed themselves to documenting built environments, which are an important part of our historical and cultural heritage whose preservation is beyond the scope of the handful of academic libraries, historical societies, and other institutions and organizations that presently maintain these documents.

Should a wider collecting program be possible, defining a collection development policy in writing, as discussed throughout this publication, is an important step in identifying and clarifying the scope of the institution's collecting focus and the types of materials the museum archives is interested in acquiring and able to manage with its given resources. The appraisal guidelines shared earlier in this chapter will be helpful in determining any categories of materials of special interest and importance, which will be particularly helpful if collecting records from active, larger-sized firms or from offices with sizable projects yielding large quantities of records. If the archives collects architectural materials created in more recent decades, the policy should also address what can be acquired in terms of born-digital content; some repositories may be equipped to take every digital file that a donor wishes to transfer, while others with a more limited capacity for preserving and providing access to digital files may wish to be more selective, accepting only certain types of file formats or only

FIGURE 11.3. Front of Yale Center for British Art tote bag, 2018. PHOTO: RICHARD CASPOLE, YALE CENTER FOR BRITISH ART. REPRODUCTION OF LOUIS KAHN DRAWING COURTESY OF THE ARCHITECTURAL ARCHIVES OF THE UNIVERSITY OF PENNSYLVANIA.

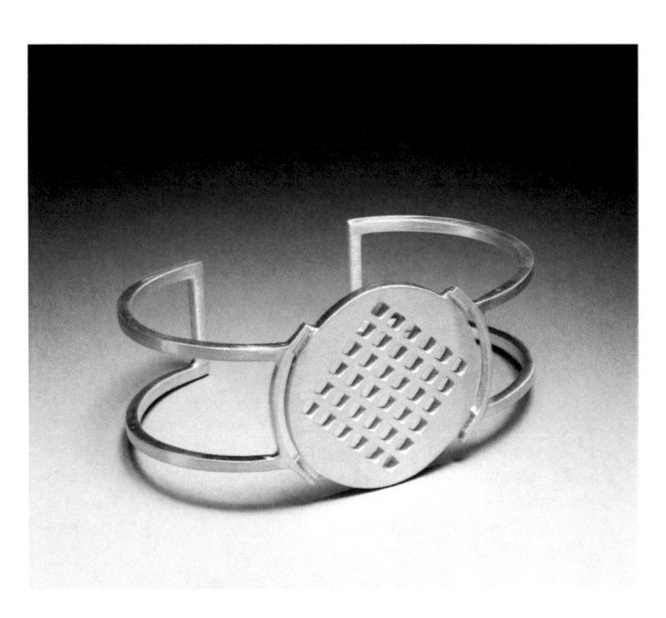

FIGURE 11.4. Glass block ceiling cuff from the moth and butterfly collection, a collaboration between the Yale Center for British Art and Pico Design, 2017. PHOTO: RICHARD CASPOLE, YALE CENTER FOR BRITISH ART.

maintaining PDFs of sections, plans, and elevations. Museum archives that choose to maintain collections of architectural materials beyond their institutional holdings will benefit from a clearly defined collection development policy, while at the same time contribute to the wider objective of preserving and providing access to valuable information on the built environment.[22]

Further Reading

Ball, Alex. *Preserving Computer-Aided Design (CAD)*. Digital Preservation Coalition Technology Watch Report 13, 2013. http://dx.doi.org/10.7207/twr13-02, captured at https://perma.cc/U49V-GEKB.

Lowell, Waverly, and Tawny Ryan Nelb. *Architectural Records: Managing Design and Construction Records*. Chicago: Society of American Archivists, 2006.

NOTES

1. See Eric Wolf, "The Role of the Museum Building in the Experience of the Museum Visit," in *American Art Museum Architecture: Documents and Design* (New York: W.W. Norton and Co., 2010): 200–11, for a discussion of museum architecture's role in a visitor's experience of a museum.

2. See Jayne Merkel, "The Museum as Artifact," *The Wilson Quarterly* 26, no 1 (2002): 66–79, for a discussion of how museum buildings have evolved through the twentieth century, "becoming objects in their own right" (p. 79). See Edwin Heathcote's article, "Age of the 'Starchitect,'" *Financial Times*, January 26, 2017, n.p., for a full discussion of the term. It could also be said that Frank Gehry's Guggenheim Bilbao kicked off the starchitect trend in the late 1990s.

3. The authors are indebted to Maygene Daniels, who authored the chapter "Architectural Records," in *Museum Archives: An Introduction*, ed. Deborah Wythe (Chicago: Society of American Archivists, 2004), 153–59; her ideas and chapter structure significantly informed this text.

4. See Peter Inskip and Stephen Gee in association with Constance Clement, *Louis I. Kahn and the Yale Center for British Art: A Conservation Plan* (New Haven: Yale University Press, 2012) for an example of how a building might be studied and stewarded as seriously as all other objects in a museum's collection.

5. For a more detailed overview of the design process and information about types of architectural drawings, see Waverly Lowell, "Creation of Design Records," in *Architectural Records: Managing Design and Construction Records*, ed. Waverly Lowell and Tawny Ryan Nelb (Chicago: Society of American Archivists, 2006), 19–35.

6. Published resources that provide more information about digital technologies in architectural firms and current approaches to preserving digital design records include Kathryn Pierce, "Collaborative Efforts to Preserve Born-Digital Architectural Records: A Case Study Documenting Present-Day Practice," *Art Documentation: Journal of the Art Libraries Society of North America*, 30, no. 2 (2011): 43–48, and Alex Ball, *Preserving Computer-Aided Design (CAD)*, Digital Preservation Coalition Technology Watch Report 13, 2013, http://dx.doi.org/10.7207/twr13-02. Additionally, the authors would like to note two forthcoming publications on architectural records that were not yet available at the time this chapter was written, but are certain to prove useful for museum archivists working with these records in future. The first is a fall/winter 2021 issue of *American Archivist* focusing on design records. The second is the SAA publication *Born-Digital Design Records*, edited by Samantha Winn.

7. Daniels, "Architectural Records," 156.

8. Lowell and Nelb, eds., *Architectural Records: Managing Design and Construction Records*, 84–85.

9. Common software packages used by design firms are AutoCAD and Revit, both licensed by Autodesk.

10. As of this volume's publication, free readers include DWG TrueView and Bentley View.

11. These are formats that maintain the layered structure typical of CAD drawings.

12. Sources to consult on digital preservation standards are Matthew G. Kirschenbaum et al., *Digital Forensics and Born-Digital Content in Cultural Heritage Collections* (Washington, DC: Council on Library and Information Resources, 2010), https://www.clir.org/wp-content/uploads/sites/6/pub149.pdf, captured at https://perma.cc/39FW-8D7C; Gabriela Redwine et al., *Born Digital: Guidance for Donors, Dealers, and Archival Repositories* (Washington, DC: Council on Library and Information Resources, 2013), https://www.clir.org/wp-content/uploads/sites/9/pub159.pdf, captured at https://perma.cc/Q6C9-C535.

13. Construction drawings can often measure 36 by 48 inches.

14. For further information about the material properties of different types of architectural drawings and their preservation and care, see Eléonore Kissel and Erin Vigneau, *Architectural Photoreproductions: A Manual for Identification and Care* (New Castle, DE: Oak Knoll Press and the New York Botanical Garden, 2009); Maygene Daniels and David Peyceré, eds., *A Guide to the Archival Care of Architectural Records, 19th and 20th Centuries* (Paris: International Council on Archives, 2000); and Lois Olcott Price, *Line, Shade, and Shadow: The Fabrication and Preservation of Architectural Drawings* (New Castle, DE: Oak Knoll Press and the Winterthur Museum, 2015).

15. For more information on format possibilities, see Ball, *Preserving Computer-Aided Design (CAD)*.

16. Daniels, "Architectural Records," 157.

17. Kelcy Shepherd and Waverly Lowell, *Standard Series for Architecture and Landscape Design Records: A Tool for the Arrangement and Description of Archival Collections* (Berkeley: University of California Regents), https://archives.ced.berkeley.edu/uploads/stdseries.pdf, captured at https://perma.cc/F23U-U896. A standards-series-based approach to arrangement and description of architectural records is also presented in Lowell, "Arrangement and Description," *Architectural Records: Managing Design and Construction Records*, 89–105.

18 Adapted from Shepherd and Lowell, *Standard Series for Architecture and Landscape Design Records*, 9 and 12.

19 Daniels, "Architectural Records," 157.

20 If it is important to restrict some materials, the best strategy may be to provide access to files on a secure server or laptop in the reading room and put in place policies that prevent copying of restricted files. Otherwise, common practice at many institutions is to transmit digital files to researchers through electronic file transfer or a file sharing platform.

21 This jewelry collection was created out of a partnership between Pico Design and the Yale Center for British Art in 2017.

22 The authors wish to acknowledge the invaluable contributions of Tessa Walsh and Ines Zalduendo, who provided significant comments and recommendations on this chapter.

12 DOCUMENTING ARTISTS IN MUSEUM ARCHIVES

Rachel Chatalbash and Heather Gendron

Imagine opening a box of curatorial records to find a trove of correspondence between a curator and a major twentieth-century artist. The correspondence includes important details from the artist's life, discussion of extant artwork, plans for upcoming exhibitions, and sketches for new works. Photographs of the artist in their studio are also enclosed among the letters, as are sample paint swatches on torn pieces of canvas. The records are as informative as they are illustrative, and they are no doubt of great interest to art museum archivists and users alike, providing a valuable glimpse into an artist's creative process, output, and personal and professional life. How should these records be kept? Where do they belong: in the museum's art collection, in curatorial object files, or in its archives?

The answers to these questions will vary from institution to institution. However, this chapter seeks to provide some general guidance for museum archivists who work with artists' records.[1] First, it will lay out the unique qualities of artists' records and the distinct challenges associated with their management and care. Second, it will describe the crucial role of archivists—either as the main stewards of a collection or in support of a curatorial department—in caring for artists' records. It will go on to identify opportunities for collaboration between archivists and living artists. Finally, it will provide some strategies for using artists' records in outreach initiatives and public programming.

Collection Development

While museum archivists often focus on collecting institutional records, archivists who work in art museums might also work with a plethora of records relating to and created by artists. Artists' records typically come to museum archives in one of two ways: as part of the documentation of museum operations or through external collecting. In the first case, artists' records most often exist as documentation of the curatorial process—the development of a museum's permanent collection and exhibition program—which regularly includes the direct participation of artists or their estates, especially in the case of modern and contemporary art museums. These records can be analog or in born-digital format. Together with other institutional records, they provide context for an artist's work and can serve as a significant and unique resource for users.

Artists' records collected externally are usually processed and managed as discrete archival collections. An archivist might collect the records of an artist whose artwork the museum is acquiring, an artist whose works are already well represented in the museum's collection, or one who fits the museum's collecting mission in some other way, such as their geographic location, time period, or participation in an artistic movement.[2] Art museums might also acquire artists' records as part of other archival collections, such as the records of dealers, collectors, researchers specializing in certain artists, or other art organizations.

Sometimes, museums obtain artists' archives and art objects as part of a single acquisition; these records may be the personal and professional corpus of a particular artist. Both art objects and artists' records are of value to the institution and therefore collected because they may be of interest to donors, staff members, and users. In other cases, an artist's archival materials may also serve a documentary or supplementary role for particular art objects, documenting how a work is made, providing provenance information, and offering other contextual details.

Museums often acquire an artist's archives after the artist's death through a bequest or promised gift and work with an heir or a representative from the artist's estate to make sure the artist's wishes are honored. However, some artists deposit their records in an archives while they are still living and actively creating new works. This scenario is becoming more common as an understanding of the fragility of born-digital records grows and artists learn more about archival repositories and the value of placing records with them. Additionally, arranging for the deposit of records while the artist is alive can be advantageous for both the artist and the collecting institution, as the artist's heirs and/or studio staff may not fully comprehend the value of the artist's records or the overall impact of the artist's legacy on broader cultural heritage. They also may not be familiar with the artist's practice, values, or priorities regarding their legacy. The archivist can meet with the artist at their studio and other locations where their records are kept to determine in advance what should be included in a deposit.[3] At this stage, the archivist secures a deposit or gift agreement, with a deed of gift to follow. Additionally, a development representative from the museum may also discuss other arrangements with the artist such as a monetary gift to help cover the cost of processing the collection. In other scenarios, the museum may be in a position to purchase collections.

Some archivists conduct "donor interviews"—oral history interviews with artists whose records were acquired.[4] A donor interview allows an archivist to collaborate closely with the artist in the processing and cataloging stages.[5] While more time consuming than a less collaborative approach, this allows the archivist to gain more context about the life and work of the artist and assistance in identifying which materials were central to the creation of art objects and those that were ancillary.[6]

In acquiring artists' records, securing a nonexclusive distribution license from the artist or estate is advisable so the museum may be granted the right to reproduce, display, and distribute records digitally and use the content without alteration for the purpose of preservation, migration, or continued distribution. A license of this kind does not take away copyright from the artist. Deeds of gift will also state the terms of use negotiated between the artist or the estate and the museum upon the transfer of materials.

Types and Examples

As is the case with any individual's records, artists' records may include a wide range of materials: personal correspondence and other writings such as diaries and journals, biographical documentation, legal and financial papers, and ephemera such exhibition announcements and posters. As mentioned, more specific to artists' records are items that document the creation of artwork, including processes, tools, and materials. Most artists maintain an artwork inventory that tracks works they create. In its simplest form, the artwork inventory is a list, spreadsheet, or database of works with title information and date of completion, but it can also include an image or several images of each work, materials used, location if the work was site specific, places where the work was exhibited, installation instructions, price at which the object was sold and to whom, documentation of conservation treatments, and any other information the artist found useful to track.[7] Some artists also keep inventories of artwork by other artists that they have collected, which can later help users better understand the influence the artist had on others and their social networks. Documentation of processes, such as written notes, video recordings of the artist at work, sketches, and photographs of artworks in different stages of conception are also considered artists' records. Museum archives may also include source materials for an artist's artwork and inspirational objects that contributed to their creative process. For example, the Andy Warhol Museum's archives includes source imagery for Warhol's paintings, and the Getty Research Institute's Harry Smith collection includes objects ranging from toys to eggshells.[8]

Some contemporary artists work in ephemeral media, such as performance and temporary site specific installations, which produce no corporeal final object. In those cases, visual documentation of the work and the process of creation are critical to the description and understanding of it. For instance, Mel Chin's temporary conceptual and site-specific work entitled *Revival Field* was a collaboration with a USDA research agronomist using hyperaccumulators to remediate polluted soil. The project was first installed at Pig's Eye Landfill in St. Paul,

Minnesota, and has subsequently been repeated at other sites in Pennsylvania, the Netherlands, and Germany. Documents such as blueprints and photographs provide more tangible information about temporary sites like *Revival Field*.[9] Art documentation can often be perceived as "the work" itself and

ART OR ARCHIVES?

Not unusually, items discovered in an artist's archives resist neat categorization and challenge traditional notions of what belongs there. Andy Warhol's *Time Capsules*, a collection of 610 cardboard boxes housed at the Andy Warhol Museum archives comprises over 8,000 cubic feet of ephemera, original artwork, and photographs by Warhol and others, correspondence, source materials for completed artworks, and collectibles that Warhol personally assembled on an almost daily basis beginning in 1974 until his death in 1987. Some of the more unusual objects found in *Time Capsules* include a mummified human foot and Warhol's signature platinum blonde wigs. Although they began as a regular habit of boxing things up in his studio and home to control his outsized collecting habits, Warhol's initial intentions for his *Time Capsules* (as he called them) were blurred by his subsequent comments about the project. In his book, *The Philosophy of Andy Warhol: From A–B and Back Again*, the artist wrote step-by-step instructions for creating the *Time Capsules* and mentions his interest in exhibiting them at a gallery or selling them to a gallery, thus elevating what originally was a mundane task to that of a long-term art project.[10] John W. Smith, the Andy Warhol Museum's former assistant director for Collections and Research, considers *Time Capsules* "Warhol's most extensive, complex, and personal work."[11] Archivists at the museum completed basic cataloging and continue with item-level cataloging, estimated to take four people working full time fifty years to fully describe the collection item-by-item.[12] In the act of encapsulating materials picked from his studio and home, Warhol created his own meta-archive of sorts, demonstrating what the most interesting artists' archives can accomplish—the painting of a cohesive picture of the life and work of an artist through the materials they kept, along with a good dose of mystery for scholars and fans to pursue.

along with that designation comes greater intrinsic value placed on the records by curators and artists alike, leading to sometimes difficult discussions between archivists and curators about the placement of materials.

While an artist's archives, artist files, or publications (e.g., books, zines) can overlap, artist files and publications are typically treated as collections distinct from archival ones, and can end up in a library collection or curatorial department. Artist files are collections of ephemera related to an individual artist, collective, or art agency and are created by curatorial departments or by libraries for reference or research purposes.[13] Records such as these might remain with a museum archives, however, if they are accessioned as part of a particular artist's archival collection and a compelling argument exists to keep print materials with the collection to maintain provenance.

Collection Management

While artists' records may be among the most significant in a museum archives' collection, many challenges accompany their stewardship. Letters from the artist James Lee Byars, known for his unconventional correspondence with friends and members of the art world, to former Guggenheim director Thomas Messer offer a useful case study.

Figures 12.1 and 12.2 show two separate letters to Messer, each demonstrating a completely different approach to correspondence: one is a letter written on crumpled white tissue paper and the other is a red-painted, accordion-like letter comprised of multiple pieces of paper that have been glued together. The first letter describes a work of art; the second is an elaborate request for a meeting with Messer. The housing and preservation of these unusual formats in artists' archives are often more complicated than those of traditional archival records. Caring for a typed letter on a standard letterhead or a handwritten message on a greeting card is easy; it is harder to care for a handmade accordion booklike assemblage or an artfully crumpled sheet of tissue paper. Despite any challenges presented by the often singular nature of artists' records, archivists and their archival techniques must play a central role in the physical and intellectual management of these materials.

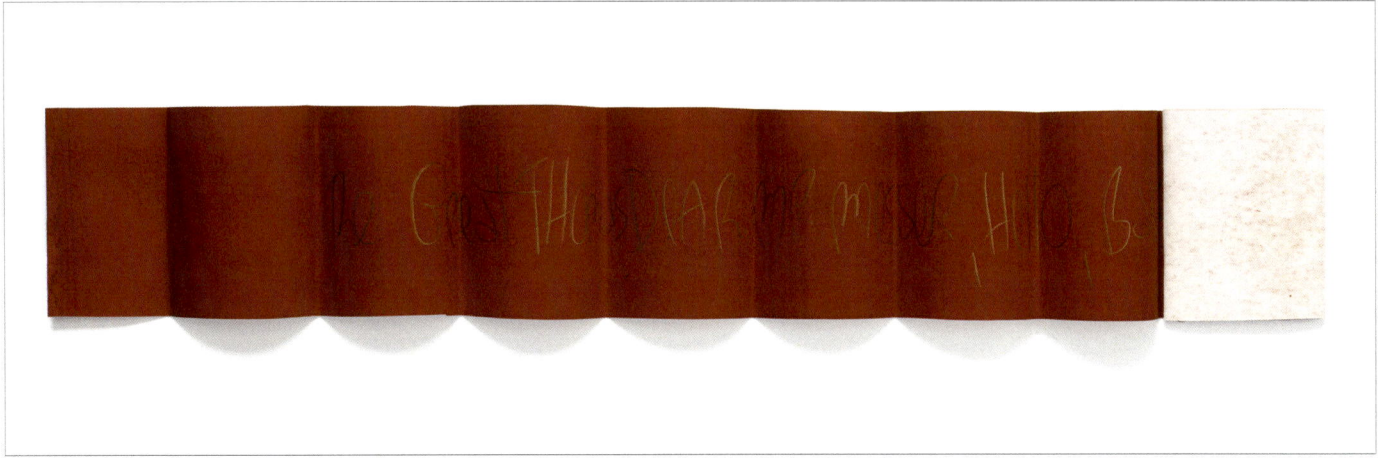

FIGURES 12.1 AND 12.2. James Lee Byars's correspondence with Thomas Messer, 1965–1968. Solomon R. Guggenheim Museum Archives, New York. © The Estate of the Artist.

Documenting Artists in Museum Archives 119

That artists' records belong in the custody of museum archives may not be immediately clear. Byars's letters, for instance, draw attention to the inexact distinction between records and art objects. If they are records, they seem to belong in the archives; if they are art objects, they seem to belong in curatorial departments. With artists' records, a case can often be made for both categories. "One is meant to experience the letters as an aesthetic occasion," notes the text from a MASS MoCA exhibition of Byars's correspondence in 2004, "quite the opposite of how one normally experiences a letter."[14] The letters are as performative and visually complex as any art object. Given these "gray areas" between definitions, museum archivists may need to advocate for their role in managing documents like these.

Librarian D. Vanessa Kam offers one argument for the role of the archivist in preserving artists' records, even when such records are considered objects. No inherent contradiction exists, she says, in an archives collecting objects. In fact, objects are often part of archival collections, "especially if the objects are part of a larger collection with qualities that invite scholarly study and research. Special Collections librarians and archivists have historically recognized the research value of collecting a 'critical mass' of documentation. This idea parallels the principles behind preserving the integrity of archives. . . ."[15] Kam's argument holds particularly true for artists' records kept in institutional archives. Some of the records in an artist's collection might well be considered art objects in their own right, but that does not necessarily mean those objects belong in curatorial departments. Keeping the records of an artist together is far more important, so that objects of artistic interest can be viewed in the full context of an artist's life and historical moment.[16] As Kam suggests, an archivist should emphasize archival concepts, such as original order, when working with diverse collections of artists' records, as adherence to archival philosophies and frameworks might better provide the context necessary to understand an artist's creative process, influences, and/or how specific works of art can be interpreted.

FIGURE 12.3. Horace E. Potter cabinet, circa 1900. Frederick A. Miller Collection, Cleveland Museum of Art Archives.

Considering the function of an object might also help.[17] Figure 12.3 shows Cleveland enamelist Horace Potter's vials of vitreous glass powders, color samples, and tools, all used in the production of enamels.

These are three-dimensional, like art objects might be, but the role they play is primarily archival: they document the artist's creative process. Rather than asking whether an item is physically more like the object held by a curatorial department or the documents held by an archives, museum staff might ask, "Does it *function* as a record?" SAA's *Dictionary of Archives Terminology* says that archival records tend to include "documents rather than artifacts or published materials, although collections of archival records may contain artifacts and books."[18] Archivist Jill Severn notes:

> As long as archivists expect to learn about artifacts from curators and curators expect to learn about records from archivists, neither profession will recognize each other's functions as their own. Archivists do not need collaborators to recognize the "recordness" of the artifacts in collections.[19]

Evaluating whether or not an item or collection is functioning primarily as a record may be a useful framework for determining whether an item belongs in the museum's archives or in a curatorial department. Potter's tools document his art processes in such a way that they are, in Severn's words, "imbued" with "recordness"; they form a record of his artistic methods, and, therefore, belong with other archival records as documentation, comprising part of the Cleveland Museum of Art Archives.[20] The artist's original intent may also be a factor when conducting a functional analysis of the item(s) in question.

Despite a museum archives' contributions to a museum's mission and its service to users in the art historical field, museum archives' collections are often considered less significant than other collections at a museum, especially its art collections. This perception inevitably fuels debate over where artists' records ought to reside; these records are as privileged as the art they document and, for that reason, curatorial departments often seek or retain them. Thus, while all other correspondence at the museum might be transferred to the museum archives once inactive, correspondence with artists often stays in the hands of curatorial departments, possibly placed in object files or in collection storage, and often dealt with inconsistently by different curatorial departments in the same museum. Facing this challenge, museum archivists should advocate for their role in stewarding the legacies of artists at their institutions. At the very least, once a collection reaches the museum, best practices should be in place to ensure dialogue and collaboration across curatorial, archival, and conservation departments, and to foster good intellectual control and easy accessibility by outside researchers.

Standard archival procedures are not always followed when caring for these types of materials because of their perceived value and differences in the professional training and approaches of curatorial and archives staff. The tendency exists to forego traditional appraisal when it comes to documentation of artists, especially those who are well known; everything is kept, under the assumption that everything is potentially valuable or useful. Furthermore, artists' records are often described in far more detail than other archival collections, sometimes even at the item level. Museum archivists should assess whether this privileging is prudent—the resources and work that can be devoted to a museum's repository are finite, and it may not always make sense to allocate so much time and labor to artists' records. On the one hand, treating an archival collection in such a way might allow it to be better integrated into existing museum databases, preserving the item-level focus that museums use for objects and for their online catalogs. On the other hand, putting so much effort into some collections may come at a cost to others.

With the shift to digital media over the course of the second half of the twentieth century, some of the issues inherent in the management of artists' archival materials have disappeared. Archivists care for fewer physical objects, fragile documents, and items with complex material makeup than they once did. However, born-digital stewardship poses a new set of challenges that archivists face with other museum records: digital impermanence, technological obsolescence, and bit rot, to name a few. In particular, artists' born-digital records may feature unusual file types or very large file sizes associated with their art practice. For repositories that collect artists' archives, a lack of awareness of the significance of born-digital records or a lack of resources to preserve them on the part of artists may result in the obliteration of these records soon after creation. Archivists are well positioned to deal with these issues, given their professional training in these areas. They can also draw upon established policies, procedures, and workflows for born-digital records, which already exist in many museum archives. Without active stewardship, born-digital artists' records may be lost. Therefore, the stewards of these records must be familiar with the risks and challenges associated with caring for digital media and the significance of born-digital records.

Insofar as born-digital records do not bear the mark of the artist's hand, does this change their significance in the museum context? In the past, artists' correspondence, no matter how it was constructed, almost always included a signature. That signature carried intrinsic documentary value and conveyed authenticity—the signature and/or other embellishments of correspondence such as sketches were material things to be preserved. With email, however, no signature exists in the traditional sense. Sketches may be sent as attachments or generated in design or illustration software. Regardless of the digital formats or software used, the literal mark of the artist is no longer present. Without question, these records are still valuable—they document the very same things as their analog counterparts—but some of the traditional allure of the physical trace of the artist no longer exists. As a result, the museum archives may no longer need to compete so actively with curatorial departments to manage these types of records; with the switch to born digital and the loss of the artist's mark, their place in the museum archives has in many ways become more evident. Museum archivists should use this transition to demonstrate that the records' analog counterparts might also be transferred to the same repository.

Working with Artists' Foundations

Artists' foundations may also collect and steward artists' records. Foundations are often established after artists die and less so during artists' lifetimes, hence the designation "artists' lifetime foundations."[21] A lifetime foundation likely focuses on charitable activities and does not typically include the archives of an artist; these materials constitute the intellectual property of the artist, as does the artwork. This is largely because owning and managing an artist's archives while they are still alive can result in legal issues related to self-dealing.[22] An Aspen Institute study on artists' foundations notes that the estates responsible for the administration of artists' copyrights and intellectual property must follow the same rules regarding the administration of copyrights for scholarly and academic purposes that other agencies, like universities and public institutions, do and advises estates and foundations to post their copyright permissions policy publicly on their website. Again, this can help ensure that a foundation is operating in line with laws restricting foundations from favoring insiders.[23] While many foundations charge for the use of copyrighted materials, the Robert Rauschenberg Foundation has led the way for foundations to embrace fair use policies to enhance their educational and research missions.[24]

Not uncommonly, an artist's records are dispersed across both a foundation and a museum archives. In such cases, the foundation typically owns the copyrights of the artist while the museum archives has physical ownership of the materials in its collection, unless such rights have been signed over in the deed of gift. Use of the copyrighted materials for other than scholarly or academic purposes must be negotiated with the foundation.

Outreach

The enticing visual nature of artists' archives and their relationship to art objects studied by curatorial departments mean that they will always be prime materials for use in museum exhibitions and publications. This provides archivists with the opportunity to support the initiatives of curatorial programs as well as to chart their own course. Collaborating with colleagues by providing them with materials from the archives will demonstrate the significance of the archives, further potential contributions that it can make to overall institutional goals, and the museum archivists' value to their colleagues. Similarly, developing one's own programmatic elements, such as working with an artist on an exhibition of their archival materials or inviting an artist to research or work in their collection, may have similar effects.[25]

Outreach activities may also support the museum archivist in achieving several collecting and service goals aligned with the mission of the institution. Local and regional community outreach can in turn help facilitate collecting opportunities and increase use of existing collections. Training activities for local and regional artists provide more general understanding and knowledge of museum archives and possibly skill building for artists in managing their personal archives. Museum archivists can draw on their expertise and experience to guide artists in the long-term care and maintenance of their personal archives.[26] The free guide *Artists' Studio Archives: Managing Personal Collections and Creative Legacies* was written for artists and those assisting artists with their personal archives and can be used as a toolkit for archivists who wish to develop workshops for artists on this topic.[27] In 2015 and 2016, the North Carolina Museum of Art in Raleigh and the Mint Museum in Charlotte hosted workshops cosponsored by UNC Chapel

Hill and the Institute for Museum and Library Services for artists from across the state in studio archives management.[28]

Museum archivists can look to outreach programs in which their colleagues are engaged for ideas and partnerships in reaching artists' communities. The Nelson-Atkins Museum of Art's Research Library has hosted events for local artists as part of its Artist File Initiative. The aim of the program is to build a collection documenting artists in the region, and each file includes: "an artist statement, a resume, a gallery or museum exhibition announcement, published reviews, annotated exhibition checklists, annotated exhibition gallery shots, as well as any other additional supporting material."[29] The library works with local arts organizations to host workshops for artists on maintaining their documentation and establishing an artist file. Activities like this could help archivists identify and connect with local artists whose records they wish to collect and seed discussions with artists about the deposit of their records. Archivists might bring their records management expertise to the table and proactively help an artist and/or studio staff deal with their active records, so their materials will be more complete, better organized, and in good condition when they arrive at a museum archives.

Conclusion

Artists' records provide many opportunities for collaboration both inside and outside of the museum. Artists' stories, which are woven throughout a museum archives, are essential to the preservation of these museums' histories, the understanding of their legacies, and the interpretation of their art objects. As these collections are developed, stewarded, and shared, they will no doubt continue to provide significant opportunities for museum archivists to advocate for the value of their collections as well as their contributions to the mission of the museum as a whole.[30]

Further Reading

Artist-Endowed Foundations Initiative. The Aspen Institute. https://www.aspeninstitute.org/programs/program-on-philanthropy-and-social-innovation-psi/artist-endowed-foundations-initiative, captured at https://perma.cc/J2XW-SV9P.

Ambrose-Smith, Neal, Joan E. Beaudoin, Heather Gendron, and Eumie Imm Stroukoff. *Artists' Studio Archives: Managing Personal Collection and Creative Legacies*, 2016. https://www.arlisna.org/publications/arlis-na-research-reports/1013-artists-studio-archives, captured at https://perma.cc/MBE6-C393.

Reed, Marcia. "From the Archive to Art History." *Art Journal / College Art Association of America* 76, no. 1 (2017): 121–28.

NOTES

1 Typically, "records" refers to institutional documents, while "papers" refers to personal documents. For the purposes of this chapter, "artists' records" include all documents created by artists, regardless of whether they are institutional or personal in nature.

2 This same process occurs with museums of other subject specialties, such as natural history and science museums. Chapter 13 will explore this process in relation to field notes.

3 A museum curator or director may also be involved in this process, especially if the artist is significant or is already well represented at the museum.

4 Other museum staff such as conservators and curators may also conduct such interviews. Oral history in the museum archives context is considered in detail in chapter 9 of this publication.

5 For more discussion of donor interviews, see Melissa Gill, "News from the Field: Artist Archives at the Getty Research Institute," *Visual Resources* 32, nos. 3–4 (2016): 306–9, and Andra Darlington, "Winnowing with George Herms: Lessons for Collaboration between Archivists and Artists," *Artists' Records in the Archives: Symposium Proceedings* (2011): 45–47, https://www.nycarchivists.org/resources/Pictures/Metropolitan_Archivist/Artists-Records-in-the-Archives-Symposium-Proceedings.pdf, captured at https://perma.cc/L253-9ZGB.

6 In the case of George Herms's collection at the Getty Research Institute, Herms ultimately created a new artwork called *The Winnowed* based on the "winnowing" process he engaged in with a GRI research assistant to identify and catalog individual items and those "out of scope." Gill, "News from the Field," 46.

7 Inventories such as these may require special consideration by the museum archivist, such as migrating data about artwork into a museum's collection management system or emulating the original database in the museum archives while keeping snapshots of the original in preservation storage.

8 Gill, "News from the Field," 307.

9 See Peter Boswell, "Invisible Aesthetic: Revisiting Mel Chin's *Revival Field*," *Sightlines* (blog), https://walkerart.org/magazine/mel-chin-revival-field-peter-boswell-rufus-chaney-eco-art, captured at https://perma.cc/F7UH-2DFP.

10 John W. Smith, "Saving Time: Andy Warhol's Time Capsules," *Art Documentation: Journal of the Art Libraries Society of North America* 20, no. 1 (2001): 8; Peter Nesbett, "Unpacking Andy's Boxes," *Art on Paper* 11, no. 2 (2006): 31; and Thomas Sokolowski and Udo Kittelmann, Forward, in *Andy Warhol's*

Time Capsule 21, ed. The Andy Warhol Museum (Pittsburgh: The Andy Warhol Museum, 2003), 14.

11 Smith, "Saving Time," 11.

12 Nesbett, "Unpacking Andy's Boxes," 31.

13 An artist file typically includes gallery show announcements, resumes, photographic documentation of artwork, newspaper clippings, and other ephemera related to the artist.

14 MASS MoCA, "James Lee Byars: Letters from the World's Most Famous Unknown Artist," https://massmoca.org/event/james-lee-byars-letters-from-the-worlds-most-famous-unknown-artist, captured at https://perma.cc/B3EP-C36A.

15 D. Vanessa Kam, "On Collecting and Exhibiting Art Objects in Libraries, Archives, and Research Institutes," *Art Documentation: Journal of the Art Libraries Society of North America* 20, no. 2 (2001): 13.

16 One might argue that such collections could be split across museum departments, with records managed by the museum archives and art objects managed by curatorial departments; however, maintaining the integrity of the collection *in toto* is important and could be facilitated by bringing the disparate elements of the collection together in a reading room, gallery, or online, for access, study, and use. However, with the collection's stewardship spread across the institution, some connections would undeniably be lost, limiting users' ability to reconstruct provenance and re-create the complete context surrounding a museum's relationship to an artist and/or work of art. Removing such records from the museum archives erases the essential narrative of the relationship of the institution to artists and their works.

17 See Jill Robin Severn, "Adventures in the Third Dimension: Reenvisioning the Place of Artifacts in Archives," in *An American Political Archives Reader*, ed. Karen Dawley et al. (Lanham, MD: Scarecrow Press, 2009): 221–33, for an overview of the literature on this topic. The subject is also discussed by Kristin Hawley Good in "Artists' Archives: Institutional Contexts, Problems, and Solution" (master's thesis, University of North Carolina at Chapel Hill, April 2012), and Lisa Darms, "The Archival Object: A Memoir of Disintegration," *Archivaria* 67 (July 2009): 143–55. All of these publications have informed the authors' discussion in this chapter. The authors' thoughts on this topic have also been influenced by email discussions with archivist Maureen Callahan.

18 See the *Dictionary of Archives Terminology*, s.v. "archival record," Society of American Archivists, https://dictionary.archivists.org/entry/archival-record.html, captured at https://perma.cc/2N75-JF2S; for a full exploration of the definition archival records, see Caroline Williams "Records and Archives: Concepts, Roles and Definitions," in *Archives and Recordkeeping: Theory into Practice*, ed. Caroline Williams (London: Facet Publishing, 2013), 13–19.

19 Severn, "Adventures in the Third Dimension," 224. For another definition of recordness, see Society of American Archivists, s.v. "recordness," *Dictionary of Archives Terminology*, https://us3.campaign-archive.com/?u=56c4cfbec1ee5b2a284e7e9d6&id=82bd286947, captured at https://perma.cc/JT4Z-4NC2.

20 Severn, "Adventures in the Third Dimension, 223.

21 Christine J. Vincent, *The Artist as Philanthropist: Strengthening the Next Generation of Artist-Endowed Foundations, A Study of the Emerging Artist-Endowed Foundation Field in the U.S.*, Aspen Institute Program on Philanthropy and Social Innovation, vol. 1 (November 2010), 125, https://www.aspeninstitute.org/publications/volume-one-artist-philanthropist-strengthening-next-generation-artist-endowed-foundatio/, captured at https://perma.cc/46MT-FC4Z.

22 Christine J. Vincent, *The Artist as Philanthropist: Strengthening the Next Generation of Artist-Endowed Foundations, A Study of the Emerging Artist-Endowed Foundation Field in the U.S.*, Aspen Institute Program on Philanthropy and Social Innovation, vol. 2 (November 2010), 150–151, https://assets.aspeninstitute.org/content/uploads/2010/11/AEF_V2.pdf, captured at https://perma.cc/RPW5-7YFK.

23 Vincent, *The Artist as Philanthropist*, vol. 2, 154.

24 "Fair Use Policy," Robert Rauschenberg Foundation, https://www.rauschenbergfoundation.org/foundation/fair-use, captured at https://perma.cc/DGW6-GZT5.

25 See Andra Darlington, "Winnowing with George Herms: Lessons for Collaboration between Archivists and Artists," 45–47, in *Artists' Records in the Archives: Symposium Proceedings* (2011), ed. Rachel Chatalbash, Celia Hartmann, Denis Lessard, and Mario Ramirez, https://www.nycarchivists.org/resources/Pictures/Metropolitan_Archivist/Artists-Records-in-the-Archives-Symposium-Proceedings.pdf, captured at https://perma.cc/4K4B-CAT8, for a discussion of how one artist, George Herms, worked with Getty Research Institute archives staff to engage with his own records in their collection.

26 Some well-resourced artists and artist foundations are able to hire an assistant or a professional archivist to organize their studio archives.

27 Neal Ambrose-Smith, Joan E. Beaudoin, Heather Gendron, and Eumie Imm Stroukoff, *Artists' Studio Archives: Managing Personal Collection and Creative Legacies* (Art Library Society of North America, 2016), https://www.arlisna.org/publications/arlis-na-research-reports/1013-artists-studio-archives, captured at https://perma.cc/4CQ4-YXBJ.

28 Colin Post, "Ensuring the Legacy of Self-Taught and Local Artists," *Art Documentation: Journal of the Art Libraries Society of North America* 36, no. 1 (2017): 73–90. Related programs include Joan Mitchell Foundation's Creating a Living Legacy (CALL) program and related career documentation guide (see *Career Documentation for the Visual Artist: An Archive Planning Workbook and Resource Guide* [Joan Mitchell Foundation, 2016], http://joanmitchellfoundation.org/artist-programs/resources, captured at https://perma.cc/L6GJ-KE6H); and Dance Heritage Coalition's "Artist's Legacy Toolkit,"https://www.danceusa.org/archiving-preservation-artists-legacy-toolkit, captured at https://perma.cc/XN4Q-Q6U6.

29 Fanny Ouyang, "Preserving Artists' Legacies with Marilyn Carbonell," Artists' Studio Archives, http://artiststudioarchives.org/2016/02/15/preserving-artist-legacies-with-marilyn-carbonell, captured at https://perma.cc/QL7W-29DT.

30 The authors would like to acknowledge and thank Susan Anderson for her insightful comments and feedback on an early draft of this chapter.

13 NEGOTIATING BOUNDARY MATERIALS: FIELD NOTES IN MUSEUMS

Christina Velazquez Fidler, Rebecca Morgan, and Lesley Parilla

For museum archivists, field notes present a particular challenge: as "boundary materials," they comprise a mix of the professional and the personal, and they exist on the border between museum and archival practice.[1] Naturalists record details about time and place in field notes during specimen collecting trips; as a result, a museum might choose to define field notes primarily as specimen documentation, inadvertently obscuring personal accounts scientists include, whereas an archives might choose to define the same item as personal papers, thus obscuring their scientific components. Neither characterization is optimal—especially because their unique mix of content

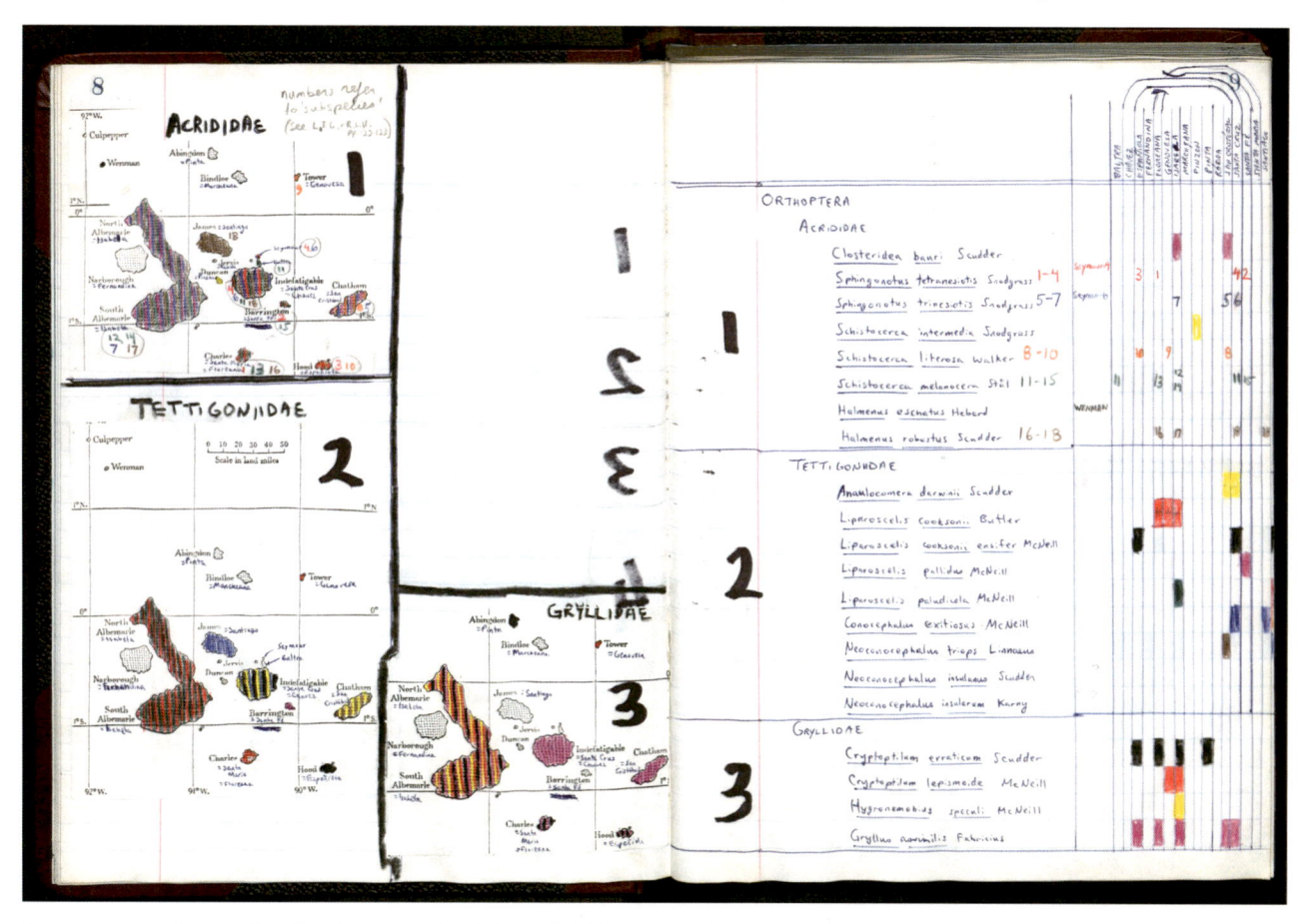

FIGURE 13.1. Insect distribution maps in Robert E. Silberglied's field notes. Pages 8 and 9 from an undated volume of field notes of Robert E. Silberglied from work conducted on the Galapagos Islands in 1967 to 1971 and unknown years. It includes a series of photocopied maps of the Galapagos Islands that have been hand colored to show the distribution of insects by order/suborder, species, and locality (island name). SIA2012-9757, HTTPS://WWW.FLICKR.COM/PHOTOS/SMITHSONIAN/8361431417/IN/ALBUM-72157631559857724.

means field notes continue to be active records for the specimens they document and are important to many kinds of users.[2] Given this, the archival profession has been considering better ways to make field notes and scientific notebooks more discoverable and accessible.[3] This chapter will examine how and why field notes need special care and stewardship, and how such attention can benefit scientists, historians, and other user communities. Furthermore, it will consider recent projects that provide improved discoverability and access to field materials via aggregators and address the inherent challenges of managing these materials in museums, where curatorial and archives departments may share their stewardship.

What Are Field Notes?

The term "field notes" is used throughout this chapter as a general term to encompass the typically bound records of observations and related notes made by field researchers in a variety of disciplines, often referred to as "field books," "field notebooks," "field diaries," "field journals," or "field documentation." This chapter employs these more specific terms as appropriate. The Smithsonian Field Book Project notes that the resulting records are "primary source documents that describe the events leading up to and including the collection of specimens or observations during field research. Field notes can take many forms depending on the information needs of the collector."[4] Generally, they are small to medium-sized bound notebooks containing handwritten entries and may contain notes, observations, diary entries, sketches, photographs, maps, and inserts alongside information about specific specimens, recorded with dates, times, and often specific weather and location data. Field notes can also be unbound mixed materials in unexpected formats such as photographs and loose correspondence, sound recordings, and even film. Increasingly, scientists are using new e-applications, including GIS-related programs, to capture important field data.[5]

FIGURE 13.2. Carla Cicero, staff curator of birds at the Museum of Vertebrate Zoology, University of California, Berkeley, recording songs of Bell's sparrows near Red Bluff, California, 2012. Courtesy of the Museum of Vertebrate Zoology Archives, University of California, Berkeley.

Most of the scientific disciplines have used and continue to use field notes to gather field data. These data are useful to researchers across the sciences, not only to those who study the changes in the environment, but also to those using new investigative techniques to study existing specimen holdings.

While natural history museums and other scientific research institutions primarily hold field notes, they can also be found in cultural institutions such as art museums, historical societies, academic institutions, government agencies, and professional organizations.[6] In these cases, the field notes often exist in the personal papers of individuals who took part in expeditions or personal collecting trips and who may have subsequently moved on to other careers. In art museums, field notes may be collected for their illustrations as well. The field notes may often only be described in a general way as diaries or journals, but making the effort to recognize, fully describe, and manage these rich primary source materials is a great service to researchers across disciplines.[7] Museum archivists may also find themselves working with field notes from disciplines like anthropology; these in particular present ethical considerations, such as restrictions on access, culturally sensitive content, and "knowledge repatriation," which affect how they are managed and made available.[8] Field notes in the form of photographic and moving image collections are especially significant to culturally sensitive content and can help to guide important outreach work.[9]

This chapter focuses both on historical field notes and on more recently collected scientific data found in museums. As the media used to record field data change over time, museum archivists can play an important role in providing guidance on good data management practices.[10]

Acquisition

Scientists going on a large expedition journey to a location and carry out their fieldwork as a group. Each scientist records data based on the mission of the expedition and their particular research focus, collects visual documentation in various formats, and often records environmental data that can be helpful to everyone in the group. Upon their return, the documentation travels back to the individual scientists' home institutions and departments. This results in a dispersal of archival materials pertaining to a single expedition.

Even when all of a scientist's field notes and documentation return to a single museum, the materials can become separated over time. Iconic or otherwise special expedition field notes are sometimes deposited in the museum's rare book collection. Visual materials may stay with the field notes in the department, be stored with the scientist's research files, or be centralized by format within the museum's larger research library and archives. In each scenario, these related materials are usually held separately with nothing connecting them other than a staff member's institutional knowledge. This disconnect is problematic for other scientists and researchers, particularly so for museum staff revisiting geographic locations for additional study.

Field notes are essentially permanently active records, like accession files, conservation reports, and other object documentation in a museum. Curatorial staff use them for cataloging specimens, and researchers for their work. As scientific concepts are regularly revisited over time, the field notes that support the research data always need to be discoverable and accessible.[11] Scientists and researchers often hold the materials separate from other papers and close to specimens or in labs for this reason, frequently keeping them all but hidden from anyone outside of the museum's science department. Museum staff can forget that related materials could reside in other science departments or that the main library and archives may have a film or images related to the field notes.

Whether the museum archivist should advocate for the field notes to be transferred to the archives or stay in another department depends on how the materials are currently being stored and handled as well as the culture of the department. If the curatorial department sees the materials as historically valuable, and/or they are mindful stewards who care for the materials as carefully as they care for the related specimens or objects, it may be appropriate to support permanent retention there. This scenario provides the museum archivist an opportunity to partner with the staff member in charge of these materials to offer expertise and provide information on how the items may relate to others throughout the museum. Additionally, senior museum staff may have personal connections with field notes' creators and can help the museum archivist secure missing field notebooks.

In other cases, the museum archivist may be the best steward for the materials; however, record creators' misperceptions about what the archives is and how it will support museum staff might challenge the archivist. Some may believe that if field notes are deposited into the archives, they will never again have easy access to them. Archivists must mitigate this concern by prioritizing access and maintaining a consistent and active dialogue with staff through the phases of acquisition, rehousing, and description.

Although not usually mandatory for an internal transfer, a deed of gift can be useful in this process, even if the institution requires deposit of field notes relating to work done by staff affiliated with the institution. Staff often have a personal connection to their work, so a deed of gift can work as a tool for recognizing the donor and may result in more field documentation being transferred into the museum archives beyond what was created during the period of affiliation, such as field notes from academic training. Furthermore, such recognition can be useful when working with family members who often end up in possession of important field materials after a museum staff person's death. The deed of gift is also an opportunity to ask specifically if field notes can be made available online. Some scientists need to protect sensitive habitats and do not want those locations published. Scientists have numerous valid ethical, legal, and personal reasons to protect their data, and a deed of gift can address these concerns.[12]

Expedition EAC-CPF Records

Relationship-based description such as Encoded Archival Context for Corporate Bodies, Persons, and Families (EAC-CPF) records can be used as part of the acquisition process to document contextual information for an expedition. Often used for recording contextual information for historical expeditions, EAC-CPF provides a unique opportunity to encode institutional memory for contemporary expeditions as well.[13] Many museums are continually working toward a future where collection management systems might be able to speak to each other; providing these authority records may help to facilitate this goal.[14]

If the museum archivist is working with an active creator, generating an expedition EAC-CPF record for contemporary fieldwork is a chance for the museum archivist to ask about the stewardship of born-digital files relating to the expedition, including whether they are being backed up or if any long-term storage plans exist for them. Through this interaction, the museum archivist gains a better understanding of the types of field documentation being created. The exercise provides an opportunity to work proactively with museum staff and allows for guidance on data management that is in line with the institution's standards. It also ensures an open channel for asking and answering questions down the road. Ideally, working with active records creators can help the museum archivist to address the field data of the past and prepare for the work of today and tomorrow.

Description

Because of the complexity of field notes, multilevel description addressing an item's content and its creator's connections with other entities is important to making them usable. Field notes frequently contain specific localities such as latitude, longitude, and elevation, and environmental conditions, as well as information about the appearance and behavior of specimens. This data's value has only grown as scientists study the specimens to understand broader questions relating to how the environment has changed over time. Researchers prefer description to be at the data level: for instance, some field notes contain information organized by specimen number, and a one-to-one relationship at the data

Collection level: Provides context, e.g., describes scientist's method of recording field data (taking pictures, annotating maps, etc.), research interests, and formal and informal relationships with colleagues and institutions.

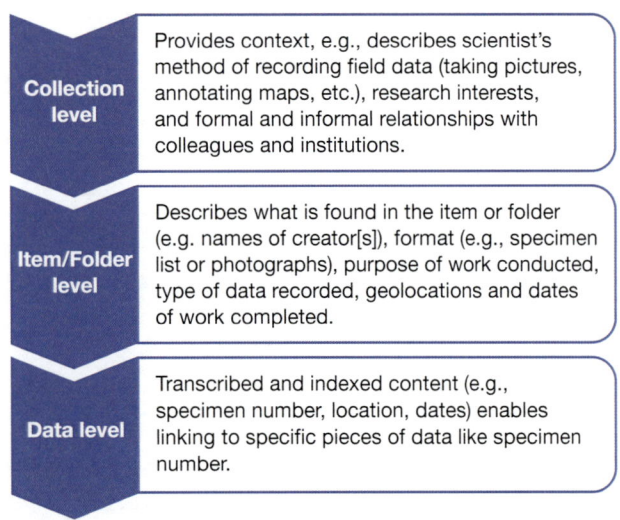

Item/Folder level: Describes what is found in the item or folder (e.g. names of creator[s]), format (e.g., specimen list or photographs), purpose of work conducted, type of data recorded, geolocations and dates of work completed.

Data level: Transcribed and indexed content (e.g., specimen number, location, dates) enables linking to specific pieces of data like specimen number.

FIGURE 13.3. Description of information found at different levels of description

FIGURE 13.4. "Rollo H. Beck and ship engineer in workshop with frigate bird specimen, aboard schooner the France."
Neg. 107956, AMNH.

level would enable the museum's specimen record to link to the specimen description in the field notes. However, this level of description, which goes beyond even page level, is not feasible unless the institution can transcribe and index the content. Generally, museum archives manage to describe field notes at the item or folder level, despite the fact that field notes typically contain data for dozens, if not hundreds, of specimens. For example, if a folder holds several notebooks or a notebook and a distinct group of other materials like correspondence or photographs, it might make more sense to describe the contents as separate items rather than at the folder level.

Though researchers often focus on information found at the folder level, such as collecting in a location on a specific date, the importance of collection-level description that can lead researchers to pertinent information in other field notes

DESCRIBING EXPEDITIONS

Creating an expedition EAC-CPF record allows the museum archivist to capture the expedition's official or authoritative name and any variations; to describe and cite its mission and scope; to list the individuals who were part of it, including any locals hired if appropriate, as well as any participating institutions, departments, and funders. A timeline and expedition locations can be added, and, most important, all related archival collections, no matter where they might be held and managed, can be listed. If the museum archivist is working with a living creator, they might offer information on how the trip relates to their other research, point out published literature about the expedition, and provide other helpful details and resources.

cannot be disregarded. Knowing which institution funded the fieldwork, whether it was the result of an expedition, or if work was done alongside a colleague or mentor can lead to other useful field data. Collection-level description can inform a researcher of the field note data from an expedition and supply the names of participants with whom they worked. This is particularly important, as the field notes of other expedition members may reside in the scientists' home institutions, not with the institution that led the expedition. For instance, the United States Exploring Expedition was funded by the US government and led by officers in the US Navy, but field notes reside in more than twelve public and private institutions.[15] Collection-level description can provide information about long-term informal relationships between scientists, who describe fieldwork observations in their correspondence. It can clarify unexpected collecting locations, like those of Edgar Alexander Mearns, who was an army surgeon and often collected at his military duty stations; his collecting expertise was so well established that he was invited to participate in expeditions with Theodore Roosevelt for the Smithsonian Institution.

Institutions are still developing best practices for item- and data-level description; they frequently employ a combination of schemas to meet the needs of each level and utilize a combination of systems to make materials available. Additional access points can lead to portions of the same description being duplicated in several schemas, especially for digitized materials. For instance, Smithsonian Institution Archives' field notes are in collections with full EAD-encoded finding aids, but the archives also creates collection-level records using EAD-friendly schemas like natural collection description (NCD) for field notes collections, and item-level description in metadata object description schema (MODS).[16] Other institutions, like the American Museum of Natural History, have created EAD-encoded finding aids and separate item-level records in MARC.[17] They have also captured higher contextual description utilizing EAC-CPF, which proves to be a good tool for documenting relationships and enabling the discovery of research overlap.[18] Examples of description relating to the Whitney South Sea Expedition appear in figures 13.5, 13.6, and 13.7.

Data-level description standards are still in development, thus archivists are reaching out to colleagues in museum collections management to discover and develop resources.[19] Museum collections management systems—especially those designed for specimen data—include controlled vocabulary and a highly appealing level of granularity, and natural sciences personnel already know how

FIGURE 13.5. Example of an EAC-CPF Expedition record in consortium SNAC based on https://snaccooperative.org/view/83667609, captured at https://perma.cc/GTK8-55KA.

AMERICAN MUSEUM OF NATURAL HISTORY

Whitney South Sea Expedition of the American Museum of Natural History. Letters and journal of José G. Correia.

Author: José G Correia 1881–1954. American Museum of Natural History. Whitney South Sea Expedition of the American Museum of Natural History (1920-1941) American Museum of Natural History.

Show More ⌄

Manuscript [between 1930 and 1941]
[between 1930 and 1941]

Summary: Daily notes, letters, and scientific illustrations from Correia's time as expedition assistant for the Whitney South Sea Expedition including Samoa, the Society islands, and the Cook islands (in vol. 1) and the Marquesas, the Society islands, the Austral islands, the Line islands, and the Pitcairn islands (in vol. 2)

Physical Description:	2 volumes (252, 117 leaves) : illustrations (chiefly color) ; 27 cm
Contents:	V. 1. January 31, 1923-December 1, 1925 -- v. 2. June 4, 1925-October 18, 1926.
Subjects:	*Art & Architecture Thesaurus* field notes. Field notes *Faceted Application of Subject Terminology* Birds. Scientific expeditions. Travel. Cook Islands. Fiji. French Polynesia Society Islands. New Zealand. Oceania. Wallis and Futuna Uvéa. *Library of Congress Subject Headings* Correia, José G., 1881–1954. Travel Oceania. Whitney South Sea Expedition of the American Museum of Natural History (1920–1941) Scientific expeditions Oceania. Birds Oceania. Oceania Description and travel. Uvéa (Wallis and Futuna) Description and travel. New Zealand Description and travel. Cook Islands Description and travel. Fiji Description and travel. Society Islands (French Polynesia) Description and travel. Scientific expeditions Oceania. Birds Oceania. Oceania Description and travel. Uvéa (Wallis and Futuna) Description and travel. New Zealand Description and travel. Cook Islands Description and travel. Fiji Description and travel. Society Islands (French Polynesia) Description and travel. Correia, José G., 1881-1954. Travel Oceania. Whitney South Sea Expedition of the American Museum of Natural History (1920–1941)
Genre:	field notes.
AMNH Research Library Notes:	Restricted; for access, please contact libref@amnh.org. .b12161160 02-01-17 01-11-16
Notes (General):	Bound volumes. Typescript, based on original field notes written between 1925 and 1926. Vol. 1 has loose typescript sheets of corrected bound material laid in at rear and newspaper clippings lightly pasted throughout. Vol. 2 includes several hand-colored scientific illustrations, some folded. Digitized through the 2016 CLIR Biodiversity Heritage Library Field Notes Project. Cataloged through a 2015 Leon Levy Foundation Archives grant.
Ownership and Custodial History:	Part of the AMNH Ornithology Archives.
Access Restrictions:	Restricted; for access, please contact libref@amnh.org.
Database:	WorldCat
OCLC Number/Unique Identifier:	919314597

FIGURE 13.6. Example of a field notes MARC record based on https://amnhlibrary.on.worldcat.org/v2/oclc/919314597, captured at https://perma.cc/LGF9-F6B6.

Whitney South Sea Expedition of the American Museum of Natural History

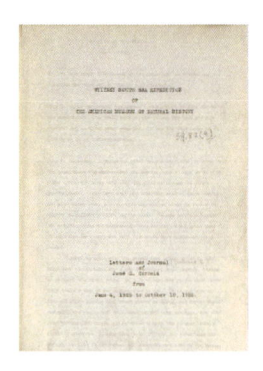

View Full Item

Created Date	1923
Description	1
Creator	Correia, José G. (José Goncalves), 1881–1954

Partner	Biodiversity Heritage Library
Contributing Institution	American Museum of Natural History Library
Subjects	1920–1941 1881–1954 Birds Correia, José G. Description and travel Field notes Scientific Expeditions Travel Whitney South Sea Expedition of American Museum of Natural History
Location	Cook Islands Fiji New Zealand Oceania Society Islands (French Polynesia) Uvéa (Wallis and Futuna)
Type	text
Format	Print
Language	English
URL	https://www.biodiversitylibrary.org/item/212269
Rights	In copyright. Digitized with the permission of the rights holder.

FIGURE 13.7. Example of a field notes record in DPLA based on https://dp.la/item/e3470f3f7b204acef5765b7789a39bd3, captured at https://perma.cc/TLJ9-3KYL.

these systems work. For instance, natural scientists increasingly collect highly accurate geolocation data in the field; if description of field notes consistently uses the same controlled vocabulary for geolocations, scientists can compare that data from field notes more precisely. In addition, in 2008 this kind of partnership resulted in the previously mentioned NCD data standard.

Access and Preservation

Natural history museums have made considerable efforts in the last two decades to digitize specimen data. iDigBio, supported by Advancing Digitization of Biodiversity Collections (ADBC), is a national effort to provide electronic access to specimen data and images, and Vertnet is an integrated data portal where researchers can access and publish data.[20] Both efforts are funded by the National Science Foundation (NSF) and are dedicated to supporting and aggregating digitization of specimen information for increased access to biodiversity data.[21] In the framework of these efforts, and the emergence of biodiversity informatics, the expectation is that archival materials, specifically field notes, will be available in a similar fashion.[22] These digitization efforts have forced many natural history museums to revisit their characterization of field notes as "ancillary" materials and to recognize their value, along with the need to digitize specimen data and conduct resurvey efforts.[23] Furthermore, increased access to specimens due to digitization will likely result in increased reference requests for the field notes that describe the collecting events surrounding them. Researchers are often puzzled by having access to individually described specimens with locality information and other details such as stomach contents and measurements, but are unable to locate the specimen-related field notes due to insufficient information on where the field notes are deposited and how, or if, they are cataloged.

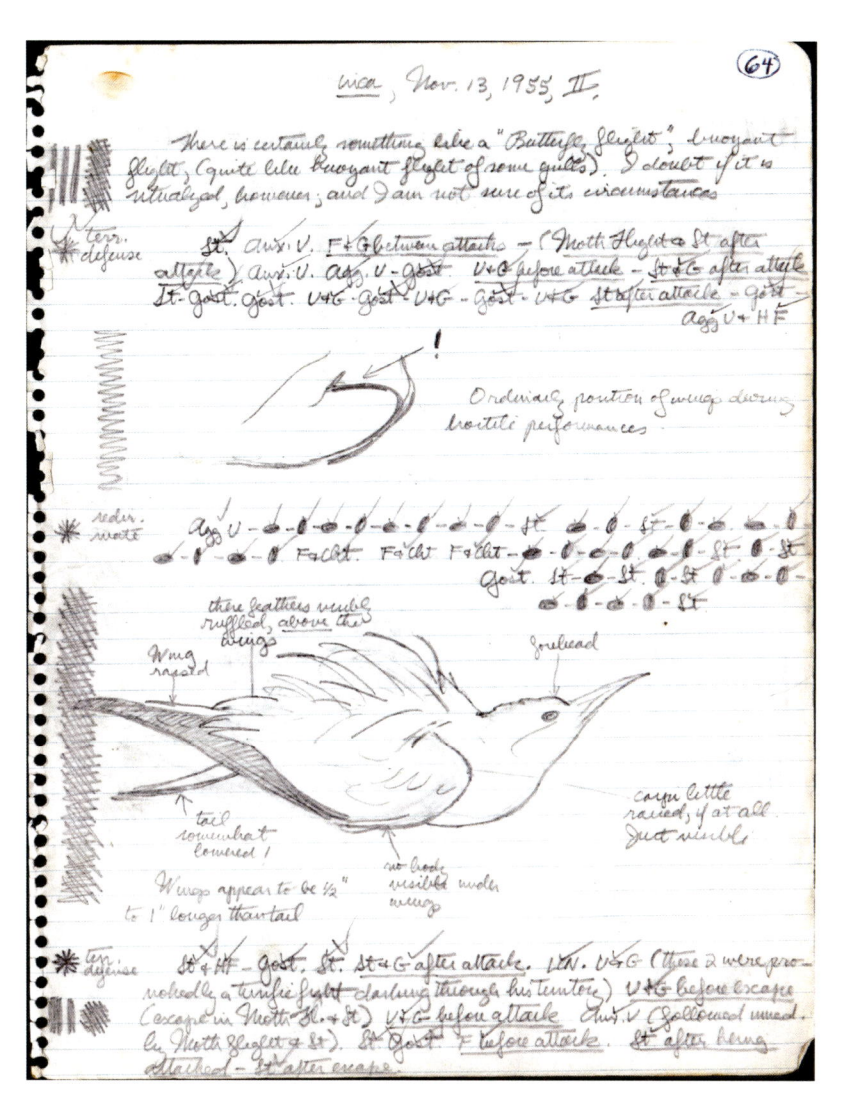

FIGURE 13.8. Martin H. Moynihan's field notes on gulls, November 13, 1955. Page of field notes documents M. Moynihan's behavioral observations of gulls (*laridae*) in South America. SIA2014-03311, HTTPS://WWW.FLICKR.COM/PHOTOS/SMITHSONIAN/14190538942/IN/ALBUM-72157644331531239.

Physical access to field notes can present a series of challenges for archivists. Researchers who create and reference field notes are likely to have high levels of access to specimens. When developing policies for accessing field notes in the archives, knowing the institution's policies for accessing specimens and other museum materials may help. Many museums do not use supervised settings like reading rooms for researchers to use specimens; generally, researchers are given a tray of specimens and trusted to peruse the collections after being introduced to their organization and relevant policies. While archival practices may not support such methods of access, knowing the context in which researchers in natural history museums normally access information at their institutions is important; this will enable museum archivists to smoothly transition users of the specimen collections to the archival collections during research visits.

Several physical barriers exist that may prevent access to field notes. Field notes are often created in the outdoors in harsh conditions, and, like many other archival collections, family members may keep field notes in basements or attics before they are gifted to a museum. These conditions make field notes susceptible to pest infestations among other issues. As a result, museum archivists should take proper preservation measures and survey materials prior to bringing them inside the museum.

Field notes come in every type of binding, or lack thereof, and may contain fragile materials such as photographs, folded maps, envelopes with feathers, scraps of paper taped inside with critical data, and every other conceivable preservation challenge. These should be treated individually and in consultation with a conservator. Keeping the field notebook intact and attempting to preserve it in its entirety may be desirable, or it may be prudent to use separation forms and remove materials to ensure their preservation.[24] For example, maps might be removed and stored in flat files, photographs interleaved with acid-free paper to prevent silvering, or they might be removed and placed in acid-free envelopes. Including a note in the catalog entry for the specimen directing researchers to the corresponding field notes with additional data might be helpful. Field notebook storage largely depends on the volume itself and institutional resources, but, in general, bound books in good condition should be stored upright and supported to prevent pages from curling and to protect the integrity of the binding.[25]

Digitizing and making scans available for research use can decrease wear and tear on the physical items and enable remote access. Archivists should be judicious about which field notes are digitized. Digitization itself can cause significant damage to a field notebook if it has conservation issues, and field notebooks with fragile bindings could be further damaged if scanned on a flatbed scanner.[26] However, digitizing field notebooks with careful consideration of their physical condition can assure long-term access to data, preventing overhandling of the original objects.

When undertaking digitization, archivists should consider citizen science–based transcription projects to provide further access to field notes. Citizen science is the use of the general public to aid scientific research, and it can be harnessed to provide text-based transcription of primary source materials. In addition to specimen- and object-specific data, field notes also contain important observational data, which can be challenging to extract in their analog form. Emerging transcription projects such as Notes for Nature and the Smithsonian Transcription Center provide researchers with text-searchable field notes and provide researchers with unprecedented levels of access to data.[27] Transcription projects have the potential to provide excellent opportunities for linked data whereby the archivists, in collaboration with museum curators, can link field note transcriptions and relate field notebooks to other museum collections.

The majority of field notes are still created in physical books, but as technology improves, more field notes are created digitally. Researchers were once unable to take laptops or tablets into remote field sites without power sources. However, with the development of solar-powered battery chargers and other advancements in battery technology, researchers can take more technology into the field. Born-digital field notes require different access and preservation strategies, and museum archivists should implement a digital preservation plan to ensure the integrity and longevity of field notes files.

Emerging technologies are also changing the level to which the creator can manipulate field data for study. Increasingly, field data are stored as structured data, especially data from long-term field studies.[28] Structured data are still field documentation but in a format more traditionally supported by an institution's technical support staff. Depending on how the institution structures its data support, the archives may be a logical place to store this data alongside other born-digital materials and physical copies of field notes.

The Role of Museum Archivists

Because of the unique nature of field notes and their specific research value, museum archivists, collection managers, and curators have much to gain by working together. The key to encouraging optimal stewardship of field notes is building trust with other departments through the development of strong administrative frameworks for accessioning, describing, preserving, and providing access.

Collection managers and curators may not be aware of the standards and best practices followed by archivists, just as archivists may not be aware of standards and best practices used by collection managers and curators.[29] Holding workshops or brown bag lunch seminars to demonstrate how archivists approach management of collections is an excellent way to foster collaboration and start conversations with colleagues. Asking collection managers and curators for tours of their collections and holding Q&A sessions to better understand their use of field notes and the other museum records they create are other useful ways to reach across departments.

Building subject knowledge can also help the museum archivist develop these important relationships and understand the full research value of their collections. Attendance at the annual Society for the Preservation of Natural History Collections (SPNHC) meeting, iDigBio workshops, or institutional seminars shows a commitment to supporting researchers and to learning about the technology tools scientists use that will affect future collections. Staying abreast of research efforts conducted by the museum's scientists as well as any resulting publications is also helpful. This knowledge enables the archivist to ask better questions and aids advocacy efforts.

Once curators and collection managers are assured that the museum archivist understands the research value and access needs of field notes, they are more likely to transfer these materials to the archives. This trust has a domino effect; when departments begin transferring materials, donors are directed to the archives and understand that their materials will be professionally managed. Donors are part of the museum's culture and mission, and the idea that their field notes will be shelved in the archives, next to the icons of the past, is a powerful concept.

Collegial relationships with other departments can lead to additional benefits such as access to walk-in freezers and climate-controlled spaces, and opportunities for collaborative grant projects, as specimen collections require equipment and data resources similar to archival collections. Because natural history museum specimen collections are intimately tied to field notes, numerous collaborative opportunities exist for digitizing and enhancing

FIGURE 13.9. Theresa Barclay, preparation lab manager of the Museum of Vertebrate Zoology, University of California, Berkeley, writing field notes at Mahogany Flat, Death Valley, California, June 27, 2018. COURTESY OF THE MUSEUM OF VERTEBRATE ZOOLOGY ARCHIVES, UNIVERSITY OF CALIFORNIA, BERKELEY.

access to collections. Also, biodiversity informatics provide an opportunity for museum archivists to collaborate with staff in other disciplines to develop innovative solutions for extracting and relating data contained in field notes.

Museum archivists should also raise awareness of long-term risks associated with some digital file formats with their colleagues and remind creators of the importance of ensuring that discoveries made today are available in the future. Becoming familiar with departmental practices and curatorial workflows better positions the archivist to assert the role of the museum archives in the records life cycle. Museum archivists should recommend metadata and file management improvements based on local institutional best practice; this will ensure higher quality files and metadata when the materials are eventually deposited into the archives.

Negotiating Boundary Materials: Field Notes in Museums   135

Collaboration with Other Institutions

Collaboration is essential not just across museum departments but also among institutions. Collaboration helps museum archivists develop profession-wide practices for description and presentation, and it enables researchers to locate field notes that may not have been deposited with the specimen collections they document and to discover pertinent field data. Several existing consortiums provide places for archivists to share field book content online.[30] The Biodiversity Heritage Library (BHL), working in partnership with the Internet Archive, is a consortium of natural history and botanical libraries that cooperate to digitize the legacy biodiversity literature held in their collections and to make that literature available for open access and responsible use as a part of a global "biodiversity commons."[31] BHL was designed to provide online access to published materials, but has begun to support unpublished materials like field notes. In 2016, BHL led a collaborative CLIR-funded grant among a number of partners to make field notes available in a number of platforms and aggregators.[32] This grant provided an opportunity to fulfill the great need of local and collaborative documentation and workflows for field notes description and digitization.[35] The BHL consortium also works with the international taxonomic community, rights holders, and other interested parties to make biodiversity documentation available globally for research and education.[36]

Conclusion

As this chapter has demonstrated, field notes are truly "boundary materials," a unique mix of scientific data, environmental observation, and personal reflection; these characteristics spawn perplexing questions regarding care, description, and access. Archivists from natural history museums have a responsibility to advocate for field notes within the profession; to do this, museum archivists must build on and look beyond the profession's descriptive methods, build relationships with creators, and seek collaborative opportunities within and beyond their own institutions. This work has the added benefit of helping the archival community develop best practices for these unique resources, strengthening connections with communities and researchers, and managing the challenges of born-digital records.

Further Reading

Jones, Michael. "Artefacts and Archives: Considering Cross-Collection Contextual Information Networks in Museums." In *Museums & the Web: Selected Papers and Proceedings from Two International Conferences*, edited by Nancy Proctor and Rich Cherry. Silver Spring, MD: Museums and the Web, 2016, 123–35.

Nakasone, Sonoe, and Carolyn Sheffield. "Descriptive Metadata for Field Books: Methods and Practices of the Field Book Project." *D-Lib Magazine* 19, nos. 11–12 (2013). https://doi.org/10.1045/november2013-nakasone, captured at https://perma.cc/X6X3-V8U9.

Primack, Richard B., and Abraham J. Miller-Rushing. "Uncovering, Collecting, and Analyzing Records to Investigate the Ecological Impacts of Climate Change: A Template from Thoreau's Concord." *BioScience* 62, no. 2

COLLABORATIONS

The American Museum of Natural History's (AMNH) Department of Ornithology has been a partner with the AMNH archives for a number of grants from the Council for Library and Information Resources (CLIR) and the Leon Levy Foundation. These grants have allowed collection inventories to be written, condition assessments to be made, and finding aids and EAC-CPF records to be written for a number of field notes collections. Field notes for one important collection, the Whitney South Sea Expedition (1920–1941), were cataloged by item, digitized, and uploaded to the Internet Archive, Biodiversity Heritage Library, and the Digital Public Library of America (DPLA).[33] Making the Whitney South Sea Expedition materials available in this way has been beneficial to many researchers working on conservation efforts in the areas the expedition visited. It also supports initiatives such as the AMNH Science Research Mentoring Program (SRMP), where students work with the department collections manager to develop expedition visualization projects.[34]

(2012): 170–81. https://doi.org/10.1525/bio
.2012.62.2.10.

Sanjek, Roger. *Fieldnotes: The Makings of Anthropology*, edited by Roger Sanjek. Ithaca, NY: Cornell University Press, 1990.

Woller, Derek A., and Jovonn G. Hill. "Melanoplus foxi Hebard, 1923 (Orthoptera: Acrididae: Melanoplinae): Rediscovered after Almost 60 Years Using Historical Field Notes Connected to Curated Specimens." *Transactions of the American Entomological Society* 141, no. 3 (2015), 545–74. http://www.jstor.org/stable/43746571.

NOTES

1. Michael Jones, "From Personal to Public: Field Books, Museums, and the Opening of the Archives," *Archives and Records* 38, no. 2 (2017), http://dx.doi.org/10.1080/23257962.2016.1269645.

2. For instance, biologists rely on the original literature and original sources of species information perhaps more than any other science discipline, and recent grant-funded research projects support this work. Rusty Russell, "Biological Field Book Project Receives CLIR Funding," http://nmnh.typepad.com/the_plant_press/2010/01/plant-press-2010-vol-13-issue-1-6.html, captured at https://perma.cc/H9NJ-AWSJ.

3. This chapter will cover issues that relate to both natural sciences and anthropology field notes, such as the creator's use of a wide variety of formats to record observations, field notes' value to ongoing research, and aspects relating to housing and conservation. It will not address issues surrounding the culturally sensitive content often found in anthropological field notes or their impact on access and custodianship. Museum archivists are encouraged to review resources such as the Council for the Preservation of Anthropological Records (CoPAR), http://copar.org, captured at https://perma.cc/72CW-88MJ. This site is in the process of being moved to http://copar.umd.edu.

4. BHL Wiki, "The Field Book Project," 2017, http://biodivlib.wikispaces.com/The+Field+Book+Project, captured at https://perma.cc/R7GT-S4J7.

5. Archivists managing these resources should follow data management workflows that are in line with the institution's policies for research and collecting electronic data.

6. Nancy J. Parezo, "Preserving Anthropology's Heritage: CoPAR, Anthropological Records, and the Archival Community," *American Archivist* 62, no. 2 (1999): 271–306, https://doi.org/10.17723/aarc.62.2.j475270470145630.

7. Eira Tansey, "The Necessary Knowledge," November 3, 2017, *Eira Tansey* (blog), http://eiratansey.com/2017/11/03/the-necessary-knowledge/, captured at https://perma.cc/XA8L-L8FC.

8. Robert Leopold, "The Second Life of Ethnographic Fieldnotes," *Ateliers d'anthropologie* (2008), https://doi.org/10.4000/ateliers.3132, captured at https://perma.cc/3H2E-RDY8.

9. For examples of outreach work, see "Setting the Record Straight," American Museum of Natural History, https://www.amnh.org/explore/margaret-mead-film-festival/archives/margaret-mead-film-festival-2013/mead-dialogues/setting-the-record-straight, captured at https://perma.cc/Q9GX-5US8, and "Shalako Film Remade," A:shiwi A:wan Museum and Heritage Center, http://ashiwi-museum.org/collaborations/shalako-film-remade/, captured at, https://perma.cc/3624-4TLF.

10. Roger Sanjek and Susan W. Tratner, "E-fieldnotes: The Makings of Anthropology in the Digital World" (Philadelphia: University of Pennsylvania Press, 2016).

11. Sarah Ramdeen and Alex Poole, "Using Grounded Theory to Understand the Archival Needs of Geologists," in *The Archival Multiverse*, ed. Anne Gilliland and Sue McKemmish (New South Wales: Monash University Press, 2016), 998–1027.

12. See chapter 6 for further description of acquisition processes.

13. The AMNH Archives creates EAC-CPF records for AMNH historic expeditions and related individuals, AMNH Research Library "Authorities," http://data.library.amnh.org/archives-authorities, captured at https://perma.cc/9TF3-UULY.

14. EAC-CPF records describe the creators of archival collections either as persons, families, or organizations. As EAD is used to describe the "what" of archival collections, EAC-CPF records define and describe the "who." EAC-CPF records are now being aggregated into the SNAC (Social Networks and Archival Context) research tool for discovery of related creators and collections, http://snaccooperative.org, captured at https://perma.cc/4WBA-N247.

15. Collections relating to the US Exploring Expedition are in numerous institutions across the country. Examples can be found in the collections of Gray Herbarium Library at Harvard University, the American Philosophical Society, Yale University, the US Naval War College, and New York Botanical Garden's LuEsther T. Mertz Library, among others. For example: Records of the United States Exploring Expedition, 1838–1842, Archives of the Gray Herbarium, Harvard University, https://id.lib.harvard.edu/ead/gra00016/catalog, captured at https://perma.cc/AZR9-JJXR; Journal of William L. Hudson, comdg. US Ship *Peacock*, one of the vessels attached to the South Sea Surveying and Exploring Expedition under the command of Charles Wilkes Esq. [Journal no. 1, Aug. 18, 1838–Aug. 11, 1840], American Museum of Natural History, http://libcat1.amnh.org/record=b1107970, captured at https://perma.cc/4535-KWRT; George Foster Emmons Papers, Yale Collection of Western Americana, Beinecke Rare Book and Manuscript Library, Yale University, https://archives.yale.edu/repositories/11/resources/1176, captured at https://perma.cc/NXE8-73K8.

16. Metadata Object Description Schema (MODS) is an XML schema developed for bibliographic description and is maintained by the Library of Congress Network Development and MARC Standards Office. It maps well to MARC and provides additional flexibility in the online environment. NCD is used to describe collections of natural history materials at the collection level and maps to Dublin Core and EAD, "Natural Collections Description (NCD)," http://www.biodiversidad.gob.mx/especies/colecciones/pdf/NCD_090.pdf, captured at https://perma.cc/QT42-P9R2.

17. MAchine-Readable Cataloging (MARC) was developed in the 1960s so that libraries could share machine-readable bibliographic records (and later authority records) primarily between libraries, but the format is also used by archives to create collection-level records. In general, archivists grappling with item-level description show a preference for using MARC or MARC-mapped options like MODS. MARC provides a decades-tested, robust structure that not only makes the item-level description searchable in a way users already know, it also aids sharing the description when putting the digital copies online. Online catalogs like Digital Public Library of America and Biodiversity Heritage Library make available digital materials and already have workflows in place for ingesting MARC records or MARC-friendly options like MODS. These

MARC and MODS records also tend to search better alongside records for related materials like science publications.

18. Christina Fidler, Barbara Mathe, Rusty Russell, and Russell D. (Tim) White, "Grinnell to GUIDs: Connecting Natural Science Archives and Specimens," in *Innovation, Collaboration and Models: Proceedings of the CLIR Cataloging Hidden Collections and Archives Symposium*, ed. Cheryl Oestreicher (November 2015), 177–91, https://www.clir.org/pubs/reports/pub169.

19. See "Collaboration with Other Institutions" section for more information on the Biodiversity Heritage Library.

20. iDigBio, https://www.idigbio.org, captured at https://perma.cc/4BZK-2DBU; Vertnet, http://vertnet.org/, captured at https://perma.cc/F7QT-229R.

21. Carla Cicero et al., "Biodiversity Informatics and Data Quality on a Global Scale," in *Emerging Frontiers in Collections-based Ornithological Research: The Extended Specimen. Studies in Avian Biology*, ed. M. S. Webster (Boca Raton, FL: CRC Press, 2017).

22. Biodiversity informatics is the application of information technology to address problems surrounding organization, access, visualization, and analysis of primary biodiversity data. Jorge Soberón and Townsend Peterson, "Biodiversity Informatics: Managing and Applying Primary Biodiversity Data," *Philosophical Transactions of the Royal Society B* (2004) 689–98, doi:10.1098/rstb.2003.1439.

23. Rebecca J. Rowe, "Looking to the Past to Plan for the Future: Using Natural History Collections as Historical Baselines," in *Stepping in the Same River Twice: Replication in Biological Research*, ed. Ayelet Shavit and Aaron M. Ellison (New Haven; London: Yale University Press, 2017), 64–80, http://www.jstor.org/stable/j.ctt1n2tvtj.10.

24. Any materials removed and separated from the field notes should be cross-referenced back to each other, both on paper and in the related archival management system.

25. If a volume is too tall and shelving cannot be adjusted to fit its size, the book may be shelved spine side down. Like other paper materials, field notes should be housed in environmentally controlled spaces with average temperatures of 60°F ± 5° and a relative humidity of 40° ± 3°. Field notebooks should be protected from light damage and stored out of direct light.

26. Field notebooks with fragile binding could be further damaged if scanned on a flatbed scanner and should either be photographed or scanned with a "v" cradle book scanner.

27. Notes from Nature, "The Notes from NatureProject," https://www.zooniverse.org, captured at https://perma.cc/4LUE-3QPX; Smithsonian, "What Is the Smithsonian Transcription Center?," https://transcription.si.edu/about, captured at https://perma.cc/578E-4WB4; Lesley Parilla and Meghan Ferriter, "Social Media and Crowdsourced Transcription of Historical Materials at the Smithsonian Institution: Methods for Strengthening Community Engagement and Its Tie to Transcription Output," *American Archivist* 79, no. 2 (2016), 438–60, https://doi.org/10.17723/0360-9081-79.2.438.

28. Eric Riddell, "Plasticity Reveals Hidden Resistance to Extinction under Climate Change in Global Hotspot of Salamander Diversity," OSFHome (April 24, 2018), 25, https://doi.org/10.17605/OSF.IO/E4SP6, captured at https://perma.cc/C9UG-Z65R.

29. These include examples such as DarwinCore, Audubon Core, and PaleoCore, as well as the Biodiversity Information Standards, also known as the Taxonomic Databases Working Group (TDWG).

30. SNAC's (Social Networks and Archival Context) research tool for discovery of related creators and collections brings materials together by creator; as the description of field notes improve so will their discovery, http://snaccooperative.org, captured at https://perma.cc/4WBA-N247.

31. Biodiversity Heritage Library, https://www.biodiversitylibrary.org, captured at https://perma.cc/VFE3-SMGF; Internet Archive, Biodiversity Heritage Library, https://archive.org/details/biodiversity, captured at https://perma.cc/YRZ7-DJ6L.

32. BHL, "Field Notes Project," https://about.biodiversitylibrary.org/projects/past-projects/field-notes-project/#Participating%20Institutions, captured at https://perma.cc/7ZBU-QGWM.

33. American Museum of Natural History, "Hidden Connections: Expeditionary Field Work at the American Museum of Natural History," http://images.library.amnh.org/hiddencollections/field-books, captured at https://perma.cc/V7BJ-QRGK.

34. Carto, "Mapping the Historical Biodiversity of the Solomon Islands with the American Museum of Natural History (October 20, 2016), https://carto.com/blog/mapping-solomon-islands/, captured at https://perma.cc/L6PY-C6S6.

35. AMNH, "The Field Book Project at the American Museum of Natural History," http://images.library.amnh.org/hiddencollections/field-books, captured at https://perma.cc/3JYZ-8FBR.

36. BHL supports increased access to content through Global Names Recognition and Discovery (GNRD) and UBio's taxonomic name finding tools. These link publications about species to related content in the Encyclopedia of Life. BHL serves as the foundational literature component of the Encyclopedia of Life, which is a free, online collaborative encyclopedia intended to document all of the 1.9 million living species known to science. For another example of a collaboration, see Wendy Wasman, "News from The Cleveland Museum of Natural History," *Museum Archivist* 27, no. 1 (2017), 13, http://www2.archivists.org/sites/all/files/MAS%20Newsletter%20Winter%202017_final.pdf, captured at https://perma.cc/2ANF-VE6H.

PART III

14 HOLISTIC FUNDRAISING: A LOGICAL EXTENSION OF MANAGEMENT, OUTREACH, AND ADVOCACY

Susan Anderson

As is the case with their parent institutions, museum archives are often tasked with raising additional funds, especially for special projects. Related nonprofit environments, such as libraries, historic houses, historical societies, and other cultural heritage institutions, face the same challenge. Fundraising is often the only way to get collections processed or digitized, especially when the museum archivist is a solo records professional.[1] In contrast to other museum departments that may have dedicated funding streams to build their collections and/or support their operations, however, the museum archives may also consider the development of purchase funds to acquire archival materials of special interest to the repository. In acknowledgment of these all-too-frequent scenarios—whatever the funding need may be—this chapter will provide a basic overview of fundraising for museum archives to support colleagues with holistic strategies to enrich their programs.

Just as a good policy framework will support a museum archives in all aspects of its operation, having a well-developed set of policies and procedures based on current best practice standards will be a necessary component to any fundraising endeavor. This framework will allow a museum archivist to provide intelligent workflows in a grant application or to assure donors that they are contributing to a stable and professionally run department.[2] Following ethical standards and legal considerations are equally important, as funders will likely require the management of their allocations to follow specific guidelines, depending on the conditions of the donation or award. Museum archives often fundraise within similar donor pools and foundations as their home institution does, so it is best practice for museum archivists to exercise due diligence and avoid conflicts of interest, not only for their own professional reputation, but also for the institution they represent.[3] The archivist, as well as a museum's development department and/or general counsel whenever applicable, should carefully review all gift forms, donor agreements, and grant funding stipulations prior to finalizing a gift.

"As for fundraising ethics, the general principle is that development should seek consonance between a donor's wishes and [an archives] need, and it should proceed in an open and balanced way. A fundraising program can be considered to be successful when it results in gifts that contribute to the strategic vision. . . . A program is not successful when it results in gifts that are, in fact, tangential, distracting, or come with cumbersome strings attached."

–Victoria Steele[4]

Another point of consideration is tying the goals set during a strategic planning process, whether on an institutional or departmental level, to any fundraising objectives. Funders are usually interested in long-range management strategies and want to know how a particular project will fit with an overall vision of an archives to ensure its sustainability over time.[5] The more institutional support a museum archivist can demonstrate—such as endorsements from a director, mission statements, or aligning a project with a larger museum initiative—the more likely the possibility of future funding.[6] Such evidence could

FIGURE 14.1. Susan Anderson giving a behind-the-scenes tour to the Fiske Kimball Society, a philanthropic group at the Philadelphia Museum of Art.
Photo by Andrea Nunez.

Working with Development Professionals

While museums vary greatly in terms of size and staffing, for purposes of illustration, fundraising departments in museums generally include staff devoted to the following functions: annual giving, major gifts, planned gifts, corporate relations, and foundation and government grants.[9] More than one of these areas might be headed by a single staff member, not fully developed, or not present at all. Colleagues in development can be good allies, and their fundraising expertise will complement the museum archivist's knowledge of collections and potential projects to be initiated. Development staff often serve as "gatekeepers" of the relationships with the museum's donors and ensure against competing requests. If an institution does not formally match the museum archives (or library, if that is the archivist's home department) with a development liaison to assist with fundraising, then various ways exist to make their acquaintance and get on their agenda. This would include senior management identifying common causes and suggesting collaboration, scheduling a meeting to review the archives' strategic plan in light of the museum's overarching fundraising goals, doing informational interviews, or offering to collaborate on a donor event with a behind-the-scenes tour with special items on display. Highlighting a museum's history, accomplishments, and contributions to the cultural community can be mutually beneficial for both departments.[10]

A development department can assist with specific funding opportunities, such as endowed positions, special projects, and creating an advisory board. Colleagues in development can also identify potential funders and present the museum archives' financial needs to them through a case statement or a funding opportunities document tailored to promoting support for the archives.[11]

provide the necessary leverage to convince a funder that they will be contributing to an ongoing legacy and not a one-off "boutique" project that will end as soon as the external funds are expended.

Developing good advocacy skills is another important component in fundraising. Museum archivists often need to diplomatically educate potential donors, who may not understand the unique nature of archival collections and the complexities related to managing them. On the other hand, archivists must also compete for funding within a limited pool of grant agencies. While these organizations may be more familiar with the archival enterprise, they are also flooded with similar proposals. In both cases, the archivist must articulate what makes an archival collection especially unique, how the project is on the cutting edge of the profession, and why the proposal is particularly well suited for a funder's philanthropic goals.[7] Just as advocacy for the archives within a home institution is needed, the archivist's elevator speech or "story" needs to be clearly articulated and framed according to the funder's priorities. It is a matter of grabbing their attention, holding their interest, creating a compelling narrative, and presenting a careful work plan that will inspire them to make an investment in an archives' program.[8]

> "A case statement is a formal, written (it can also be orally presented) presentation by a program addressed to prospective private sector sources to raise money. It is equivalent to the formal grant proposal. . . . They generally include a brief summary of the program's mission, a concise history of the repository, descriptions of the strengths and needs of the program, potential of the program and the use of the solicited funds, and a description of a vision for the programs' future, including what the new funds can help the program accomplish and the difference the new moneys will make."
> –Richard J. Cox[12]

Another form of team building could include reference work with development colleagues—assuming the department has been transferring records to the museum archives—and empowering them to review successful fundraising techniques from the past, rather than reinventing the wheel. Such topics would include the review of previous capital campaigns, researching the history of different fundraising groups, determining important anniversaries to tie into donor events, and looking into biographical information about major donors prior to a specific "ask," or request for funding. Reviewing previous grant applications can provide valuable insights about a museum's history with different funding organizations, as well as ideas for grant-writing approaches (the recycling of existing boilerplate is a tried-and-true strategy). Ephemera such as sample invitations, newsletters, and promotional materials can be referenced for future fundraising events.[13] As a side benefit, the process of completing research together, along with underscoring records management procedures with colleagues, can serve as a mutual learning opportunity between the museum archives and development departments, as well as keeping the lines of communication and collaboration flowing.

Collaborating with the Library and Allied Departments

Depending on how an archives is positioned within the larger museum, collaborating with a library, special collections division, and/or allied departments, such as registration or conservation, may be possible. The archivist would also be well served to create a "wish list" of giving opportunities alongside a yearly budget to identify budgetary shortfalls and areas where supplemental income could support special projects and initiatives.[14] Part of the planning process should involve determining which opportunities are appropriate for the archives to pursue. In large institutions, more than one department may be interested in approaching a common funder, such as the National Endowment for the Humanities or the Institute of Museum and Library Services (IMLS), during a given funding cycle. If the archivist is interested in applying to a grant program, checking with the development staff well in advance of the next grant cycle is in good form, so as not to submit competing proposals.[15]

With that said, departments should be able to collaborate on many levels. For example, open houses for donor groups can shed light on the complementary work of allied departments and how additional resources can help advance common causes. A collaborative grant could enable the museum archives to partner with another department and work with a vendor, such as an on-site digitization service. Specific campaigns could be geared toward promoting a shared resource, such as endowing a study center for an archives and library, which would provide mutual benefit and help make a philanthropist's gift go even farther.

Donor Cultivation

As already mentioned, partnering with the development department, given its responsibility in stewarding donors on behalf of the parent institution, is important.[16] Development staffers are well positioned to identify individuals who may be interested in supporting the archives and projects that can advance the department's programs.[17] Museum archivists and development colleagues can cultivate donors through outreach events with an educational component, such as behind-the-scenes tours, exhibitions, and special lectures on historical topics. The archivist could organize a field trip to a related institution to provide perspective beyond the immediate context and enable donors to see a successful initiative that colleagues have realized and create a vision for future implementation on home turf.

FIGURE 14.2. Philadelphia Museum of Art staff standing on the steps of the Perelman Building, demonstrating a creative way to say "thank you" to Ray Perelman, the benefactor who generously provided funds to purchase the building with his wife, Ruth. PHOTO BY JASON WIERZBICKI.

Another strategy for cultivating relationships is to complete oral histories with trustees and donors. The connection and rapport that develop during the time spent together is difficult to re-create, and an interview offers a unique opportunity to get to know a potential donor intimately. If nothing else, even if they choose not to donate, an informative interview can be added to the museum archives.[18]

After a relationship has been cultivated, the next step with a donor is solicitation.[19] In concert with the development staff, the archivist might set up a private meeting, a luncheon, or a visit to their home. A donor could be potentially interested in providing funds for a specific cause or donating their papers to the museum archives. The archivist should research these possibilities ahead of time and be prepared for both scenarios. Requesting funds with the donation of a collection to ensure its processing, conservation, and/or digitization is also possible.[21]

As the process of making an "ask" begins, fund-raising requests should be balanced with good manners and proper etiquette. Beyond the common courtesy of a timely response and follow-up, the archivist should thank donors frequently, both in person and in writing (hence the oft-repeated rule to thank donors at least seven times).[22] Philanthropists donate for a variety of reasons: to do good in the community, to support causes they believe in, and to be acknowledged for making a difference. A museum archivist's role is to provide the acknowledgments, both privately in one-on-one interactions and publicly in meetings, presentations, and publications.[23] All expressions of gratitude are appreciated, even by the shyest and most unassuming donor. Credit lines should be carefully noted and used consistently in conjunction with a funded project, space, or program. Privacy should also be respected if the donor chooses to remain anonymous, and the details of their gift should only be shared with colleagues on a need-to-know basis.[24]

Another corollary to good donor relations is to keep appropriate documentation. Just as development departments keep files about specific funders,

> "The most effective fund-raising technique is one person asking another to give. Most of us are very uncomfortable doing this, but in my experience, if you believe in what you are doing, it works extremely well. I frequently have turned to friends or family of donors for support, often with a promise to provide half of the funding from internal sources so that the donors know I am committing resources to the effort."
>
> –Ben Primer[20]

Susan Anderson

museum archivists will be well served by maintaining documentation about each gift and grant solicited and all related communications. Reviewing such files before a donor interaction helps to keep their information in mind as possible gifts or projects are discussed. While this activity could be seen as somewhat mercenary, most donors appreciate—even expect—fundraisers to know such details and tailor a funding request to the issues they care about. Making a personal investment in a donor relationship is much like being involved with colleagues in the development department. These people have the ability to connect resources with a repository's funding needs. Keeping allies in the loop and enlisting their support can be beneficial on multiple levels, such as requesting an outright gift or the donation of a collection, and/or advocating on a museum archivist's behalf with fellow donors and trustees. Sending regular progress reports about a project their gift or grant has made possible is another vital feature of any archivist/donor relationship.[25] Keeping a donor apprised of positive developments is a good way to keep in touch, assure them that their funds are being well managed, and potentially pave the way for future support.[26]

> "For any archives, the prime subjects of advocacy are most often decision makers within the larger organization. But identifying and developing advocates outside the organization to help influence these internal decision makers usually is helpful, and it may be the only way for some archives to obtain some important objectives. External supporters can help in other ways, as well. For example, they can make financial gifts and grants, provide in-kind contribution and technical assistance, offer access to potential donors of collections, facilitate media relations, introduce the archives to their peers and to organizations that might help the archives, and influence other external decision makers and supporters."
> –Audray Bateman Randle[27]

Friends Groups

Friends groups for a museum archives, library, and/or special collections department can be another way to create support for programs. Rather than

> "The relationship of the Friends to the repository must be made clear to everyone from the outset. Those who govern the Friends must understand that the policy, operation, and management of the repository is *not* their responsibility, but that of the director. The director, in turn, must do all that is necessary to assure the Friends that the group is making a valuable contribution to the repository. The Friends board, with guidance from the director, will make decisions about meetings of the organization, fund raising, spending money that will be raised, special events and projects, and membership dues and benefits."
> –Larry J. Hackman[28]

relying on a major "ask" for one philanthropist or grant agency to fulfill, the desired funding amount is distributed among a group of people committed to the work of the department and advocating for its causes. Friends groups can provide a collective benefit, and their contributions can range from paying annual dues, usually on a sliding scale, to making individual donations. While such groups can provide funding for general operating expenses, capturing people's interest with potential acquisitions, processing plans, or digitization projects can help with projects that could benefit from focused support. Another aspect of working with these groups includes annual meetings to display the results of their generosity, such as new acquisitions or processed collections. Newsletters and blog postings are other ways to keep friends groups apprised of the museum archives' efforts.[29]

While a general "friends" group may provide unrestricted annual support for the museum at large, an institution may be receptive to creating other friends groups dedicated to a specific department, if branding, events, and messaging can be kept straight.[30]

Advisory Boards

An advisory board or departmental committee is another way to deepen the involvement of a group of committed individuals, often trustees of a museum, who have a higher level of interest and dedication to the archives. An advisory board is more formally structured than a friends' group and may play a more proactive role by funding ambitious projects and lending greater support to a department's activities in general.[31]

Given this higher degree of involvement, care should be taken in appointing members, with the understanding that advisory board members will provide advice and advocacy as opposed to directly administering the museum archives—the same caution extended to friends' groups.[32] Rules and regulations may already be in place at the home institution if other departmental committees are active. The archivist should follow the existing policies, often established by museum governance, rather than reinvent the wheel. These guidelines have been established for good reason, and speaking with a consistent message to trustees and higher-level donors who may serve on more than one committee is important. Clearly defined expectations will ensure appropriate engagement for all parties and should be communicated by senior management, another constituency usually included on such boards.

An advisory board usually requires regular yearly donations, which are typically on a higher tier than the dues requested for a friends' group. Regular meetings are also part of this traditional structure; staff presentations and progress reports can demonstrate the benefits of their support and keep board members interested and involved with the progress of the department. Wish lists can be compiled, based on specific needs for projects, acquisitions, supplies, and/or conservation treatments. Larger funding requests can also be made for special projects, such as implementing a digital asset management system. As a result, more ambitious programming can be realized, albeit with a greater investment of staff time, effort, and involvement with the selected group of advisers.[33]

Foundations and Grants

Grant-giving agencies operate on a number of levels, such as entities providing funding on behalf of the federal government, like the National Historical Publications and Records Commission, which is part of the National Archives and Records Administration.[34] Grant organizations operate on the state level as well, such as the Pennsylvania Historical and Museum Commission, along with large private funders, such as the Andrew W. Mellon Foundation.[35] Across the United States, nearly 100,000 independent foundations exist, each with its own geographic focus, mission, grant-writing guidelines, and requirements for fiscal management.[36]

While applying for grant funding can seem like an intimidating process, thinking of a grant proposal as a business plan can help. At the heart of each proposal is a plan of work—what the archives plans to do with the funding—supported by a narrative to substantiate the applicant's fitness for support. This will describe the significance of the collections, the importance of the project, the respectability of the standards to be employed, and the expertise of the staff committed to doing the work. Other sections lay out an accurate and realistic assessment of costs in the budget (including a portion of cost-sharing or matching funds, to demonstrate an investment of resources on the institution's part), as well as the long-term viability and sustainability of the project.[37] In this day and age, funders consider the ongoing costs of digital preservation, as well as how to aggregate assets and resources to benefit more than one institution—going beyond the enhancement of a single collection as a limited information silo—and throw their weight behind projects that promote collaboration and/or serve as models for similar institutions, if not entire communities.[38]

Regardless of the scale of a project, whether within a repository, a collaboration between two, or on a consortial level, finding a good match with a foundation is key, even if it will take repeated attempts and refinement of a proposal to eventually secure funding. The archivist should remember that some funding agencies receive hundreds of requests during a grant cycle. To ensure that a proposal will make the first cut, the archivist should carefully research possible grant organizations and select a program that is the most appropriate for the project.[39] Even within a single funding organization, such as the IMLS, there are multiple categories.[40] The archivist should first meet with a supervisor and other stakeholders to review strategic goals and see how a potential grant project could map onto the museum archives' priorities, schedule, collections, and staffing. They should also consult with a grant writer or liaison from the development department, who may know of an alternative agency or approach that would be a more appropriate fit for the project and might also partner with the archives staff on the writing and/or submission process.

Another aspect of preparing a funding proposal is to develop appendixes or support information. The review panels at grant organizations are sticklers for detail, and they expect applicants to do their homework and provide accurate estimates for everything to be done in a project, such as the linear feet to be processed, the number of items to be digitized, costs for supplies, and fees for consultants. Doing sufficient research and survey work is important here, so the archivist can speak authoritatively about the details of the project and explain exactly what needs to be done to make collections fully accessible to researchers. This information must be made consistent throughout the proposal, which can be an issue if the survey work happens over time and/or when more than one person contributes to the narrative, which is sometimes the case. Just as donors can never be thanked enough, a grant proposal cannot be proofread too many times.[41]

Looking at similar proposals written by other institutions, which can sometimes be obtained through a colleague, is another helpful strategy. While recipients usually hesitate to share their budgets, given the confidential information relating to salaries, the narrative portion of a grant request can usually be shared. Reviewing successful proposals can provide many helpful insights, such as an optimal sequence of events in a work plan, or emerging standards that a colleague is choosing to follow. Informational interviews can also be useful, and, depending on the grant organization, speaking with a representative or program officer to get feedback on eligibility and projects that are more likely to be funded may be possible. A development colleague could also initiate the conversation and/or participate in a conference call with the museum archivist.

An additional useful approach, if the funder in question offers the opportunity, is to submit a proposal ahead of time for preliminary feedback. This input can help the archivist correct issues that may jeopardize the proposal, as well as provide information that may strengthen the case for funding. Circulating the proposal to other stakeholders who may be involved in the project, such as the library and information technology departments, is also a good idea, especially if they will be contributing staff time to an institutional match (i.e., in-kind costs), or if the museum archives will be drawing on some aspect of their technical expertise and/or infrastructure with a digital project.[42]

As far as categories of grants are concerned, obtaining a planning grant or seed money before making a request for full implementation funding may be possible. While this approach will lengthen the timeline of an overall project, when embarking on a major initiative without much experience in an area and/or when the preparations will exceed what is reasonable to expect during a normal grant-writing period, then investigating the possibility of a planning grant is worthwhile. If it is an option, the archivist can approach the entity that will eventually fund full implementation, because sometimes a preliminary investment can work in favor of subsequent funding (i.e., initial support would not be provided if the funder didn't think a project was worthwhile in the first place). Other organizations can be approached for seed money too, especially if their mission meshes well with the archives' planned preparatory work.[43]

> "As we look into the future at what we're going to fund, I think a trend you're going to see—and something that will be in the funding mix—is how will you come together as a collaborative unit? . . . We need to be . . . going in together and applying for funding with one voice and looking at the kind of impact we can have."
>
> –Lisa Peet[44]

Another type of grant funding to consider is a collaborative or consortial project, which could involve a group of organizations with a preexisting affiliation, such as the Philadelphia Area Consortium of Special Collection Libraries, or PACSCL (which includes museum archives), or a group of institutions that come together for a specific purpose, like the American Art Collaborative.[45] A consortial grant can provide a broad-based group benefit, which is appealing to certain funders and allows them to extend their reach of support beyond one institution. While this collaborative approach certainly has its benefits, including a more efficient use of resources, sharing project documentation between institutions, and aggregating complementary collection data online, the added complexity of working across institutions needs to be considered.

Usually, one entity has to step forward as the fiscal agent, which includes such duties as managing the grant funds, compiling and submitting reports to the funder, and assuming administrative responsibility for project staff. One or more participants, usually those responsible for writing the proposal, will also need to act as principal investigator(s) and oversee project activities across the consortium, as well as supervise the project staff. This can be a demanding role to play on top of regular job duties, so the responsibilities for various collaborators need to be clearly defined for the success of the project. Methods developed by the tech industry can be used to good advantage here, such as instant message and project management software to keep on top of the distributed teams and make sure that project goals are met according to schedule.[46]

Resources for grant writing include the information provided by foundations through their grant staffs and websites, as well as the perspectives of previous recipients. The Foundation Center is an excellent resource; it has an extensive website, as well as branches in New York, Atlanta, Cleveland, San Francisco, and Washington, DC.[47] Its Grantspace wiki is a helpful compendium of grant-related information.[48] The Society of American Archivists (SAA) also offers a day-long workshop on grant writing, as do many professional regional archives organizations.[49]

Endowments

Endowments are a way to facilitate long-term planning and security for a museum. They entail a major gift being made by a donor or foundation to an institution. The process is somewhat like establishing a trust fund within a nonprofit institution to provide ongoing support for a specific purpose. As with other fundraising scenarios enumerated in this chapter, the archivist best undertakes any discussion relating to a possible endowment with their supervisor and colleagues in the development department, as established policies and financial protocols will surely exist. An investment of this magnitude will likely need a special level of donor cultivation and close cooperation with everyone involved, including an institution's senior management team.[50]

Endowments can take many forms and include naming opportunities for a physical space, such as a reading room; purchase funds for future acquisitions; outreach programs for lectures and exhibitions; as well as fellowships and staff positions. After the initial investment, the fund may take some time to develop sufficient interest for the staff to draw upon it. Most museums have a board-approved spending formula for the annual draw. Working with colleagues in the finance department to track the balance and use of such funds ensures they are not overdrawn, diminishing the principal amount as a result.[51]

A museum archives might also participate in some larger endowment-related initiatives happening at a museum. For instance, in 2008, the Lenfest Challenge at the Philadelphia Museum of Art endowed the positions of twenty-nine employees at the institution, including the archives. The program was initiated by H. F. (Gerry) Lenfest, who was a major philanthropist and former chairman of the board, along with his wife, Marguerite. They offered to make a 50/50 matching gift to establish endowed positions at the museum. The naming opportunity for a position was given to the other donor, which created an extra incentive to participate.[52]

> "[Archivists] should be well versed in the motivations behind a donor's charitable giving as well as in the forces governing the nonprofit sector and all the giving and investment options at their disposal to help a donor achieve his or her philanthropic objectives. For just as our donors will profit from long-term strategies, so will libraries benefit from long-term development strategies that are unwavering in their goals and objectives but flexible enough to respond to the volatilities of a market economy. It is only by taking the same long view that philanthropists and the beneficiary libraries will share a vision that will insure long-term institutional growth and survival."
>
> –Lisa Browar and Samuel A. Streit[53]

Changing Landscape of Fundraising

The uncertain political environment of recent years has made advocacy more important than ever. Educational efforts undertaken by professional organizations, such as the American Library Association and SAA, and their members helped rally support and spread awareness of the high return of cultural enrichment for a small investment of taxpayers' money.[54] While developments with the federal budget will continue to evolve over time, fundraising professionals have been looking to other methods of bridging possible gaps in philanthropic giving, which were already being explored in the face of a competitive grant environment and the need to look for alternative funding sources.[55]

Along with an increased focus on private sector funding with individual donors and philanthropic groups, other approaches in the new funding landscape include submitting grant proposals to smaller community foundations and social venture partners, or "angel investors."[56] Some museum archives are looking to other options of bringing in needed support, such as online fundraising. Providing an online giving component is vitally important; it is one of the few areas where fundraisers are seeing growth.[57] Webpages can serve as pointers to different categories of an institution's giving program, complete with detailed descriptions and contact information, as well as provide the option of making contributions directly online.[58] Some museum archives also have fundraising pages devoted solely to their departments, such as the Cleveland Museum of Art's Ingalls Library and Museum Archives.[59] Adopting an archival collection is also an interesting trend—in the spirit of adopt-a-book programs—and can be applied to analog or digital archives.[60]

Other institutions are starting to explore crowdsourced fundraising to raise money for special projects. In some ways, this is analogous to friends' groups combining their resources to fund a particular cause; only in this case, the "friends" are coming together momentarily in a virtual context.[61]

As these trends continue to evolve, the foundational principles of fundraising are important to remember. Just as good archival practice is format-agnostic and high standards should apply to all records, the basic principles of strong policy framework, strategic planning, advocacy, careful research, partnering with development professionals, and maintaining a courteous and professional demeanor organically inform all fundraising opportunities. While a focused effort is necessary to engage with funders, this should be a logical extension of good management practice and will help an institution gain a better overall grasp of programs, collections, and projects than before. Enlisting the support of a community of interested donors is an excellent way to educate them on all aspects of the archival enterprise. Fundraising can be the ultimate form of outreach and advocacy, and, through the process of communication and making a personal investment—on both sides—a shared vision can develop, and opportunities that once seemed completely unattainable can be successfully realized.

Further Reading

Candid (formerly known as the Foundation Center). https://candid.org/, captured at https://perma.cc/B5HR-98ZH.

Hackman, Larry J., editor. *Many Happy Returns: Advocacy and the Development of Archives.* (Chicago: Society of American Archivists, 2011).

Hartsook, Herbert J. "By Fair Means If You Can: A Case Study of Raising Private Monies to Support Archival Programs." *Archival Issues* 25, no. 1 (2000): 49–56.

Hohmann, Judy. "Money Talk: An Introduction to Private Sector Fund Raising for Archives." In *Advocating Archives: An Introduction to Public Relations for Archivists*, edited by Elsie Freeman Finch. Metuchen, NJ: Society of American Archivists and Scarecrow Press, 1994, 23–37.

Primer, Ben. "Resources for Archives: Developing Collections, Constituents, Colleagues, and Capital." *Journal of Archival Organization* 7, nos. 1–2 (2009): 58–65.

NOTES

1. Richard J. Cox, *Managing Institutional Archives: Foundational Principles and Practices* (New York: Greenwood Press, 1992), 161.
2. Ben Primer, "Resources for Archives: Developing Collections, Constituents, Colleagues, and Capital," *Journal of Archival Organization* 7, nos. 1–2 (2009): 61–62.
3. "Code of Ethical Standards," Association of Fundraising Professionals, http://www.afpnet.org/Ethics/EnforcementDetail.cfm?ItemNumber=3261, captured at https://perma.cc/LB2R-8C8X.
4. Victoria Steele, "The Role of Special Collections in Library Development," in *Library Fundraising: Models for Success*, ed. Dwight F. Burlingame (Chicago: American Library Association, 1995), 77.
5. Bruce W. Dearstyne, *Leading the Historical Enterprise: Strategic Creativity, Planning and Advocacy for the Digital Age* (Lanham, MD: Rowman & Littlefield, 2015), 20–21.

6. Cox, *Managing Institutional Archives: Foundational Principles and Practices*, 175.

7. Judy Hohmann, "Money Talk: An Introduction to Private Sector Fund Raising for Archives," in *Advocating Archives: An Introduction to Public Relations for Archivists*, ed. Elsie Freeman Finch (Metuchen, NJ: Society of American Archivists and Scarecrow Press, 1994), 26.

8. Vanessa Chase-Lockshin, "How Nonprofits Can Steward More Donors with Stories," Association of Fundraising Professionals, http://www.afpnet.org/ResourceCenter/ArticleDetail.cfm?ItemNumber=38512, captured at https://perma.cc/JKS5-BXVA.

9. Museums Association, "Fundraising" (series of instructional essays), *Museum Practice*, no. 42, https://www.museumsassociation.org/museum-practice/fundraising, captured at https://perma.cc/U3WH-3QKE.

10. Lisa Browar and Samuel A. Streit, "Mutually Assured Survival: Library Fundraising Strategies in a Changing Economy," *Library Trends* 52, no. 1 (2003): 70.

11. Cox, *Managing Institutional Archives*, 176.

12. Cox, *Managing Institutional Archives*, 176.

13. Bernadette A. Lear, "The Hippest History: The Detritus of Your Library's Past Can Help with Your Present-Day Marketing, Fundraising, and Professional Pride," *Library Journal* 130, no. 9 (2005): 52–53.

14. Browar and Streit, "Mutually Assured Survival: Library Fundraising Strategies in a Changing Economy," 75–76.

15. Susan Klier Koutsky, "Getting Started," in *Museum Archives: An Introduction*, 2nd ed., ed. Deborah Wythe (Chicago: Society of American Archivists, 2004), 21.

16. "About 80%—or $4 out of every $5 contributed to charity—comes from individuals, not foundations or corporations. A lot of people don't realize how striking the balance is, and overestimate the role of grants. I've experienced this on the ground—in fact, with a library fundraising project—where the leadership wasn't thinking of their best prospect, a man who loved the library. When they asked him, he gave, but people don't give if we don't ask." Genevieve Richardson (grants manager at the Philadelphia Museum of Art), email message to author, July 25, 2018. This is aptly illustrated in "See the Numbers," Giving USA, https://givingusa.org/see-the-numbers-giving-usa-2018-infographic/, captured at https://perma.cc/5XZY-TU5Q.

17. Hohmann, "Money Talk: An Introduction to Private Sector Fund Raising for Archives," 31.

18. Herbert J. Hartsook, "By Fair Means If You Can: A Case Study of Raising Private Monies to Support Archival Programs," *Archival Issues* 25, no. 1 (2000): 52. Oral history in the museum archives context is described in detail in chapter 9 of this publication.

19. "Building Relationships with Donors: Identification, Cultivation, Solicitation and Stewardship" (training module), http://www.ala.org/advocacy/advleg/frontlinefundraising/buildingrelationships, captured at https://perma.cc/6PS6-4PEG.

20. Primer, "Resources for Archives: Developing Collections, Constituents, Colleagues, and Capital," 62–63.

21. "Capitalize on Collections Care," Heritage Preservation in partnership with Institute of Museum and Library Services, https://www.imls.gov/sites/default/files/publications/documents/caponcc_0.pdf, captured at https://perma.cc/SW9H-8ALN.

22. Michael Rosen, "Get More Repeat Gifts; the Rule of 7 Thank Yous," *Michael Rosen Says* (blog), https://michaelrosensays.wordpress.com/tag/rule-of-seven-thank-yous/, captured athttps://perma.cc/6Y72-6FD7.

23. Hohmann, "Money Talk: An Introduction to Private Sector Fund Raising for Archives," 34.

24. Association of Fundraising Professionals, "Code of Ethical Standards," https://afpglobal.org/ethics/code-ethics, captured at https://afpglobal.org/ethics/code-ethics.

25. "Fundraisers call this the BOY principle: Because of You. We are supposed to use this phrase often." Genevieve Richardson in an email to author, July 25, 2018.

26. Primer, "Resources for Archives: Developing Collections, Constituents, Colleagues, and Capital," 63–64.

27. Audray Bateman Randle, "Volunteers and Friends: Recruitment, Management, and Satisfaction," in *Advocating Archives: An Introduction to Public Relations for Archivists*, 96–97.

28. Larry J. Hackman, ed., *Many Happy Returns: Advocacy and the Development of Archives* (Chicago: Society of American Archivists: 2011), 20.

29. Randle, "Volunteers and Friends: Recruitment, Management, and Satisfaction," 96.

30. "I think in many cases these groups commit to annual support of the organization by, for example, maintaining a current membership, and then they give special dues in addition to that baseline support." Genevieve Richardson, email message to author, July 25, 2018.

31. Hartsook, "By Fair Means If You Can: A Case Study of Raising Private Monies to Support Archival Programs," 54.

32. Linda Henry, "Archival Advisory Committees: Why?," *American Archivist* 48, no. 3 (1985): 316–17, https://doi.org/10.17723/aarc.48.3.t00q46g24133rl13.

33. Henry, "Archival Advisory Committees: Why?," 318–19.

34. "National Historical Publications and Records Commission," National Archives and Records Administration, https://www.archives.gov/nhprc, captured at https://perma.cc/28HR-B5BB.

35. "Grants and Funding," Pennsylvania Historical and Museum Commission, https://www.phmc.pa.gov/Preservation/Grants-Funding/Pages/default.aspx, captured at https://perma.cc/ZK6S-ZKHF; "Grants," The Andrew W. Mellon Foundation, https://mellon.org/grants/, captured at https://perma.cc/8J5K-NTKR.

36. "Foundation Directory Online," Foundation Center, https://fconline.foundationcenter.org/, captured at https://perma.cc/P3X9-CRZD.

37. Primer, "Resources for Archives: Developing Collections, Constituents, Colleagues, and Capital," 64.

38. "Digitizing Hidden Special Collections and Archives," Council for Library and Information Resources, https://www.clir.org/hiddencollections/, captured at https://perma.cc/J39Q-SD2Z.

39. Koutsky, "Getting Started," 20–12.

40. "Apply for a Grant," Institute for Museum and Library Services, https://www.imls.gov/grants/apply-grant/available-grants, captured at https://perma.cc/LJG3-ZX88.

41. Primer, "Resources for Archives: Developing Collections, Constituents, Colleagues, and Capital," 64.

42. Both NEH and NHPRC offer the opportunity to submit a preliminary proposal for feedback.

43. The Conservation Center for Art and Historic Artifacts offers preservation needs assessments, subsidized by the National Endowment for the Humanities, which can be used for grant planning purposes. "Surveys and Consultations," Conservation Center for Art and Historic Artifacts, last modified 2018, https://ccaha.org/services/surveys-consultation, captured at https://perma.cc/GKX3-V99G.

44 Lisa Peet, "The New Fundraising Landscape: Budgets and Funding," *Library Journal* (January 6, 2016), https://www.libraryjournal.com/?detailStory=the-new-fundraising-landscape-budgets-funding, captured at https://perma.cc/WT7T-ZHUX.

45 "PACSCL Projects," Philadelphia Area Consortium of Special Collection Libraries, http://pacscl.org/pacscl-projects, captured at https://perma.cc/5JQV-6FCK; "About the AAC," American Art Collaborative, http://americanartcollaborative.org/about/, captured at https://perma.cc/VQV7-LB35.

46 This approach is being taken by the Duchamp Research Portal project, which is a collaboration between the Philadelphia Museum of Art, the Association Marcel Duchamp, and the Centre Pompidou. The project is being funded by the National Endowment for the Humanities, the Delmas Foundation, the Women's Committee of the Philadelphia Museum of Art, and the Museum's Library and Archives Committee.

47 The Foundation Center, http://foundationcenter.org, captured at https://perma.cc/FS2Q-UQEX.

48 "Grantspace," The Foundation Center, https://grantspace.org, captured at https://perma.cc/2YZ4-BWDD.

49 "Grant Proposal Writing," Society of American Archivists, last modified 2018, https://www2.archivists.org/prof-education/course-catalog/grant-proposal-writing, captured at https://perma.cc/RD2L-ZMDX.

50 Carol Norris Vincent, "Creating and Building Endowments for Small Museums" (1997), http://download.aaslh.org/AASLH-Website-Resources/IHS-CreatingAndBuildingEndowments.pdf, captured at https://perma.cc/KHR3-APJU.

51 Vincent, "Creating and Building Endowments for Small Museums."

52 "Philadelphia Museum of Art Raises $54M to Endow 29 Key Staff Positions," Philadelphia Museum of Art, December 18, 2013, https://philamuseum.org/press/releases/2013/994.html, captured at https://perma.cc/9TME-CH6S.

53 Browar and Streit, "Mutually Assured Survival: Library Fundraising Strategies in a Changing Economy," 85.

54 "Issue Brief: Federal Funding for Archives," Society of American Archivists, https://www2.archivists.org/statements/issue-brief-federal-grant-funding-for-archives, captured at https://perma.cc/PQT8-MJ7U.

55 Peet, "The New Fundraising Landscape: Budgets and Funding," 1.

56 Peet, "The New Fundraising Landscape: Budgets and Funding," 4.

57 "Online Giving to Nonprofit Organizations Reaches a Record High in 2016," Association of Fundraising Professionals (March 1, 2017), http://www.afpnet.org/Audiences/ReportsResearchDetail.cfm?ItemNumber=42552, captured at https://perma.cc/93BG-HQ7C.

58 For instance, the "Support" section on the New-York Historical Society Museum and Library's website is a good example, https://www.nyhistory.org/support, captured at https://perma.cc/8Y48-BCZW.

59 "Support the Library and Archives," http://www.clevelandart.org/join-and-give/why-support-the-museum/scholarship/support-the-library, captured at Cleveland Museum of Art, https://perma.cc/8DF8-AES4.

60 "Adopt a Digital Collection," Duke University Libraries, last modified July 13, 2018, https://library.duke.edu/about/adopt-digital-collection, captured at https://perma.cc/5GHD-4VYL.

61 For further information and case studies, see cultural heritage technologist Mia Ridge's compilation for her online British Library course, "Resources for Crowdsourcing in Libraries, Museums and Cultural Heritage Institutions," last modified June 2016, https://www.miaridge.com/resources-for-crowdsourcing-in-libraries-museums-and-cultural-heritage-institutions/, captured at https://perma.cc/4KG2-CM9P.

15 ARCHIVAL VALUES IN MUSEUMS

Melissa Gonzales, Dawn Sueoka, and
Susan Hernandez

Museums, like other cultural and educational institutions, are intertwined with the social, cultural, political, and economic forces that shape our lives. Indeed, these forces have shaped museums—and consequently what they have historically collected, whom they have admitted, and which perspectives they have represented—since their very beginnings. Museums and their archives often confront legacies of colonialism, a lack of diversity, and paternalistic histories. Marjorie Schwarzer, a museum scholar and educator, writes that the typical late nineteenth-century museum ". . . was a place for the elite and privileged to teach the nation's working men and women what it meant to be cultured, civic-minded Americans."[1] Furthermore, as Dr. Johnnetta Betsch Cole, director of the National Museum of African Art, Smithsonian Institution, put it in her keynote address to the 2015 American Alliance of Museums (AAM) Annual Meeting, "When we look back at the history of American museums, we see that they were products of and reflections of the political, economic and social times."[2]

This is the context in which museum archivists work. Decisions archivists make on a daily basis, whether what to acquire, what to make available to the public, how to describe and represent archival collections, or how to engage with user communities, may have far-reaching implications that can ultimately help museums become more fair and equitable stewards of the collections entrusted to them. So, how should museum archivists proceed? In addition to relying on their professional training and considering practical circumstances like their institutional context, what moral or ethical concerns should they take into account?

Museum archivists, like other archivists and museum professionals, are guided by core values and codes of ethics adopted by a variety of professional organizations.[3] These statements are useful resources to museum archivists while they navigate the complex issues that arise in their work and can serve as frameworks for constructively questioning and critically examining established practice. This chapter will discuss the ethics of access restrictions, privacy, and staffing, and will consider diversity of museum archives collections and staff in the context of the traditional influences that have historically shaped the perspectives, audiences, and collections of museums.

Access and Privacy

SAA CORE VALUES OF ARCHIVISTS: ACCESS AND USE

Archivists promote and provide the widest possible accessibility of materials, consistent with any mandatory access restrictions, such as public statute, donor contract, business/institutional privacy, or personal privacy. Although access may be limited in some instances, archivists seek to promote open access and use when possible.[4]

SAA CODE OF ETHICS FOR ARCHIVISTS: PRIVACY

As appropriate, archivists place access restrictions on collections to ensure that privacy and confidentiality are maintained, particularly for individuals and groups who have no voice or role in collections' creation, retention, or public use. Archivists promote the respectful use of culturally sensitive materials in their care by encouraging researchers to consult with communities of origin, recognizing that privacy has both legal and cultural dimensions.[5]

Museums are charged with the stewardship of cultural heritage for the benefit of the public and therefore have a vested interest in maintaining public confidence through accountability and transparency.[6] In the last ten years, museums around the world have been making information about their collections, including images and metadata, more and more accessible.[7] Whether they use cultural heritage information for the purposes of analysis, creative work, scholarship, or play, users are increasingly coming to expect high levels of access to museum collections.

Museum archivists similarly support accountability, transparency, and public service, as well as user expectations regarding access, by making museum records in their care as accessible as possible. Yet, museum archivists are also obligated to respect the privacy of individuals, the proprietary and security interests of the museum, and the intellectual property rights of artists and others whose work may appear in archival records.[8] Museum archivists must also take into consideration the concerns of Indigenous groups whose traditional cultural expressions (TCE) and traditional knowledge (TK) may be documented in archival collections.[9] Thus, decisions about access can sometimes be highly charged. Indeed, "access to records can have important political consequences," archivist and professor Randall Jimerson writes. "The archivist plays an essential role in mediating conflicting interests of researchers, donors, and third parties. This is not a passive or neutral position."[10]

In the sections that follow, the factors that affect access to museum records will be explored, and practical solutions for providing access to those records will be discussed. Careful management of legal, ethical, cultural, and institutional concerns can mitigate risk, promote scholarly dialogue, and ensure that the museum archives is perceived as a trustworthy repository with the expertise and capacity to administer access to its present and future collections equitably.[11]

FIGURE 15.1. Researchers in the newly redecorated reading room of the Robert Allerton Library, November 9, 1956. HONOLULU MUSEUM OF ART ARCHIVES (PHOTO: RAYMOND SATO).

Institutional Considerations and Commonly Restricted Record Types

Certain categories of museum records have traditionally been restricted to protect the museum's assets, its relationships, its reputation, and its strategic position. Additionally, records are sometimes restricted to protect the privacy of the individuals named in them, whether they be donors, museum officials, or other groups. Though privacy is defined as the right of a living individual to be "left alone," it is perhaps more clearly explained in terms of what constitutes an invasion of privacy: intrusion into one's solitude, public disclosure of embarrassing private facts, misrepresentation, and appropriation of one's name or likeness.[12] Information commonly considered private includes facts about a living individual that would be regarded as "highly offensive to a reasonable person," employment information, medical information, financial records, educational records, Social Security numbers, credit card numbers, passwords, research data identifying the subjects of a study, and select traditional knowledge and traditional cultural expressions of Indigenous communities.[13] Furthermore, externally collected materials such as manuscripts and special collections could include correspondence or other documents that contain intimate details about individuals and organizations.[14]

Restrictions may also be based on whether the museum is a public, private, or hybrid institution—a designation dependent on funding. For example, the records of a museum solely funded by the public through tax dollars are subject to state and/or federal open records laws. A critical examination of historically restricted museum record types follows, with suggested strategies for balancing institutional privacy with greater access. Best practice requires archivists to consult with their institutions' legal counsel when determining what materials to restrict and when drafting policy around them.

Board of Trustees Records

Board meeting minutes and associated materials likely contain information considered by the museum to be sensitive or proprietary as they may reference property negotiations, acquisitions, capital projects, compensation and other personnel decisions, financial decisions, and strategic initiatives and projects. Yet, these records document many of the most consequential and visible decisions affecting the museum and its communities. Most potentially sensitive information contained in these records becomes less sensitive over time, particularly as decisions, policies, and projects are enacted or completed and become public knowledge. The museum archivist should weigh the research value of the records against the potential risk of disclosing sensitive information and consider opening board records for research after sufficient time has elapsed, for example, twenty-five, thirty, forty, or fifty years from creation.[15] Once records are opened for research, the archives may still reserve the right to restrict portions of them—such as items relating to personnel issues, for example—provided that these restrictions are justified, documented, and administered equitably.

Director's Records

Director's records, like board records, document the museum's decisions and activities at the highest levels, and therefore have significant research value. At the same time, they are likely to contain sensitive or protected information relating to finances, personnel matters, litigation, restitution claims, and ongoing relationships and projects. Taking into consideration both risk and research value, the museum archivist should consider treating these records similarly to board of trustees records, opening them after a prescribed number of years and reserving the right to continue to restrict select records that remain sensitive even after this time period has elapsed.

Records Revealing the Monetary Value of Objects in the Collection

Valuations and prices are often embedded in many of the most frequently accessed and historically significant records in a museum archives: exhibition records, loan records, directors' papers, and curatorial files. Yet, revealing the financial history surrounding purchases and gifts of artwork can negatively impact their market value, as well as the institution's relationships with dealers and artists. Restricting entire swaths of records to keep historical valuations confidential would render much of the associated materials inaccessible. Neither is redaction a practical strategy, as the ubiquity of this information would make that work prohibitively time consuming for most museum archivists. As such, archivists may consider restricting only current values, most of which would be found in active records not yet transferred to the archives, or in recently transferred materials not yet processed and accessible to researchers.

Conservation Reports

Conservation reports are often incorporated into museum object files, which the archives does not typically manage. Nevertheless, copies may make their way into the archives via exhibition files, loan files, registrar's files, grant files, curatorial files, and conservation department files. Information contained in these records could be used to create counterfeit objects or otherwise compromise the security or value of objects.[16] These records may also contain information about materials, techniques, or historical repairs that is critical to understanding the complex history of an object. As always, the archivist is urged to consult with colleagues and museum counsel when weighing the likelihood of a potential forgery or theft against the research value of the records and should consider opening these files when the information contained therein no longer poses a significant risk.

Architectural Records

Museum buildings and grounds are often architecturally significant, and the associated design records have great research potential for users. Some design records, however, could jeopardize the safety of visitors, staff, and collections if they were to fall into the hands of thieves or other bad actors. Archivists should work with security and operations staff to identify which records might be appropriate to open for access and which to restrict. For example, the museum archives might make accessible conceptual drawings, presentation drawings, landscaping plans, drawings of unrealized additions, and drawings depicting publicly accessible spaces because they have high research value and pose little security risk to the institution. Conversely, they may restrict systems and security plans, as well as drawings of vaults and other nonpublic spaces, as that information has little research value but presents significant risk if disclosed.[17]

Donor and Development Records

Donor and development records most certainly contain private information about individuals, such as contact information, personal financial information, and information about donors wishing to remain anonymous. They also likely contain information that the museum would prefer to keep confidential to protect its strategic position and ongoing relationships, such as solicitation lists of individuals and corporate sponsors, internal strategy documents, and amounts paid for different types of funding opportunities. Records may also contain sensitive information relating to the settling of estates. That said, museum funding is a topic of legitimate public interest, especially with regard to how funding sources may or may not affect exhibitions, programming, and hiring. Museum archivists will want to exercise caution given these reasons, but access should be granted to public-facing documents, such as literature prepared for fundraising campaigns, widely distributed solicitations, published reports, and federally and state-mandated disclosures. Archivists should consult with colleagues in development, finance, and legal departments to keep abreast of changing legislation and to determine restrictions for other types of records in this category.

Personnel Records

Personnel records contain information that, if disclosed, would constitute an invasion of a living individual's privacy. This may include personally identifying information, medical information, grievances, salaries (in private institutions), performance reviews, and investigative information.[18] With the exception of dates of employment, job titles, and materials intended for public dissemination, personnel information is typically restricted at least until the death of the staff member, or destroyed in accordance with the institution's records schedule.[19]

Legal Records

Legal records, such as correspondence with attorneys, research files, notes, strategies, and drafts of reports, may be restricted to protect the privacy of the museum and also to comply with regulations relating to attorney-client privilege and attorney work product.[20] Collections being used as legal exhibits may need to be restricted for the duration of the case. Destruction of records—both paper and digital—must also be halted during ongoing litigation to ensure that no potentially admissible materials are destroyed before a case is resolved.

Expressions of Indigenous Knowledge

Indigenous communities may consider some records in museum archives confidential, sensitive, or sacred. These include, but are not limited to, still and moving images; recordings; transcripts; cartographic materials that document sacred sites, ceremonies, burials and funerals; religious or sacred objects; songs and chants; genealogies; community histories; and folklore.[21] Documentary records such as these were typically created by non-Indigenous researchers and deposited in museums without the knowledge or consent of the communities documented.[22] An institutional commitment to building and sustaining reciprocal relationships with Indigenous communities, as well as an understanding of Indigenous systems of knowledge, are essential for museums seeking Indigenous partnerships in identifying, preserving, interpreting, and providing access to expressions of Indigenous knowledge.[23] For more information on this topic, see chapter 16.

Email

Appraisal of email accounts is a complicated endeavor due to the sheer volume of messages comprising them, and the high potential for the presence of personal information increases its complexity. To manage this issue, museum employees should be educated on the email capture process at their time of hire and upon their separation from the institution at minimum and encouraged to manage their email as it is created, isolating personal correspondence whenever possible. Museum archives staff might go a step further and collaborate with human resources staff to develop a form, which employees could sign at their time of hire, describing the process of retaining emails in the archives in detail.[24]

Noninstitutional Collections

Gifts of special collections to the museum archives require additional considerations. The terms of an acquisition should always be guided by a deed of gift; most legal language in deeds of gift clearly dictates the opportunity to transfer copyright of the materials from the donor to the archives, in addition to outlining the caretaking responsibilities promised by the archives as a result of the donation. The deed of gift presents an opportunity for the museum

---

GUARDING INSTITUTIONAL AND PERSONAL PRIVACY DURING EMAIL PRE-APPRAISAL

In 2016–2017, the Solomon R. Guggenheim Museum Archives, through research sponsored by the Metropolitan New York Library Council (METRO) Fellowship program, developed workflows and procedures for the capture and archiving of museum staff email.[25] The resulting set of recommendations advocates for the annual export of significant department-level correspondence, as well as a select group of staff accounts.

An ethical concern was identified during email appraisal however: reviewing the contents of staff emails while an individual is still employed—or even shortly after their departure—could reveal sensitive information about active projects. Additionally, although employees are informed upon hire that their emails are property of the institution, personal messages can inevitably become intermixed with work messages.

To address this without viewing the emails directly, museum archivists conduct regular interviews with museum employees to capture contextual metadata about the collected correspondence. Employees are asked about their role at the museum, the projects they have worked on over the past year, the newsletters they subscribe to, and the personal contacts (e.g., spouse, dentist) they correspond with whose messages should not be archived. Collecting this data will assist in identifying privacy issues in staff email prior to capture and will also aid future appraisal by highlighting important professional contributions as well as identifying information for potential restriction or redaction.

archivist to discuss with the donor potential restrictions on the materials, the transfer of copyright of the materials to the archives, and issues of privacy.[26]

Taking the time to review the deed of gift in detail and discuss restrictions will assure the donor that the museum archivist will protect their privacy while providing access to their collection. Restrictions on collections imposed by donors are often governed by timeframes, such as until death, a set number of years after death, or until the death of a spouse or family member. An ideal deed of gift would include no restrictions, but sometimes this is not possible; the museum archivist should strive for an agreement that allows as few restrictions as possible.[27]

Legal Considerations

The Freedom of Information Act, the Privacy Act of 1974, the Family Educational Rights and Privacy Act, the Health Insurance Portability and Accountability Act, the European Union's General Data Protection Regulation, and the Federal Policy for the Protection of Human Subjects, which governs research conducted on human subjects, are federal regulations that identify categories of protected information and define criteria for exemptions. They generally hold that individuals have the right to know what information an organization maintains about them and prohibit organizations from disclosing that information to third parties without the consent of the individual. Even in cases where these laws may not directly apply to records in the museum archives—private institutions, for example, are not subject to Freedom of Information Act requests—their principles, provisions, classifications, restriction terms, and exemptions can provide a useful reference point when crafting and providing justification for access and other archival policies.[28]

Access Strategies

As noted, providing access to records inevitably carries some degree of risk.[29] Indeed, an archivist's goal is not to avoid or eliminate risk but to manage it. A reasonable, mission-aligned collections access policy tailored to the institution and approved by the museum's administration and legal counsel is the best way to balance access with the need to protect private and other sensitive information. For more on access policies, see chapter 7.

Being realistic about the capacity of the museum archives to administer any proposed restrictions is important. For example, suggesting that only fully processed collections be open to the public when few collections are processed and staffing levels are inadequate to address processing backlogs is not a feasible way to administer access. For most institutions, equally unrealistic is for the museum archivist to examine collections item by item to redact insurance valuations or purchase prices. In cases like these, temporarily closing groups of records that likely contain private or confidential information may make more sense, opening them only after a certain amount of time has elapsed, as previously detailed, at which point, any sensitive information is potentially less damaging.[30]

Internal researchers—that is, staff—in museum archives, as in other institutional archives, commonly have a higher degree of access to records. For example, unprocessed collections may be closed to the public but accessible to staff members in the course of their work for the museum; records containing information about donors may be accessible only to the development department, or to other staff whose duties necessitate regular access to that information.[31] Providing different levels of access in this way is often an effective means to meet the research needs of the museum archives' different constituencies.

Diversity

SAA CORE VALUES OF ARCHIVISTS: DIVERSITY

Archivists collectively seek to document and preserve the record of the broadest possible range of individuals, socio-economic groups, governance, and corporate entities in society. . . . They work actively to achieve a diversified and representative membership in the profession.[32]

Moving toward inclusion, diversity, equity, and social justice in museums and archives is complicated and nuanced, and a comprehensive treatment of the topic is beyond the scope of this publication.[33] However, the following sections outline possibilities for a way forward for museum archivists. Rose

Paquet Kinsley and Aletheia Wittman, founders of incluseum.com, a website dedicated to inclusion in museums, propose three broad first steps to museums, which demonstrate how the museum archives can provide valuable support to its parent institution: confronting institutional legacies, examining museum staffing, and evaluating the use of language.[34] Following discussions of these three points, the chapter will turn to strategies for diversifying museum archives collections.

Institutional Legacies

Kinsley and Wittman list several questions that can assist a museum wishing to understand how its institutional legacy influences current interactions with communities: "Who are my museum founders? Where did their money come from? Where did the collections come from. . . . What does my museum not have in its collections and why? Did my museum practice active exclusion during, for example, the Jim Crow era? How else has my museum maintained practices over the years that reinforce service to some groups over others? Today, who are the authors of the stories that my museum tells?"[35] That some view museums with mistrust is more understandable, they contend, when that mistrust is viewed in its historical context. Furthermore, they write, "Museums' desires to form inclusive relationships with their communities cannot be disassociated from the relationship they had in the past. Even if that history predates everyone on staff, we must educate ourselves and make amends for them today."[36] If museums choose to take this self-reflective path, their archives will be vital partners. As keepers of the institution's history, museum archivists are uniquely positioned to understand the motivations of its founders and the history of whom it has and has not historically served or represented. Records such as correspondence of the museum's leaders, internal documents relating to the production of programming, and many others can be used to study topics such as who has historically been included in and excluded from museum activities like exhibitions and collecting and to help shed light on the motivations behind the museum's decisions and actions.[37] Archivists should also be prepared to consider the historical—and current—role of the archives itself in representing a museum's complicated and sometimes problematic history.

Staffing and Diversity, Equity, and Inclusion Initiatives

Curatorial, education, conservation, and leadership staff of most museums and archives are homogenous.[38] SAA and AAM have recognized and articulated the need to diversify along intersecting lines of race, class, sexual orientation and gender expression, and disability.[39] Moving from statements to action, however, requires self-reflection, commitment, and work. As columnist Anna Holmes writes, the word "diversity" has become so ubiquitous that it "has become both euphemism and cliché, a convenient shorthand that gestures at inclusivity and representation without actually taking them seriously."[40] In other words, contending that diversity is important while not taking meaningful action to achieve it can be seen as self-serving and devalues any future use of the word. Consequential and sustainable diversity, equity, and inclusion (DEI) initiatives require museums to critically examine structural issues—such as unpaid internships, low wages, ableism, and institutional legacies of racism and colonialism—that have excluded people from the profession.

Low salaries are a significant impediment to diversification. As part of their proposed self-assessment for museums, Kinsley and Wittman urge them to "ponder the role of intersecting privileges, such as race and class, in determining who works and studies in the field."[41] For example, someone without financial security has difficulty choosing to work in a field that requires high levels of education and yet pays relatively low wages. Furthermore, completion of graduate education and entry into the profession often require internships, which may be unpaid, a problem discussed later in greater depth. To help address these systemic inequities, museum archivists should advocate for competitive salaries and benefits, wage transparency, and paid internships. Archivists can advocate for greater wage equity with support from their professional organizations such as the Society of Southwest Archivists, which does not accept job advertisements that do not include a salary range.

Since its inception in 1990, the Americans with Disabilities Act has served to prohibit discrimination against individuals with disabilities across all areas of life, in addition to ensuring institutions make their facilities more physically accessible for this group of people.[42] Museum archivists acting as hiring managers should also provide equal opportunities to applicants with disabilities by creating reasonable accommodations and by eliminating job requirements that exclude these individuals, such as requiring archivists to be able to lift at least forty pounds.[43] In 2019, SAA Council approved a proposal to create the Accessibility and Disability Section, whose microsite provides many resources for those with disabilities and their allies, in addition to promoting intersectionality.[44] For instance, "Guidelines for Accessible Archives for People with Disabilities" covers eliminating harmful stereotypes, respecting privacy and boundaries, and factoring accessibility into all facets of institutional spaces, policies, and services.[45]

Museums can welcome and support LGBTQ+ staff by expressing public support for LGBTQ+ campaigns and initiatives, actively recruiting LGBTQ+ employees, providing equitable benefits to LGBTQ+ individuals and their families, and ensuring safe access to appropriate restrooms. The AAM LGBTQ Alliance's 2019 "Welcoming Guidelines for Museums" identifies benchmarks based on AAM National Standards of Excellence.[46] AAM's Taskforce for Transgender Inclusion has created resources that provide guidance for transitioning individuals, coworkers and allies, and institutions.[47]

Indeed, inclusion efforts do not end at the point of hire. Requiring cultural competency training for all staff, ensuring that diverse perspectives are represented at all decision-making levels, supporting professional development, providing advancement opportunities, and changing institutional culture are additional ways in which museums can demonstrate an institutional commitment to inclusion and help staff to thrive and excel.[48]

Unfortunately, many museums rely heavily on their staff who are Black, Indigenous, and/or People of Color (BIPOC) to serve on or lead DEI groups, placing them in precarious, hostile situations when they must already negotiate white fragility and microaggressions daily.[49] Additionally, expecting BIPOCs to lead this endeavor when they already work and live in spaces with a history of colonialism steeped in white supremacy generates an immense amount of invisible emotional labor.[50] If institutions desire a healthy, diverse profession and wish to promote retention among BIPOCs, it is highly recommended that leadership hire a skilled third-party facilitator to direct DEI initiatives and training.

Whether they are acting as hiring managers, supervisors, internship advisers, or simply colleagues and allies, museum archivists can support coworkers across the museum and advocate for greater equity within the institution. Diversity in staffing is, after all, not an end in itself, but rather a step toward transformation.[51]

Language

Language is a powerful tool. As Kinsley and Wittman write, "We are at an exciting moment in the museum field, in which a host of individuals are interrogating how commonly used words reinforce exclusion or distract us from its root causes."[52] Evaluating the use of language in museum archives descriptive tools, an approach some libraries and archives are already embracing, is one way for museum archivists to employ their knowledge to help their museums with DEI efforts.[53] In 2018, Karen Smith-Yoshimura, a senior OCLC program officer, summarized a discussion held by the OCLC Research Library Partnership Metadata Manager Focus Group. She noted that metadata managers agree that implicit bias exists in standard library and archives descriptive metadata. The group agrees that "Our metadata is currently created according to Western Knowledge constructs, and our systems have been designed around them."[54] Acknowledging that description is not neutral, sharing the actions the archives will take—and the resources the archives will consult— to identify and either change or contextualize harmful descriptions and providing a means for researchers to contact the archives when they encounter something potentially problematic are some of the steps that archivists can take to begin to address the issue of bias in descriptive language.[55]

Diversifying Collections

Museum archivists should consider ways to make their collections more diverse and inclusive, and to actively contribute to museum-wide efforts to the same effect. Dominique Luster, Teenie Harris archivist at the Carnegie Museum of Art, writes, "In its simplest terms, the selection of certain records over others is an assertion of power, and these decisions affect our history by uplifting or silencing certain individuals and groups over others."[56] Furthermore, archivist Randall Jimerson argues that archivists should proactively seek out records that will most equitably document society.[57] Research shows that many libraries and archives are already taking steps to this effect. A 2017 OCLC Research survey found that 79 percent of respondents had changed collection building activities as a result of their parent organization's DEI efforts.[58]

Institutional museum archivists may find such diversification challenging, although nontraditional approaches to appraisal such as documentation strategy offer possibilities.[59] Institutional museum archivists may want to consider why some areas of museum work are more fully documented than others. For example, some vital museum functions, such as custodianship of museum buildings, art handling, and security may not be represented in the archival record. Collecting records of these functions, or creating documentation through programs such as oral histories, could establish a more equitable collection and provide future researchers interested in museum work or other related topics with important documentation.

Museum archives that collect externally can look to the wider landscape of archival scholarship to find strategies to diversify their collections. For example, Valerie Love and Marisol Ramos suggest working to regain the trust of communities that may view institutions like museums with suspicion; being willing to reconsider established collection development and arrangement and description practices; recognizing that all individuals—including archivists—have multiple, shifting identities; and engaging communities as partners in the documentation and interpretation of their stories as ways to begin this work.[60]

Focusing collecting efforts for external collections on current records is another strategy. Recognizing that not all individuals will save materials or accrue collections that find their way to a repository, some museums have begun "rapid response collecting," where curators attend events as they are happening to solicit the donation of objects and materials.[61] Collaborating with colleagues at the museum, such as curators or educators who may already have established helpful relationships, could assist with thoughtful diversification efforts for the archives' collections.

Interns and Volunteers

Both the museum and archival professions have histories of utilizing interns and volunteers, and museum archivists routinely manage both types of workers. Internships and volunteer positions can be extremely rewarding and beneficial to the individual as well as to the institution. However, to ensure that interns and volunteers are treated appropriately, ethical questions must be addressed. For example: What are appropriate duties for interns and volunteers? Is it ethical to offer unpaid internships?

Several key differences exist between interns and volunteers, including the duration of the relationship with the institution, expectations regarding tasks and assignments, and compensation.[62] An intern is usually a student who works for a limited amount of time on a distinct project, is seeking supplemental experience to theoretical coursework, and, ideally, is paid for their work. Volunteers, on

FIGURE 15.2. Image of an intern digitizing the Hebrew Immigrant Aid Society (Boston) records. JEWISH HERITAGE CENTER AT NEW ENGLAND HISTORIC GENEALOGICAL SOCIETY.

the other hand, can work for an organization indefinitely, knowingly engaging in unpaid work that provides personal satisfaction. Thus, assignments for interns and volunteers should vary greatly as the former is receiving professional-level experience that will make them more proficient, and the latter is providing charitable services that are not expected to enhance a professional knowledge base. For example, an appropriate project for an intern would be helping to process a collection, which provides arrangement and description experience, whereas a volunteer might assist with data entry, a task that is not the equivalent of vocational training.[63]

BEST PRACTICES FOR WORKING WITH INTERNS

Successful internship relationships should be reciprocal and balanced; to assure a mutually beneficial relationship, museum archivists should be aware of best practices for interns.[64]

- Provide interns with a clear understanding of the work they will be expected to perform and what criteria will be used to evaluate their performance.
- Be sure to create projects that will fit into the required timeframe. Many internships are intended to be performed within one semester, so project management will play a large role.
- Intern projects should be designed with the understanding that the intern should benefit from the opportunity.
- A high level of supervisory engagement is associated with positive student outcomes. Holding regular meetings with interns will help ensure expectations are met on both sides by allowing for any adjustments that need to be made along the way.
- If the intern is not associated with a program that requires the host repository to fill out an evaluation, creating one for interns will provide insight into your management process and ultimately help future internships.

Museum archivists should be aware of several issues regarding intern compensation. Although unpaid internships are not necessarily more readily available to wealthy individuals than to others, the nature of the system excludes lower-income students and graduates who cannot afford to work for free.[65] Second, unpaid interns do not qualify for the benefits legally available to paid employees, such as federal protections against discrimination and harassment and protection under the Civil Rights Act, which may put them at risk for unfair treatment.[66] Finally, some contend that unpaid internships devalue archival work. For example, information studies scholars Marika Cifor and Jamie A. Lee suggest that using unpaid internships to counter a lack of funding for professional staff members establishes "an unstable, often short-term workforce and the perception thereby that archives' needs have been met and at a low cost means that such conditions of deprivation can easily become the new status quo. This puts the long-term survival of archives at risk, which challenges the archival paradigm of long-term preservation and historical importance."[67] In other words, archivists should be careful not to replace permanent paid positions with intern labor, as doing so could compromise the ability of the archives to appropriately steward its collections. SAA's *Best Practices for Internships* echoes this concern by stating, "Given the value of archives work and the skills possessed by archives graduate students, interns should receive compensation (in the form of academic credit or a stipend) for their work commensurate with the qualifications required for the position. Graduate internships without any form of compensation should be rare to avoid devaluing the professional nature of archival work."[68] Given these concerns, museum archivists should advocate for paid internships. Information science professional Karly Wildenhaus notes that employers can undertake several additional strategies including developing an "Intern Bill of Rights" and elevating internship job titles to reflect paid status such as "Paid Intern," or "Grant-Funded Intern."[69]

Funding for interns is competitive in the museum environment. As part of a strategy to secure appropriate internship funding, museum archivists should familiarize themselves with any museum-wide internship initiatives at their institutions. Working closely with colleagues in charge of recruiting and coordinating interns can help museum archivists secure and manage these opportunities while ensuring that the museum archives is contributing to the work of its parent institution in the same way as other departments. Advocating for paid internship funding is also an opportunity for museum archivists to articulate the potential intern's contributions—and thus the archives'—to the overall mission and strategic goals of the institution.

Conclusion

Museums, as reflections of the social, political, racial, and economic tensions of the times, are in the midst of a period of reckoning and transformation.[70] Archivists can lead during this time, advocating for greater access to institutional records, thereby helping the museum to acknowledge its history and past practices with honesty and transparency. Archivists can also lead by example, embodying equity, fairness, and care in the way they work with collections, staff, interns, volunteers, and researchers. Codes of ethics, along with professional literature and discussions in both formal and informal spaces, can serve as a guide and a basis for such advocacy within the museum. This difficult but necessary work will ultimately help museums to become true community partners and more equitable, empathetic, and generative civic spaces.

Further Reading

Behrnd-Klodt, Menzi L., and Christopher J. Prom, editors. *Rights in the Digital Era*. Trends in Archives Practice Series. Chicago: Society of American Archivists, 2015.

Caldera, Mary, and Kathryn Neals, editors. *Through the Archival Looking Glass: A Reader on Diversity and Inclusion*. Chicago: Society of American Archivists, 2014.

Kowalsky, Michelle, and John Woodruff. *Creating Inclusive Library Environments: A Planning Guide for Serving Patrons with Disabilities*. Chicago: ALA Editions, 2017.

Ng, Wendy, Syrus Marcus Ware, and Alyssa Greenberg. "Activating Diversity and Inclusion: A Blueprint for Museum Educators as Allies and Change Makers." *Journal of Museum Education* 42, no. 2 (2017): 142–54.

Paquet Kinsley, Rose, and Aletheia Wittman, "Bringing Self-Examination to the Center of Social Justice Work in Museums." *American Alliance of Museums Blog*. http://ww2.aam-us.org/docs/default-source/resource-library/bringing-self-examination-to-the-center-of-social-justice-work-in-museums.pdf?sfvrsn=0, captured at https://perma.cc/5B7G-5A8X.

NOTES

1 Marjorie Schwarzer, *Riches, Rivals, and Radicals: 100 Years of Museums in America* (Washington, DC: American Association of Museums, 2006), 3.

2 Johnnetta Cole, "Museums, Diversity, & Social Value" (keynote address to the American Alliance of Museums' Annual Meeting, 2015), https://aamd.org/our-members/from-the-field/johnnetta-cole-museums-diversity-social-value, captured at https://perma.cc/A7YS-KZ82. See also the work of La Tanya S. Autry at http://artstuffmatters.wordpress.com; La Tanya S. Autry and Mike Murawski at #MuseumsAreNotNeutral; and the work of Aletheia Wittman and Rose Paquet Kinsley at http://incluseum.com.

3 Although this chapter will focus on the core values and code of ethics approved by the Society of American Archivists (SAA), those published by the American Alliance of Museums (AAM), and other allied organizations such as the International Council on Archives, the American Library Association, and the College Art Association are also relevant. See American Alliance of Museums, "Code of Ethics for Museums," https://www2.archivists.org/statements/saa-core-values-statement-and-code-of-ethics, captured at https://perma.cc/LE57-N6JG; Society of American Archivists, "Core Values Statement and Code of Ethics," https://www2.archivists.org/statements/saa-core-values-statement-and-code-of-ethics, captured at https://perma.cc/LBP2-TCHB; International Council on Archives, "Code of Ethics," https://www.ica.org/sites/default/files/ICA_1996-09-06_code%20of%20ethics_EN.pdf, captured at https://perma.cc/79AG-5AWY; American Library Association, "Professional Ethics," http://www.ala.org/tools/ethics, captured at https://perma.cc/88E7-DN5W; College Art Association, "CAA Guidelines," http://www.collegeart.org/standards-and-guidelines/guidelines, captured at https://perma.cc/B577-E6LM.

4 Society of American Archivists, "Core Values Statement and Code of Ethics."

5 Society of American Archivists, "Core Values Statement and Code of Ethics."

6 According to AAM's "Code of Ethics," "Museums in the United States are grounded in the tradition of public service. They are organized as public trusts, holding their collections and information as a benefit for those they were established to serve.... Museums and those responsible for them must do more than avoid legal liability, they must take affirmative steps to maintain their integrity so as to warrant public confidence"; according to AAM's "Characteristics of Excellence," "The museum is committed to public accountability and is transparent in its mission and its operations," http://www.aam-us.org/resources/ethics-standards-and-best-practices/characteristics-of-excellence, captured at https://perma.cc/T58R-SLQZ.

7. For example, by sharing 375,000 images under a Creative Commons Zero license in 2017, the Metropolitan Museum of Art joined the British Library, the National Gallery of Art, LACMA, the Getty, the Walters Art Museum, the Penn Museum, and others that have together made hundreds of thousands of high-resolution images freely available for public use.

8. Sarah S. Hodson, "In Secret Kept, In Silence Sealed: Privacy in the Papers of Authors and Celebrities," in *Privacy and Confidentiality Perspectives Archivists and Archival Records*, ed. Menzi L. Behrnd-Klodt and Peter J. Wosh (Chicago: Society of American Archivists, 2005), 145.

9. "Archivists promote the respectful use of culturally sensitive materials in their care by encouraging researchers to consult with communities of origin, recognizing that privacy has both legal and cultural dimensions." Society of American Archivists, "Code of Ethics for Archivists," https://www2.archivists.org/statements/saa-core-values-statement-and-code-of-ethics#code_of_ethics, captured at https://perma.cc/HPR5-L7UY.

10. Randall C. Jimerson, *Archives Power: Memory, Accountability, and Social Justice* (Chicago: Society of American Archivists, 2009), 348.

11. Christopher A. Lee and Kam Woods, "Automated Redaction of Private and Personal Data in Collections, in *Conference Proceedings of the Memory of the World in the Digital Age: Digitization and Preservation* (Vancouver, BC: UNESCO, 2012).

12. Gary M. Peterson and Trudy Huskamp Peterson, *Archives & Manuscripts: Law* (Chicago: SAA, 1985), 40.

13. William L. Prosser, "Privacy," *California Law Review* 48, no. 3 (1960): 383; Ben Goldman and Timothy D. Pyatt, "Security without Obscurity: Managing Personally Identifiable Information (PII) in Born-Digital Archives," *Library and Archival Security* 26, nos. 1–2 (2013): 37–55; Kay Mathiesen, "A Defense of Native Americans' Rights over Their Traditional Cultural Expressions," *American Archivist* 75, no. 2 (2012): 473–81, https://doi.org/10.17723/aarc.75.2.0073888331414314; First Archivist Circle, *Protocols for Native American Archival Materials*, http://www2.nau.edu/libnap-p/protocols.html, captured at https://perma.cc/D8JW-W7HV. SAA endorsed the Protocols as an external standard of the organization on August 13, 2018; the Association of College and Research Libraries endorsed the Protocols in early 2020.

14. For more information about privacy concerns in manuscript collections, see Hodson, "In Secret Kept, In Silence Sealed, 131–48.

15. "Board of Trustees records in another repository," SAA Museum Archives Section mailing list discussion, October 27–28, 2015.

16. Susan K. Anderson, "Research Use: Ethics, Restrictions, and Privacy," in *Museum Archives: An Introduction*, ed. Deborah Wythe (Chicago: Society of American Archivists, 2004), 58.

17. Maygene Daniels, "Architectural Records," in *Museum Archives*, 159.

18. Peterson and Huskamp Peterson, *Archives & Manuscripts: Law*, 41.

19. Society of American Archivists, Museum Archives Section, "Access Policies," "Standards and Best Practices Resource Guide," https://www2.archivists.org/groups/museum-archives-section/standards-best-practices-resource-guide, captured at https://perma.cc/4GBK-ST4L.

20. Attorney-client privilege protects confidential communications (communications not intended to be disclosed) between an attorney or an attorney's staff and the client. To disclose privileged materials, the client's consent is needed, though no agreement exists on the duration of such privilege. Attorney work product privilege protects "mental impressions, analyses, strategies, conclusions, opinions, legal theories, research, and investigations prepared by the lawyer or third parties in contemplation of litigation." Menzi L. Behrnd-Klodt and Christopher J. Prom, eds. *Rights in the Digital Era*, Trends in Archives Practice Series (Chicago: Society of American Archivists, 2015), 151–60.

21. First Archivists Circle, "Protocols for Native American Archival Materials."

22. Jennifer R. O'Neal, "'The Right to Know': Decolonizing Native American Archives," *Journal of Western Archives* 6, no. 1, (2015); see also Linda Tuhiwai Smith, *Decolonizing Methodologies: Research and Indigenous Peoples*, 2nd ed. (London: Zed Books, 2012.).

23. For more on Indigenous knowledge organization, see Sandra Littletree, Miranda Belarde-Lewis, and Marisa Duarte, "Centering Relationality: A Conceptual Model to Advance Indigenous Knowledge Organization Practices," *Knowledge Organization* 47, no. 5, 410–26. The American Philosophical Society, the Autry Museum of the American West, and the Smithsonian Institution's National Anthropological Archives are among the institutions that are incorporating elements of the Protocols into management of archival collections. See Brian Carpenter, "Archival Initiatives for the Indigenous Collections at the American Philosophical Society," SAA Case Studies on Access Policies for Native American Archival Materials, February 2019, https://www2.archivists.org/sites/all/files/Case_1_Archival_Initiatives_for_Indiginous_Collections.pdf, captured at https://perma.cc/A8U9-3MVD; Diana E. Marsh, Robert Leopold, Katherine Crowe, Katherine S. Madison, "Access Policies for Native American Archival Materials in the National Anthropological Archives, Smithsonian Institution," SAA Case Studies on Access Policies for Native American Archival Materials, October 2020, https://www2.archivists.org/sites/all/files/Case_3_Access_Policies_for_Native_American_Archival_Materials.pdf, captured at https://perma.cc/S2WP-42TK; Karimah Kennedy Richardson, Anna Liza Posas, Lylliam Posadas, and Paige Bardolph, "New Discoveries and New Directions for the Archaeological Archives at the Autry Museum of the American West," *Advances in Archaeological Practice* 5, no. 3 (2017): 280–88; Brian Carpenter, Caitlin Haynes, Diana Marsh, Liza Posas, Ricky Punzalan, Gina Rappaport, and Melissa Stoner, "Providing Culturally Responsive and Ethical Access to Indigenous Collections," *Archival Outlook* (May/June 2019): 4–5, 21.

24. Care should be taken to restrict or redact personally identifiable information before providing access to email. Tools have been developed to assist with redaction and access. For example, ePADD uses archivist-built taxonomies to flag messages for sensitive content. "ePADD," Stanford Libraries, https://library.stanford.edu/projects/epadd, captured at https://perma.cc/ZZF3-75JZ.

25. Tali Han, Jenny Korns, and Katherine Martinez generously provided background for this case study.

26. Society of American Archivists, "Notes on Copyright, Restrictions, and Unprocessed Collections," https://www2.archivists.org/usingarchives/notesoncopyright, captured at https://perma.cc/X8T8-2KDQ.

27. Creating a privacy and confidentiality checklist that the archivist and the donor can work through together during the acquisition process is a prudent way to ensure the needs of the repository are met while making the donor as comfortable as possible. For an example checklist prepared for archivists acquiring born-digital materials, see Gabriela Redwine et al., "Born Digital: Guidance for Donors, Dealers, and Archival Repositories," *CLIR Publication* no. 159 (October 2013): 25–26, https://www.clir.org/wp-content/uploads/sites/6/pub159.pdf, captured at https://perma.cc/9JKH-VY5J.

28 For more information, see Behrnd-Klodt and Prom, eds. *Rights in the Digital Era*; Peterson and Huskamp Peterson, *Archives & Manuscripts: Law*; International Federation of Library Associations and Institutions, "General Data Protection Regulation: What Do the New EU Rules Mean for Libraries?," webinar, https://www.ifla.org/node/36104, captured at https://perma.cc/BC26-JMD2; and Diane E. Kaplan, "The Stanley Milgram Papers: A Case Study on the Appraisal of and Access to Confidential Data Files," *American Archivist* 59, no. 3 (1996): 288–97, https://doi.org/10.17723/aarc.59.3.k3245057x1902078.

29 Goldman and Pyatt, "Security," 8.

30 Anderson, "Research Use," 58.

31 SAA Museum Archives Section, "Access Policies."

32 SAA, "Core Values Statements and Code of Ethics." The American Alliance of Museums also explores ideas about inclusivity and diversity, as well as other topics, through the Center for the Future of Museums, and many museums have released statements or policies on diversity and inclusion. Just a few examples include the Science Museum of Minnesota, "Statement on Equity and Inclusion," https://www.smm.org/equity, captured at https://perma.cc/26S2-BNYR; the Cleveland Museum of Art, "Diversity, Equity and Inclusion Plan," http://www.clevelandart.org/diversity-equity-and-inclusion-plan, captured at https://perma.cc/DD6U-SYM8, and the Minneapolis Institute of Art, "Inclusion, Diversity, Equity, and Accessibility Policy," https://new.artsmia.org/about/diversity-and-inclusion-policy, captured at https://perma.cc/633S-QX4T.

33 A good resource to begin with is the *Museum as Site for Social Action Toolkit* (2017), https://static1.squarespace.com/static/58fa685dff7c50f78be5f2b2/t/59dcdd27e5dd5b5a1b51d9d8/1507646780650/TOOLKIT_10_2017.pdf, captured at https://perma.cc/R5WS-2MV6.

34 Rose Paquet Kinsley and Aletheia Wittman, "Bringing Self-Examination to the Center of Social Justice Work in Museums," *Museum* (January/February 2016), http://ww2.aam-us.org/docs/default-source/resource-library/bringing-self-examination-to-the-center-of-social-justice-work-in-museums.pdf?sfvrsn=0, captured at https://perma.cc/5B7G-5A8X.

35 Kinsley and Wittman, "Bringing Self-Examination to the Center of Social Justice Work in Museums."

36 Kinsley and Wittman, "Bringing Self-Examination to the Center of Social Justice Work in Museums."

37 In 2019, the Museum of Modern Art published *Among Others: Blackness at MoMA*, an examination of the museum's history with regard to acquiring and presenting the work of Black artists. See Carolina A. Miranda, "How One Art Museum Has Reckoned with Race and Its Past," *Los Angeles Times*, October 22, 2020, https://www.latimes.com/entertainment-arts/story/2020-10-22/how-one-art-museum-has-reckoned-with-race-and-its-past, captured at https://perma.cc/Z5AF-LSKS.

38 An Andrew W. Mellon Foundation Art Museum Staff Demographic survey found that 84 percent of curators, conservators, educators, and leadership in American art museums identified as non-Hispanic white. Roger Schonfeld and Mariet Westermann, "The Andrew W. Mellon Foundation Art Museum Staff Demographic Survey" (2015), https://mellon.org/media/filer_public/ba/99/ba99e53a-48d5-4038-80e1-66f9ba1c020e/awmf_museum_diversity_report_aamd_7-28-15.pdf, captured at https://perma.cc/3FWS-RDWJ. A 2004 survey of archivists in the United States found that 87.7 percent of the profession identified as white and 7 percent indicated that they identified as nonwhite and belonged to one or more minority ethnic or racial groups. Victoria Irons Walch, Elizabeth Yakel, Jeannette Allis Bastian, Nancy Zimmelman, Brenda Banks, Susan E. Davis, and Anne P. Diffendal, "Special Section on A*CENSUS (Archival Census & Education Needs Survey in the United States)," *American Archivist* 69, no. 2 (2006): 333, https://doi.org/10.17723/aarc.69.2.d474374017506522.

39 See American Alliance of Museums, "Diversity, Equity, Accessibility and Inclusion," https://www.aam-us.org/programs/diversity-equity-accessibility-and-inclusion/, captured at https://perma.cc/WW4R-KCX6; and Society of American Archivists, "SAA Statement on Diversity, Equity, and Inclusion," https://www2.archivists.org/statements/saa-statement-on-diversity-equity-and-inclusion, captured at https://perma.cc/J93K-TGZW.

40 Anna Holmes, "Has 'Diversity' Lost Its Meaning?," *The New York Times Magazine*, November 1, 2015, https://www.nytimes.com/2015/11/01/magazine/has-diversity-lost-its-meaning.html, captured at https://perma.cc/J52H-4KHG.

41 Kinsley and Wittman, "Bringing Self-Examination to the Center of Social Justice Work in Museums." See also Alyssa Greenberg and Nina Pelaez, "Unsafe Ideas: Building Museum Worker Solidarity for Social Justice," *Center for the Future of Museums Blog*, June 2, 2015, https://www.aam-us.org/2015/06/02/unsafe-ideas-building-museum-worker-solidarity-for-social-justice, captured at https://perma.cc/4WNM-LTUJ.

42 For more information regarding the Americans with Disabilities Act, see ADA National Network, "What Is the Americans with Disabilities Act (ADA)?," https://adata.org/learn-about-ada, captured at https://perma.cc/Q5A5-ZFNM.

43 Bridget Malley, Lydia Tang, Chris Tanguay, and Zachary Tumlin, "Toward Inclusion: Best Practices for Hiring People with Disabilities," *Archival Outlook* (July/August 2020): 4.

44 Society of American Archivists, "Accessibility & Disability Section," https://www2.archivists.org/groups/accessibility-and-disability-section, captured at https://perma.cc/LRR3-5LVB.

45 Society of American Archivists, Accessibility & Disability Section, "Recommended Resources," https://www2.archivists.org/groups/accessibility-and-disability-section/recommended-resources, captured at https://perma.cc/5SDK-E9VA.

46 American Alliance of Museums, "Welcoming Guidelines for Museums," https://www.aam-us.org/wp-content/uploads/2019/05/2019-Welcoming-Guidelines.pdf, captured at https://perma.cc/3MN6-ZSDV.

47 These resources, which acknowledge that every individual's situation is different, include background information and vocabulary, plans for transitioning at work or supporting transitioning employees, sample scripts for situations like being misgendered or accidentally misgendering someone, and guidelines on using gender-inclusive language across the institution. American Alliance of Museums, "Resources," https://www.aam-us.org/professional-networks/lgbtq-alliance/resources, captured at https://perma.cc/FR3N-8FUB.

48 Joseph Gonzales, Nicole Ivy, Porchia Moore, Rose Paquet Kinsley, and Aletheia Wittman, "Michelle Obama, 'Activism,' and Museum Employment Part 3," The Incluseum, November 6, 2015, https://incluseum.com/2015/11/06/michelle-obama-activism-museum-employment-part-iii/, captured at https://perma.cc/SVD6-WLX2. For more information on cultural competency, see the work of Helen Wong Smith; see also Ellen Engseth, "Cultural Competency: A Framework for Equity, Diversity, and Inclusion in the Archival Profession in the United States," *American Archivist* 18, no. 2 (2018): 460–82, https://doi.org/10.17723/0360-9081-81.2.460.

49 We Here (www.wehere.space) is one organization working to create safe and supportive spaces for BIPOC library workers and students to collaborate, support each other, and seek mentorship. Much has been written about white fragility across many disciplines. Just a few resources include Jessica Caporuscio, "Everything You Need to Know about White Fragility," *Medical*

News Today, June 12, 2020, https://www.medicalnewstoday.com/articles/white-fragility-definition, captured at https://perma.cc/74TZ-REVP; Robin DiAngelo, *White Fragility: Why It's So Hard for White People to Talk about Racism* (Boston: Beacon Press, 2018); Melanie A. Adams, "Deconstructing Systems of Bias in the Museum Field Using Critical Race Theory," *Journal of Museum Education* 42, no. 3 (2017): 290–95. For more on microaggressions, see Andrew Limbong, "Microaggressions Are a Big Deal: How to Talk Them Out and When to Walk Away," NPR, June 9, 2020, https://www.npr.org/2020/06/08/872371063/microaggressions-are-a-big-deal-how-to-talk-them-out-and-when-to-walk-away, captured at https://perma.cc/9FBL-5S87.

50 Porchia Moore, "Cartography: A Black Woman's Response to Museums in the Time of Racial Uprising," The Incluseum, June 10, 2020, https://incluseum.com/2020/06/10/cartography-a-black-womans-response-to-museums-in-the-time-of-racial-uprising, captured at https://perma.cc/F3BL-K27S; and Theresa Suico, "Emotional Labor and Women of Color in the Workplace: A Reality Check," City of Portland, Oregon, May 29, 2018, www.portlandoregon.gov/article/686010, captured at https://perma.cc/TJA3-LMF5. For more on white supremacy in museums, see Mike Murawski, "Interrupting White Dominant Culture in Museums," Art Museum Teaching: A Forum for Reflecting on Practice, May 31, 2019, https://artmuseumteaching.com/2019/05/31/interrupting-white-dominant-culture, captured at https://perma.cc/D69P-7TCA.

51 Sara Ahmed, *On Being Included: Racism and Diversity in Institutional Life* (Durham: Duke University Press, 2012), 17, quoted in Wendy Ng, Syrus Marcus Ware, and Alyssa Greenberg, "Activating Diversity and Inclusion: A Blueprint for Museum Educators as Allies and Change Makers," *Journal of Museum Education* 42, no. 2 (2017): 142–54. For more on inclusion in museums, see Laura-Edythe Coleman, *Understanding and Implementing Inclusion in Museums* (Lanham, MD: Rowman & Littlefield, 2018).

52 Kinsley and Wittman, "Bringing Self-Examination to the Center of Social Justice Work in Museums."

53 A 2017 OCLC Research report found that 55 percent of respondents "have changed metadata descriptions in archival collections due to their institutions' EDI goals and principles." Karen Smith-Yoshimura, "Creating Metadata for Equity, Diversity, and Inclusion," *Hanging Together: The OCLC Research Blog*, November 7, 2018, http://hangingtogether.org/?p=6833, captured at https://perma.cc/HPZ8-Z59Q. See Christine Bone et al., "Decolonizing Descriptions: Finding, Naming and Changing the Relationship between Indigenous People, Libraries and Archives," an OCLC Works in Progress Webinar, for a discussion of efforts to modify description to fit with EDI efforts, https://www.youtube.com/watch?v=w4HGdWx2WY8, captured at https://perma.cc/4BL7-PM4W.

54 Smith-Yoshimura, "Creating Metadata for Equity, Diversity, and Inclusion."

55 For examples of statements from museum archives about potentially harmful language in archival description, see Philadelphia Museum of Art, "Ethical Cataloging Statement," https://philamuseum.libguides.com/c.php?g=929979&p=7463787, captured at https://perma.cc/8AWL-TJ5B; and Presbyterian Historical Society, "Digital Collection Offensive Language Policy," https://digital.history.pcusa.org/dig_collection_offensive_lang_policy, captured at https://perma.cc/8RYR-YDYD. For examples of statements and policies from academic libraries, see Stanford Libraries, "Stanford Special Collections and University Archives Statement on Potentially Harmful Language in Cataloging and Archival Description," https://library.stanford.edu/spc/using-our-collections/stanford-special-collections-and-university-archives-statement-potentially, captured at https://perma.cc/6XGP-U6JS; Temple University Libraries, "SCRC Statement on Potentially Harmful Language in Archival Description and Cataloging," https://library.temple.edu/policies/scrc-statement-on-potentially-harmful-language-in-archival-description-and-cataloging, captured at https://perma.cc/L335-NYYZ; and Drexel University, "Statement on Harmful Content in Archival Collections," https://www.library.drexel.edu/archives/overview/HarmfulContent/, captured at https://perma.cc/T9AD-3Z2H. See also Archives for Black Lives in Philadelphia, "Anti-Racist Description Resources," https://archivesforblacklives.files.wordpress.com/2019/10/ardr_final.pdf, captured at https://perma.cc/PH3T-UTLA.

56 Dominique Luster, "Archives Have the Power to Boost Marginalized Voices," *Archival Outlook* (November/December 2018): 10.

57 Randall Jimerson, "Embracing the Power of Archives," *American Archivist* 69, no. 1 (2006), 25, https://doi.org/10.17723/aarc.69.1.r0p75n2084055418.

58 OCLC Research, "Equity, Diversity, and Inclusion in the OCLC Research Library Partnership Survey," https://www.oclc.org/research/themes/community-catalysts/rlp-edi.html, captured at https://perma.cc/Z67M-6UY2.

59 Information on documentation strategy can be found in chapter 5.

60 Valerie Love and Marisol Ramos, "Identity and Inclusion in the Archives: Challenges of Documenting One's Own Community," in *Through the Archival Looking Glass: A Reader on Diversity and Inclusion*, ed. Mary Caldera and Kathryn Neals (Chicago: Society of American Archivists, 2014), 1–22. See also Mark Greene, "Into the Deep End: One Archivist's Struggles with Diversity, Community, Collaboration, and Their Implications for Our Profession," in the same volume.

61 For an example, see Graham Bowley, "In An Era of Strife, Museums Collect History as It Happens," *The New York Times*, October 1, 2017, https://www.nytimes.com/2017/10/01/arts/design/african-american-museum-collects-charlottesville-artifacts.html, captured at https://perma.cc/5PMC-FZS2. For an example of a community-driven archives, see the University of North Carolina's Southern Historical Collection at https://library.unc.edu/wilson/shc/community-driven-archives, captured at https://perma.cc/AWS8-3HXF.

62 See US Department of Labor Wage and Hour Division, "Fact Sheet #71: Internship Programs under the Fair Labor Standards Act," January 2018, https://www.dol.gov/whd/regs/compliance/whdfs71.htm, captured at https://perma.cc/X7ZY-MYBQ, which "provides general information to help determine whether interns and students working for 'for-profit' employers are entitled to minimum wages and overtime pay under the Fair Labor Standards Act (FLSA)." A footnote adds, "Unpaid internships for public sector and non-profit charitable organizations, where the intern volunteers without expectation of compensation, are generally permissible." See also Jordan Weissmann, "The Court Ruling that Could End Unpaid Internships for Good," *The Atlantic*, June 12, 2013, https://www.theatlantic.com/business/archive/2013/06/the-court-ruling-that-could-end-unpaid-internships-for-good/276795/, captured at https://perma.cc/88UB-PNBK.

63 For guidance on the appropriate use of volunteers, in contrast to interns, see Society of American Archivists, "Best Practices for Volunteers," 2014, https://www2.archivists.org/sites/all/files/BestPract-Volunteers.pdf, captured at https://perma.cc/DSW9-FXKS.

64 For a review of literature on internships, as well as lists of factors associated with positive student outcomes, see Matthew T. Hora,

Matthew Wolfgram, and Samantha Thompson, "What Do We Know about the Impact of Internships on Student Outcomes?" (Center for Research on College-Workforce Transitions, Wisconsin Center for Education Research, University of Wisconsin–Madison, September 2017), http://ccwt.wceruw.org/documents/CCWT-report-Designing-Internship-Programs.pdf, captured at https://perma.cc/RC2S-FUKQ. See also Jeannette Bastian and Donna Webber, *Archival Internships: A Guide for Faculty, Supervisors, and Students* (Chicago: Society of American Archivists, 2008).

65 Blair Hickman, "What We Learned Investigating Unpaid Internships," ProPublica, July 23, 2014, https://www.propublica.org/article/what-we-learned-investigating-unpaid-internships, captured at https://perma.cc/GZ3Q-RCTB; and Phil Gardner, "The Debate Over Unpaid College Internships," Intern Bridge, https://citeseerx.ist.psu.edu/viewdoc/download?doi=10.1.1.372.1710&rep=rep1&type=pdf, captured at https://perma.cc/4NNH-VCK8.

66 Karly Wildenhaus, "Wages for Intern Work: Denormalizing Unpaid Positions in Archives and Libraries," in "Evidences, Implications, and Critical Interrogations of Neoliberalism in Information Studies," ed. Marika Cifor and Jamie A. Lee, special issue, *Journal of Critical Library and Information Studies* 2, no.1 (2019): 8.

67 Marika Cifor and Jamie A. Lee, "Towards an Archival Critique: Opening Possibilities for Addressing Neoliberalism in the Archival Field," *Journal of Critical Library and Information Studies*, no. 1 (January 2017): 13.

68 Society of American Archivists, "Best Practices for Internships as a Component of Graduate Archival Education," https://www2.archivists.org/sites/all/files/BestPract-Internships.pdf, captured at https://perma.cc/W2SM-N4FX. Museum archivists should be aware of the ongoing debate about the ethics of receiving course credit in exchange for completing an internship, which essentially entails the intern paying a college or university to work for no monetary compensation. For a summary of the issues involved in this debate, see Ellen Wexler, "Paying to Work," *Inside Higher Ed*, May 17, 2016, https://www.insidehighered.com/news/2016/05/17/when-students-pay-tuition-work-unpaid-internships, captured at https://perma.cc/E799-PNSX; Association of Art Museum Directors, "Association of Art Museum Directors Passes Resolution Urging Art Museums to Provide Paid Internships," June 20, 2019, https://aamd.org/for-the-media/press-release/association-of-art-museum-directors-passes-resolution-urging-art-museums, captured at https://perma.cc/3JCH-277J.

69 Wildenhaus, "Wages for Intern Work," 15–16.

70 In the summer of 2020, amid protests against the police killing of George Floyd and Breonna Taylor, and widespread layoffs across the sector, museums across the country were called on to address issues of racism, particularly anti-Blackness, in hiring, institutional culture, interpretation, education, and other aspects of museum operations. See Aaron Randle, "'We Were Tired of Asking': Why Open Letters Have Become Many Activists' Tool of Choice for Exposing Racism at Museums," artnet news, July 15, 2020, https://news.artnet.com/art-world/museum-open-letters-activism-1894150, captured at https://perma.cc/F5Z7-X892. In June 2020, the American Museum of Natural History decided to remove the iconic *Equestrian Statue of Theodore Roosevelt* from its entrance. See "Addressing the Statue," American Museum of Natural History, https://www.amnh.org/exhibitions/addressing-the-theodore-roosevelt-statue, captured at https://perma.cc/HT5S-J5J9. Prior to 2020, there were increasing calls for accountability relating to exhibitions, corporate sponsorship, the affiliations of donors and board members, and repatriation.

16 PROVENANCE RESEARCH IN MUSEUM ARCHIVES: RESTITUTION, REPATRIATION, AND RETURN OF CULTURAL HERITAGE

Emily Connell and Michael Pahn

As long as objects of cultural heritage have religious, cultural, social, or monetary value, a market will exist for their illegal and unethical acquisition for profit. History is known to repeat itself, as evidenced by cultural heritage objects becoming the pawns of currency and power through war looting and unscrupulous collectors and dealers, or out of the dire circumstances of the minority, such as refugees and immigrants escaping nations in conflict. However, international awareness of the importance of ethical return of certain cultural heritage objects to their rightful owners is growing. To do so requires complete and accurate understanding of the provenance of these objects.

Provenance, for the purposes of this chapter, is "information regarding the origins, custody, and ownership of an item or collection."[1] The concept of provenance is fundamental to the work of archivists as well as that of museum professionals, although each may approach the concept in different ways. The archivist refers to it as "the individual, family, or organization that created or received the items in a collection"—did these files come, for example, from the director's office or the development office?[2] This chapter will focus on the museum professional's perspective: their interest in provenance deals with ownership or authenticity—who bought the object, when, and from whom, and how it was acquired by the museum. The museum archivist must have a firm grasp of both interpretations to arrange and describe records, assist internal and external users with provenance research, and perhaps even function as an institutional provenance point person.

Provenance research has the potential to play a crucial role in uncovering an object's true history, which may ultimately result in its restitution, repatriation, or return. Each is a means by which objects may be deaccessioned out of museum collections and returned to their rightful owners. The categories share a similar context, but their definitions are unique and specific, either as a matter of law or of moral obligation.

- *Restitution* is generally used when an object has been looted, illegally exported, stolen, or otherwise removed from its owner in infringement of the law. In other contexts, *restitution* may refer to monetary compensation for stolen property.
- *Repatriation*, in the context of relevant laws, refers to the transfer of physical custody of and legal interest in Native American human remains and cultural items to lineal descendants, culturally affiliated Indian tribes, and Native Hawaiian organizations.[3]
- *Return* can be used in a general sense to cover all methods of getting an object back to its owner, but is also "based on a moral or ethical obligation to restore the cultural heritage rather than an obligation which arises from a breach of some legal norm."[4] Providing duplicates of archival records to communities whose cultural heritage is documented in them is often referred to as "return."

"Return" and "repatriation" are both used when referring to antiquities or objects removed from their owners during occupation by colonial powers.

The provenance landscape for museums has shifted massively in the past several decades. Until World War II, provenance was a concern most often related to the attribution or authenticity of an object rather than to the circumstances of its previous owners and whether ownership could legally be transferred.[5] Although highly publicized scandals about illegally excavated antiquities purchased by museums began to move attention to awareness of how objects had been obtained, museums were often reluctant to share information about provenance widely and might do so only in *catalogues raisonné* or scholarly publications not broadly available. Most museums and collectors around the world now embrace the value of a deep understanding of the provenance of the objects in their care. Provenance and exhibition histories are available on many museum websites, and objects in museum collections with now-questionable provenances regularly make their way back into the hands of their original owners, their descendants, or their communities.

Provenance and the Museum Archivist

Registrars are typically museums' custodians of the records that document the last link in the chain of provenance—the deeds of gift, contracts, or receipts that demonstrate that the museum has legally acquired the objects in their collections. Nevertheless, archivists in museum settings steward myriad records that speak to research activities, exhibitions, sales, exchanges, trades, or other transfers of ownership or custody that are important when determining the provenance of objects or human remains. The history, value, and authenticity of cultural heritage objects can be documented in a dizzying variety of archival materials. The Archives of American Art, in its *Guide to Provenance Research*, states that "holdings of dealer, art historian, artist, collector, and gallery correspondence, stock inventories, estate records, oral histories, sales ledgers, photographic images, as well as exhibition and bibliographic materials, offer remarkable opportunities for provenance research and scholarship."[6] Further provenance information for artwork and Judaica looted by Nazis may also be found in interrogation reports and other Allied military records.

For archaeological materials, the field notes, maps, photographs, correspondence, and other documentation of excavation are vitally important for demonstrating whether objects may be of a funerary nature. Permits from tribal, national, and state authorities can be important sources of information, as well. Specific details of an excavation may support or contradict a tribe's claim of cultural affiliation with the remains that were removed.

Ethnographic materials—those acquired from living individuals—may be documented in field notes, receipts, object lists, letters, permits, photographs, and other records that demonstrate both their acquisition history and their cultural purpose.

Commonly, the records that document the provenance of archaeological and ethnographic objects and human remains in museums' collections are widely dispersed among museums and archives all over the world. This often leads to widely varying degrees of researcher access. Multiple institutions often sponsored anthropological expeditions, excavations, and collecting trips, with anthropologists from any number of museums or universities participating. The diaspora of these materials and records has made provenance research particularly challenging. The increasing availability of digitized archival records online, as well as emerging standards and tools such as EAC-CPF (Encoded Archival Context—Corporate Bodies, Persons, and Families) and Social Networks and Archival Context (SNAC) are beginning to make this research easier.[7] Organized provenance research and data-sharing initiatives, discussed here, are tremendously helpful as well.

The vast majority of provenance documentation relevant to current restitution or repatriation claims was generated between the late nineteenth and mid-twentieth centuries. These records are often unique physical papers that reside in archival collections or registrars' records. Given the attention to the legal and ethical issues that looted art, objects, and human remains present, most museums no longer intentionally acquire materials that may fall into these categories and are careful to scrutinize proposed acquisitions that may be subject to the laws and regulations discussed later. That said, contemporary records, including born-digital records such as email correspondence and permit applications, may be useful in researching provenance.[8] The ethical obligations of museum archivists—to provide access to the full archival record to re-create the most complete provenance history possible—are the same whether these records that support claims have been digitized or not.

Nazi-Era Objects

Many publications focused on cultural heritage in the Nazi era are available and worth reading for detailed histories of the theft, looting, and, in some cases, destruction of fine and decorative arts, books, and manuscripts by the Nazi regime.[9] Hitler and his cohorts were cognizant of the value and power of these objects and were determined to use them to both fund war operations and control their narrative. From the moment the Nazis took power in 1933, they attempted to purge works of art that did not fit the national identity they envisioned, punishing German museums that owned or exhibited modern art. They held exhibitions of "degenerate" and "acceptable" art to further spread their condemnation of modernism and eventually confiscated or seized through forced sale untold numbers of objects from museums as well as dealers and collectors who were fleeing for their lives.[10] Cultural heritage in each country Germany occupied faced the same fate.

Even the novice museum archivist will likely have some familiarity with the issues related to the restitution of Nazi-era objects. As an ongoing focus of both news stories (the trove of modern art with questionable provenance uncovered in an Austrian apartment) and popular media (the widely seen movies *The Monuments Men* and *Woman in Gold*), rarely a week goes by without news that either a museum is returning an object to the heirs of a Holocaust victim or that a claim has been made for one.[11] With motivation from policies established by the American Alliance of Museums (AAM) and the Association of Art Museum Directors (AAMD), most museums have spent years researching and clearing the provenance of suspect works in their collections, and an increasing number have published the results on their own online collections search sites, established formal provenance research projects, or contributed results to the AAM's Nazi-Era Provenance Internet Portal database.[12] This shift was a dramatic change from the prevailing attitudes of the last decades of the twentieth century, when museums were just beginning to acknowledge their culpability in acquiring and holding onto objects from the World War II period with dubious or unclear ownership history.

One of the turning points that led to this change in the United States was a meeting in 1998—the Washington Conference on Holocaust-Era Assets.[13] Representatives from a wide array of countries attended the conference, which attracted the attention of high-level governmental officials as well as museum leaders. What set it apart from other meetings about restitution of Nazi-era objects was the outcome: a statement with eleven accompanying principles to address the problems museums were facing.[14] These principles, originally drafted by the AAMD and thus with fundamental support from art museums, formed the basis of new policies from the AAM all the way down to individual museums. The changes the principles recommended for international claims and restitution processes have seen less dramatic implementation, particularly when it comes to art that made its way to the Soviet Union during and after World War II. Although the Nazis documented their actions in detail, many records were destroyed as the war was ending, and those that survived were dispersed across Europe, the United States, and Israel. Very few records related to objects in the Soviet Union have been released by either the Soviet or post-Soviet Russian government.[15] Because of the significance museums place on provenance in the Nazi-era, museum archivists should be familiar with the history of the Nazis' activities regarding cultural heritage objects, as well as with the names of government officials, dealers, and collectors involved in carrying them out.[16] Expertise is not required, knowing the basics to guide staff and users to the most appropriate records in the museum archives is helpful, as is being aware of institutional needs when acquiring new records or working on processing projects. Knowing, for example, whether former museum staff members served in the Monuments, Fine Arts and Archives program (popularly known as the Monuments Men) can be useful. The service members who worked under this program protected the cultural heritage under siege in Europe during the war and helped to document and return as much as possible afterward. Many of these people went on to have long careers in museums, and records of their work as well as personal papers can be important resources. Knowing, as another example, that Hildebrand Gurlitt and Theodor Fischer played a role in the sale of thousands of works of art taken from museums and Jewish owners enables museum archivists to be alert for correspondence or receipts for purchases from these dealers during the Nazi era and to bring them to the attention of other museum staff, as well as to highlight them in finding aids and other documentation.

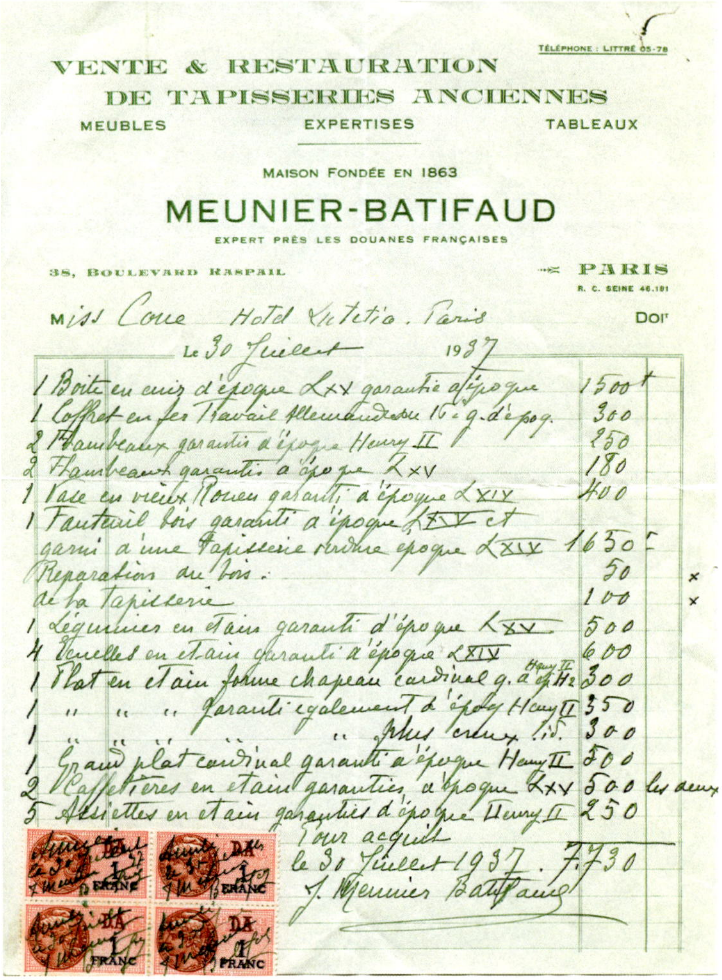
Téléphone : Littré 05-78

VENTE & RESTAURATION
DE TAPISSERIES ANCIENNES
MEUBLES EXPERTISES TABLEAUX

Maison Fondée en 1863
MEUNIER-BATIFAUD
EXPERT PRÈS LES DOUANES FRANÇAISES

38, Boulevard Raspail PARIS
R. C. Seine 46.181

Miss Cone Hotel Lutetia. Paris Doit
Le 30 Juillet 1937

1 Boite en cuir d'époque Lxv garantie d'époque	1500
1 Coffret en fer Travail Allemand du 16e s. g. d'époq.	300
2 Flambeaux garantis d'époque Henry II	250
2 Flambeaux garantis d'époque Lxv	180
1 Vase en vieux Rouen garanti d'époque Lxiv	400
1 Fauteuil bois garanti d'époque Lxv et garni d'une tapisserie brodée époque Lxiv	1650
Réparation du bois	50
de la tapisserie	100
1 Légumier en étain garanti d'époque Lxv	500
4 Écuelles en étain garanti d'époque Lxiv	600
1 Plat en étain forme chapeau cardinal g. d'ép. H2	300
1 " " garanti également d'époque Henry II	350
1 " " "	300
1 Grand plat cardinal garanti d'époque Henry II	500
2 Caffetières en étain garanties d'époque Lxv	500 les deux
5 Assiettes en étain garanties d'époque Henry II	250

Pour acquit
le 30 Juillet 1937. 7.730
J. Meunier Batifaud

FIGURE 16.1. Museum archives may contain receipts such as this one from a dealer who handled looted art during the Nazi era. *Receipt from Meunier-Batifaud to Etta Cone*, July 30, 1937. Claribel Cone and Etta Cone Papers, Archives and Manuscripts Collections, The Baltimore Museum of Art, CP24.15.21.1.

The Native American Graves Protection and Repatriation Act and the National Museum of the American Indian Act

Repatriation law exists because of the often-unjust manner in which Native American human remains, funerary objects, and sacred objects of cultural patrimony came to be in US museum collections. These objects were excavated and removed without any regard for the descendant Native American communities affected. The subject of repatriation rarely enters the public discourse, except for extraordinary circumstances such as that of the Kennewick Man/Ancient One controversy.[17] Two federal laws define the terms of repatriation, the processes, the parties covered, and their respective obligations.

The first federal law to address repatriation directly was the National Museum of the American Indian Act (NMAI Act), signed into law by President George H. W. Bush in 1989.[18] This law established the National Museum of the American Indian within the Smithsonian Institution and required the establishment and execution of a repatriation policy regarding Native American human remains and certain cultural items. In 1996, the NMAI Act was amended to broaden the categories of materials covered.

The more widely known law is the Native American Graves Protection and Repatriation Act (NAGPRA), signed into law by President Bush in 1990.[19] NAGPRA covers any entity within the United States that receives federal funding of any kind, except the Smithsonian Institution. Due to the 1996 amendment of the NMAI Act, the categories of repatriatable materials are the same in both laws. The processes outlined in each, while different, are similar enough that this chapter will treat them as the same. They both concern the transfer of physical custody and legal interest in Native American or Native Hawaiian human remains, funerary objects, and objects that are either sacred or of cultural patrimony from a museum to either lineal descendants, culturally affiliated Native American tribes, or Native Hawaiian nonprofit organizations.

The passage of these laws represented a hard-won victory for Native American activists, leaders, and scholars. Many of the same individuals and organizations that fought for tribal sovereignty and Native American civil rights, including

American Indian Movement activists and the National Congress of American Indians, were actively engaged in the struggle to recognize the human rights of Native Americans for the return of their ancestral remains and certain cultural items wrongfully alienated from their communities.

It was also the beginning of long and complex processes. Under both laws, institutions were required to publish inventories of human remains and funerary objects and summaries of other materials in their collections that fell within the repatriable categories. Some institutions published inventories of all repatriable materials because the summaries are less detailed and informative. These inventories are organized geographically and by tribe and are updated by institutions if and when they discover previously unreported human remains or objects.[20] Based on these published inventories, tribes and Native Hawaiian organizations submit claims to the institutions requesting the repatriation of specific objects or remains. Archives and administrative records are crucial for investigating these claims, which are also supported by religious practices, oral histories, statements from tribal political and religious leaders, and anthropological studies. If the evidence supports a claim, the material will move forward through the institution's internal process and the Department of the Interior's NAGPRA claims process before being deaccessioned and repatriated.

Archival records such as field notes, photographs, receipts, object lists, correspondence, and meeting minutes that describe or document these types of materials are of great research value and provide the necessary context to trace objects' provenance and to determine other characteristics required for successful repatriation claims. They may also contain culturally sensitive information. The documentation of an object's context, for instance a religious practice, may include descriptions of esoteric knowledge typically restricted to religious leaders or clan members. Ethical management of these records is thus an important responsibility in its own right.

While NAGPRA represents important progress, Native American activists, museum professionals, art historians, and anthropologists criticize the law and the processes it mandates. Tribal authorities may submit repatriation claims for human remains or objects, but, ultimately, the museum or the Department of the Interior investigates the claims, leaving decisions in the hands of the institutions that have already compromised the trust of Indigenous people. When NAGPRA was first enacted, many curators feared that museums would be "emptied of their treasures." However, this did not happen; the law defines a narrow range of materials subject to claim, the burden of proof may be high, and—in some cases—tribes have chosen not to repatriate materials, instead actively deciding to work with museums to properly steward their cultural patrimony. Some physical anthropologists express concern that the reburial of Native American remains limits the diversity of human remains available for study in museum collections. While this may be true, the manner in which these remains came to be in museums' and medical schools' collections was often ethically questionable and, at times, illegal.[21]

NAGPRA and the NMAI Act not only specify the categories of materials eligible for repatriation, but also who may make such claims. Only federally recognized Native American tribes and Native Hawaiian nonprofit organizations are identified in the laws. Native Hawaiian society is not organized in tribes, and hence nonprofit organizations were formed as the authorized entities to make repatriation claims. Unfortunately, neither law addresses several common circumstances. Native American tribes that have state or local recognition, or no formal recognition at all, can legally be denied otherwise legitimate claims. In many cases, a religious society or clan may be the culturally appropriate entity to make a claim, but this is not possible. Both laws also only apply to materials held in institutions in the United States.

Nothing in either law prevents museums from choosing to return objects that fall outside of the narrow scope of those defined in the law, or to repatriate objects or human remains to Native American tribes that do not have federal recognition or to Indigenous communities outside of the United States. NAGPRA and the NMAI Act outline minimum requirements that entities must meet. They place no limits on what can be done, and museums are free to go beyond the letter of the law and to develop relationships with native communities represented in their collections to develop ethical stewardship plans, which may or may not include repatriation.

International Conventions Protecting Cultural Heritage during Armed Conflict

Only after World War II did the international cultural heritage community begin to fully recognize the destruction to cultural heritage that modern warfare and armed conflict are capable of rendering. In light of this, the Convention for the Protection of Cultural Property in the Event of Armed Conflict, also known as the 1954 Hague Convention, was adopted. Several later agreements have subsequently reinforced it.[22] The treaty covers fixed and movable artwork, monuments, archaeological sites, books, scientific collections, and other cultural heritage materials. Among its many provisions, the Hague Convention calls for the establishment of special units within military forces specifically for the protection and safeguarding of cultural heritage materials by both state and occupying forces. The Hague Convention additionally prohibits the direction of hostilities against cultural heritage properties. By attempting to limit the destruction, looting, and seizure of cultural heritage during conflict, this treaty has the effect of keeping provenance of cultural heritage property from becoming obscured through illegal sale, smuggling, or forced transfer.

Internal revolts and shifts in power such as the Bolshevik Revolution in Russia and the Cuban Revolution have also led to seizure and either destruction or nationalization of objects from a country's own citizens. In Russia, for example, beginning in 1917, government officials deemed works of art and valuable objects of all kinds to be state property and confiscated them from churches, museums (most notably the Hermitage), and individuals (textile merchant and collector Sergei Shchukin and nobleman and collector Sergei Shcherbatov, among others).[23] Some objects were destroyed, but, particularly during the 1920s and 1930s, thousands more were sold off to fund the operations of the state and gain access to Western markets. A significant amount of Russian cultural heritage made its way into collections outside the country during this period and continued to flow out as successive regimes following World War II used similar tactics to find funding. Because these objects were nationalized and ostensibly sold legally, international law does not favor their return. US courts have affirmed this, but the potential for claims remains.[24] Additionally, after the fall of the Soviet Union, previously nationalized collections were privatized again in a chaotic fashion that left many questions remaining about ownership. The story is much the same for nationalized art from the collections of Cubans.[25] Museum archivists should consider that very few records from either regime are publicly available, and any relevant documentation in the museum archives is of value in both claims for return and in improving understanding of the history of these revolutions.

European colonial-era powers such as France, Germany, and England often considered objects owned by Indigenous people to be for the taking, and many works of art were looted from Asia, Africa, and the Americas during this period. The Benin Bronzes are a notable and contentious example, now widely dispersed and found in museums throughout the United States. These objects were part of the riches owned by the ruler of the Kingdom of Benin (now in Nigeria) taken by British forces in 1897 to punish the regime for an earlier attack and to force the opening of new trade routes. Several factors complicate the return of these objects: the long period that has passed since the objects were taken, the fact that no lists were made of what was taken, and the lack of support in international law for restitution of objects taken during colonial rule, most of which do not favor developing countries (often former colonies) with limited funds and personnel to devote to the cause.[26] Nigeria and other countries seeking return of objects have more recently stepped up efforts to apply diplomatic and political pressure on Western governments and museums to attempt to influence the decision to return on moral grounds. As discussion about the destructive impact of colonial rule on these nations has increased, popular protests aimed at museums that hold colonial-era objects, development by European museums of guidelines for repatriation, and successful return of some objects are encouraging signs of progress.[27] Advocacy within museums for transparency in provenance information and action regarding repatriation, particularly in terms of non-Western collections, has also begun to yield results.[28] While the long-term impact of these developments is unclear, museum archives that hold records related to non-Western collections

REPATRIATION

Provenance information is not only documented in receipts, letters, and deeds of gift. Historical photographs, such as those typically held in museum archives, can also provide valuable context. In 2012, the Smithsonian National Museum of the American Indian (NMAI) repatriated a clan hat to the Central Council of the Tlingit and Haida Indian Tribes of Alaska (CCTHITA) on behalf of the Naanya.aayi Clan. The hat, known as Tsax S'aaxw (Marmot Hat), was claimed as a "sacred object" and an "object of cultural patrimony" under the NMAI Act. Clan crest hats are among the most important items in Tlingit culture. The symbolic beings embodied by the crest identify the relationship and place that individuals and the clan have within the Tlingit social world. And, the practice of their ceremonial rites serves as a legacy bond to their ancestors. In addition, clan crest hats are typically considered the property of the clan. Therefore, no individual would have the authority to alienate it from the community.

Virtually no written record exists of the provenance of Tsax S'aaxw. The Museum of the American Indian/Heye Foundation, the National Museum of the American Indian's predecessor institution, acquired it from the de Menil family in 1970. No prior documentation of its acquisition or ownership exists. Without this documentation, identifying the clan of origin of an object such as this hat can be very difficult due to the complex nature of traditional Tlingit society.

In the absence of written documentation, the CCTHITA provided photographic evidence that Tsax S'aaxw is culturally affiliated with the Naanya.aayii Clan. Several photographs taken between 1887 and 1909, found in archival collections at the Alaska State Library, Seattle's Museum of History and Industry, the Sealaska Heritage Institute, and the University of Washington Libraries, depict the hat in ceremonial use. Most important, a funeral photograph inside the home of a Naanya.aayi chief lying in state provides a compelling indication that this particular hat was considered the property of the clan.

Careful analysis of this archival photographic evidence, in addition to Tlingit oral tradition and anthropological research, provided a reasonable basis for confirming the cultural affiliation of this clan hat as Tlingit and more specifically associating it with the Naanya.aayi Clan. As a result, the NMAI repatriated the clan hat as a sacred object and an object of patrimony to the CCTHITA on behalf of the Naanya.aayi Clan. Shortly thereafter, the NMAI received photos of the clan hat in a ceremony fulfilling its intended purpose.[29]

FIGURE 16.2. Tsax S'aaxw (Marmot Hat). Image by the National Museum of the American Indian, used with permission of the Central Council of the Tlingit and Haida Indian Tribes of Alaska.

FIGURE 16.3. Detail of Tlingit Chief Coonk Shakes's funeral showing Tsax S'aaxw in the right corner, directly above a different clan hat. MOHAI, 1995.38.36.29B.

will want to make sure that they are prepared for further shifts in practices and focus attention on efforts to process, digitize, and otherwise provide access to these records.

Laws protecting cultural heritage in the United States long predate NAGPRA. The American Antiquities Act of 1906 was enacted, in part, to limit the damage that amateur archaeologists could do to historic Native American sites and objects.[30] The Archaeological Resources Protection Act of 1979 is essentially an update of the Antiquities Act and expressly prohibits the sale, purchase, exchange, transport, or receipt of archaeological resources taken from federal or tribal land without a permit.[31]

International agreements such as the Convention on the Means of Prohibiting and Preventing the Illicit Import, Export, and Transfer of Ownership of Cultural Property and the Convention on the International Trade of Endangered Species strictly limit the movement of objects and specimens, create frameworks for international cooperation, and have created restitution provisions of their own.[32]

The laws that govern restitution and repatriation are far from uniform across the world and are constantly changing. While an object may now be part of a museum collection in the United States, legislation enacted in other countries where ownership claims for it might be made can still impact it. Conversely, cultural objects subject to repatriation within the United States may be sold in Europe, much to the dismay of Native Americans and tribal governments who have no legal means of stopping the sales.[33] Native American activists continue to strategize about means of stopping these transactions, but until laws in other countries recognize the cultural and moral rights of Indigenous communities, the struggle will continue.[34]

Theft of Cultural Heritage

Even as museum security practices and technology have vastly improved, art and cultural objects continue to be valuable and desirable on the black market, and thus thieves continue to target collectors and museums, and stolen objects remain missing, sometimes for decades. While returning a stolen object to its rightful owner might seem to be a simple undertaking, this is often not the case, and archival collections and museum archivists can be instrumental in making a difficult case for return successful.

State and international laws about stolen property vary greatly, and many factors come into play. Considerations include where the object was stolen, where it was discovered or recovered, where the person from whom it was stolen resides, when it was stolen, how long it took to discover that it was stolen, how much effort went into trying to get it back, and more. The most significant of these are often statutes of limitations and the concept of good faith purchase, which occurs when someone who purchases a stolen item without knowing it has been stolen can be seen to have purchased it in "good faith" and retains ownership rights over the person or museum from which it was stolen.[35] Archival records that establish ownership, provide evidence of when a theft was discovered and how efforts to find it were handled, and any communications with or payments from insurers will be valuable. These might include purchase receipts, shipping documents or waybills, correspondence, press releases about the theft, meeting minutes, exhibition installation photographs, or accounting documents.

Provenance Research and Data-Sharing Efforts

Digital resources play an increasingly significant role in many aspects of museum archives work; provenance research and repatriation/restitution claims efforts are no exception. An ever-expanding number of museums now make not only images of works in their collection available online but also detailed descriptions of them, including their provenance. This availability of information is the result of significant shifts in policies and practices in the museum field that emphasize open and proactive sharing of information about collections. In the past, and even still today, museums have been reluctant to share this information fearing that some part of it will be incorrect, incomplete, or misleading and could result in untold misfortune for the institution. Museums have had to confront their legacy policies that tightly controlled access to information, perhaps only allowing certain types of researchers to look through object files or to see complete provenance records.

THEFT

The importance of museum archives' records to the return of stolen objects was highlighted in the case of a small landscape painting by Pierre-Auguste Renoir that turned up at auction with an intriguing backstory. The painting was in a bin at a flea market and purchased only for the attractive frame. Numerous news outlets picked up on this trash-to-treasure tale noting that labels on the back of the painting indicated it had once belonged to Herbert May. Staff at the Baltimore Museum of Art (BMA) knew that May was the husband of Saidie Adler May, a major donor to the museum, and checked object files to see if the Renoir had any connection to the museum. When nothing turned up, the museum pursued it no further, but the story had already piqued the interest of a journalist at the *Washington Post*. The journalist made an appointment to go through Saidie May's papers in the BMA's archives and discovered a list of works in May's collection that included a painting by Renoir with a similar size and title to the one up for auction. A loan number on the list allowed museum staff to check paper loan files and discover a card noting that the painting had been stolen from the galleries in 1951. Quickly, the police, FBI, and lawyers were involved, and the painting was pulled from the auction while the circumstances of its theft and whereabouts for the intervening six decades were investigated. Many significant questions regarding the ownership of the painting needed to be untangled. The painting was marked as from the collection of Herbert May, and he and Saidie May divorced long before she gave or loaned the majority of her collection to the BMA. To further complicate matters, Saidie May died a few months before the painting was stolen, and some long-term loans from her collection had not yet been formally cleared by her estate and accessioned by the museum. The possibility also lingered that an insurance payout had been made for the painting and that the insurance company could be the owner. Information found in the BMA's archives made a major impact on the museum's legal argument: accounting ledgers, records about security procedures in 1951, photographs of the painting in Saidie May's apartment after her divorce from Herbert May, correspondence from Saidie May about sending the Renoir to the BMA and her intention to give her collection to the museum, board of trustees minutes about the theft—all were essential in the final determination that the painting would be returned to the BMA.

FIGURE 16.4. The photograph shows the Renoir painting hanging in Saidie May's apartment following her divorce from Herbert May. *Saidie A. May's rooms in the Park Lane, New York City, circa 1923–1933.* SAIDIE A. MAY PAPERS, ARCHIVES AND MANUSCRIPTS COLLECTIONS, THE BALTIMORE MUSEUM OF ART, SM5.6.4A.

The Getty Provenance Index databases have been searchable online for several decades and remain an essential resource for researching European and American art.[36] The databases that make up the Provenance Index aggregate data from auction catalogs, dealer stock books, and archival sources to provide details about sales and ownership of works of art, in most cases from the early modern period through World War II. The Getty is not alone in providing data for the Index, and it collaborates with other American and European institutions to contribute additional resources and increase the scope of coverage.

The Carnegie Museum of Art's Art Tracks project is a grant-funded effort begun in 2014 to simplify and standardize provenance information using structured data.[37] Because provenance information often varies considerably from museum to museum, where gaps may be or where connections could be made to other objects across museums is often unclear. Implementation of the proposed standard and the software created by the project would enable museums to share provenance information more easily without requiring on-site access to a museum's files.

The National Gallery of Art (NGA) conducted extensive provenance research on its collection and now makes that information publicly available on its website.[38] NGA has identified over thirty works in its collection that were looted during World War II and returned to their rightful owners prior to acquisition by the NGA.

Ethical Obligations

The Society of American Archivists' "Core Values of Archivists" and "Code of Ethics for Archivists" contains important principles that can help guide archivists' decision-making and actions as they pertain to records of provenance. Access and Use, Responsible Custody, and Social Responsibility are just some of the core values of the profession that demand that archivists both safeguard records of provenance and make them available to researchers, descendants, Indigenous communities, and others.

Provenance documentation is often most readily accessible by museum professionals, as they reside within institutional archives or registrars' records. Museum archivists, however, are obliged by the SAA code of ethics to be "honest, fair, collegial, and equitable" in all professional relationships.[39] These professional values require archivists to provide individuals, families, communities, or their representatives with access to records of provenance even when it may result in the restitution, repatriation, or return of materials from institutions.[40]

Museum archivists confront a glaring irony when addressing repatriation: archival materials are not in and of themselves subject to repatriation as defined by NAGPRA or the NMAI Act. Under current law, Native American communities may claim for repatriation the material culture of religious and traditional practices, but not the documentation of these religious and traditional practices. For instance, a community may successfully repatriate an object of cultural patrimony, such as a drum, while no longer having the complete record or memory of the ceremony of which that drum was a part. Field notes, photographs, motion picture films, or audio recordings may in part document the role of the drum. This documentation may have been made without tribal knowledge or permission, which is now recognized as unethical; nevertheless, it may be a valuable record of these traditions.

Museum archives have a special obligation to share cultural heritage documentation with source communities to support the revitalization and continuance of religious expressions and traditions, languages, and artistic expressions. The return of cultural heritage documentation is not repatriation. Repatriation is the complete return of both physical custody and legal interest in the materials in question. This usually is not possible with archival materials and is often not the goal, which is the return of knowledge and traditions to communities. Substituting high-quality reproductions, when paired with ethical stewardship of originals, is often satisfactory.

Guidelines exist to support museums and archives in these types of potentially sensitive interactions. In 2006, a group of Native American and non-Native archivists, librarians, and other cultural heritage professionals developed the *Protocols for Native American Archival Materials*. SAA Council endorsed this document in 2018.[41] They provide guidelines and best practices for ethical stewardship of Native American materials, particularly those held by non-Native institutions. These protocols are based on codes of ethics, other guidelines, and international agreements such as the United

Nations Declaration on the Rights of Indigenous Peoples.[42] Some of the principles they articulate are the importance of consultation with tribal communities, an understanding of Native American values and knowledge, rethinking access in the context of culturally sensitive materials, and mutual respect.

Conclusion

Provenance research is one of the most complex and challenging areas in which museum archivists work. When questions of the ownership of valuable cultural heritage arise, the stakes can be incredibly high for both the institution and those making claims for its return. Understanding provenance-related issues and history discussed in this chapter will prepare museum archivists to act ethically, provide access to appropriate records, and ultimately assist in making the best possible case for whether an object remains in an institution's collection or not.

Further Reading

Chari, Sangita, and Jaime M. N. Lavallee, editors. *Accomplishing NAGPRA: Perspectives on the Intent, Impact, and Future of the Native American Graves Protection and Repatriation Act*. Corvallis, OR: Oregon State University Press, 2013.

Fitz Gibbon, Kate, editor. *Who Owns the Past?: Cultural Policy, Cultural Property, and the Law*. New Brunswick, NJ: Rutgers University Press, 2007.

Forrest, Craig. *International Law and the Protection of Cultural Heritage*. Hoboken, NJ: Taylor and Francis, 2010.

Mathiesen, Kay. "A Defense of Native Americans' Rights over Their Traditional Cultural Expressions." *American Archivist* 75, no. 2 (2012): 456–81, https://doi.org/10.17723/aarc.75.2.0073888331414314.

Yeide, Nancy H., Konstantin Akinsha, and Amy L. Walsh. *The AAM Guide to Provenance Research*. Washington, DC: American Association of Museums, 2001.

NOTES

1 *Dictionary of Archives Terminology*, s.v. "provenance," Society of American Archivists, https://dictionary.archivists.org/entry/provenance.html, captured at https://perma.cc/8P5P-JVN4.

2 *Dictionary of Archives Terminology*, s.v. "provenance."

3 "Native American Graves Protection and Repatriation Act," National Park Service, https://www.nps.gov/nagpra/mandates/25usc3001etseq.htm, captured at https://perma.cc/YTZ9-9WES.

4 Craig Forrest, *International Law and the Protection of Cultural Heritage* (Hoboken, NJ: Taylor and Francis, 2010), 142.

5 Gail Feigenbaum and Inge Jackson Reist, *Provenance: An Alternate History of Art* (Los Angeles: Getty Research Institute, 2013).

6 "A Guide to Provenance Research in the Archives of American Art," Archives of American Art, https://www.aaa.si.edu/collection-features/a-guide-to-provenance-research-at-the-archives-of-american-art, captured at https://perma.cc/94R9-SW7H.

7 Social Networks and Archival Context (SNAC) Cooperative, http://snaccooperative.org/, captured at https://perma.cc/4WBA-N247.

8 For discussion of a recent project dedicated to preserving born-digital provenance documentation, see Cate Peebles, "A New Paradigm for Preserving Born-digital Art Collection Records: National Digital Preservation Stewardship Residency Final Report," Yale Center for British Art, http://ndsr-pma.arlisna.org/wp-content/uploads/2018/08/Peebles-NDSR-Art-Final-Report.pdf, captured at https://perma.cc/X69F-GQLV.

9 Resources about the history of Nazi-era objects include Lynn H. Nicholas, *The Rape of Europa: The Fate of Europe's Treasures in the Third Reich and the Second World War* (New York: Alfred A. Knopf, 1994); Melissa Müller and Monika Tatzkow, *Lost Lives, Lost Art: Jewish Collectors, Nazi Art Theft, and the Quest for Justice* (New York: The Vendome Press, 2010); and Michael J. Kurtz, *America and the Return of Nazi Contraband: The Recovery of Europe's Cultural Treasures* (Cambridge: Cambridge University Press, 2006).

10 The *Degenerate Art* exhibition was held in 1937 concurrent with the contrasting first annual *Great German Art* exhibition. The *Degenerate Art* exhibition was re-created by the Los Angeles County Museum of Art in 1991, see Stephanie Barron, *Degenerate Art: The Fate of the Avant-Garde in Nazi Germany* (Los Angeles: Los Angeles County Museum of Art, 1991), and more recently contextualized in a Neue Galerie exhibition, see *Degenerate Art: The Attack on Modern Art in Nazi Germany, 1937* (New York: Neue Galerie, 2014).

11 Alison Smale, "Report of Nazi-Looted Trove Puts Art World in an Uproar," *The New York Times*, November 4, 2013, https://www.nytimes.com/2013/11/05/arts/design/trove-of-apparently-nazi-looted-art-found-in-munich-apartment.html, captured at https://perma.cc/N3DZ-L7NB; *The Monuments Men*, directed by George Clooney, Columbia Pictures Corporation, Fox 2000 Pictures, Smokehouse Pictures, Obelisk Productions, Studio Babelsberg, 2014, film; *Woman in Gold*, directed by Simon Curtis, Origin Pictures, BBC Films, 2015, film.

12 "Art Museums and the Identification and Restitution of Works Stolen by the Nazis," Association of Art Museum Directors, https://aamd.org/sites/default/files/document/Nazi-looted%20art_clean_06_2007.pdf, captured at https://perma.cc/H9AC-SLGY; "Standards Regarding the Unlawful Appropriation of Objects During the Nazi Era," American Alliance of Museums, http://www.aam-us.org/resources/ethics-standards-and-best-practices/collections-stewardship/objects-during-the-nazi

-era, captured at https://perma.cc/VE5W-T2GF; "Nazi-Era Provenance Internet Portal," American Alliance of Museums, http://www.nepip.org, captured at https://perma.cc/U34U-A8NB.

13. "Washington Conference on Holocaust-Era Assets," US Department of State, https://1997-2001.state.gov/regions/eur/wash_conf_material.html, captured at https://perma.cc/F3XS-AUSH.

14. "Washington Conference Principles on Nazi-Confiscated Art," US Department of State, https://www.state.gov/p/eur/rt/hlcst/270431.htm, captured at https://perma.cc/Y4AE-326E.

15. Patricia Kennedy Grimsted, "Reconstructing the Record of Nazi Cultural Plunder: A Guide to the Dispersed Archives of the Einsatszt Reichsleiter Rosenberg (ERR) and the Postwar Retrieval of ERR Loot," https://www.errproject.org/guide.php, captured at https://perma.cc/67B4-XMH8.

16. "The Art Looting Investigation Unit (ALIU) List of 'Red Flag' Names," in *The AAM Guide to Provenance Research*, ed. Nancy H. Yeide, Amy L. Walsh, and Konstantin Akinsha (Washington, DC: American Association of Museums, 2001).

17. "Kennewick Man, The Ancient One," Burke Museum, http://www.burkemuseum.org/blog/kennewick-man-ancient-one, captured at https://perma.cc/AZ7J-Z7KJ.

18. "National Museum of the of the American Indian Act," https://americanindian.si.edu/sites/1/files/pdf/about/NMAIAct.pdf, captured at https://perma.cc/H5P7-GL2S.

19. "National Native American Grave Protection and Repatriation Act," United States Park Service, https://www.nps.gov/nagpra.

20. NAGPRA inventories are aggregated by the National Park Service's NAGPRA Office into databases that can be found online at https://www.nps.gov/nagpra/ONLINEDB/index.htm, captured at https://perma.cc/8P2L-LKC4.

21. Sonya Atalay, Jen Shannon, and John G. Swogger, Journeys to Complete the Work: Stories about Repatriation and Changing the Way We Bring Native American Ancestors Home, https://coahrepat.com/system/files/atoms/file/Journeys_to_Complete_the_Work_Comic_0.pdf, captured at https://perma.cc/J2JV-HBKH. Licensed under CC BY-NC-SA 4.0, 2017.

22. "1954 Hague Convention of the Protection of Cultural Property in the Event of Armed Conflict," United Nations Educational, Scientific and Cultural Organization, http://www.unesco.org/new/en/culture/themes/armed-conflict-and-heritage/convention-and-protocols/1954-hague-convention, captured at https://perma.cc/FU2G-GSCP.

23. Rifat Gafifullin, Nicholas V. Iljine, and Natalja Semyonova, *Selling Russia's Treasures: The Soviet Trade in Nationalized Art 1917–1938* (New York: Abbeville Press, 2013).

24. See for example, Pierre Konowaloff, Paris, France, Plaintiff–Appellant, v. The Metropolitan Museum of Art, New York, New York, Defendant–Appellee (United States Court of Appeals, Second Circuit, December 18, 2012), http://caselaw.findlaw.com/us-2nd-circuit/1618007.html, captured at https://perma.cc/VAA4-94MD.

25. Mari-Claudia Jiménez, "The Future: Restituting Looted Cuban Art," *Proceedings of the ASIL Annual Meeting* 109 (2015): 116–23.

26. Salome Kiwara-Wilson, "Restituting Colonial Plunder: The Case for the Benin Bronzes and Ivories," *DePaul Journal of Art, Technology & Intellectual Property Law* 23, no. 2 (2013): 375–425, http://via.library.depaul.edu/cgi/viewcontent.cgi?article=1052&context=jatip, captured at https://perma.cc/K9L9-G9CU.

27. "Guide to Dealing with Collections from Colonial Contexts, 2nd version, 2019," Deutscher Museums Bund, https://www.museumsbund.de/publikationen/leitfaden-zum-umgang-mit-sammlungsgut-aus-kolonialen-kontexten, captured at https://perma.cc/P5JB-2DVW; Robin Scher, "Better Safe than Sorry: American Museums Take Measures Mindful of Repatriation of African Art," *ARTnews*, June 11, 2019, https://www.artnews.com/artnews/news/african-art-repatriation-american-museums-12750, captured at https://perma.cc/H2L7-2HCK; Alex Marshall, "This Art Was Looted 123 Years Ago. Will It Ever Be Returned?," *The New York Times*, January 23, 2020, https://www.nytimes.com/2020/01/23/arts/design/benin-bronzes.html, captured at https://perma.cc/W8ZX-CPQ7.

28. "UMMA's Ongoing Commitment to Anti-Racist Action and a More Inclusive Museum," University of Michigan Museum of Art, https://umma.umich.edu/blm?utm_source=miragenews&utm_medium=miragenews&utm_campaign=news, captured at https://perma.cc/P6YV-ABMY.

29. Risa Diemond Arbolino, *Tlingit Repatriation Claim Assessment: Central Council of the Tlingit and Haida Indian Tribes of Alaska (CCTHITA) on Behalf of the Naanya.aayí Clan* (Suitland, MD: Unpublished report on file, Smithsonian Institution, National Museum of the American Indian, Repatriation Department, 2012).

30. "American Antiquities Act of 1906," National Park Service, https://www.nps.gov/history/local-law/anti1906.htm, captured at https://perma.cc/MXG2-9XL4.

31. "Archaeological Resources Protection Act of 1979," National Park Service, https://www.nps.gov/Archeology/tools/laws/ARPA.htm, captured at https://perma.cc/ZP7T-VRSG.

32. "Convention on the Means of Prohibiting and Preventing the Illicit Import, Export and Transfer of Ownership of Cultural Property—1970," United Nations Educational, Scientific and Cultural Organization, http://www.unesco.org/new/en/culture/themes/illicit-trafficking-of-cultural-property/1970-convention, captured at https://perma.cc/Y2V7-HYWP; "Convention on International Trade in Endangered Species of Wild Fauna and Flora," CITES, https://www.cites.org, captured at https://perma.cc/LXU6-TXPS.

33. For example, "Hopi Restitution Suits: Questions of Standing and Rights," Center for Art Law, https://itsartlaw.com/2015/10/01/hopi-restitution-suits-questions-of-standing-and-rights, captured at https://perma.cc/DWB3-W2Q5.

34. One approach to addressing the sale of Native American sacred objects in Europe is to simply buy them and return them to the tribes. This was the case in 2013 when a French auction house sold highly sacred Hopi and San Carlos Apache objects to an anonymous buyer. The buyer turned out to be Gregory Annenberg Weingarten, who immediately returned the objects to their respective tribes. While this was a positive outcome, the tactic is not without problems. Aside from requiring a generous benefactor, it maintains the monetary value of cultural patrimony and may actually encourage future sales of similar materials.

35. Ashton Hawkins and Judith Church, "A Tale of Two Innocents: The Rights of Former Owners and Good-Faith Purchasers of Stolen Art," in *Who Owns the Past: Cultural Policy, Cultural Property and the Law*, ed. Kate Fitz Gibbon (New Brunswick, NJ: Rutgers University Press, 2007).

36. "Getty Provenance Index Databases," the Getty Research Institute, http://www.getty.edu/research/tools/provenance/search.html, captured at https://perma.cc/6UY3-QS3G.

37. "Art Tracks," Carnegie Museum of Art, http://www.museumprovenance.org, captured at https://perma.cc/QJ5M-GXRY.

38. "Resources Relating to World War II," National Gallery of Art, https://www.nga.gov/research/gallery-archives/world-war-ii-resources.html, captured at https://perma.cc/Q23X-R5QU.

39 "SAA Core Values Statement and Code of Ethics," Society of American Archivists, https://www2.archivists.org/statements/saa-core-values-statement-and-code-of-ethics, captured at https://perma.cc/LBP2-TCHB.

40 See chapter 15 for a discussion of the balance between institutional procedures and ethical considerations.

41 *Protocols for Native American Archival Materials*, http://www2.nau.edu/libnap-p, captured at https://perma.cc/GP4V-SDC6; "SAA Council Endorsement of Protocols for Native American Archival Materials," https://www2.archivists.org/statements/saa-council-endorsement-of-protocols-for-native-american-archival-materials, captured at https://perma.cc/D68D-8XZB.

42 "United Nations Declaration on the Rights of Indigenous Peoples," United Nations Department of Economic and Social Affairs, Indigenous People, https://www.un.org/development/desa/indigenouspeoples/declaration-on-the-rights-of-indigenous-peoples.html, captured at https://perma.cc/Y5Z9-KNUK.

17 WE ARE WHAT WE SHARE, OR MAKING THE CASE FOR MUSEUM ARCHIVES

Kathleen Williams

This publication has emphasized collaboration and advocacy throughout as vital to the skill set of museum archivists; this is how they deliver their knowledge and expertise in support of the museum's mission and advance and enhance many of its stewardship, curatorial, and educational functions. Sharing that knowledge and expertise is of crucial importance to the success of museum archives programs and makes collaboration and advocacy possible. If colleagues and constituencies are not aware of the work of the archives, they will not understand its value. With that idea as its basis, this chapter introduces the concept of aggressive sharing and argues that through it and its many facets—advocacy, collaboration, and leadership to name a few—the museum archives has the potential to become not only the locus for narratives of the institution's past but an active place of contemporary engagement.

Fully implementing the concept of sharing opens a vital gateway to communicating the relevance of the archival enterprise in museums to parent institutions and to the communities that they serve. Archivists prepare materials for access and use and then create data about those materials, sharing that information with, in effect, everyone. This is the primary way museum archivists share, in their manifold work as stewards of collections. Although this sharing of holdings is significant, and very familiar to archivists, it does not fully capture the important mindset and skill set of aggressive sharing that museum archivists should be encouraged to actively adopt. In the campaign waged every day for museum archives, museum archivists must embody the idea that we are what we share.

Inviting the public into the museum archives to engage with the core work of the repository, whether in person or online, is a deliberate sharing that enables a deep exploration of collections and unlimited applications of the knowledge gained from them. Beyond traditional research visits or volunteer arrangements, these are larger-scale undertakings with a potentially unknown public, whether hack-a-thons, Wikipedia parties, document transcription activities, tag-a-thons, or the like. How does this approach to sharing advance a museum archives and its cause? When the public is asked to participate substantively in the archival workflow, a new community of supporters, fans, and stakeholders is created, and that community, which is not necessarily confined to a museum archives' physical location, can be regularly augmented with further outreach initiatives. Significant, largely untapped advantages can be realized by the museum archives and its parent organization when archivists move beyond their traditional researchers and encourage active public participation in archival work.

While reaching a diverse constituency of external users is essential, proving the museum archives' value to its own institution is often the most significant challenge museum archivists face, and one that this publication has tried to address. How does the museum archivist increase a museum archives program's value so that the institution sees it as essential for what it has, what it does, and what it knows? An often-overlooked activity that, if undertaken, can communicate value to select museum colleagues like nothing else is records management. This function, on its face, may not seem the most exciting, but critical sectors of every museum care more about efficiency, space management, and accountability, and far less about historical evidence and cultural landscapes. Knowing the values that various parts of the museum hold dear is a key aspect of advocating for the archives. If the museum's records management program falls under the archives' purview, museum staff who value that program should be important allies and partners.

Another type of aggressive sharing that museum archivists might employ leverages the incredible oceans of knowledge that they possess about their parent institutions. Using that knowledge at every opportunity is to the museum archivist's great advantage, as it demonstrates the value of their museum archives program, as they likely know better than anyone exactly how the museum fits into the community, the museum's connections to that community, and its place in the cultural heritage landscape. The museum archivist's expertise and the archival holdings in their care serve as unique assets: the former a master of context and meaning, and the latter providing the evidence that supports that meaning. In the end, it is as much about using management and social skill sets as anything else, but these are often the most difficult skills to employ to enable aggressive sharing, as they require archivists to regularly advance their programs and their knowledge in complex and often highly competitive museum environments.

This effort must move beyond simply reporting the museum archives' activities through regular chains of command: that is not aggressive sharing, but rather a routine accounting of daily work. Straight chain of command communications, even when following archivist Mark Greene's suggestion for using "strong words" with superiors, will likely see limited results when program advocacy is the goal.[1] Archivist Kathleen Roe implored archivists to take on a more robust "Year of Living Dangerously" approach to advocacy:

> We need to make opportunities to do this—online, live, in writing, anywhere, and everywhere we can. We cannot wait around for someone to button hole us in an elevator and ask "so what's an archivist? What's an archives?" We cannot wait for our bosses to ask us what the archives actually contributes and why it needs resources; we cannot wait patiently for the researchers to find our websites or come to our repositories. We have to step forward and engage.[2]

This may seem risky but will likely gain more traction for a museum archives in the long term.

Associating the archives mission with the broader mission, goals, and strategic plans of the museum is essential in demonstrating ongoing relevance. This requires the museum archivist to constantly put the archives program in a larger, and proper, context: the museum archives and its staff do not simply collect and document an institution's past but actively contribute to its future. The museum archives can participate in the museum's collection development efforts, organize exhibitions, create programming, and produce publications, all in service of preserving and stewarding the institution's historical and intellectual legacy. When those dots are connected on behalf of a museum archives program, senior leaders and decision-makers see its value in improving the institution's current activities, as well as contributing to its future directions.

In sum, through archival collections, opportunities to augment and enhance the public's interaction with the institution, professional expertise, and vast and growing knowledge about "the bigger picture," museum archivists have the opportunity to advocate for the essential nature of the archives program on multiple levels. Is it easy? Of course not. It requires more time and significant effort, stretching of skill sets, maybe leaving comfort zones, and staying well informed about the work of others at the museum. It means the museum archivist must be confident and consistent in seeking advocacy opportunities for the archives program daily. This holds true even if a museum archives' staff is small in number; if the museum archivist cannot just "do it all," they must prioritize the projects, initiatives, and work that is most important to the museum and be strategic about where to focus efforts.

But, above all else, museum archivists must aggressively share. Making the case for a museum archives calls for a finely honed ability to prove its relevance on a host of levels and situations at the parent institution but also for an impetus to share that is active, engaged, and sometimes even relentless. Toward this end, the museum archives community maintains a strong legacy of perseverance in promoting its work both within its local context and the profession at large. Today's museum archivists share the same passion for their collections, and they are well prepared to see this heightened level of advocacy accomplished. The museum archivist faces no greater challenge, perhaps, than advocating for their archives. How the challenges of aggressive sharing are addressed will vary among professionals, and each chapter of this publication has outlined possible tools and strategies. But let the work begin, secure in the knowledge that those who specialize in museum archives are fully equipped to meet the challenge.

NOTES

1   Mark A. Greene, "Putting Archives on the Agenda: How and Where to Use Strong Words in Continual Internal Advocacy," *Archival Outlook* (July/August 2015): 12.

2   Kathleen D. Roe, "Why Archives?," *American Archivist* 79, no. 1 (2016): 6–13, https://doi.org/10.17723/0360-9081.79.1.6.

CONTRIBUTORS

Seth Anderson is an expert in digital preservation technology and strategy for digital archives and media collections. As the software preservation program manager at Yale University Library, he oversees efforts in collection and preservation of software resources, as well as tools for access to preserved software and digital collections. Anderson received his MA in moving image archiving and preservation from New York University. He has previously worked as project manager of the Museum of Modern Art's Electronic Records Archive (MERA) and worked with Carnegie Hall, the Smithsonian Institution, and the United States Holocaust Memorial Museum as a consultant with AVP.

Susan Anderson is an archivist at the American Philosophical Society. She has been involved with the archives profession for more than twenty-five years and worked at the Philadelphia Museum of Art from 1998 to 2019. She is a member of the Museum Archives Section of the Society of American Archivists and served as cochair from 2009 to 2011. Anderson has worked closely with development departments throughout her career. She is grateful to colleagues for mentoring her on grant writing, member programs, and major funding initiatives; writing this chapter has been a way of paying it forward and sharing that generous expertise. Anderson received an MFA from Southern Illinois University, Carbondale, and an MS-LIS from Drexel University.

Brad Bauer is head of archives and special collections at New York University Abu Dhabi (NYUAD), United Arab Emirates. Prior to joining NYUAD in 2017, he served as chief archivist at the United States Holocaust Memorial Museum in Washington, DC, where he worked across various museum departments on the acquisition, arrangement, description, and digitization of archival materials. He has written and given presentations about the similarities and differences between the practices of archivists and other museum professionals. He has also held archival positions at Stanford University, NARA, and the Thousand Oaks (CA) Public Library. He earned his MLIS at the University of California, Los Angeles, and has an MA in liberal arts from Stanford University.

Ellen Brooks is an oral history producer and consultant who currently works with Wisconsin Library Systems (WiLS) on the IMLS grant-funded Accelerating Promising Practices project, mentoring and supporting a cohort of practitioners as they take on oral history initiatives, community digitization events, and other projects to document and share their unique local stories. Prior to her current role, Brooks worked as the oral historian for the State Archives of North Carolina from January 2019 to August 2020 and as the oral historian for the Wisconsin Veterans Museum from 2013 to 2018. Before graduating from the oral history master of arts program at Columbia University, she interned at several cultural institutions, including the Chicago History Museum, the Chicago Cultural Alliance, and the Lower East Side Tenement Museum. Brooks is a founding member of the Oral History Association Emerging Professionals

Committee and is active with the Society of American Archivists and the Columbia Oral History Alumni Association. She is passionate about welcoming new voices into the oral history space.

Rebecca Chandler is a senior consultant at AVP, where she specializes in collection care and management in support of preservation, planning, and advocacy. Chandler is an experienced audio engineer, having worked in postproduction at Broadway Video, Creative Group, and Sony Music Studios. She earned her MLIS with an archives certificate from Pratt Institute. Chandler teaches and presents throughout the United States on the topics of audiovisual preservation, collection management, and digitization.

Rachel Chatalbash is deputy director for research at the Yale Center for British Art, where she established a museum archives and records management program. She served three terms as secretary of the Society of American Archivists' Museum Archives Section and has led the section's Standards and Best Practices Working Group since its inception. Over the past fifteen years, she has organized symposia, outreach programs, and publications on artists' records, advocacy, and born-digital records in a museum archives setting. She previously held museum archives positions at the Solomon R. Guggenheim Museum and the MIT Museum, received her MS in archives management from Simmons College, and received her PhD in art history from the CUNY Graduate Center.

Emily Connell is manager of technical services in the Greenfield Library at St. John's College. She worked in the library and archives of the Baltimore Museum of Art (BMA) beginning in 2000, serving as head librarian and archivist from 2013 to 2019. Throughout her tenure at the BMA, Connell was involved in the museum's provenance research. Additionally, Connell managed two National Historical Publications and Records Commission grant projects at the BMA, establishing a records management program and processing significant museum records. She has an MLS from the University of Maryland.

Maygene Daniels was chief of gallery archives at the National Gallery of Art from 1984 to 2016. Before joining the museum staff, she served in a number of positions in the National Archives of the United States, including special assistant to the deputy archivist and director of the Modern Archives Institute. She has lectured internationally, written extensively, and curated exhibitions of archival materials. Among other professional activities, she served as president of the Society of American Archivists (SAA), president of the Academy of Certified Archivists, and chairman of the International Council on Archives Section on Architectural Records. She is a fellow of SAA.

Sarah R. Demb has been a records professional for twenty-five years. She is currently senior records manager/archivist at Harvard University Archives. Much of her career has been in museum records and archives at the Peabody Museum of Archaeology and Ethnology (Harvard University), the National Museum of the American Indian (Smithsonian Institution), and the Museum of London. She wrote four chapters of the 2004 edition of *Museum Archives: An Introduction* (Society of American Archivists) and coauthored *Records Management for Museums and Galleries: An Introduction* (Chandos Publications, 2012).

Nancy Enneking is the head of institutional records and digital stewardship at the Getty Research Institute in the J. Paul Getty Trust. She helped found, and has responsibility for, all records management and institutional archives functions for each of the Getty's four operating programs (the Conservation Institute, Foundation, Museum, and

Research Institute) and for the overarching Trust Administration. Enneking has also served on the ArchivesSpace User Advisory Council and on the California Historical Records Advisory Board. She received her MLIS from the University of Texas at Austin and, prior to her arrival at the Getty in 2004, worked in several university archives and at the Texas State Archives.

Christina Velazquez Fidler is the digital archivist at the Bancroft Library at the University of California, Berkeley. Prior to her role at the Bancroft Library, she was the museum archivist at the Museum of Vertebrate Zoology at the University of California, Berkeley (MVZ). While at the MVZ, her work centered on linking archival resources and description with related museum collections and finding the intersections in library and information sciences with bioinformatics. Fidler also previously worked at the California Academy of Sciences as the digital projects coordinator and as the project manager for the Academy Library's IMLS Grant, Connecting Content. Fidler received her MLIS from San José State University.

Jessica Gambling has been the museum archivist at the Los Angeles County Museum of Art (LACMA) since it was established in 2010. There, she is responsible for all description, access, reference, and outreach activities for the institutional archives as well as records management at the museum. Before joining LACMA, she worked as an archivist at the Huntington Library, Art Galleries, and Botanical Gardens and the Los Angeles Public Library after earning her MLIS from the University of California, Los Angeles.

Heather Gendron is director of the Robert B. Haas Family Arts Library at Yale University and is coauthor of the free guide for visual artists, *Artists' Studio Archives: Managing Personal Collections and Creative Legacies*. Her research on the personal archives of living artists has been funded by the Joan Mitchell Foundation, Art Libraries Society of North America (ARLIS/NA), IMLS, and the University Research Council at the University of North Carolina at Chapel Hill. Gendron has served in several leadership roles within ARLIS/NA, including as a member of the executive board and most recently as ARLIS/NA's president.

Melissa Gonzales is the director of records management at Houston Community College and has worked in academic and museum archives for the past ten years. In addition to receiving an MSLIS with an archives management concentration from Simmons College, she is also a Certified Archivist and Digital Archives Specialist. Gonzales has experience creating and implementing restriction and policy protocols for the Texas History Room in the Goliad County Library, the University of Texas at Arlington Special Collections, the Witte Museum, and the Museum of Fine Arts, Houston.

Susan Hernandez is the digital archivist and systems librarian at the Cleveland Museum of Art. Her duties include records management, accessioning and managing born-digital records, and overseeing library and archives systems, web presence, and digitization programs. Hernandez served as cochair of the SAA Museum Archives Section Standards and Best Practices Working Group from 2013 to 2016. She received her MA in history, archives, and museum studies from Duquesne University.

Rebecca Morgan is the special collections archivist at the American Museum of Natural History (AMNH). Her work centers on improving the discoverability of the museum's archives, and, since 2010, she has been leading efforts to survey, describe, digitize, and steward the museum's extensive archival collections. She has served as the Society of

American Archivists' Museum Archives Section web liaison and participated in the section's Standards and Best Practices Working Group. Morgan received her MLIS in archives, records management, and preservation from the City University of New York, Queens College.

Samantha Norling is the digital collections manager at the Indianapolis Museum of Art at Newfields. In this role, she manages digital assets and data related to the museum's art, archival, and horticultural collections. Prior to moving into this role, Norling spent more than three years working as the institution's archivist and continues to collaborate closely with the Library and Archives department on born-digital records management and related projects. As a former member and chair of the SAA Committee on Public Awareness, Norling is particularly interested in raising the profile of the archival profession through advocacy and outreach.

Suzanne Noruschat is Southern California studies specialist in Special Collections at the University of Southern California Libraries, where she oversees the Regional History Collection. From 2012 to 2017, she was the architectural records archivist in Manuscripts and Archives at Yale University Library. Noruschat received an MLIS from the University of California, Los Angeles, and a PhD in art history, with a specialization in modern architecture, from Emory University.

Michael Pahn is the head of archives and digitization at the Smithsonian Institution's National Museum of the American Indian (NMAI). He was the media archivist at NMAI from 2003 until 2014, when he became the head of Archives and Digitization. His prior professional experiences include Save Our Sounds project librarian at the Smithsonian Center for Folklife and Cultural Heritage and librarian at the Nature Conservancy. He is a past chair of SAA's Indigenous Archives Section. Pahn has an MLS from the University of Maryland.

Lesley Parilla is the technical services librarian at George Washington's Mount Vernon Library. From 2011 to 2016, she worked on the Smithsonian Field Book Project, a joint initiative at the Smithsonian Institution Archives, Smithsonian Libraries, and the National Museum of Natural History to increase accessibility to field book content that documents natural history. She was cataloging coordinator and managed metadata standards, record contribution, and outreach through social media. She earned an MLIS from the University of Hawai'i at Mānoa, with a certificate in special collections and archives.

Megan Schwenke has headed the Harvard Art Museums Archives since 2013, overseeing archival accessions, cataloging, research services, and outreach as well as the museums' institutional records management program. She is currently cochair of the Society of American Archivists' Museum Archives Section's Standards and Best Practices Working Group and holds an MS with a concentration in archives management from Simmons College.

Lynette Stoudt served as the director of the Georgia Historical Society (GHS) Research Center from 2012 to 2018 and was responsible for the development, management, and preservation of the institution's archives, objects, and library collections. The collection includes a museum archives component with records dating back to the institution's founding in 1839. Prior to GHS, Stoudt held positions at the University of California, San Diego; the University of California, Irvine; the University of California, Berkeley;

and with History Associates Incorporated. She holds an MLIS with an emphasis in archival studies from San José State University.

Dawn Sueoka is the congressional papers archivist at the University of Hawaiʻi at Mānoa Library. She received her MLIS from the University of Hawaiʻi at Mānoa and has previously served on the board of the Association of Hawaiʻi Archivists. She is a Digital Archives Specialist and a former member of the Society of American Archivists' Museum Archives Section's Standards and Best Practices Working Group. She was previously archivist and lending collection manager at the Honolulu Museum of Art and archivist at the Shangri La Museum of Islamic Art, Culture and Design, where she created access policies and helped to define restrictions through records management initiatives.

Jennie Thomas is director of archives for the Rock & Roll Hall of Fame. The dual mission of the Rock Hall's Library & Archives is to serve as an archives for the institution and as a research library for the community at large. Thomas manages all archival operations, and, as such, has worked with the museum to craft an institution-wide collections development policy and to customize a collections management system to serve library, archives, and museum needs. Thomas was previously the archivist for Albion College. She holds an MLS with a specialty in archives, information and records management from the University of Maryland, and an MA in the humanities from Central Michigan University. She also collaborates with curators on donations and purchases, works with potential donors to secure collections, and devises workflows and agreements for the acquisition of materials in all formats.

Madeleine Thompson is library and archives director for the Wildlife Conservation Society (WCS), based at the Bronx Zoo. She previously held the role of WCS's photo collection manager, overseeing the institution's photograph collection, from its earliest glass-plate negatives to its current digital assets. She holds an MLS and a PhD in English, both from Indiana University at Bloomington, and has served as the Society of American Archivists' Museum Archives Section newsletter editor.

Lindsay Turley is vice president of museum collections at the Museum of the City of New York, with previous related experience at the American Civil Liberties Union Nation Archives, Brooklyn College Special Collections and Archives, and the Whitney Museum of American Art. She joined the museum as the manuscripts and reference archivist in 2010 and assumed direction of the Collections department in 2016. Turley has presented at national and regional conferences, participated in the Society of American Archivists' Museum Archives Section Standards and Best Practices Working Group, sat on committees and the board of directors for the Archivists Round Table of Metropolitan New York, and served as reviewer for the IMLS and NEH. She holds an MLIS with certificates in archival studies and museum librarianship from Pratt Institute.

Kathleen M. Williams is chief of archives at the National Gallery of Art, having served for more than twenty years in archives positions at the Smithsonian Institution; the Museum of Fine Arts, Houston; and the Corcoran Gallery of Art. From 2004 to 2017, Williams served as deputy and executive director of the National Historical Publications and Records Commission, the grant-making entity of the National Archives. Williams studied graduate-level archives and history at University of Maryland and has an MA in arts administration from Goucher College. She was named a Fellow of the Society of American Archivists in 2015.

INDEX

A
Academy of Certified Archivists (ACA), 13
access
    as aid to provenance research, 175–76
    architectural records, 112–13
    audiovisual materials, 73, 81–82
    ethical issues, 152–57
    field notes, 133–34
    oral histories, 91
    photographs, 101–2
access copies, 76
access policies, 22–23, 59–63, 112, 157
access restrictions, 41, 55, 61, 101, 152–57
access tools, 63–64, 81–82, 88–89, 101
Accessibility and Disability Section, SAA, 159
accessioning, 40, 41, 55–56
accountability, 21–23
acquisition
    artists' records, 116–17
    audiovisual materials, 76–78
    documenting, 40
    field notes, 127–28
    manuscript collections, 50–55
acquisition policies, 22, 40
Advancing Digitization of Biodiversity Collections (ADBC), 133
advisory boards and committees, 28, 30, 145–46
advocacy
    advisory board's role, 145–46
    "aggressive sharing," 180–82
    as essential aspect of museum archives enterprise, 5, 18, 148–49, 180–81
    on behalf of staff, 158–59, 161–62
    fundraising and, 142
    goals and, 23
    skills, 142
    subject knowledge and, 23
aggregate description, 42, 49, 112
American Alliance of Museums (AAM), 159, 169
American Antiquities Act (1906), 174
American Museum of Natural History, 136
American Society of Appraisers, 54
Americans with Disabilities Act (ADA), 158–59

appraisal
    about, 37–40
    architectural records, 108–10
    artists' records, 121
    email, 156
    financial, 54
    manuscript collections, 49–50
    photographs, 98–99
appraisal grid, 109
Archaeological Resources Protection Act (1979), 174
archaeologists, amateur, 174
architectural records
    about, 105–6
    access, 112–13, 155
    appraisal, 108–10
    arrangement/description, 111–12
    collection development, 113–14
    preservation, 110–11
    record types, 106–8
archival bond, 43
archival education, 4, 13, 26, 158
Archives of American Art, 4
archives systems, 18–19
armed conflict, 172
arrangement, 40–41, 111–12
Art Museum Libraries Symposium, 7
Art Tracks, 175–76
Artist File Initiative, 123
artist files, 118
artists' foundations, 122
assessment, 44
assets, records *vs.*, 74, 75
Association of Art Museum Directors (AAMD), 169
Association of Independent Museums (AIM), 5
auctions, 54
audiovisual materials. *see also* oral histories
    about, 73–74
    access, 73, 81–82
    acquisition, 76–78
    as architectural records, 108
    as artists' records, 117–18
    collection development policies, 75–76
    digitization, 78–80

file tiers, 76
institutional context, 74–75
metadata, 76
preservation, 80–81
authority records, 43

B
baseline description, 41
Belmont Conference, 4
Biodiversity Heritage Library (BHL), 136
biodiversity informatics, 135
black markets, 174
board of trustees records, 154
boards, 28, 30
born-digital materials
acquiring, 40
appraisal, 39
architctural records, 108, 109–10
artists' records, 121–22
audiovisual, 75–78
field notes, 134, 135
preservation, 19, 44, 102, 110–11
websites, 62
Breton, Arthur, 4
Brooklyn Historical Society, 88
budgets, 18, 50, 52
built environment. *see* architectural records
business systems, 28–30
Byars, James Lee, 118–20

C
capstone approach, 39
Central Council of the Tlingit and Haida Indian Tribes of Alaska (CCTHITA), 173
Chin, Mel, 117–18
citizen science projects, 134
climate control, 19, 20
Coalition to Advance Learning in Archives, Libraries, and Museums, 15
collaboration
on acquisition, 53, 56
as advocacy, 180–81
with conservation staff, 44
on fundraising, 143
on grant proposals, 147–48
with legal counsel, 13–14
on natural history collections, 134–36
with photography department, 97
collecting areas, typical, 37–38
collection development, 85–87, 113–14, 116–18, 159–60
collection development policies. *see also* appraisal
about, 48–49
architectural records, 113–14
audiovisual materials, 75, 76
importance of, 22
for photographs, 98
collections management, 18–19, 27
collections management policies, 59
communication, 23, 79, 181
compliance, 22
confidentiality, 60–61
conservation, 44

conservation reports, 155
conservators, 14, 110
construction records, 107–8
Convention on the International Trade of Endangered Species, 174
Convention on the Means of Prohibiting and Preventing the Illicit Import, Export, and Transfer of Ownership of Cultural Property, 174
Convention for the Protection of Cultural Property in the Event of Armed Conflict, 172
copyright. *see also* rights management
about, 61
artists' foundations, 122
audiovisual materials, 81
merchandising and, 66, 112–13
oral histories, 90
photographers, 97
photographs, 101
Corita Kent and the Language of Pop, 88–89
Craft and Folk Art Museum, 87
crowdsourcing, 100, 134, 149, 180
cultural competency, 159
curators
archivists' relationship with, 15, 37, 134–35
artists' records and, 118, 120–21
as records creators, 116
role of, 4–5
viewpoint of, 50

D
data migration, 81
data protection laws, 26, 33, 157
databases, 15
deaccessioning, 55
deeds of gift, 54–55, 117, 128, 156–57
Describing Archives: A Content Standard (DACS), 42
description
about, 41–43
architectural records, 111–12
field notes, 128–33
levels of, 128
museum *vs.* archival, 42, 49
photographs, 99–101
sharing, 63–64
development professionals, 142–43
development records, 155
"Dialogic Museum," 87
digital asset management system (DAMS), 18–19, 33, 81–82, 97–98
Digital Curation Sustainability Model, 75
digital negatives (DNG), 102
digital photographs, 94, 98
digital preservation, 19, 22, 44
digital technologies, 14–15
digitization, 33, 63–64, 78–80, 133–34, 136
digitization strategies, 64
director's records, 154
disaster planning, 23
discovery, 41–43, 63–64
diversification, 22, 157–60
documentation strategy, 39–40

Index **189**

donor interviews, 117
donor records, 155
donor relations, 52–54, 117, 143–45
drawings, architectural, 106–8, 110

E
email, 39, 156
Encoded Archival Context for Corporate Bodies, Persons, and Families (EAC-CPF), 128, 129, 130, 136, 168
Encoded Archival Description (EAD), 42, 63, 130
endowments, 148
ethical obligations. *see* values, archival
exhibition files, 43
exhibitions, 22–23, 65, 88–89, 95
expeditions. *see* field notes
extensible processing, 41
external audiences, 64–65
external collections, 40, 156–57. *see also* manuscript collections

F
facilities, 19–21
fees, 63
field notes
    about, 125–27
    access, 133–34
    acquisition, 127–28
    collaboration regarding, 134–36
    description, 128–33
    preservation, 134
file fixity, 81
file formats, 78, 108, 109, 111
file names, 98
file tiers, 76
financial resources, 18
finding aids, 15, 61, 63, 130
foundations, 146–48
foundations, artists', 122
freedom of information laws, 26, 33, 157
friends groups, 145
functional analysis, 39
funding agencies, 146–48
funding structures, 28–29
fundraising
    about, 141–42
    advisory boards, 145–46
    collaborating on, 143
    creative, 148–49
    development staff, 142–43
    donor cultivation, 143–45
    endowments, 148
    foundations and grants, 146–48
    friends groups, 145
    privacy concerns, 155

G
gallery shots, 95
geolocation data, 133
Getty Provenance Index, 176
GLAMs/LAMs, 5, 41–42
goals, 23, 33, 141–42

governance structures, 28–30
grants, 143, 146–48

H
Hague Convention (1954), 172
Harvard Art Museums, 88
Hess family, 51
Hirshhorn Museum, 73, 74
Hmong community, 85–87

I
identification, of photos, 100
identity, institutional, 5
iDigBio, 133
Illinois Holocaust Museum, 88
incluseum.com, 158
inclusion, 22, 157, 159
Indianapolis Museum of Art (IMA), 62
Indigenous communities, 153, 154, 156, 170–74
information management. *see* records management
information maps, 32
inreach, 67, 87–88
institutional context, 17–21
institutional knowledge, 181
institutional legacies, 158
institutional records, 37–39, 154–56
intellectual property, 55, 61
interns, 160–62
internships, 18
interviews, 89–91
IT departments, 14, 21, 30, 31–32

K
key contacts, 30

L
LAMs/GLAMs, 5, 41–42
language, 159
lawyers, 13–14
leadership, archival, 21–23
legal records, 155–56
LGBTQ+ staff, supporting, 159
libraries, 15
libraries, archives *vs.*, 15
life-cycle model, 38–39
linked data, 15, 43, 134
literature review, 5, 7
"living museums," 96
loan policies, 22–23
looted items, 33, 169–70, 172
Los Angeles County Museum of Art, 73

M
macro-appraisal, 39
management skills, 14
mandate, 18
manuscript collections
    accessioning, 55–56
    acquisition, 50–55
    appraisal, 49–50

collection development policies, 48–49
  value of, 49
media assets, 74
media producers, 14
merchandising, 65–66, 113
metadata
  audiovisual materials, 82
  digital materials, 14, 76, 135
  field notes, 135
  implicit bias in, 159
  oral histories, 88, 90, 91
  photographs, 98–101
metadata standards, 76
mezzanine copies, 76
minimal processing, 41
Minnesota Method, 30
mission, 15–16, 181
mission statement, 22, 33
mixed collections, 51
models, architectural, 110
"more product, less process" (MPLP), 41
museum architecture. *see* architectural records
Museum Archives: An Introduction, vii, 5, 7, 41, 101, 109
museum archives movement, 4–6
Museum Archives Section, SAA, 6, 26
museum archivists
  key contacts, 30
  leadership responsibilities, 21–23
  need for professional training, 17, 37
  provenance and, 168–69
  relationship with adminstrators, 21
  relationships with colleagues, 5, 30, 56, 134–36 (*see also* collaboration)
  role of, 3–4, 5, 7
  skills needed, 14–16, 142
museum history, 95
Museum of Modern Art, 43, 73
Museum of the City of New York, 66

N

National Historical Publications and Records Commission (NHPRC), 4
National Museum of the American Indian Act (NMAI Act), 170–71, 173, 176
National Science Foundation (NSF), 133
Native American Graves Protection and Repatriation Act (NAGPRA), 170–71
Native American materials, 33, 170–71, 173, 176–77
natural collection description (NCD), 130, 133
navigation, 81
Nazi-era objects, 33, 169–70
Nazi-Era Provenance Internet Portal (AAM), 169
Nelson-Atkins Museum of Art, 123

O

objects, managing, 43–44, 51, 120–21
online giving, 149
open access (OA), 61
oral histories
  access to, 88–89
  collection development, 85–87
  conducting, 90–91
  donor interviews, 117
  planning, 89–90
  raising visibility via, 87–88
  role in fundraising, 144
  value of, 85
Oral History Association, 85
Oral History Metadata Synchronizer (OMHS), 88
organizational placement, 17–18
outreach, 65–67, 87–88, 100, 122–23

P

personal data, 31
personnel records, 155
Philadelphia Museum of Art, 144
photo identification, 100
photographers, 97
photographs
  access, 101–2
  appraisal, 98–99
  description, 99–101
  in institutional context, 97–98
  in "living museums," 96
  in museum context, 94–95, 108
  preservation, 102
  role in provenance, 173, 175
  types of, 98
policies
  access, 22–23, 59–63, 112, 157
  acquisition, 22, 40
  collection development, 22, 48–49, 75–76, 98, 113–14
  collections management, 59
  loan, 22–23
  records management, 22, 27, 31–34
  use, 22–23, 61, 63
"policy umbrella," 32
postcustodial approaches, 39
preservation
  about, 44
  architectural records, 110–11
  audiovisual materials, 80–81
  field notes, 134
  oral histories, 91
  photographs, 102
preservation masters, 76
privacy, 61, 152–57. *see also* data protection laws
processing, 20–21, 40–43, 61, 111–12
professional organizations, 4
programming, 65
Protocols for Native American Archival Materials (SAA), 176–77
provenance research
  about, 167–69
  data-sharing efforts, 174, 176
  as ethical obligation, 176–77

provenance research *cont.*
    international conventions, 172, 173
    museum archivist's role, 168–69
    Native American objects, 170–71, 173
    Nazi-era objects, 169–70
    theft, 174, 175
publications, 65
publicity, 66
purchases, 54

Q
quality control, 78–79

R
reading rooms, 21, 60, 133–34, 153
"recordness," 121
records
    vs. assets, 74
    objects as, 120–21
    relationships between, 43
    types of, 37–39
records continuum model, 39
records management
    benefits of, 34
    as core function, 14, 27–28
    governance structures and, 28–30
    history of, in museums, 26–27, 38
    literature review, 7
    risk management and, 31–33
    typical content, 38
records management policies, 22, 27, 31–34
Records Management Section, SAA, 26
reference, 112
registrars, 13, 55–56
release forms, 90
repatriation, 33, 167–68, 170–71, 173, 174
reports, 28
research services, 63
restitution, 33, 167, 174
return, 167–68, 174
Revival Field (Chin), 117–18
rights management, 81–82, 98–99, 102. *see also* copyright
risk management, 22–23, 31–34, 157
risk registers, 32
Robert Rauschenberg Foundation, 122

S
salaries, 158
San Diego Air and Space Museum Archives, 100
searching, 42–43
security, 59–61
selection, 37–40, 77–78, 159–60
self-reflection, institutional, 158
Smithsonian Field Book Project, 126
Smithsonian Institution, 39, 42
social media, 66
Social Networks and Archival Context (SNAC), 130, 168
Society of American Archivists (SAA)
    core values/ethics, 152, 157, 176
    definition of "records," 120

diversity efforts, 157, 158, 159
educational guidelines, 13
internship best practices, 161
Museum Archives Section, 6, 26
Solomon R. Guggenheim Museum, 106, 107, 156
specimens, scientific, 133, 135
staffing, 158
standards, 4, 14, 42, 63, 76, 80, 130
statistics, 67–68
storage, 19–21, 44, 79, 110
StoryCorps, 88
strategic planning, 23
structured data, 134
students, 66
support, institutional, 17–21

T
"Taking Our Pulse" (OCLC), 73
Taskforce for Transgender Inclusion, AAM, 159
Teenie Harris Archive, 100, 159–60
theft, 174, 175
TIFF files, 102
Time Capsules (Warhol), 118
tours, 65, 88
transcription projects, 134

U
United States Holocaust Memorial Museum, 51
unprocessed holdings, 60–61
use cases, 64–65, 66–67
use policies, 22–23, 61, 63
user expectations, 42, 81
users
    external, 64–65
    information-seeking behavior, 49
    internal, 66–67, 75

V
valuations, 154–55
values, archival, 152, 157, 176–77
Vertnet, 133
volunteers, 160–62

W
Warhol, Andy, 118
Washington Conference on Holocaust-Era Assets, 169
web archiving, 62
Whitney South Sea Expedition, 130–32, 136
Wildlife Conservation Society Archives, 96
Wisconsin Veterans Museum, 85–87
workflows, business, 28–30
workspaces, 20–21

Z
zoos, 96